Learn to Trade Like a Professional

Sam Warner-Baker

Learn to Trade Like a Professional

A Proven Process for Consistent Success in Financial Markets

palgrave
macmillan

Sam Warner-Baker
Teach the World to Trade
Brighton, UK

ISBN 978-3-032-20124-9 ISBN 978-3-032-20125-6 (eBook)
https://doi.org/10.1007/978-3-032-20125-6

Cover Design: eStudio Calamar

This Palgrave Macmillan imprint is published by the registered company Springer Nature Switzerland AG.
The registered company address is: Gewerbestrasse 11, 6330 Cham, Switzerland

Foreword

Trading is often misunderstood. It is mistaken for speculation, equated with gambling, or framed as a shortcut to wealth. In truth, professional trading is none of these things. It is a structured discipline rooted in risk management, grounded in probabilistic thinking, and executed through consistent, process-driven decisions under uncertainty. It sits at the intersection of markets, behavior, and strategic reasoning, and its mastery demands far more than intuition or luck.

Those of us working across financial risk management and market microstructure understand that trading well is not simply about being right more often than wrong. It is about understanding how information flows through market systems and deploying a repeatable method that aligns decisions with risk-adjusted expectations. This demands resilience, composure, and a framework capable of evolving with the market.

Yet most retail traders today operate without such a framework. The rise of zero-commission trading platforms and social media "finfluencers" has led to an explosion in market participation, particularly amongst younger, digital-native traders. But access has outpaced education. Widespread misinformation, algorithm-driven hype, and unrealistic expectations dominate much of the content available online. The trading landscape is now crowded with tools but starved of discipline.

I first met Sam in 2013, when I looked into a trading competition that he was running for a student society at Sussex University, on behalf of OSTC, and his dynamic and generous character caught my attention immediately. I encouraged him to develop a third-year trading module and this option very quickly because was so popular that places were always already full within hours of opening online option selection. What set it apart was his rigorously structured, stage-based process: by the end, students could design and implement full trading strategies using real-time market data. In today's AI-saturated assessment landscape, that kind of deep practical learning has become even more vital ... and much harder to deliver.

Sam was ahead of his time then, as he still is now. Our shared interests in crypto-assets, market structure, and trading innovation have sparked a long professional friendship, during which I've watched his insight and integrity lead me to discover the important new challenges myself, from crowdfunding through token offerings to the launch of institutional ETFs. Recently, he made an uncharacteristically highly speculative, but short, foray into memecoins during which he assembled a team of young minds to sift through the thousands of these that were launched every day, identifying early signals of herding behavior. It was a textbook example of his entrepreneurial instinct: willing to engage tactically, and always with strategic awareness. So, unlike the price of bitcoin, my admiration for Sam has grown steadily, and it has never faltered for a minute. I feel so fortunate to call him not just a trusted colleague, but a close family friend.

Hove, United Kingdom
January, 2025

Professor Carol Alexander

Acknowledgements My deepest thanks go first to my wife, Kimberley, and to my children, who have been my daily motivation throughout this journey. Their love, patience, and belief in me provided the energy and purpose needed to see this book through. I am also grateful to my wider family for their constant support and encouragement over the years.

I would like to thank all those who have shared this journey with me in the markets. From learning alongside old-school trading pit traders at the very start of my career, to the students who join me today through the Teach the World to Trade scholarships, every one of you has taught me something I did not know before.

A special thank you to Colin, my man on Wall Street—a fine friend, constant cheerleader, and trusted sounding board. I am also grateful to Steve Ward for his Stoic inspiration and enduring influence on my thinking around performance and self-mastery. My thanks to Professor Carol Alexander, who planted the seed for this book many years ago and encouraged me to bring these ideas together in written form. I am equally thankful to Jimmy and Kevin for their professional insight and for lending expert eyes to several chapters when they were most needed.

Finally, to those I have not yet reached: I am here to help you on your trading journey.

Competing Interests The author has no competing interests to declare that are relevant to the content of this manuscript.

Learn to Trade Like a Professional: A Beginner's Guide to Mastering the Trading Process and Psychology

Introduction: Why Learn to Trade

My journey as a trader began when I was just eight years old. Every Sunday, my dad would get the paper, and tucked inside was the business section with the prices of shares in the FTSE 100 (I would later find out that these were the 100 biggest companies publicly listed in the UK). We'd sit down together, and he'd show me the companies that had gained over the week. He explained that someone who bought a particular share one week and sold it for a higher price the next week would have made a lot of money. Dad made it sound so simple, and from that moment, curiosity and fascination took hold of me as a young boy.

As it happens, my father wasn't your stereotypical city finance worker. Far from it—he was a bohemian market trader in the laid-back West Country, selling clothes and eccentricities from India, Thailand, Mexico, and beyond. What he did notice, though, was my aptitude for mathematics, my love of Monopoly (it turns out the world isn't all that different when you grow up), and my eagerness to learn about how things work.

Fast forward 30 years, and I won't bore you with the full details of my life story just yet. Yes, I've traded for some of the largest proprietary trading companies in the world, remained profitable for 20 years, trained thousands of professional traders globally, lectured at a top UK business school, helped build and then sell a successful trading business, and more. But this book isn't about me—it's about you. You'll find snippets of my experience throughout these pages, but only where it helps you on your journey to becoming a profitable trader.

Learning to trade is about more than just mastering a financial skill; it's about developing a mindset that drives success. It's an opportunity to unlock financial independence, experience personal growth, and take control of your future. Trading can empower you to create an income stream that aligns with your lifestyle, offering the flexibility to work when and where you choose. It challenges you intellectually, pushes your emotional boundaries, and rewards you for building discipline, resilience, and consistency.

At its core, trading is a journey of self-mastery. Success requires more than understanding the markets—it demands improving yourself: sharpening your focus, strengthening your decision-making, and mastering the ability to manage risk. For those who embrace this challenge, the rewards extend far beyond financial gain. Trading builds confidence, mental toughness, and self-awareness, enabling growth in every area of life. And yes, there's the undeniable thrill of seeing your analysis come to life as the market moves your way.

But let's face it: the trading world can be intimidating. With an overwhelming amount of information—some helpful, much misleading—it's easy to feel unsure of where to start. That's precisely why I created Teach the World to Trade: to cut through the noise, simplify the complex, and guide you step by step toward profitability.

Over the past twenty years, I've traded the markets and coached thousands of traders, from complete beginners to seasoned professionals at major institutions. I've seen what works—and, just as importantly, what doesn't. I chose to write "Learn to Trade like a Professional" with a single mission: to help people unlock their potential and change their lives through trading.

My approach is built on experience, credibility, and transparency. I don't sell "get-rich-quick" schemes or secret strategies. Instead, I focus on the trading process and mindset that professionals use to navigate the markets. Whether you're new to trading or looking to refine your skills, I aim to provide the tools, guidance, and supportive community to help you succeed.

Trading isn't easy. But with the right approach and the proper guidance, it's achievable. This book will help you become the trader you aspire to be.

Anyone, anywhere, can learn to trade.

Let me show you how.

How This Book Can Help You on Your Pathway to Profitability

If you're reading this, you're probably curious about trading—or you've already begun your journey into financial markets. Either way, you're in the right place. This book aims to help you understand the complexities of trading and guide you in developing the skills and mindset required to become a profitable trader.

Let's start with a reality check: trading is not a get-rich-quick scheme. Forget the flashy ads and stories about overnight success—they're designed to sell you dreams, not reality. One of the reasons I started Teach the World to Trade was because of an advert I saw on YouTube. It promised massive trading gains with no stress, offered by someone claiming to have "cracked the system." I immediately recognized the seller: a well-known fraud in the financial world with no actual trading experience. After conducting some market research, I discovered numerous others like him—people with flashy social media profiles and no substance, profiting from others' dreams by selling ineffective trading systems.

That's when I realized the world desperately needed ethical, professional trader training for the masses—something rooted in real experience, not false promises.

Trading is a craft. Like any craft, it takes time, effort, and practice to master. The journey isn't always easy, but the rewards—financial freedom, personal growth, and the confidence that comes from mastering a professional skill—make it all worthwhile.

This book will show you how to approach trading as a process, not a gamble. It's about understanding the markets, building a plan, managing risk, and continually improving. While no book can guarantee you'll become a millionaire trader, this one can equip you with the tools and insights to help you succeed.

Here's What You Can Expect:

1. Actionable Insights

This book breaks trading into clear, manageable steps. From understanding market mechanics to mastering the trading process, you'll gain knowledge you can implement immediately.

2. Proven Strategies and Tools

Learn the core elements that make professional traders successful—how they plan, execute, and evaluate trades. You'll also find templates and examples to help you create your trading plan and track your progress effectively.

3. The Right Mindset

Trading success isn't just about strategies—it's about how you think. This book will help you develop a professional mindset, showing you how to stay disciplined, manage emotions, and approach challenges with resilience.

4. A Long-Term Focus

Trading is a marathon, not a sprint. This book will help you approach the markets sustainably, building a strong foundation for long-term success.

Whether you're a complete novice or someone looking to refine your skills, this book is designed to meet you where you are and help you move forward. It's not about instant results—it's about progress. Trading is a continuous learning and improvement journey, and this book serves as your companion along the way.

By the end of these pages, you'll clearly understand what it takes to trade like a professional and the tools to take actionable steps toward your goals. So, let's set realistic expectations, embrace the process, and take that first step on your pathway to profitability.

You've got this—and I'm here to help.

Overview of This Book: The Three Core Sections

This book is structured around three core sections—**Preparation**, **Process**, and **Practice**—and is carefully designed to guide you through each essential phase of becoming a successful trader. Each section adopts a practical, beginner-friendly approach, ensuring traders at all experience levels can follow along and establish a robust trading foundation.

Preparation: Mindset and Market Knowledge

Effective preparation is crucial before entering the world of trading. This section equips you with the essential mental framework and foundational market insights necessary for successful trading.

Here, you will:

- Cultivate a professional trader's mindset, focusing on discipline, resilience, patience, and setting realistic goals.
- Understand the mental toughness required to handle the inevitable highs and lows of trading.
- Gain clarity on core market concepts, including supply and demand, macroeconomic influences, market efficiency, and a trader's role in the financial ecosystem.

- Explore popular asset classes such as forex, commodities, stocks, crypto, energy, and bonds, identifying the markets that resonate most with your interests and goals.
- Familiarize yourself with key trading terms through a beginner-friendly glossary, simplifying complex jargon into easily understandable language.

This preparation phase ensures you're mentally sharp, intellectually informed, and emotionally balanced—equipping you with the confidence and competence to enter the market decisively, manage volatility effectively, and seize profitable opportunities when they arise.

Process: Mastering Your Trading Approach

In this section, theory transforms into actionable trading strategies. You'll delve deeply into the trading processes that elite traders consistently rely upon, breaking down the approach into the following areas –

Identify profitable trading opportunities by effectively combining technical and fundamental analysis.

Execute trades with precision, understanding essential mechanics, including order types, strategic entry and exit points, and risk-reward management techniques.

Effectively **manage** trades from initiation to closure, adapting your strategy to overcome challenges and optimize performance.

Systematically **evaluate** each trade, adopting a win-or-learn mindset to refine and enhance your trading strategy continuously.

This structured process is rooted in practices honed by hundreds of successful professional traders, providing a proven blueprint for sustainable market success.

Practice: Mastering Trading Psychology

Ultimately, trading success relies significantly on mastering your psychology. This final section addresses the emotional and mental aspects essential for long-term achievement. You will:

Learn to recognize and manage psychological triggers such as fear, greed, impulsivity, and overconfidence, enabling better emotional control.

Establish and reinforce habits that promote consistent performance, including maintaining a robust trading plan, keeping a journal regularly, and engaging in thoughtful daily reflection.

Develop a resilient growth mindset that turns every trading experience—positive or negative—into an opportunity for personal and professional growth.

Mastering trading psychology lays the groundwork for sustained adaptability, discipline, and continuous improvement, ensuring you thrive amidst ever-evolving market conditions.

A Practical, Beginner-Friendly Approach

Each section is designed with practicality in mind, offering clear explanations, actionable steps, and tools you can use immediately. Whether it's creating a trading plan, understanding market dynamics, or mastering emotional control, you'll find clear guidance and real-world examples to help you apply what you learn.

Trading can seem complex, but with the right approach, it's achievable. I'm confident I can teach anyone to trade. Success is down to you.

This book is designed to break down barriers, demystify the process, and help you take one step closer to transforming your life through trading, step by step.

LET'S GO

Contents

Part I Preparation 1

1 A Different World Will Have Its Own Language 3
- 1.1 The Sound of the Trading Floor 3
- 1.2 Thinking in Trader Language 7

2 Developing the Trader Mindset 9
- 2.1 Goal Setting 9
- 2.2 Motivation: You are the Key to Your Success as a Trader 13
- 2.3 Overcoming Fear 16
- 2.4 The Core Traits of a Successful Trader 18

3 Building Foundations 23
- 3.1 The (Trading) Skills That Pay the Bills 23
- 3.2 How the Markets Work 27
  - 3.2.1 Efficient Market Hypothesis (EMH) 27
  - 3.2.2 Supply and Demand 29
  - 3.2.3 Circular Flow of Income 29
  - 3.2.4 Monetary Policy: The Central Bank's Key Role in the Economy 30

4 Understanding the Markets 35
- 4.1 Money—It Makes the World Go Round (Apparently) 36
  - 4.1.1 Fixed Income Markets 36
  - 4.1.2 Understanding the Currency Market (Forex/fx) 48
  - 4.1.3 Short-Term Interest Rates (STIRs) 60
  - 4.1.4 Mastering the Holy Trinity 70

4.2 Precious Metals: The Golden Thread of Wealth and Power 71
4.2.1 The Metal That Needs No Introduction-Gold 72
4.2.2 Hi Ho Silver—The Poor Man's Gold 82
4.2.3 The Doctor Will See You Now: Understanding Copper 91
4.2.4 Platinum and Palladium: The Smaller Precious Metals With Big Potential 101
4.3 The Stock Market—The Market Everyone has Heard About 104
4.3.1 Investing in Stocks Vs. Trading Stock Indices 105
4.3.2 All you Need to Know About a Stock Index 106
4.4 The Rise of Crypto: The Future of Money? 131
4.4.1 The Evolution of Crypto: From Niche to Mainstream 132
4.4.2 Bitcoin: The Birth of Decentralized Money 133
4.4.3 Ethereum: The Birth of Smart Contracts 145
4.4.4 Decentralized Finance (Defi): The New Financial Frontier 149
4.4.5 The Future of Crypto 154
4.5 Energy—The Means to Get Anything Done! 167
4.5.1 Black Gold (Oil) 167
4.5.2 OPEC: The World's Most Powerful Cartel 169
4.5.3 A Tale of Two Oils: Light Sweet Crude Vs. Brent Crude 174
4.5.4 Oil Futures and Derivatives You Can Trade 181
4.5.5 Arbitraging the Brent-WTI Spread 186
4.5.6 Anticipation Vs. Reaction in Fundamental Trading 192
4.6 Natural Gas: The Market Fueled by Mother Nature 193
4.7 Hungry for the Markets—Food 197
4.7.1 The Sugar Market: Sweet Opportunities in Soft Commodities 198
4.7.2 The Cocoa Market: I Mean, Who Doesn't Like Chocolate! 205
4.7.3 Coffee, the Original Energy Drink 212
4.7.4 Mastering Corn Trading 221
4.7.5 Wheat, Give us our Daily Bread 226
4.7.6 Soybeans and Soy-based Products 231
4.7.7 Lean Hogs: The Market that Sizzles with Opportunity 237
4.7.8 Feeder and Live Cattle: Trading the Meat Markets 241
4.7.9 Understanding the Importance of COT and WASDE Reports in Agricultural Markets 245

Part II Process 251

5 The Professional Trading Process 253
5.1 Moving from Preparation to Process 253
5.1.1 Origin and Evolution of the Professional Trading Process 254
5.1.2 Enter the Trading Process 256

6 Identifying a Trade 257
6.1 What Does the Chart Say? 257
6.1.1 The Basics of Technical Analysis 259
6.1.2 "The Trend Is Your Friend." Identifying a Market Direction 262
6.1.3 My Three Core Techniques for Spotting a Market Direction 263
6.1.4 How to Spot the Market Turn—Counter-Trending or Mean Reversion 277
6.1.5 Counter-Trend Technical Trading Ideas 277
6.2 Fundamental Analysis 287
6.2.1 Qualitative Analysis 288
6.2.2 Quantitative Analysis 290
6.3 Seasonality 294
6.3.1 Classic Seasonal Patterns 296
6.3.2 How to Find Seasonal Trades in Commodities 297
6.3.3 Connect Seasonality to Fundamentals 298
6.4 Trading Price Action 299
6.4.1 A Trader's First School: Scalping 300
6.4.2 Introducing the Price Ladder 301

7 Executing a Trade 305
7.1 The Three Golden Rules of Trade Execution 306
7.1.1 May I Take Your Order (Type) 307
7.1.2 Market Liquidity and Why it Matters 310
7.1.3 Beyond the Basics: Advanced Order Types 311
7.1.4 Trading is a Risky Business—Execution Risks 312
7.1.5 Classic Execution Profiles 314

8 Managing a Trade 317
8.1 Stop Losses: The Foundation of Trade Management 318
8.2 Scaling Risk: Adding and Reducing Positions 319
8.3 Stay on Course in the Eye of the Storm 321
8.4 Golden Rules for Managing Trades 323

9 Evaluating a Trade 325
9.1 The Power of the Journal 326
9.1.1 Reviewing Performance: Process Vs Outcome 327
9.1.2 Spotting Recurring Patterns 328
9.1.3 Building Feedback Loops 329

Part III Practice 333

10 Practicing the Process 335
10.1 A Word on Risk Before You Begin 336
10.2 Preparing the Mental Athlete for Practice in the Markets 337
10.3 Understanding Trader Profiles 338
10.4 Setting Targets and Bringing Lag Indicators to Life 340
10.5 The Checklist: Your Daily Compass 342
10.6 Follow the money, not the impulse 343
10.7 Trading Blueprint 344

11 Trader Drills to Build Trading Skills 347
11.1 Identify: Drills to Strengthen Your Market Awareness 348
11.2 Execute: Drills to Build Precision and Control 352
11.3 Management: Drills to Get You That Promotion! 359
11.4 Evaluation: Drills to Help You Win or Learn 363

12 Risk vs Reward 375
12.1 Reframing Risk 375
12.2 Probability and Expectancy 380
12.3 Value at Risk (VaR) 383
12.4 The Risk–Reward Equation 386
12.5 The Power of Process to Help the Psychology of Risk 388
12.6 The Importance of Risk 391

13 The End Is Just the Beginning 393
13.1 Transitioning From Knowing to Doing 393
13.2 The Reality of Professional Trading 394
13.3 Next Steps: Building a Professional Pathway 394
13.4 Paying It Forward 395
13.5 The End Is Just the Beginning—Final Word 396

References 397

Index 399

About the Author

Sam Warner-Baker is a trading coach, capital markets educator, and founder of Teach the World to Trade. With over twenty years of experience trading global financial markets, he has worked primarily in financial futures—spanning commodities, interest rates, bonds, currencies, equities, and, more recently, cryptocurrencies and decentralized finance—both as an active trader and as a senior figure responsible for developing others. Sam has trained and mentored thousands of traders worldwide across proprietary trading firms, broker platforms, universities, and financial institutions. He previously served as Head of Education at a leading international trading academy and lectured in Trading Strategies at the University of Sussex, where he became known for translating complex institutional concepts into clear, practical frameworks that traders could apply in real markets. What distinguishes Sam's work is his emphasis on process over prediction. His teaching blends professional trading methodology with behavioral psychology, performance coaching, and elements of Stoic philosophy, reflecting a belief that long-term success is driven less by clever ideas than by discipline, self-awareness, and repeatable decision-making. Through Teach the World to Trade, Sam works in partnership with global exchanges, brokers, and institutional clients to help individuals learn to think, act, and improve like professionals—not gamblers.

Part I

Preparation

1

A Different World Will Have Its Own Language

1.1 The Sound of the Trading Floor

Step onto a professional trading floor, and you'll notice the language before you fully understand it. Screens flicker. Voices cut through the hum. "Bid up." "Offer lifted." "Scratch that." Every word is impactful. There's no small talk—only shorthand for action and risk. Trading has its own dialect, originating in the open-outcry pits and honed in electronic markets. It's quick, efficient, and brutally clear.

A single syllable can move millions, and a mistaken word can cost just as much. Learning this language isn't about memorising jargon; it's about understanding how professionals think—how they perceive risk, express conviction, and communicate under pressure.

Before you can trade like a professional, you must learn to speak like one.

Why Language Matters

Language equals clarity, and clarity equals speed. When a trader says, "Long five Brent outrights, onside ten ticks," every part of that sentence carries precise meaning. There's no ambiguity, no emotion. Markets reward those who can process information quickly and express intent clearly.

This vocabulary also shapes mindset. Professionals talk about being onside or offside rather than winning or losing. They scratch a trade instead of breaking even. The words are neutral and procedural—they describe process, not pride. This habit keeps emotion out of decision-making and reinforces objectivity, a hallmark of professional performance.

S. Warner-Baker, *Learn to Trade Like a Professional*,
https://doi.org/10.1007/978-3-032-20125-6_1

The Grammar of the Markets

Below are the words and expressions that make up the daily language of the trading floor. They are organised by theme, just as they appear in real conversations. Keep this section bookmarked as you work through the book; it's the foundation on which everything else is built.

1. *Price and Order Flow*

Bid/Offer (Ask)—The highest price a buyer will pay (offer), and the lowest price a seller will accept (bid).

Spread—The difference between bid and offer; a quick measure of market liquidity.

Lifting the Offer/Hitting the Bid—Buying at the offer or selling into the bid for immediate execution.

Flat—No open position.

Long/Short—Buying (long) in anticipation of a rise or selling (short) in anticipation of a fall.

Onside/Offside—When the price moves for (onside) or against (offside) your entry.

Pull Orders—Cancelling resting orders before they're hit.

Traded Out—All visible volume at that price has traded.

Priority—The queue for execution; first in = first filled.

Order Flow—The sequence and intensity of buying and selling that drives short-term price moves.

Slippage—The difference between expected and actual fill price, often in fast markets.

Liquidity Trap—When a position is so large that it distorts entry or exit, trapping the trader in illiquid conditions.

2. *Market Structure and Instruments*

Futures Contract—An agreement to buy or sell a set quantity of an asset at a future date and price.

Outright—A single futures position without an offset.

Inter-market or Calendar Spread—Trading the price difference between two related contracts of the same market, products, or exchanges.

Options—Rights (not obligations) to buy or sell at a specified strike price before expiry. We don't go into Options, but it's good to know what they are.

ETF/CFD/Index—Instruments that track baskets of assets or allow synthetic exposure.

Open Interest—Total number of outstanding contracts in a particular market—an indicator of participation.

Settlement—The exchange's official daily closing price.

Basis Trade—Trading the difference between futures and the physical or spot price.

Curve—A visual of futures prices across maturities, revealing expectations about time and value.

3. *Order Types and Execution*

Market Order—Execute immediately at the best available price.

Limit Order—Execute only at a chosen price or better.

Stop-Loss Order—Automatically closes a losing trade once the price reaches a threshold.

GTC/GTD—Good-Till-Cancelled or Good-Till-Day orders.

Iceberg Order—Large order shown in small visible pieces to conceal true size.

Limit Stop—Triggers only when both price and volume conditions are met.

Missed Stop—When the price gaps through your stop without filling it.

Whipsaw—A sharp reversal that stops traders out before resuming the trend.

Stop Run—A quick move through a cluster of stops before snapping back.

Backtest—Testing a trading or execution rule on historical data to assess reliability. Essential in algorithmic trading.

4. *Risk and Money Management*

Margin—Collateral posted to maintain a leveraged position.

Risk Management—Controlling downside through position sizing, diversification, and stops.

Round Trip—Opening + closing a trade; used to measure transaction costs.

Scratch—Exiting at entry price—no gain, no pain.

Volatility—The speed and magnitude of price changes; a proxy for uncertainty.

Mean Reversion—The idea that price eventually returns to its average.

Hedge—An offsetting position that reduces exposure.

Drawdown—The peak-to-trough decline in account equity over a period.
R-Multiple—Profit or loss expressed relative to the initial risk on a trade.
Expectancy—The average return per trade after accounting for win rate and reward-to-risk.
Edge—A measurable, repeatable advantage that makes a strategy profitable over time.

5. *Trader Culture and Slang*

Fat Finger—An accidental oversized or mis-priced order.
Figure Sheet (Economic Calendar)—Schedule of key economic data releases.
Liquidity—How easily you can enter or exit without moving the price.
Market price—The best bid and offer currently available.
Caught a Bid—Market finding new buying interest.
Thin Market—Low liquidity and erratic movement.
Run the Stops—Push through obvious stop levels to flush positions.
Tape's Heavy/Light—Describes aggressive selling or buying in the flow.
Fade the Move—Taking the opposite side of an emotional or overextended market move.
HODL—Crypto slang for holding through volatility.
Swing Trader/Scalper/Position Trader—Different trading horizons.
Risk Desk—Professional teams managing traders' execution and exposure.

6. *Analysis and Edge*

Technical Analysis (TA)—Studying price, volume, and chart patterns.
Fundamental Analysis (FA)—Evaluating economic data, policy, and sentiment.
Seasonality—Recurring patterns tied to calendar cycles.
Correlation—Degree to which two assets move together.
Order-Book Imbalance—Uneven bid/offer depth hints at short-term bias.
Breakout/Breakdown—Price moving beyond key resistance or support.
Backtest—Historical testing of a strategy (also used in execution).
Edge, Expectancy, R-Multiple—The trio that defines a trader's statistical advantage and performance expectancy.

7. Digital and Modern Markets

Funding Rate—The periodic payment between longs and shorts in perpetual futures, reflecting the cost of carry.

DeFi (Decentralised Finance)—Blockchain-based financial ecosystem.

Tokenomics—Economic design of a crypto asset.

Yield Farming—Earning returns by providing liquidity to DeFi protocols.

Basis Arbitrage—Profiting from differences between spot and futures in crypto.

Exchange Outage/Liquidation Cascade—Events where forced liquidations or system halts amplify volatility.

1.2 Thinking in Trader Language

Initially, your internal dialogue might sound emotional:

"I hope this goes up." "I can't afford another loss."

Professionals think differently:

"I'm long two contracts, heavy on the offer—market's overdone."

Notice the lack of emotion. The statement is factual, detached, and data-focused. This linguistic distance creates psychological space—the gap between you and your trade. Once you master the language, your decision-making becomes clearer, quicker, and more composed.

Every phrase in this chapter emphasises a key trading truth: words shape behaviour. When you begin speaking like a professional, you start thinking like one.

From Words to Wisdom

Language is the initial layer of professionalism. It transforms noise into meaning and chaos into structure.

The vocabulary in this chapter will recur throughout the book—when we analyse charts, manage trades, or assess performance. Fluency here speeds up mastery elsewhere.

Keep this glossary close. Add to it. Make it your own. The markets are alive, and their language constantly evolves.

Fluency comes before mastery. You can't master what you can't describe.

Every industry has its language. In medicine, it's anatomy; in law, precedent; in aviation, procedure.

In trading, the language is the markets themselves. Once you're fluent, the charts speak more clearly, the data makes sense, and execution becomes instinctive.

You've just learnt to speak the market's mother tongue.

Now it's time to learn how professionals think—and that begins with developing the trader mindset.

2

Developing the Trader Mindset

2.1 Goal Setting

The Philosophy of Targinium—a foreword on target-setting

The idea of target-setting is not new. The ancient philosophers of Greece and Rome adhered to a principle called Targinium, derived from the word "targum," meaning a clear point to aim at. They believed that living a meaningful life required setting clear goals and striving for them with purpose and resolve. Aristotle famously argued that "happiness" (or eudaimonia) is not a fleeting emotion, but a state achieved through deliberate action, guided by virtue and purpose.

In trading, Targinium reminds us that we must always have a target—a reason behind every trade we undertake. Without clear objectives, we risk becoming impulsive and reacting emotionally to every market fluctuation. But with a clear target, every decision becomes part of a greater plan. Even losses become meaningful because they teach us how to adjust our aim and improve.

The philosophers also warned against the danger of setting goals that are too ambitious or unrealistic. Instead, they advocated for incremental targets—small, achievable steps that lead towards larger ambitions. This aligns directly with the growth mindset traders must nurture: every trade, whether a win or a loss, is a stepping stone towards mastery.

The Professional Approach

The traders who find success in the markets and I share one key trait: confidence in what they're doing and clarity about what they want to achieve.

S. Warner-Baker, *Learn to Trade Like a Professional*,
https://doi.org/10.1007/978-3-032-20125-6_2

But this doesn't happen by chance. It comes from spending time setting clear goals, working hard to pursue them, and staying motivated every single day.

I'm not much of a golfer or athlete in my later years, but I tend to draw a lot of inspiration from sports coaching and high performance. One of the best ways to approach target-setting in trading is to take inspiration from the principles discussed in "Golf is Not a Game of Perfect" by Dr Bob Rotella. In the book, Rotella explains that the key to excelling at golf—or any skill—is not to fixate on perfect outcomes but to focus on process-oriented goals. Instead of worrying about the result of every swing or shot, great golfers break their game down into smaller, controllable elements: their stance, their grip, and their mental state. They trust that by perfecting their process, the results will take care of themselves.

The same principle applies to trading. You can't control how the market moves, just as a golfer can't control the wind. However, you can control your preparation, process, and response to challenges. Instead of setting vague goals like "make a lot of money," set specific, actionable targets.

By focusing on the process, you build the skills and habits that lead to long-term success.

How can we apply Target-Setting in your Trading

Set Process-Oriented Goals

Don't just aim for monetary profits. Focus on improving specific aspects of your trading process, such as consistently following your plan, managing risk effectively, or maintaining a trading journal.

Some examples I use myself, and when I'm coaching traders, are as follows.

"Follow my trading plan without deviation for the next 30 days."
"Journal every trade through the correct process."
"Limit my losses to X% of my account per day."
"Paper trade (on a demo account) 5 new ideas a day for a week."

Break Goals into Daily Targets

Ancient philosophers recognised the profound impact of daily habits. Ask yourself: "What can I achieve today to get closer to my long-term trading goals?" This could be something as simple as reviewing your trades or reading market news.

Reflect and Adjust

Just as ancient archers used their misses to refine their aim, use every trade to refine your strategy. Ask: "What worked? What didn't? How can I improve next time?"

Stay Motivated with Purpose
Trading can be isolating and challenging, but you'll find the motivation to keep going when you connect your targets to a larger purpose—such as achieving financial independence, fostering personal growth, or providing for your family.

Target-setting is more than just a to–do list; it's a framework for building confidence and clarity, removing the overarching focus all new traders have—their P&L. By focusing on what you can control and aiming for steady improvement, you can achieve remarkable results in trading—just as ancient philosophers and even professional golfers understood centuries ago.

Goal Setting in Trading: Leaning on the 4DX Principle

Goal setting has always been a fundamental part of my success and that of the traders I've mentored over the years. When trading, particularly when money is at stake, having clear goals is crucial. Without them, you're like a ship without a compass, drifting aimlessly in the constantly shifting tides of the markets.

One of the first questions I often ask traders during coaching sessions is, "How much money are you hoping to make in a day, week, month, or year, and how realistic is that at the moment, doing what you're doing?" Setting your trading goals based on both ambition and reality is essential. Unrealistic expectations can lead to frustration and eventually cause traders to leave the markets. Conversely, vague or overly cautious goals fail to motivate the necessary action for genuine progress and can drain motivation.

Based on my studies in this area over the years, I tend to rely on the principles from "The 4 Disciplines of Execution (4DX)" by Chris McChesney, Sean Covey, and Jim Huling to guide my goal-setting process, and I recommend this framework to all traders. Their principles are well-documented and broadly applied in business strategy globally. The 4DX principle emphasises setting clear, achievable goals while creating a system to track progress and ensure accountability. Here's how the 4DX model directly relates to trading:

1. Focus on the Wildly Important Goal (WIG)

The first step in the 4DX framework is to identify your Wildly Important Goal (WIG)—the single most important thing you want to achieve. In trading, my WIG has always been clear: earn double my outgoings and help a million people change their lives through trading. I also lean on both intrinsic and extrinsic goal setting, but I won't delve too deeply into that now.

For you as a trader, a WIG might look like:

"Earn enough money through trading to give up my job in the next three years."
"Pay off all my debts and start saving for retirement by the time I'm 30/40."
"Supplement my income to x per month/year in the next 6 months."

Your WIG should motivate you, but stay realistic considering your current skills, experience, and resources. As you develop, your WIG can adapt to reflect your ambitions.

2. Act on the Lead Measures

The 4DX principle distinguishes between **lag measures** and lead measures. Lag measures are the results you want to achieve, like the profits in your trading account, but these are outcomes—things you can't control directly. **Lead measures**, on the other hand, are actions you can take now to drive those results.
In trading, examples of **lead measures** include:

Spending 30 minutes each day analysing the market.
Journaling every trade to identify patterns and areas for improvement.
Not losing more than x ticks per trade.

By focusing on lead measures, you develop the habits and behaviours that ultimately help you achieve your WIG. When we examine the trade process, you will have many more lead measures to consider for your goal setting. We will revisit this section when we arrive there in a few pages.

3. Keep a Compelling Scoreboard

To stay motivated, you should monitor your progress. A compelling scoreboard provides a visual representation of your progress toward your goal. I do and recommend the following:
A spreadsheet tracking your daily, weekly, and monthly profits and losses or ticks made/lost.
A process checklist including performance metrics, such as win rates, average trade duration, trade type, notes from evaluation, or adherence to your plan.
Seeing your progress in real time keeps you engaged and accountable.

4. Create a Cadence of Accountability

The final discipline of 4DX is establishing a routine of regular **accountability**. This could involve weekly or monthly reviews of your trading performance, either independently or with the guidance of a mentor or trading group. The key is to reflect on your progress, identify what's working, and adjust where necessary.

Remember, you are ultimately responsible for your results. As successful traders, we need to wear many hats, including being our own coaches.

Regularly ask yourself the following:

"Did I stick to my trading plan this week?"
"What lead measures did I follow, and how did they impact my results?"
"What can I do differently next week to get closer to my WIG?"

Holding yourself accountable creates a feedback loop that drives continuous improvement.

Balancing Trading Goals with Life Goals

One of the reasons I'm so passionate about goal setting is that it extends beyond trading. Life is about more than just profits, and a balanced approach ensures that success in one area doesn't come at the expense of another. Alongside my trading WIG, I also have goals for my energy (staying healthy and focused) and family (being present and supportive). I recommend you do the same.

When you align your trading goals with your personal values, you create a sense of balance and purpose that keeps you motivated in the long run.

Start Setting Your Goals Today

Trading is a journey, and success doesn't happen overnight. By applying the principles from Chris McChesney, Sean Covey, and Jim Huling's "The 4 Disciplines of Execution"—defining your WIG, focusing on key lead measures, tracking progress, and staying accountable—you can create a clear, actionable pathway to profitability. Combine this with balanced life goals, and you're not just building a successful trading career—you're building a life worth celebrating.

2.2 Motivation: You are the Key to Your Success as a Trader

For an inexperienced trader, motivation can often feel fleeting. The markets are complex, and the journey to success isn't always straightforward. But here's the reality: someone, somewhere—who isn't as driven, disciplined, or intelligent as you—is making money in the markets. That simple truth has been one of my most effective personal motivators, and it can be yours too.

Motivation doesn't come from waiting for inspiration—it comes from taking action, building belief in your abilities, and committing to growth. Here's some helpful advice to motivate you to start trading and stay consistent, drawing on lessons from some of the most impactful personal development books I've used over the years, combined with my own experience. You might be surprised to hear that motivating junior traders isn't easy, even with the incentive of earning more than their peers and parents.

Owning Your Journey—You Pull the Trigger

Eric Thomas, one of the most inspiring voices in personal development, emphasises in his book-*You Owe You* that success is about taking responsibility for your future. No one is coming to save you. This truth is particularly relevant in trading, where your success is entirely in your hands.

As a trader, you must commit to yourself. If you want it, you need to put in the work. No matter what they say on their Instagram account, no one will hand you winning position after winning position.

Take ownership of your learning. The market doesn't care about your excuses or why you didn't study that strategy. You owe it to yourself to prepare.

Show up every day. Thomas discusses the importance of consistency and discipline. Even when the markets feel intimidating or your trades don't go as planned, showing up to improve is half the battle.

Motivation starts with a decision: to stop blaming external factors and take responsibility for your progress. In trading, that means learning, reflecting, and never giving up on the process.

One of the main reasons I have always loved trading is the autonomy I have had in each decision from the very start. I am responsible for my own destiny in the markets and no one else. I pull the trigger (click the mouse)

The Power of Desire

Napoleon Hill's classic book *Think and Grow Rich* highlights desire as the starting point of all achievement. Without a burning desire to succeed, it's easy to falter when things get tough, like after a losing trade or a challenging run in the markets.

Hill suggests that to channel desire effectively in trading, it should be turned into a definite purpose. It would be helpful if you had read the earlier pages on goal setting.

Write those trading goals down. Get specific: "I want to grow my account by 10% this quarter by consistently following my trading plan."

Visualise your success every day. Imagine yourself trading with discipline and building your confidence. As a young trader in a trading office, I would observe the senior traders and visualise their risk profiles and positions, picturing what I would do and how I would manage their positions if it were me. I still hold a vision of myself as the best trader I aspire to be.

Hill also emphasises the importance of faith. Believe that you can succeed, even when the results aren't immediate. Combine faith with a clear action plan, and you'll have the fuel to stay motivated.

Trading is an emotive game as much as it is a mix of critical thinking and numerical reasoning. If you don't believe you will succeed, even when going through a tough patch, you never will.

Practical Steps to Build and Maintain Motivation

Here are actionable strategies which I have used over the years to stay motivated as a trader:

Create a Routine: Establish a daily schedule for market analysis, journaling, and educational activities. Consistency builds momentum. Monday through Friday, I analyse the market between 0700 and 0830 to prepare myself for the trading day, and from 1700 to 1800, I review and analyse the day. These are two of many parts of my trading routine, which I will share throughout the book.

Celebrate Small Wins: Reward yourself for progress, like sticking to your weekly trading plan or learning and testing a new trading strategy. Celebrating the small wins really helps me personally; when you're trying to reach your greater goal over a month or a year, these little dopamine hits help a big time.

Surround Yourself with Support: Join trading communities or find a mentor to keep you accountable and inspired. This has been harder post-COVID. While most people now work from home, I am accustomed to an office environment with numerous traders around me. On the other hand, social groups online have grown as more people have turned to the markets. It would help if you found your tribe.

You are your barrier and gateway to trading success.

Motivation isn't about waiting for the perfect moment to start or constantly feeling excited. It's about committing to your goals even when it's hard. Take ownership of your journey (*You Owe You*) and nurture a burning desire to succeed (*Think and Grow Rich*).

Remember: someone out there, less driven and less prepared, is already making money in the markets. Why not you?

The enemy within

While digging into our psychological selves, it's the perfect time to address the constant battle every trader faces with fear, greed, and overconfidence. Even after 20 years in the markets, I still encounter days when I must rely on my mental toolkit to overcome these challenges. Writing about these emotions is not just a reminder for you—it's a reminder for me, too. It helps keep my focus sharp and my process on track.

Overcoming these mental blocks requires daily effort. I use mantras and rituals to reinforce my mindset. Simple practices, such as reviewing my trading plan every morning or journaling my trades each evening, serve as psychological anchors, keeping me grounded. These rituals help me reset after tough days and stay disciplined after great ones.

Trading success isn't just about understanding charts or strategies, but about mastering your mind. You develop the mental resilience needed to succeed in the markets by recognising and addressing fear, greed, and overconfidence. These emotions may never completely disappear, but you can ensure they don't hinder you with the right tools and mindset.

Let's analyse these emotional black holes and explore practical ways to manage them. Understanding how to overcome these mental blocks is essential to long-term trading success.

2.3 Overcoming Fear

Fear often arises in trading due to market uncertainty or the risk of loss. It can appear as hesitation, making you miss opportunities, or as panic, leading you to close trades too early.

Have a Plan: Fear thrives in chaos. A well-defined trading plan with clear entry, exit, and stop-loss levels gives you the confidence to act decisively.

Start Small: If fear is holding you back, reduce your position size. Smaller trades help ease the psychological burden of potential losses while you build confidence. I use a trick to switch from my live account to a simulated account if I have ideas I want to test or have been through a particularly testing trading period.

Use Visualisation: Before trading, visualise yourself calmly executing your strategy, even in volatile markets. This mental rehearsal reduces the fear of the unknown. I have always visualised what to do in the event of a switch in market sentiment and how to limit losses and profit from the market moving against my initial trade idea.

Reframe Losses: View losses as part of the learning process. Fear diminishes when you accept that losing is inevitable and focus on the lessons each trade offers. We will pick this up throughout the book. Our mantra at Teach the World to Trade is 'Win or Learn'; there is no such thing as losing if you adopt the growth mindset needed for success.

Controlling Greed

Greed often stems from the excitement of winning trades and the desire to maximise profits. It can push traders to over-leverage, hold onto trades too long, or deviate from their strategy in pursuit of quick gains.

Set Profit Targets: Define your profit goals before entering a trade and stick to them. Exiting at your target ensures you don't let greed lead to unnecessary risks.

Follow a Risk-Reward Ratio: Maintain a consistent risk-reward ratio (e.g., 1:2 or 1:3) to ensure your trades align with your long-term goals. This is a favourite of mine and has kept me on the straight and narrow for many years. Falling into the trap of high-risk, low-reward trades has been the end for many traders.

Use Journaling: Document trades where greed influenced your decisions. Reflecting on these moments helps you recognise patterns and improve discipline. (Are you picking up on some of the constant themes yet?)

Focus on the Process: Shift your mindset from "How much can I make?" to "Am I following my plan?" This will keep you grounded in good trading habits. Once you start removing the financial aspect from your trading, you will begin to shine.

Taming Overconfidence

Overconfidence can emerge after a string of successful trades, making you believe you're invincible. This mindset often leads to overtrading, neglecting risk management, or taking on positions outside one's area of expertise.

Stay Humble: Remember that the market is unpredictable, and no trader wins every time. Acknowledge that luck can play a role in short-term success. The very best traders know this and continue to grow incrementally rather than exponentially.

Review Your Trades: Regularly review your journal, including trades where overconfidence led to mistakes, to identify areas for improvement. Remind yourself of the importance of sticking to your process.

Maintain Position Size Discipline: Avoid increasing position sizes impulsively after a win. Consistency is critical to long-term success. As I mentioned, this is a significant factor for myself and other seasoned traders;

the number of times I have increased size after a good run, only to see my next trade go wrong, is ridiculous. It's almost a running joke among the more senior traders I work with that the market knows you're trying to improve, and it wants to remind you to stay humble. (It doesn't, by the way)

Practice Gratitude: Take a moment to appreciate what you've already achieved. Gratitude shifts your focus from chasing more to valuing steady progress. For years (before my journey into philosophy and ancient wisdom), I would say to my trading partner at the time after a loss, 'It's okay; as long as we stick to the golden rule, we will be alright. The golden rule was to stay alive!

I am grateful that I wake up every day and have the opportunity to work in the markets. So should you be, as one day, this won't be the case.

2.4 The Core Traits of a Successful Trader

Throughout my career, I've received tens of thousands of applications from aspiring traders worldwide and interviewed thousands of individuals eager to take on the challenge of becoming professional derivatives traders. If there's one thing I've learned from this experience, it's this: there is no clear-cut profile of a person that guarantees success in the markets.

Our hiring process was surprisingly straightforward yet incredibly effective in the early years of recruiting potential trading legends. It consisted of three simple steps:

Review the CV and cover letter for anything that stood out—whether it was an exceptional academic achievement, a unique experience, or signs of an entrepreneurial spirit.

Conduct a face-to-face interview to assess their confidence, curiosity, and passion for the markets.

Administer a timed maths test—a deceptively simple exam taken alone in the interview room. It wasn't about advanced calculations but about staying calm under pressure and solving problems efficiently. This test alone proved to be an excellent filter.

As the years went by, we chose to explore deeper into what sets successful traders apart. We enlisted a team of psychology experts from a top UK university to work with our best traders, analysing their traits and characteristics to find common patterns. Although each successful trader was unique in their approach, they all shared key traits that underpinned their success: resilience, discipline, patience, and consistency.

Let's examine them and see how you can harness their benefits and why they are so helpful in the market.

Cultivating the 4 Core Traits

Success in trading is rarely determined by intelligence, background, or luck. Instead, it hinges on the following four core traits that can be cultivated throughout life: resilience, discipline, patience, and consistency. These qualities aren't just reserved for trading—they're skills that can be developed through everyday experiences and challenges. By working on these traits in your personal life, you'll find they translate seamlessly into the trading world, laying the foundation for long-term success.

Resilience: Fall 7, Rise 8 (Japanese Proverb—Thanks Angela Duckworth)

Life:

Resilience is built through adversity. It's the ability to bounce back after setbacks, whether failing an exam, losing a job, or facing personal challenges. Life constantly throws obstacles in your way, and how you respond shapes your ability to persevere. We can help cultivate resilience:

- View failures as opportunities to learn and grow.
- Surround yourself with a supportive network of friends, family, or mentors.
- Practice mindfulness or meditation to help process stress and regain focus.

Trading:

In the markets, resilience is about staying calm after losses. Every trader faces losing streaks, but resilient traders don't let these moments define them. Instead, they:

- Reflect on their mistakes, refine their strategy, and prepare for the next trade.
- Avoid emotional decisions driven by frustration or fear.
- Maintain a long-term perspective, understanding that one bad day doesn't dictate their success.
- The key is to view every loss as a lesson, not a failure. With resilience, setbacks become stepping stones.

Discipline: Sticking to the Plan

Life:

Discipline is the ability to stay committed to your goals, even when distractions or temptations arise. Whether it's exercising regularly, saving money, or studying for an exam, discipline is about doing what needs to be done, even when you don't feel like it. The following can help build a foundation of discipline:

- Create routines that make good habits automatic.
- Break big goals into smaller, actionable steps to stay focused.
- Use accountability partners or tools to track your progress.

Trading:
In the markets, discipline means sticking to your trading plan. It's about avoiding the temptation to chase profits, take impulsive trades, or deviate from your strategy.

Disciplined traders always follow pre-set risk management rules, such as limiting the percentage of their account risked on any single trade or the number of ticks they are willing to sacrifice on a trade's execution.

- Avoid revenge trading after a loss, knowing that emotional decisions often lead to further mistakes.
- Maintain their trading journal, holding themselves accountable for every decision.
- Discipline isn't glamorous—it's the daily grind of doing the right things over and over. But it's what separates successful traders from those who burn out.

Patience: Disciplines close relative.
Life:
Patience is built through waiting for results, opportunities, or even mundane annoyances like traffic or queues. It's the ability to delay gratification, trusting that the right outcome will arrive eventually. We have been striving to develop patience throughout our lives. Here are some of my tips.

- Practice mindfulness to stay present in the moment. It won't be the first or last time I tell you I meditate for 20 minutes every morning before I trade.
- Focus on the bigger picture rather than immediate results.
- Learn to tolerate discomfort, whether boredom or frustration, without reacting impulsively. No pressure, no diamonds is a phrase often used in our household.

Trading:
Patience is essential for waiting for the proper setups. The best traders know that forcing trades out of boredom or fear of missing out (FOMO) often leads to unnecessary losses.

- The most patient traders wait for setups that align perfectly with their strategy, even if it means sitting on the sidelines for hours or days.
- Avoid overtrading, knowing that less can often be more. I am guilty of this one on a hectic day.
- Trust that the markets will provide opportunities as long as they stay prepared and disciplined, a regular mantra of mine—the markets will always move!

Patience is about trusting your process and avoiding rushed decisions that could derail your progress.

Consistency: You did well; now, do it again.
Life:
Consistency is the foundation of all success. It's the ability to show up and put in the work every single day, even when the results aren't immediate. Whether it's exercising, studying, or practicing a skill, consistency turns effort into habits and habits into achievements. I call them my set of fundamentals for success. Here is an insight.

- Focus on small, repeatable actions that compound over time.
- Create systems or routines that make consistency easier to maintain.
- Celebrate progress, no matter how small, to reinforce the habit.

Trading:
In the markets, consistency is the key to long-term profitability. It's not about having one great day—it's about following your process day in and day out.

- As mentioned, the most consistent traders prepare daily for the markets with routines like market analysis and journaling.
- They stick to their strategy regardless of short-term results, trusting that consistency over time will yield success.
- Keep their emotions in check, trading with the same focus and discipline after wins or losses. This is easier said than done, as we are only human.

Consistency isn't exciting, but it ensures that progress continues, even when motivation wanes. Consistency is the most potent trait; once you nail a consistent approach, you can compound your success in life and the markets.

While every trader's journey is unique, these core traits—resilience, discipline, patience, and consistency—are the common threads that run through every success story I've witnessed. They're not qualities you're born with; they're skills you can develop with time, effort, and the right mindset.

In trading, these qualities become your advantage. They enable you to navigate market fluctuations, stay focused on your objectives, and improve steadily over time. Remember, success in trading isn't just about the markets—it's about mastering yourself. These traits lay the groundwork for that mastery.

Life is a trade!

3

Building Foundations

3.1 The (Trading) Skills That Pay the Bills

When developing successful traders, recognising the right character traits is just part of the equation. Equally vital is evaluating and nurturing specific skills that traders need to succeed in the markets. Over the years, I've observed that these skills often stand out in individuals who excel at activities such as gaming, poker, chess, or playing a sport or an instrument at a high level. These pursuits demand focus, strategy, and discipline—qualities that easily transfer into trading.

Here are the core skills we recognise as essential for success. As you read through them, consider how they resonate with you and how you could incorporate them into your daily life.

Critical Thinking

The ability to analyse information, identify patterns, and make sound decisions is crucial in trading. Markets are complex, and traders must approach them with a logical and systematic mindset.

How to Enhance It:

Challenge yourself with strategy games like chess, or my inner geek enjoys battle simulation games on the PS5.

Practice analysing market news and reports to discern actionable insights. I still do this now, imagining what each piece of news I read could do to the price of an asset—it's a game for me.

S. Warner-Baker, *Learn to Trade Like a Professional*,
https://doi.org/10.1007/978-3-032-20125-6_3

Reflect on your decision-making processes to identify areas for improvement. Bringing it back to that coaching piece again!

Numerical Reasoning

Strong numerical reasoning allows traders to process and interpret data quickly and accurately. Whether calculating risk, determining position sizes, or spotting trends, comfort with numbers is key.

How to Enhance It:

Practice mental maths or use apps designed to sharpen numerical skills.

Explore basic statistics and probabilities to understand risk-reward dynamics. Using trial and error with market probabilities is an excellent way to learn and will ultimately be rewarding over time.

Regularly review trading data to become accustomed to interpreting charts and figures. We will discuss using technical analysis, which examines numerical data on charts. A confident approach to numbers is all that is needed.

Focus

Successful traders excel at maintaining focus, even during long periods of inactivity or high-pressure situations. They don't let distractions pull them away from the task at hand.

How to Enhance It:

Try mindfulness or meditation exercises to improve your ability to stay present. I am a 20-minute-morning kind of guy before I even look at the screens.

I regularly practice breathing techniques, especially when markets are hectic. A simple round of 6 seconds in and 8 seconds out, three times, always brings me into focus.

Engage in activities that demand concentration, such as learning a musical instrument or gaming, to cultivate focus away from screens by doing something that helps us relax.

Curiosity

Curiosity drives the desire to explore new ideas, strategies, and market trends. It's the fuel for continuous learning and adaptation in an ever-changing industry.

How to Enhance It:

Dedicate time to reading about market trends, trading strategies, or economic principles.

Experiment with small, low-risk trades in new markets to expand your understanding. I have unearthed some great trade ideas by doing this; the possibilities are endless.

Develop a habit of asking "why" when analysing market movements or results. You learn this way retrospectively and prepare yourself for future moves.

Work Ethic

Trading demands a strong work ethic to prepare, analyse, and improve consistently. It's not about occasional bursts of effort—it's about showing up every day. Effort counts twice.

How to Enhance It:

Build a daily routine that includes market preparation, journaling, and reflection.

Set short-term goals that align with your long-term trading ambitions.

Learn to embrace the grind, knowing that steady effort pays off over time. This is your opportunity to change your life. It isn't impossible; it's simply hard work.

Growth Mindset

Perhaps the most powerful skill of all is a growth mindset, the belief that abilities and intelligence can be developed through effort, learning, and perseverance. Traders with a growth mindset view setbacks not as failures but as opportunities to improve. They understand that the markets will test them, but each challenge is a chance to grow stronger.

How to Enhance It:

Reframe failures as learning experiences. After a losing trade, ask: "What can I do better next time?"

Seek feedback from mentors or peers to identify blind spots in your approach.

Celebrate progress, not just results. Acknowledge minor improvements in your skills, discipline, or understanding.

Practice self-awareness by tracking your emotional and psychological responses to market conditions.

Adaptability

The markets are volatile, and no two trading days are alike. Successful traders are flexible and able to adjust their strategies when market conditions shift. In my 20 years of trading, I have had to change both what and how I trade many times.

How to Enhance It:

Practice switching between different task types or environments to build mental flexibility.

Stay open to feedback and continuously refine your approach; also, try not to overload yourself with new ideas that may distract from your focus.

Simulate various market scenarios in a demo account to prepare for unexpected events.

Enhancing Your Skills Daily

These skills aren't just for trading—they're life skills that can be developed and applied in countless ways. Whether playing poker, devising a business strategy, or mastering an instrument, activities that challenge your mind and build discipline are excellent training grounds for the market.

You can start cultivating your edge as a trader by identifying which skills come naturally to you and which need more development. A growth mindset ties all these skills together—it's the belief that every day is an opportunity to learn, improve, and get closer to your goals.

So, which of these skills resonates with you, and how will you enhance them starting today? And next time someone tells you to stop wasting time playing that PlayStation, you can proudly tell them you're building an elite skill set that will one day set you apart.

From Traits and Skills to Market Knowledge

In the previous chapter, we explored the traits and skills that set successful traders apart: resilience, discipline, patience, consistency, and abilities such as critical thinking, numerical reasoning, and curiosity. These qualities form the core of a trader's mindset and the tools they employ to navigate the market's challenges.

However, mindset and skills alone are not enough. To trade successfully, you must understand the environment in which you are operating. Trading isn't a game of chance—it's a strategic engagement with complex, dynamic systems. To succeed, you need to understand how those systems function.

The next step in your journey is to master some essential market fundamentals. These ideas aren't just theoretical—they form the foundation of how markets operate and why prices fluctuate. Without a firm understanding of these principles, even the best strategies and attitudes will struggle to establish a foothold.

This chapter will introduce four essential concepts:

- Efficient Market Hypothesis
- Supply and Demand
- Circular Flow of Income
- Monetary policy

Understanding these concepts will give you insight into market behaviour and help you make informed decisions, interpret trends, and anticipate opportunities.

3.2 How the Markets Work

3.2.1 Efficient Market Hypothesis (EMH)

The Efficient Market Hypothesis (EMH) is a theory proposing that markets are "efficient," implying that all available information is already embedded in asset prices. According to EMH, it's impossible to consistently "beat the market" because prices already incorporate all known data.

There are three levels of market efficiency:

Weak Form Efficiency: Past price data is reflected in current prices, so technical analysis alone won't give you an edge.

Semi-Strong Form Efficiency: Prices also reflect all publicly available information, making fundamental analysis less useful.

Strong Form Efficiency: Prices even account for insider information, making it theoretically impossible to outperform the market.

Why It Matters for Traders:
While EMH is a useful framework, markets are not always perfectly efficient. Traders can find opportunities by identifying inefficiencies caused by human behaviour, news events, or market anomalies. Understanding EMH helps you focus your strategies on where inefficiencies might occur, such as during periods of heightened emotion or when new information is unevenly digested.

More than ever, this concept, documented as an economic principle by Eugene Fama in the 1970s, has been shown to be outdated. While the market will move on to new data and information, it will also try to outsmart itself by predicting far into the future and getting things wildly wrong. This has produced huge opportunities in markets.

In his book Efficiently Inefficient: How Smart Money Invests and Market Prices Are Determined, Lasse Heje Pedersen presents a compelling theory that markets operate in a state of equilibrium he terms "efficiently inefficient." According to Pedersen, financial markets are not perfectly efficient, as traditional economic theory might suggest, but neither are they entirely inefficient. Instead, they are structured to provide limited opportunities for skilled investors to exploit inefficiencies while remaining efficient enough to deter widespread arbitrage by less sophisticated participants.

Pedersen's theory is based on the idea that informed and skilled investors, like hedge funds and institutional traders, help correct pricing anomalies and bring markets closer to their fair value. However, the costs, risks, and competition involved in trading limit these profit opportunities. The balance created by these forces ensures that inefficiencies exist but are not easy to exploit, maintaining what Pedersen describes as the "efficiently inefficient" nature of the market.

Sources of Market Inefficiency

Pedersen identifies several key sources of inefficiency that create opportunities for traders while also imposing limits on their ability to exploit them. One major source is behavioural biases among investors, including overconfidence, herding behaviour, and emotional decision-making, which can lead to mispricing in the market. For instance, retail investors might overreact to news events, creating short-term inefficiencies that more sophisticated traders can exploit. Computer-driven trading systems (algos) can more commonly extend market moves, creating huge opportunities.

Another critical factor is the limit to arbitrage. Even when mispricing is clear, arbitrageurs' ability to act is limited by risks such as liquidity shortages, transaction costs, and the possibility that market conditions might worsen before the inefficiency is corrected. These limits ensure that inefficiencies last long enough to give informed traders opportunities, while discouraging reckless or excessive risk-taking.

Arbitrage explained.
Suppose gold is priced at £1,000 per ounce in London but £1,020 per ounce in New York due to differences in supply and demand. A trader can:

1. *Buy gold in London at £1,000.*
2. *Sell gold in New York at £1,020.*
3. *Pocket the £20 per ounce difference minus transaction costs.*

Arbitrage plays a critical role in maintaining market efficiency. It helps align prices across markets, ensuring that discrepancies are corrected quickly.

Finally, information asymmetry is a key factor. Access to timely, accurate, and comprehensive information is not consistent across financial markets. Traders with better analytical tools, expertise, or access to exclusive information can use this advantage to identify and capitalise on inefficiencies.

However, competition among informed investors and the eventual spread of information ensure these opportunities are short-lived.

Pedersen's insights highlight the importance of understanding the ever-changing relationship between market efficiency and inefficiency. For us as traders, this means recognising that although opportunities are present, seizing them requires skill, discipline, and an understanding of the forces that limit their availability, all of which we seek to develop through the chapters in this book.

3.2.2 Supply and Demand

The principle of supply and demand is one of the most fundamental concepts in economics and trading. At its core, it explains how prices are determined in a market based on the balance (or imbalance) between buyers and sellers.

Supply: The quantity of a good or asset available for sale.

Demand: The desire and ability of buyers to purchase that good or asset.

Prices rise when demand exceeds supply (more buyers than sellers) and fall when supply exceeds demand (more sellers than buyers). In trading, this dynamic plays out on price charts as buyers (bulls) and sellers (bears) compete for control.

Why It Matters for Traders:

Understanding supply and demand allows traders to anticipate price movements. For example:

Look for support and resistance levels on a chart where demand or supply concentrations might cause price reversals.

Monitor economic events or earnings reports that can shift demand or supply dynamics, such as a central bank interest rate decision or a crop yield report.

Supply and demand form the heartbeat of the markets, and recognising their patterns gives you an edge.

3.2.3 Circular Flow of Income

The Circular Flow of Income is an economic model that shows how money flows among households, businesses, and governments. It's a cycle of spending and income generation that drives economic activity.

Key components include:

Households (this is you): Provide labour and consume goods and services.

Businesses: Produce goods and services while paying wages to households.

Government: Collects taxes and spends on public services and the ever-increasing public employment sector, influencing the flow of money.

Financial Markets: Facilitate saving, investment, and capital allocation (mortgages, loans).

Why It Matters for Traders:

The circular flow of income underpins macroeconomic trends and market movements. For example:

A surge in household spending can drive economic growth, increasing demand for stocks or commodities.

Government fiscal policies, like stimulus packages or tax changes, can influence market sentiment and asset prices.

Changes in savings and investments, such as shifts in interest rates or bond yields, impact currency and equity markets.

By understanding how money flows through the economy, traders can better interpret the broader context of market moves and position themselves accordingly.

3.2.4 Monetary Policy: The Central Bank's Key Role in the Economy

Monetary policy refers to the actions taken by a central bank, such as the Bank of England, the Federal Reserve, or the European Central Bank, to manage the economy by controlling the money supply and interest rates. It's a vital tool for influencing inflation, employment, and overall economic growth.

Central banks set specific targets and use monetary policy to achieve them. These targets often include:

Stable inflation: Typically, around 2% per year, ensuring prices don't rise or fall too quickly.

Full employment: Maintaining a low and sustainable unemployment rate.

Economic growth: Encouraging steady GDP growth without overheating the economy.

Stable currency: Ensuring exchange rates don't fluctuate excessively, supporting trade and investment.

Financial stability: Preventing market crashes or systemic risks that could harm the broader economy.

Central banks aim to balance these objectives using interest rates, open market operations, and other tools, fostering an environment conducive to long-term economic prosperity.

Key Components of Monetary Policy

Interest Rates
Central banks set a benchmark interest rate (e.g., the Federal Funds Rate or the Bank of England Base Rate) that influences the cost of borrowing and returns on savings.
Lower interest rates encourage borrowing and spending, stimulating economic growth.

Higher interest rates curb excessive spending and inflation by making borrowing more expensive.

Open Market Operations (OMO)
Central banks buy or sell government bonds to regulate the money supply:
Buying bonds injects money into the economy, lowering interest rates and encouraging spending.

Selling bonds reduces the money supply, raising interest rates and slowing economic activity.

Quantitative Easing (QE)
In times of economic crisis, central banks may implement QE, in which they purchase financial assets such as government bonds or mortgage-backed securities to inject liquidity into the financial system.

Reserve Requirements
Central banks can dictate how much money commercial banks must hold in reserve, limiting or expanding the amount of money available for lending.

Forward Guidance
Central banks provide signals about future policy intentions, influencing market expectations and economic behaviour in advance.

Why Monetary Policy Matters for Traders
Monetary policy directly affects macroeconomic conditions and market dynamics, emphasising the importance for traders to understand its influence. Here's how it impacts the markets:

Interest Rates and Bond Yields
Rising interest rates usually cause higher bond yields and lower bond prices, while falling rates have the opposite effect.
Equity markets often react negatively to rate hikes, as higher borrowing costs reduce corporate profits.

Currency Markets (Forex)
Higher interest rates generally strengthen a country's currency because they attract foreign investment looking for higher returns.
Conversely, lower rates can weaken a currency, promoting exports but discouraging foreign investment.

Stock Markets
Expansionary monetary policy (low rates, QE) supports equity markets by making borrowing cheaper for companies and boosting consumer spending.
Tightening policy (higher interest rates, bond sales) can damp stock market growth by raising borrowing costs and reducing liquidity.

Commodity Prices
Loose monetary policy often leads to higher commodity prices, as a weaker currency increases demand for dollar-denominated assets such as gold and oil.

Conversely, stricter policy can reduce demand for commodities as the cost of financing increases.

Real-World Examples
2008 Financial Crisis: Central banks slashed interest rates and implemented QE to stabilise the global economy. This injected liquidity supported financial markets and prevented a deeper recession.

2020 COVID-19 Pandemic: Central banks worldwide introduced emergency measures, including near-zero interest rates and large-scale QE, to support businesses and households during the economic shutdown.

2022–2023 Inflation Surge: Central banks, including the Federal Reserve, aggressively raised interest rates to combat high inflation, leading to sharp corrections in stock and bond markets.

How Traders Can Benefit from Understanding Monetary Policy
Understanding how monetary policy functions is essential, as it enables us to anticipate central bank actions based on available information and data. Any change in monetary policy—whether it's a modification of interest rates,

quantitative easing, or tightening—will influence every market, impacting bonds, currencies, equities, and commodities. To succeed, we must position ourselves appropriately, adjusting our strategies to exploit these movements or reduce potential risks.

Getting to grips with the basic economic principles

Efficient Market Hypothesis, supply and demand, monetary policy, and the circular flow of income are more than theoretical ideas—they're the forces that shape every trade you'll make. Understanding these concepts will help you:

Recognise the drivers behind price movements.
Anticipate how markets react to new information.
Build a framework for analysing opportunities, risks and trading success!

In the next chapter, we'll explore these concepts and their influence on several markets, showing how they apply in real-world trading scenarios and how you can use them to your advantage. Mastering these basics will enhance your confidence as a trader and build the foundation for sustained success.

4

Understanding the Markets

Moving From Theory to Real-World Markets

Having covered the fundamental principles of how markets operate—the Efficient Market Hypothesis, supply and demand, and the circular flow of income—it's now time to explore the real-world trading dynamics in more depth. While theory provides the framework, experience and market knowledge truly set successful traders apart.

Over the years, I've traded a broad range of markets—from interest rates and oil to commodities, metals, bonds, stock markets, and more recently, cryptocurrencies and decentralized finance. Each market has its own rhythm, quirks, and specific challenges. Markets are dynamic, evolving systems influenced by economic fundamentals, human psychology, and external shocks. Understanding their behaviors, what moves them, and the risks involved is vital for trading with confidence.

You need to understand your market's characteristics, drivers, and risks to trade effectively. This chapter aims to provide practical market profiles for various asset classes accessible through retail brokers, offering good liquidity and clear trading opportunities. Over the years, I have not only traded these markets but also mentored traders on how to navigate them. Although each market group has its own unique dynamics, they all share one key truth: the better you understand them, the more informed your trading decisions will be, increasing your chances of success.

In the following pages, I'll share insights from my years of experience navigating these markets and training traders to succeed. We'll cover:

S. Warner-Baker, *Learn to Trade Like a Professional*,
https://doi.org/10.1007/978-3-032-20125-6_4

- Essential facts about each market, including its characteristics and trading nuances.
- Market drivers influencing price movements, including economic data, geopolitical events, and global trends.
- Risk factors to watch for and manage.
- Opportunities and trade ideas that these markets consistently provide.
- Real-world experience is often the best teacher. I'll share stories of extraordinary market moves I've witnessed and traded on throughout my career, highlighting the lessons they've taught me.

By the end of this chapter, you'll have a practical understanding of the markets, what drives them, and how to approach them with a professional mindset.

To give this section structure—and to help you connect more naturally with the material—I've focused on markets across three everyday categories: money, energy, and food. These are markets that directly influence your life, often more than you realize. By understanding how they work and why they move, you're more likely to stay engaged, build genuine curiosity, and ultimately develop the depth of insight needed to trade them with confidence.

Let's dive in and build your market knowledge, one market at a time.

4.1 Money—It Makes the World Go Round (Apparently)

Understanding Fixed Income, Currency, and Interest Rate Markets
These three interconnected market groups—fixed income, currency, and interest rates—are at the heart of the modern global financial system. They influence everything from economic policy to the value of your money and serve as vital indicators of global economic health. To trade them effectively, you must understand their origins, what they are, why they move, who trades them, and key risk-management factors.

4.1.1 Fixed Income Markets

Fixed-income markets involve trading debt securities such as government, corporate, and municipal bonds. The aim is to help governments and companies raise funds while providing investors with a steady income through interest payments (coupons). Similar to when you and I want to borrow money for a house or a car, we would approach a bank. Governments, however, must access the broader money markets, promising to repay the borrowed amount and pay interest. Still, the figures involved are much larger than anything you or I could imagine.

The most actively traded bonds are government securities issued by politically stable countries such as the USA, the UK, and Germany. Their economies and political systems have remained steady since the post-World War II period, and they have experienced strong growth and, most importantly, met their debt obligations when required.

Bond futures are widely traded worldwide. When issued, they consist of a set of characteristics, including the underlying bond's maturity, coupon rate, face value, and the delivery month specified in the contract. These characteristics ensure standardization, allowing efficient trading and hedging across different markets.

On the day a bond is issued, often at auction, the market sets the coupon (interest rate) based on the current cash market rate for that particular bond. Once the bond is issued, a delivery date (maturity) is established, when the government is obliged to repay the money. The holder of that bond can keep it and claim the interest. They can also trade this bond on the futures market to benefit from market volatility (which can be significant).

Historical Origins

From their origins in 12th-century Venice, government bonds have been a cornerstone of financial systems, enabling governments to fund wars, infrastructure, and economic recovery. Over the centuries, bonds have played pivotal roles in some of history's most significant economic events and continue to be a vital part of our modern financial system, ensuring the stability of the world order.

Here's a look back at some key moments in history

1. US Treasury Bonds During the Revolutionary War (1775–1783)

The United States issued its first government bonds to fund the war for independence. These bonds were a crucial tool for financing the fledgling nation's military efforts, marking the beginning of what would become the world's most liquid and trusted bond market. At the end of 2024, the total outstanding value stood at around \$53 trillion!

2. The Marshall Plan (1948)

In the aftermath of World War II, the US government used bond financing to support the Marshall Plan, which funded the reconstruction of Europe. This demonstrated the power of fixed-income markets to drive large-scale economic rebuilding, stabilize economies, and foster global growth. The US was (literally) building bridges with the EU and ensuring a path to its global dominance.

3. Argentinian Debt Crisis (2001)

Argentina defaulted on $95 billion in sovereign debt, the largest default at the time. This event sent shockwaves through global financial markets, highlighting the risks associated with emerging market debt and the domino effect such crises can have on investor confidence. As a result, the premium (interest rate) on bonds from developing countries has increased. The more likely a country is to default, the higher the interest rate it must pay to investors.

What is so interesting about this piece of history is that the Argentinian government was allowed to issue more bonds on the condition that it would never default again . . . Guess what? They did!

4. Eurozone Debt Crisis (2010–2012)

The sovereign debt crises in Greece, Ireland, and Portugal revealed the vulnerabilities of some EU nations. Bond yields soared as default fears grew, leading to massive EU and IMF bailouts. This period of volatility underscored the interconnectedness of bond markets and their influence on regional stability.

Due to the nature of the EU, all countries issued government bonds at low interest rates because Germany was very successful and accounted for the bulk of the EU's economy (30%). The market bought bonds from all EU countries, assuming their growth and stability would eventually match. The 'weaker' countries in the EU borrowed more than they should have at very low interest rates and couldn't pay it back, leading the EU to the brink of collapse and forcing Germany to pay the debts of those who borrowed too much and couldn't repay the market.

Economic Impact of Fixed Income Markets

Fixed-income markets are the backbone of public and corporate financing, allowing governments and companies to raise capital efficiently. Beyond funding, these markets play a vital role in monetary policy:

During the Global Financial Crisis (2008), governments issued unprecedented amounts of debt to stabilize economies and fund stimulus packages, preventing what we thought at the time was a complete collapse of the modern financial system.

Central banks, such as the Federal Reserve and the European Central Bank, relied heavily on bond-buying programs (quantitative easing) to inject liquidity into the financial system.

As a student of economics and the world, I understand that most economies operate on a Keynesian model, named after the renowned economist John Maynard Keynes. In essence, this model seeks to balance the economy using interest rates and taxation to achieve three key goals: stable growth, high employment, and manageable inflation. I think of these as the 'gauges' of an economy, with interest rates and taxation acting as the dials used to adjust them.

A fundamental principle of the Keynesian model is that printing money to sustain the system is dangerous, as it can lead to uncontrollable inflation that ultimately derails an economy. History offers stark warnings:

Pre-World War II Germany (Weimar Republic): Hyperinflation rendered its currency practically worthless, leading to an unhappy uprising and a change in government (Mr Hitler).

Zimbabwe (2000s): Inflation soared to over 1000%, collapsing the value of the currency.

In today's world, quantitative easing (QE)—issuing bonds to inject money into the economy—is the modern equivalent of printing money. Unlike historical examples, QE allows governments to direct where the money is spent. During the 2008 financial crisis, QE was used to prevent a collapse of the banking system. More recently, it was employed to cover the costs of the global pandemic.

However, this strategy has consequences. The massive injection of funds into the system has contributed to rampant inflation—too much money chasing too few goods, driving prices sharply higher. This aligns with a warning issued by Keynes decades ago: an uncontrolled money supply risks destabilizing the entire system.

These examples illustrate that government bonds are more than just financial instruments—they are tools of economic policy, crisis management, and recovery. Understanding their historical importance gives traders insights into their enduring role in shaping financial and economic landscapes.

I have been analyzing and trading bond markets for 20 years. The first book I ever read about trading was Michael Lewis's Liar's Poker, a fascinating account of bond trading in the 1980s. The book captures the explosive rise of the investment bank Salomon Brothers, in which mortgage bonds transformed Wall Street, and traders reveled in their newfound wealth and power. It paints a vivid picture of a high-stakes world where ambition, bravado, and cunning were the keys to success.

It was the modern mortgage bond market that nearly brought the world to its knees during the 2008 financial crisis. The very instruments that had made traders in Liar's Poker so powerful—securitized mortgage bonds—became the ticking time bomb that detonated the global economy. Risky lending practices, combined with overconfidence and greed, created a house of cards that eventually collapsed.

The once-mighty "Masters of the Universe" were no more, their hubris exposed as the world grappled with the fallout. This event was a stark reminder of the importance of understanding and managing the risks inherent in financial markets, even in instruments once considered safe.

What struck me most when reading Liar's Poker was the fact that I had never even considered bonds as a way to make money. Yet here were these traders, cleaning up and calling themselves the "Masters of the Universe." The book opened my eyes to the vast potential of the bond markets and set me on a path to explore and master this critical financial arena.

Like most markets I will discuss in these pages, I have a wealth of facts, stories, and memories to share with you. The aim is to help you, the reader, begin to understand the opportunities that arose during these times and how these experiences can better prepare you to succeed in each market.

A Little Context Is Always Helpful

That was a great history lesson, but why should you care about government bonds? They seem like the market for hedge funds, pension funds, and central banks, but what about trading them as an individual?

Well, I have always had a saying that I used to inspire the new traders who I would be training over the years, as well as still using it myself—'if it moves, you can make money out of it'—Bond markets move, a lot, there are a lot of them (see table below), the ones from economically developed countries are liquid (easy to get in and out of a trade), and have clear market drivers, more on this later. By the time you read this, the total market capitalization of all bonds around the world will be at a new high, creating more opportunities than ever before.

That last point is bold, as you might be reading this ten years from now, but it is based on solid reasoning: inflation is raising the cost of doing anything, and politicians keep telling voters they will cut taxes and increase spending to get elected, or at least one of these. Either of these political promises will require more bonds to fund these commitments. Only time will tell if this is a sustainable way to manage an economy, but as seen in Argentina's case, sometimes the money to settle debts runs out, and investors lose their shirts.

We will explore the factors affecting supply and demand in each market covered in this book, as well as the key fundamentals that influence price movements. This will form the foundation for our fundamental analysis of a market, which we will examine further as our journey together continues.

For bonds, supply is primarily controlled by the government or the country's central bank.

Supply-side, price-driven moves in the bond market can be particularly extreme, often signaling a shift in economic health or government policy. For instance:

A sudden surge in bond issuance may indicate that a government faces rising fiscal (tax) deficits or needs to finance major infrastructure projects. This increase in supply can shake investor confidence, driving bond prices down and yields up.

Conversely, reduced bond issuance may signal tighter fiscal policies or economic improvement, which can drive prices higher and yields lower as demand outweighs supply.

These moves reflect broader economic shifts, such as changes in GDP growth (how well a country is performing), inflation, or geopolitical risks. Recognizing these signals early can provide valuable opportunities to capitalize on market trends or protect against volatility.

For example, if a government wants to invest heavily in infrastructure, it needs to raise funds. To do this, it issues more bonds, which increases the supply. This additional supply typically leads to decreased bond prices and increased yields (since price and yield move inversely).

In contrast, during quantitative easing (QE)—a tool used during economic crises—a central bank issues bonds and then buys them back itself to inject money into the economy. This process reduces the effective supply of bonds in the market, causing prices to rise and yields to fall.

QE was used extensively during the 2008 financial crisis and the COVID-19 pandemic to stabilize financial markets and stimulate economic activity. While this strategy prevents short-term economic collapse, it also introduces risks, such as inflation and asset bubbles, which traders must carefully monitor.

Grasping these dynamics is essential to spotting opportunities and managing risks in the bond market. Whether it's an abrupt change in government policy or a central bank intervention, bond traders who can predict and respond to supply and demand shifts are better equipped to succeed. By understanding the forces that influence bond prices, you can create a clearer trading strategy and gain a sharper edge in this crucial financial market.

I have kept the list of bonds I would recommend trading to the ones I believe have a very low chance of default in the foreseeable future. I have included a volatility rating for each of them as a guide.

High—can trade a 50 + price range in a day
Medium—trades on average between 20 and 50 prices a day
Low—trades, less than a 20-price range on average each day

The names Bond … Government Bond

Country	Name of Bond	Duration	Futures Exchange	Tick Value	Opening Times (GMT)	Volatility
United Kingdom	Gilt	5, 10, 30 years	ICE Futures Europe	£10 per tick (0.01)	01:00–23:00	High
United States	Treasury Note (T-Note)	2, 5, 10 years	Chicago Board of Trade (CBOT)	$15.625 per tick (0.01)	23:00–22:00 (next day)	2—low 5—Med 10—High
United States	Treasury Bond (T-Bond)	20, 30 years	Chicago Board of Trade (CBOT)	$31.25 per tick (0.01)	23:00–22:00 (next day)	High
Germany	Bund	10, 30 years	Eurex	€10 per tick (0.01)	07:00–21:00	High
Japan	Japanese Government Bond (JGB)	10, 20 years	Tokyo Financial Exchange (TFX)	¥1,000 per tick (0.01)	23:45–06:15 & 07:30–20:30	High
France	OAT	10 years	Eurex	€10 per tick (0.01)	07:00–21:00	High
Italy	BTP	10, 30 years	Eurex	€10 per tick (0.01)	07:00–21:00	High
Canada	Government of Canada Bond	10, 30 years	Montréal Exchange (MX)	CAD 10 per tick (0.01)	11:00–21:30	Medium
Australia	Australian Government Bond	3, 10 years	ASX 24	AUD 10 per tick (0.01)	21:30–07:30 (next day)	Medium
India	Government of India Bond	10 years	NSE India (Interest Rate Futures)	₹10 per tick (0.0025)	03:30–11:30	Medium

What makes a bond market move?

The bond market is often referred to as the "smart money," a crucial financial barometer that reflects economic conditions, investor sentiment, and government policy. Bond prices and yields move for various reasons, ranging from shifts in monetary policy to changes in global risk sentiment. Understanding these drivers is essential for traders, investors, and policymakers alike. This section explores the factors that move bond markets (the fundamentals) and provides historical examples to illustrate their impact.

Key Drivers of Bond Market Movements—(what makes the price move up and down)

Interest Rates and Central Bank Policy
The most significant driver of bond market movements is the relationship between bond prices and interest rates. Bond prices and yields move inversely: when interest rates rise, bond prices fall, and vice versa. Central banks are pivotal in setting short-term interest rates and influencing the broader bond market.

Monetary Policy Changes:
Central banks such as the Federal Reserve and the European Central Bank employ tools such as interest rate adjustments and open market operations to meet their economic objectives. When a central bank raises rates to tackle inflation, bond yields generally rise, as new bonds offer higher returns, lowering the prices of existing bonds.

Forward Guidance:
Central banks often indicate their intentions through forward guidance, shaping bond market expectations. Traders and investors adjust their positions in response to expected changes in monetary policy. Central bankers are akin to politicians; they enjoy sharing their opinions and are frequently invited to speak at events worldwide to comment on the economy they represent. Traders interpret this forward guidance and then execute trades based on any shifts in sentiment.

In the early 1980s, Federal Reserve Chairman Paul Volcker implemented aggressive rate hikes to combat soaring inflation, pushing interest rates above 20%. This caused bond prices to plummet while yields skyrocketed, shaking the bond market and the broader financial system. Think about that when you're looking at the current rates of borrowing (hopefully, at the time of reading, we have a sensible world order and relatively stable interest rates).

Inflation Expectations
Inflation erodes the purchasing power of future bond payments, making bonds less attractive to investors. As inflation expectations rise, bond yields typically increase to compensate for the diminished value of future cash flows, leading to a decline in bond prices.

During the 1970s, the United States and the UK experienced "stagflation," a period of high inflation and stagnant economic growth. Bond yields soared as investors demanded higher returns to offset the rapid price rise, leading to a prolonged downturn in the bond market. The UK needed a bailout from the International Monetary Fund as things got so bad!

Supply and Demand

We covered this before, but it's always worth a timely reminder: some of the biggest moves in bond markets have been driven by supply events. These include large-scale bond issuances to finance government budgets or central bank interventions such as quantitative easing (QE). When a government needs to raise significant funds, such as for infrastructure projects or economic stimulus, it increases the supply of bonds, pushing prices down and yields up.

A recent and notable example occurred in September 2022, when then-UK Prime Minister Liz Truss unveiled a controversial budget that included unfunded tax cuts and increased borrowing. The announcement spooked investors, leading to a sell-off in UK government bonds (gilts). Yields on 10-year gilts surged from around 3.5% to over 4.5% in just a few days, causing significant turmoil in financial markets. The Bank of England was forced to intervene by buying long-dated gilts to stabilize the market and protect pension funds from potential collapse. This event highlighted how rapidly supply-driven events can affect bond markets and the broader economy.

In contrast, during periods of quantitative easing, central banks purchase large amounts of government bonds to inject liquidity into the economy. This reduces the effective supply in the market, driving bond prices higher and yields lower. There is a limit to how much QE a country can do. However, governments can't just issue and buy their bonds infinitely, rendering them worthless; this would collapse the financial system entirely.

Economic Data Releases

Economic indicators such as GDP growth, unemployment rates, and retail sales can significantly influence bond markets. Strong economic data often leads to expectations of tighter monetary policy, which can push yields higher as bond prices fall. The opposite holds for weak data readings. We will discuss data releases further when examining fundamental analysis; the data indicates how well those economic indicators are performing.

Geopolitical Events and Risk Sentiment

The bond market is highly sensitive to geopolitical risks and changes in global investor sentiment. During periods of heightened uncertainty, such as wars or financial crises, investors often flock to government bonds as safe-haven assets. A safe-haven asset is an investment that retains or increases in value during market turbulence, thereby providing stability when other assets decline. This behavior, known as a flight to safety, involves reallocating capital from riskier investments, such as equities, to more secure instruments, such as government bonds. This shift in demand pushes bond prices up and yields down.

The COVID-19 pandemic in 2020 triggered a global flight to safety, driving US Treasury yields to record lows as investors sought refuge in government debt. The same can be said when the Russian invasion of Ukraine happened in 2022; bonds in all major economies were bought.

Understanding what moves bond markets is crucial for traders, investors, and policymakers to make informed decisions. Bond markets influence borrowing costs, corporate investment, and government spending, and serve as leading indicators for the broader economy. By studying historical moves and the factors that drive bond markets, participants can better anticipate future trends, identify opportunities, and manage risks effectively.

A complex interplay of economic, political, and market-specific factors influences bond market movements. Recognizing these drivers and learning from historical examples offers valuable insights for navigating this vital financial arena. Now that we understand why bond markets move, the next step is to translate this knowledge into actionable trading strategies. The following section will examine how to profit from trading bonds, covering the key techniques, tools, and approaches employed by professional traders.

Do you want to be a Master of the Universe?

Trading bonds can be highly lucrative, but it requires a solid understanding of strategies tailored to the unique dynamics of fixed-income markets. Unlike equities, where the focus is often on capital gains, bond trading involves interest rate movements, yield fluctuations, and macroeconomic trends. In this chapter, we'll explore several trading strategies to help you profit from bond markets, whether you're a novice or a seasoned trader.

Yield Curve Trading

To trade bonds effectively, you need to understand the yield curve. The yield curve is a graphical representation of the relationship between bond yields (interest rates) and their maturities. It typically slopes upward, reflecting the higher yields investors demand for longer-term investments to compensate for increased risk and uncertainty. However, the curve's shape can vary—it may steepen, flatten, or even invert—depending on economic conditions and investor expectations.

Types of Yield Curves:

Normal Yield Curve: Long-term yields are higher than short-term yields, indicating economic growth.

Steep Yield Curve: Suggests strong future growth but may also signal inflation concerns.

Flat or Inverted Yield Curve: Often seen as a warning of economic slowdown or recession.

Strategies Involving the Yield Curve:

Steepener Trade: Profit from an expected steepening of the yield curve by going long on long-term bonds and short on short-term bonds.

Flattener Trade: Expect the curve to flatten by shorting long-term bonds and going long on short-term bonds.

Example: During periods of economic expansion, yield curves often steepen, presenting opportunities for steepener trades as long-term yields rise faster than short-term yields.

Duration Trading

Duration measures a bond's sensitivity to changes in interest rates. By trading bonds with different durations, traders can position themselves to benefit from anticipated rate movements.

Examples of Duration:

Short-Duration Bonds: Treasury bills (T-bills) with maturities under a year.

Medium-Duration Bonds: US Treasury notes with maturities of 2–10 years.

Long-Duration Bonds: US Treasury bonds with maturities of 20–30 years.

Key Tactics:

If interest rates are expected to rise, focus on short-duration bonds, which are less sensitive to rate increases.

Long-duration bonds offer greater potential for price appreciation if rates are expected to fall.

Central bank announcements are critical indicators for duration trades. A dovish policy stance—favoring lower interest rates to stimulate the economy—signals opportunities for long-duration positions. A hawkish stance—favoring higher rates to combat inflation—indicates a preference for short-duration bonds.

Spread Trading

Spread trading involves taking positions based on the yield difference between two bonds. This strategy allows traders to profit from relative value discrepancies.

Popular Spread Trades:

Government vs. Corporate Bonds: Exploit differences in risk premiums.

Treasury Spread Between Countries: Compare the yield on US Treasuries with similar bonds from other countries, such as German Bunds or UK Gilts. Variations in economic conditions, inflation rates, and monetary policy can create profitable opportunities.

Trade idea: If corporate bond spreads widen due to increased market risk, shorting corporate bonds while going long on treasuries can be profitable. Similarly, a spread trade can exploit this differential if US yields exceed German Bund yields due to stronger economic growth.

Bond Futures

Derivatives like bond futures enable traders, hedge funds, investment banks, and pension funds to leverage their positions and hedge risks. These are the most accessible types of bonds for retail investors, and the ones you and I are most likely to trade.

Using Bond futures allows us to speculate on bond price movements without owning the underlying asset.

It is our duty to decide whether a bond's price will be bid (up) or offered (down) and to position ourselves appropriately with respect to market movements. Although it is easier said than done, we will aim to improve our accuracy by studying the book's pages.

Interest Rate Swaps

Interest rate swaps are advanced instruments that allow traders to exchange fixed-rate payments for floating-rate payments or vice versa. In essence, they function similarly to fixing your mortgage. When you lock in a fixed mortgage rate, you protect yourself from future interest rate hikes, like entering an interest rate swap to hedge exposure.

How It Works:

If you expect interest rates to rise, enter into a swap to pay a fixed rate and receive a floating rate.

Conversely, if rates are expected to fall, pay a floating rate and receive a fixed rate.

Trade Idea: Companies frequently use swaps to hedge their interest rate exposures, but traders can use them to speculate on rate changes. Most people engage in interest rate trading without realizing it when they choose between fixed and variable mortgage rates.

Event-driven trading with Fundamental Analysis
Bond markets are susceptible to events such as central bank meetings, inflation reports, and geopolitical developments. Combining event-driven trading with fundamental analysis enables traders to make informed decisions informed by data and market expectations.

How to Trade Events with Fundamentals:
Analyze key economic data releases, such as GDP, employment figures, and inflation reports, to gauge the health of the economy.

Assess central bank policy statements and minutes to understand the trajectory of interest rates and monetary policy.

Monitor geopolitical developments that could affect global risk sentiment and drive demand for safe-haven assets such as government bonds.

Trade Idea: During the 2020 COVID-19 crisis, Federal Reserve rate cuts and bond-buying programs created significant trading opportunities as yields plummeted. Traders who combined fundamental analysis with event monitoring were better positioned to anticipate these moves, buying bond futures in their thousands.

Trading bonds successfully requires a deep understanding of market dynamics, macroeconomic trends, and the tools available. You can capitalize on market opportunities by employing strategies such as yield curve trading, duration management, and event-driven trades supported by fundamental analysis. The bond market offers countless ways to profit—a little background knowledge from the pros and the upcoming chapters will give you what you need on your pathway to profitability.

4.1.2 Understanding the Currency Market (Forex/fx)

The currency (forex or FX) market is the largest and most liquid financial market in the world. It facilitates the exchange of one currency for another. With a daily trading volume exceeding $7 trillion as of 2025, it operates 24/7 and plays a vital role in global trade, investment, and economic stability.

For many years, forex has been the primary market for retail traders, attracted by its volatility and the allure of "get-rich-quick" marketing schemes. While I have traded forex extensively, I've found it to be one of the most inconsistent markets, not just in how it moves but also in my profit and loss! This inconsistency highlights the challenges of navigating a market often oversaturated with misinformation and unrealistic expectations.

Forex is also the market I receive the most questions about in public forums and online discussions. Its popularity may be linked to the fact that we all use money in our daily lives, giving us a false sense of familiarity with currency markets. A certain mental elasticity tricks us into thinking we understand forex better than we do—when, in reality, most of us don't.

The rise of self-proclaimed "forex experts" advertising on social media, promising massive gains with little effort, further fuels misconceptions about the market. Witnessing these misleading claims motivated me to embark on a mission to provide honest, open trader education. I wanted to provide aspiring traders with the tools, insights, and skills they need to succeed, based on real-world experience rather than empty promises.

In this chapter, we'll explore the nature of currency markets, delve into their historical origins, and examine the key drivers of price movement. By the end, you'll gain a deeper understanding of the opportunities and challenges of forex trading, empowering you to approach it with greater clarity and confidence.

What Are Currency Markets?

Currency markets exist to facilitate international trade and financial transactions. Whether a business in Germany imports goods from Japan or an individual travels abroad, currency markets enable these exchanges by determining the value of one currency relative to another.

Currencies are traded in pairs, such as EUR/USD or GBP/JPY, where the first currency is the base currency and the second is the quote currency. The exchange rate reflects how many units of the quote currency are needed to buy one unit of the base currency.

The idea of currency isn't new. The earliest use of currency dates to Mesopotamia around 3000 BCE, when people used silver and other commodities as a medium of exchange. These early forms of currency were essentially bills of trust between parties, enabling them to trade goods and services without direct barter. Over time, this developed into the coinage and paper money systems we recognize today.

For most people today, currency markets are most familiar through travel, when exchanging their money for a foreign currency while on holiday. This process connects them, albeit briefly, to the global currency market. The daily exchange rates they encounter are determined by the exact mechanisms that drive trillion-dollar trades among banks, corporations, and investors.

A Brief History of Currencies

The Origin Story

The history of currency dates back to around 3000 BCE in Mesopotamia, in what is now modern-day Iraq, where silver and other commodities were first used as means of exchange. Traders in this region exchanged goods such as grain, livestock, and textiles, using silver as a standard of value. These early forms of money served as tokens of trust between parties, facilitating trade and reducing the inefficiencies of barter. The advent of currency marked a revolutionary milestone in economic history, laying the foundation for organized trade and commerce across societies. By enabling long-distance trade and economic specialization, these innovations connected regions and cultures in unprecedented ways.

Roman Coins and Economic Integration

The Roman Empire (27 BCE—476 CE) advanced the idea of currency by creating standardized coinage across its vast territories. Coins like the denarius bore the emperor's image, symbolizing authority and building trust in their value. This system enabled smooth trade across Europe, the Middle East, and North Africa, encouraging economic integration and marking one of the earliest examples of a global monetary system. The stability of Roman currency supported the empire's prosperity by facilitating effective tax collection, funding military expansion, and sustaining consistent trade over great distances. This economic cohesion underpinned the empire's political and social stability, allowing it to thrive for centuries, even as economic difficulties arose in later years.

Long live the King/Queen

By the ninth century, the Vikings introduced standardized coinage to the British Isles. These silver coins often bore the image of the reigning monarch, a practice that reinforced the currency's legitimacy and its issuer. The image also guaranteed that the silver coin would be of a certain weight and quality, which was crucial for establishing trust in transactions. This innovation helped establish trust and facilitated trade within and beyond the British Isles. It set the precedent for modern monetary systems, in which coins and banknotes continue to bear national symbols and government endorsements.

The Invention of Central Banks

The establishment of central banks, beginning with Sweden's Riksbank in 1668 and followed by the Bank of England in 1694, revolutionized monetary systems. Central banks provided a framework for regulating the money supply, managing inflation, and ensuring financial stability. By the twentieth century, central banks like the Federal Reserve (established in 1913) became key players in shaping economic policy, influencing currency values, and stabilizing financial systems. We will take a deeper look at the role and functions of central banks later in the book.

The Gold Standard and Its Legacy
The gold standard appeared in the late nineteenth century as nations aimed to stabilize their currencies by linking them to a fixed amount of gold. This system allowed paper money to be exchanged for gold, offering a reliable store of value and supporting international trade. However, the rigidity of the gold standard limited monetary policy flexibility, especially during economic downturns.

The Great Depression, which started in 1929 and continued through much of the 1930s, further revealed its weaknesses. The global economic collapse resulted from a mix of factors, including stock market crashes, bank failures, and declining consumer spending. Under the gold standard, governments found it difficult to implement effective monetary policies to boost their economies. Consequently, many countries abandoned the system in favor of more adaptable monetary frameworks, which enabled them to adjust currency values and respond more effectively to economic crises.

Hyperinflation in Weimar Germany
After World War I, Germany's economy was weakened by reparations and debt. Reparations were financial penalties imposed on Germany by the Treaty of Versailles (1919), requiring Germany to compensate the Allied nations for the destruction caused during the war. These payments put a heavy burden on Germany's economy, leading to more borrowing and debt. Germany's currency was the mark, which quickly lost value as the Weimar Republic tried to meet its obligations by printing large amounts of money.

This unchecked money printing led to hyperinflation between 1921 and 1923. Prices skyrocketed, with basic goods costing millions of marks, and the currency became nearly worthless. It was rumored that burning money was cheaper than buying coal with it, highlighting the scale of the crisis. This catastrophic economic collapse contributed to widespread social unrest, eroded trust in the government, and created fertile ground for extremist political movements. The Nazi Party capitalized on this discontent, eventually rising to power and starting World War II in 1939.

We discussed this topic earlier in the chapter with quantitative easing (QE), a modern method of injecting money into the economy. Unlike the unchecked printing of physical currency seen in Weimar Germany, QE involves central banks ‘controlled issuance and purchase of government bonds. This targeted approach helps direct liquidity into specific sectors of the economy and reduces the risk of hyperinflation, making it a more effective tool for managing financial crises. Let’s hope it doesn’t lead to global chaos as we saw early in the twentieth century.

Bretton Woods and the Post-WWII Era
In 1944, the Bretton Woods Agreement established a new global monetary system, pegging major currencies to the US dollar, which was itself tied to gold. Representatives from 44 Allied nations, including the United States, the United Kingdom, and France, convened in Bretton Woods, New Hampshire, to create this system. It aimed to ensure global economic stability and foster post-war reconstruction. However, by 1971, the strain on US gold reserves and growing international trade imbalances led President Richard Nixon to end the dollar’s convertibility into gold, collapsing the Bretton Woods system and ushering in an era of floating exchange rates.

The Plaza Accord (1985)
The Plaza Accord was a coordinated effort by the US, Japan, Germany, France, and the UK to devalue the US dollar and address trade imbalances. By the early 1980s, the dollar had appreciated significantly due to a combination of factors: high Federal Reserve interest rates to combat inflation, robust U.S. economic growth, and strong inflows of foreign capital seeking higher returns. This made American exports less competitive on the global stage. The agreement at New York’s Plaza Hotel involved governments and central banks selling dollars and buying other major currencies, such as the yen and the mark. This intervention successfully weakened the dollar, highlighting the influence of coordinated government action in shaping currency markets.

Black Wednesday (1992)
On 16 September 1992, the UK faced a currency crisis when it was forced to withdraw from the European Exchange Rate Mechanism (ERM). The ERM was designed to stabilize exchange rates and prepare European countries for monetary union by maintaining their currencies within agreed-upon bands. Member nations included the UK, France, Germany, Italy, and others in the European Community.

Speculators, including George Soros, bet heavily against the pound, believing it was overvalued within the ERM and that the government would not be able to defend it. To maintain the pound’s value, the Bank of England raised interest rates dramatically, from 10% to 15% in a single day—one of the UK's largest interest rate moves. Despite these efforts, the pound continued to plummet, and the UK ultimately exited the ERM.

At the time, key decisions were being made by the UK government, led by Prime Minister John Major and Chancellor of the Exchequer Norman Lamont. Soros reportedly made over $1 billion in profit from his speculative bets, and Black Wednesday became a pivotal moment in the history of currency markets, demonstrating the power of market forces over government policies.

The Formation of the Euro

In 1999, the euro was introduced as the common currency of the European Union, marking a significant step toward economic integration. Initially used for electronic transactions, euro banknotes and coins entered circulation in 2002. Just like when the Romans and Vikings developed a standard currency, this was the modern version of the same principle, designed to enable seamless trade and economic cohesion across Europe. The euro eliminated exchange rate fluctuations within the eurozone, facilitating trade and investment. However, differing fiscal policies among member states led to challenges, particularly during the Eurozone Debt Crisis (2010–2012), which tested the currency's resilience.

The Swiss Franc Shock (2015)

In January 2015, the Swiss National Bank (SNB) shocked markets by removing its currency peg to the euro, which had been set at 1.20 CHF per euro. The peg was established in 2011 to prevent the Swiss franc from appreciating too much, as a stronger franc would harm Switzerland's export-driven economy by making Swiss goods more expensive for foreign buyers. Traders had been selling the franc against the euro at 1.20, assuming the peg would hold and profiting from any dips below that level. However, when the SNB removed the peg, the value of the franc soared nearly 30% in a single day, and traders couldn't exit their positions quickly enough. This caused significant losses for those who had relied on the peg being unbreakable. The SNB's move underscored the risks of depending too heavily on central bank policies and highlighted the volatility that can arise when market expectations are disrupted.

The Ever-Changing World of Currencies

From silver in Mesopotamia to the euro and beyond, the evolution of currencies reflects the constant interplay between innovation, policy, and economic forces. In the digital age, we are witnessing the rise of cryptocurrencies like Bitcoin and Ethereum, which challenge traditional notions of money and central banking. As blockchain technology advances, the future of currencies could see even greater decentralization and democratization. The journey of currency is far from over, and traders, investors, and policymakers must adapt to the ever-changing landscape of global finance.

What Makes the Currency Markets Move?

The currency (forex or FX) market is the largest and most liquid financial market in the world, with daily trading volumes surpassing $7 trillion. This huge volume results from the vast number of currency pairs traded globally. With 195 recognized countries, there are 18,915 possible currency pair combinations, as each country's currency can be traded against every other. However, not all of these currencies are actively traded due to insufficient demand to establish fair market prices.

This is why the world has a reserve currency: the US dollar. Most international trade is conducted using the American greenback, further cementing its role as the backbone of the global financial system.

This chapter and throughout the book will focus on the top 10 currency pairs by market capitalization. Below is a table outlining these currency pairs and their respective countries of origin for context:

Currency Pair	Country of Origin
EUR/USD	Eurozone/United States
USD/JPY	United States/Japan
GBP/USD	United Kingdom/United States
AUD/USD	Australia/United States
USD/CHF	United States/Switzerland
USD/CAD	United States/Canada
NZD/USD	New Zealand/United States
EUR/GBP	Eurozone/United Kingdom
EUR/JPY	Eurozone/Japan
GBP/JPY	United Kingdom/Japan

However, the theories and practices we will discuss apply to any currency pair you wish to trade. These pairs form the basis for international trade, investment, and speculation. If you consider every country's currency paired with every other country's currency, the result is an enormous number of combinations, each requiring a value for trade to take place. Understanding what drives this market is crucial for traders and investors. A complex interaction of economic, political, and psychological factors influences currency values. Over the following pages, we will explore the main factors affecting currency movements and how traders can anticipate and respond to them.

Interest Rates and Central Bank Policies

Central banks, such as the Federal Reserve (Fed), European Central Bank (ECB), and Bank of England (BoE), play a critical role in determining currency values. Setting interest rates and implementing monetary policies influence the demand and supply of money in the economy.

- Higher Interest Rates: Attract foreign investors seeking better returns, leading to currency appreciation. Investors typically seek to profit by purchasing assets such as government bonds, equities, or other high-yield investments in countries offering higher interest rates. To do this, they convert their currency into the target country's currency, increasing demand and causing it to appreciate. For instance, when the Federal Reserve raises interest rates, foreign investors often rush to buy U.S. Treasury bonds, strengthening the dollar.
- Lower Interest Rates: Reduce returns for investors, often causing a currency to depreciate. When interest rates are low, investors tend to seek higher yields in other economies for better returns. For example, they may sell the low-yielding currency to buy assets such as bonds, stocks, or real estate in countries offering more attractive returns. This increased selling pressure on the low-yield currency results in its depreciation. Additionally, lower interest rates can discourage savings and boost borrowing within the domestic economy, thereby further influencing currency demand and valuation.

One notable strategy related to interest rate differentials is the carry trade, especially involving Japan. The carry trade involves borrowing money in a currency with low interest rates, such as the Japanese yen, and investing in a currency with higher interest rates, like the Australian or US dollar. This strategy benefits from both the interest rate differential and potential currency appreciation. Japanese households and global financial institutions benefited significantly from this strategy when Japan kept interest rates near zero for decades. However, it carries risks, particularly during market instability, when exchange rates can shift suddenly.

Central banks also use forward guidance to signal their future policy intentions, affecting trader sentiment and currency movements before actual rate changes take place. The central bank board always has a chairperson and several voting members, which we will discuss later. Their statements are closely monitored to determine the direction of future policy.

Example: When the Fed raised interest rates aggressively in 2022 to combat inflation, the US dollar strengthened considerably as investors sought higher yields on dollar-denominated assets.

Economic Indicators

Currencies reflect the health of their respective economies. Key economic indicators provide insight into a nation's economic performance and influence currency values. We will cover the economic calendar in full later in the book, but essentially, to run an economy, you need to monitor how it's doing through a regular series of monthly data releases. I will highlight the big three again for good measure:

- Gross Domestic Product (GDP): Higher-than-expected GDP growth can boost a currency by signaling economic strength.
- Unemployment Rates: Lower unemployment rates suggest a robust economy, often supporting currency appreciation.
- Inflation Data: Moderate inflation is ideal, but runaway inflation can weaken a currency by eroding purchasing power.

This figure is known as Non-Farm Payrolls and is published on the first Friday of each month. Strong employment figures in the US often boost the dollar, as they indicate economic resilience and the possibility of Fed rate increases.

Trade Balances and Current Accounts

A country's trade balance—the difference between exports and imports—significantly affects currency value.

- Trade Surplus: A country exporting more than it imports creates demand for its currency, leading to appreciation.
- Trade Deficit: A country importing more than it exports creates an excess supply of its currency, leading to depreciation.

Example: China's trade surplus has historically supported the yuan, as foreign buyers need to purchase yuan to pay for Chinese goods. However, due to a loose peg with the dollar, they have remained competitive. This strategy has been criticized as anti-competitive because it artificially keeps Chinese exports cheaper on the global market. Governments in other countries began to fight back by imposing tariffs on Chinese imports, highlighting the ongoing tensions in international trade.

Political Stability and Geopolitical Events

Currencies thrive on confidence, and political instability can erode this trust. Wars, elections, policy uncertainty, and geopolitical tensions often lead to volatility in currency markets.

- Political Instability: Weakens investor confidence and can cause currency depreciation.
- Safe-Haven Flows: In times of crisis, investors often flock to stable currencies like the US dollar, Japanese yen, or Swiss franc.

Example: During the Russian invasion of Ukraine in 2022, the euro weakened amid concerns about energy supplies and geopolitical uncertainty.

Another notable example happened in September 2022 when UK Prime Minister Liz Truss announced a contentious budget that included unfunded tax cuts and increased borrowing. This sparked panic among investors, causing a sharp drop in the British pound. The Bank of England had to intervene with emergency bond-buying measures to stabilize the financial markets. Truss's budget and its poorly received economic consequences underscored the significant influence of political decisions on currency stability.

Market Sentiment and Speculation

Trader psychology plays a massive role in currency markets. Speculative flows driven by expectations of future events can cause significant short-term price movements. For both human and computer-driven traders, this can spill over into a herd mentality, amplifying trends and creating feedback loops that exacerbate market volatility.

- Bullish Sentiment: This leads to increased buying and appreciation of a currency.
- Bearish Sentiment: Results in selling pressure and depreciation.

Example: During the 2016 Brexit referendum, market sentiment strongly favored a vote to remain in the European Union, keeping the value of the British pound artificially high in the run-up to the vote. However, when the vote resulted in a decision to leave, the unexpected outcome sent the pound plummeting. This sharp depreciation reflected the market's reassessment of the UK's economic prospects outside the EU. It also highlighted the risks of trading on consensus expectations without preparing for shocks from unexpected outcomes.

Commodity Prices and Resource Dependency

For countries heavily dependent on the export of commodities such as oil, gold, or natural gas, currency values are closely linked to fluctuations in commodity prices. Most of these commodities are priced in US dollars, reinforcing the dollar's role as the global reserve currency.

- Oil-exporting nations: Rising oil prices often strengthen currencies like the Canadian dollar (CAD) and the Norwegian krone (NOK).
- Gold-Dependent Economies: Nations like Australia and South Africa see their currencies move in tandem with gold prices.

Government and Central Bank Interventions

Governments and central banks often actively influence currency values through direct intervention or the establishment of currency pegs. These actions can significantly impact global forex markets and reveal the political and economic priorities of the countries involved.

Currency Pegs:

A currency peg happens when a country fixes its currency's value to another, usually the US dollar or the euro. This system stabilizes and encourages trade by lowering exchange rate volatility. For example, the Hong Kong dollar has long been pegged to the US dollar, keeping a steady exchange rate through active intervention by the Hong Kong Monetary Authority.

However, pegs can disrupt market forces and cause imbalances. If a central bank cannot defend the peg due to limited reserves or external pressures, it may collapse, leading to considerable volatility.

In 2015, the Swiss National Bank removed its 1.20 CHF-per-euro peg, causing the franc to surge by nearly 30% in a single day. This decision, prompted by unsustainable intervention costs, disrupted global forex markets and led to massive losses for traders who had bet on the peg's stability.

Currency Wars:

Sometimes, countries participate in what is called "currency wars," intentionally devaluing their currencies to gain a competitive edge in global trade. A weaker currency makes exports cheaper and more appealing to foreign buyers, but can lead to retaliatory measures.

In the late 2000s, as countries emerged from the global financial crisis, several engaged in competitive devaluations to stimulate growth, creating tension in international markets. For instance, the US Federal Reserve's quantitative easing policies were criticized by some nations as a form of currency manipulation.

Tariffs and Trade Policies:
Government interventions, such as tariffs, can also influence currency values. For example, trade disputes between the US and China caused significant fluctuations in the yuan's value, as both nations used tariffs and currency policies to exert economic pressure.

A system that works or working the system?
Central bank interventions often aim to stabilize their economies or maintain competitiveness. These interventions may involve purchasing or selling currencies on the open market, adjusting interest rates, or using foreign reserves to influence exchange rates.

By understanding these mechanisms, traders can better anticipate market movements and navigate the complexities of currency markets.

Some countries peg their currency to another (e.g., the Swiss franc to the euro or the Hong Kong dollar to the US dollar). Central banks intervene to maintain these pegs, buying or selling their currency as necessary.

Anticipating Currency Market Moves
A dynamic combination of economic fundamentals, geopolitical influences, and market sentiment drives currency markets. Understanding these factors helps traders predict price movements and create informed strategies. As the world progresses with new technologies and shifting global power structures, the currency market will remain an intriguing and constantly evolving arena for traders and investors.

So you want to make money from money?
Currency trading can be undertaken from minutes to months and everything in between. The forex market operates 24/7 to facilitate the seamless flow of global trade, making it one of the most accessible and dynamic financial markets. The scenarios highlighted in previous chapters demonstrate how pivotal events in the history of money have created monumental opportunities for traders to capitalize on significant moves. To seize these opportunities, however, you need more than luck—you need a comprehensive understanding of how currency markets operate.

Sadly, most trading influencers on social media, along with many who sell online courses, tend to offer overly simplified solutions to trading forex.

These methods usually emphasize technical analysis heavily while neglecting the complexities behind how and why currencies fluctuate so significantly. Without understanding the key moments in the history of money and the factors influencing currency values, traders overlook the bigger picture and miss out on the full potential for profits.

This isn't to discount the value of technical analysis—it's a powerful tool that we will delve into in its own dedicated chapter later in the book. However, the most significant profits I have witnessed, both in my career and from historical examples, stem from major fundamental shifts. These shifts are often tied to a country's changing economic outlook, geopolitical events, or how global markets perceive its stability and growth potential.

Your biggest opportunity for substantial gains lies in understanding the economies linked to the currency pair you're trading. By assessing whether the pair's price reflects the underlying health of each country's economy, you can identify mispricing and position yourself to profit. There are often lucrative trading opportunities every month within the top currency pairs we highlighted earlier in the table. And that's without even considering the more exotic pairs, which tend to exhibit even greater volatility and profit potential, albeit with increased risk.

As will be a recurring theme throughout your trading journey, the key to success lies in knowing your market inside and out. Currency trading isn't about following trends blindly; it's about understanding the forces driving those trends and positioning yourself accordingly. With the proper knowledge, patience, and strategy, you'll be well-equipped to unlock the riches this dynamic market has to offer.

4.1.3 Short-Term Interest Rates (STIRs)

Trading Interest Rates and Interest Rate Futures

If you are reading this book, I will assume you are familiar with interest rates. You have either borrowed or saved money at some point in your life and paid or received interest on the funds in question, whether through personal loans, savings accounts, or mortgage payments. The interest rate market is a dynamic, thriving system. Interest rates represent the cost of borrowing money and the return on saving it. Central banks presently set them, and they are a fundamental aspect of monetary policy, influencing inflation, employment, consumer spending, and financial markets. Traders and investors closely watch interest rate movements, affecting everything from bond yields to stock market performance and currency fluctuations.

One of the most effective ways to trade interest rates is through Short-Term Interest Rate (STIR) futures, including Euribor (Europe), SONIA (UK), and SOFR (USA) futures. These financial instruments enable traders to speculate on future interest rate changes, hedge risks, and manage exposure to fluctuations in interest rates. Understanding how these markets operate offers significant opportunities to profit from shifts in monetary policy.

The Most Liquid STIR Futures Markets

Contract	Region	Exchange
Euribor	Europe	ICE Europe
SONIA	United Kingdom	ICE Europe
SOFR	United States	CME Group
Fed Funds	United States	CME Group
3-Month BAX	Canada	Montréal Exchange
3-Month JGB	Japan	Tokyo Financial Exchange
90-Day Bank Bill	Australia	ASX
3-Month HIBOR	Hong Kong	HKEX

What Are Interest Rates?

Interest rates represent the cost of money over time. When you borrow money, you pay interest; when you save money, you earn interest. They are essential to economic decision-making, influencing everything from mortgage payments to business investments. Central banks, such as the Federal Reserve (Fed), the European Central Bank (ECB), and the Bank of England (BoE), set benchmark interest rates that affect the rates banks charge customers for loans, mortgages, and credit, ultimately guiding financial markets and economic growth.

Central banks usually meet at scheduled intervals to evaluate economic conditions and decide on policies. The Federal Open Market Committee (FOMC) in the U.S. meets eight times a year, the ECB Governing Council gathers every six weeks, and the Bank of England's Monetary Policy Committee (MPC) meets monthly. During these meetings, policymakers analyze economic data, including inflation trends, employment figures, and GDP growth, to decide whether interest rate adjustments are needed.

Their decisions, and even their public statements, can strongly influence financial markets as traders and investors respond in anticipation of policy changes.

Types of Interest Rates:

Nominal Interest Rate:
The stated interest rate before adjusting for inflation. For example, suppose a bank offers a savings account with a nominal interest rate of 5% per year, but inflation is running at 3%. In that case, the real return on savings is effectively 2% when adjusted for inflation.

Real Interest Rate:
The interest rate is adjusted for inflation to reflect the actual cost of borrowing. For example, suppose a bank offers a savings account with a nominal interest rate of 5% per year, but inflation is running at 3%. In that case, the real return on savings is effectively 2% when adjusted for inflation. Similarly, if an investor purchases a bond yielding 4% annually while inflation runs at 2%, their real return is only 2%.

Conversely, if inflation rises above the nominal return, the real return can turn negative, meaning the investor effectively loses purchasing power over time.

Policy Interest Rate:
The rate set by central banks influences economic activity and guides inflation, employment, and overall economic growth. This includes key benchmark rates such as the Fed Funds Rate (Federal Reserve), the ECB's Main Refinancing Rate (European Central Bank), and the Bank Rate (Bank of England). These rates form a basis for borrowing costs across the financial system, impacting everything from consumer loans to corporate investments and government bond yields.

Market Interest Rate:
The rate set by supply and demand for credit in financial markets. For example, during periods of strong economic growth, businesses and consumers seek more credit for expansion and spending, driving market interest rates higher. Conversely, during economic downturns, demand for credit decreases, resulting in lower market interest rates as lenders compete to attract borrowers.

The bottom line:
Interest rates directly affect investment decisions, consumer spending, corporate borrowing, and government fiscal policies. When interest rates are high, borrowing becomes expensive, slowing down economic growth. Conversely, lower interest rates stimulate borrowing and investment, driving economic expansion.

A Brief History of Interest Rates

Interest rates have shaped economic policies and financial markets for centuries. Understanding their historical trends helps traders anticipate how central banks may act in different economic conditions.

Ancient Civilizations: The concept of charging interest dates back to Mesopotamia (circa 3000 BCE), where loans were recorded on clay tablets, and lenders charged interest on grain and silver loans.

The Medici Banking System (fifteenth Century): Modern banking emerged in Renaissance Italy, where the Medici family pioneered lending practices that relied on interest payments.

The Establishment of Central Banks (17th-twentieth Century): The creation of institutions such as the Bank of England (1694) and the Federal Reserve (1913) enabled governments to regulate monetary policy more effectively.

Post-WWII Bretton Woods System (1944–1971): Fixed exchange rates were established, tying major currencies to the US dollar, which was pegged to gold. This system collapsed in 1971 when the US abandoned the gold standard, leading to modern floating interest rates.

The 1980s Interest Rate Hikes: In response to rampant inflation, Federal Reserve Chairman Paul Volcker raised US interest rates above 20%, demonstrating the power of monetary policy in controlling inflation.

The Global Financial Crisis (2008): Central banks worldwide slashed interest rates to near-zero levels and introduced Quantitative Easing (QE) to prevent economic collapse.

The Post-COVID Inflationary Spike (2022-Present): In response to high inflation, the Federal Reserve and ECB aggressively raised interest rates, demonstrating the cyclical nature of monetary policy.

Interest rates remain a powerful economic tool, affecting everything from mortgage costs to the stability of financial markets. They fit within the Keynesian economic framework as a key method for managing economic cycles, controlling inflation, and encouraging growth.

Central banks seek to balance employment, consumer demand, and price stability by adjusting interest rates. For instance, lowering interest rates during a recession encourages borrowing and spending, which boosts economic activity. Conversely, when inflation is high, central banks increase interest rates to reduce excessive demand and stabilize prices.

In the next chapter, we will explore the role of central banks in more detail, examining their decision-making processes and the ways in which monetary policy influences financial markets.

What Makes Interest Rates Move?

Interest rates are fundamental to monetary policy and one of the most powerful tools central banks use to influence economic activity. They affect variables such as inflation, employment, borrowing costs, corporate investment, and currency strength. Basic supply-and-demand principles also determine interest rates. When demand for credit increases—such as during periods of economic growth—interest rates tend to rise as borrowers compete for funds.

Conversely, when demand for credit decreases, rates generally fall as lenders seek to attract borrowers. Likewise, the money supply, managed by central banks and financial institutions, significantly affects interest rate movements. An increase in the money supply usually results in lower rates, whereas a reduction typically causes rates to rise.

Understanding the factors driving interest rate changes is crucial for traders, investors, and businesses seeking to anticipate market movements and economic shifts.

The Role of Central Banks in Setting Interest Rates

Central banks, such as the Federal Reserve (Fed), European Central Bank (ECB), and Bank of England (BoE), are responsible for setting benchmark interest rates. These rates act as a reference for commercial banks, influencing everything from mortgage rates to corporate lending and bond yields. The main aim of central banks is to maintain economic stability by managing inflation, promoting growth, and ensuring sustainable employment levels.

Each central bank meets regularly to assess economic conditions and decide whether to change interest rates. These decisions are made by committees composed of senior economists, policymakers, and central bank officials:

Federal Reserve (USA)—8 meetings per year (Federal Open Market Committee, FOMC)

European Central Bank (ECB)—Every 6 weeks (Governing Council)

Bank of England (BoE)—Monthly (Monetary Policy Committee, MPC)

During these meetings, policymakers review various economic indicators to determine whether to raise, lower, or keep interest rates steady. Their decisions, along with forward guidance on future policy moves, significantly impact financial markets.

Forward Guidance: Why It Matters

Forward guidance refers to statements made by central banks that signal their future policy intentions, affecting market expectations even before actual rate changes occur.

Why It's Important: Markets respond not only to rate changes but also to expectations of future moves. If a central bank hints at hikes months in advance, traders and investors immediately price them in.

How Traders Use It: Investors carefully analyze speeches, meeting minutes, and statements from central bank members, especially those with voting power. A shift from a "dovish" (lower rates) to a "hawkish" (higher rates) stance can trigger significant market movements.

Example: In 2013, then-Fed Chair Ben Bernanke hinted at slowing asset purchases (known as the "Taper Tantrum"). Even though no rate hike had occurred, bond yields surged, stock markets fell, and emerging market currencies depreciated as investors anticipated tighter monetary policy.

In 2012, the Federal Reserve used explicit forward guidance, stating it would keep rates near zero until unemployment fell below a specific threshold. This influenced long-term bond yields and shaped investor sentiment, demonstrating the power of forward guidance.

Key Factors That Affect Interest Rate Movements

Inflation and Price Stability

Inflation is one of the most important factors influencing interest rate changes. Central banks aim to keep inflation within a target range—usually around 2% annually—to maintain price stability and sustainable growth.

Rising inflation: Central banks raise interest rates to curb borrowing and spending, avoiding uncontrolled inflation.

Falling Inflation or Deflation: When inflation is too low or negative, central banks decrease interest rates to encourage borrowing and investment.

In the early 1980s, the U.S. faced double-digit inflation. To address this, Federal Reserve Chairman Paul Volcker raised interest rates to over 20%, leading to a recession but ultimately successfully lowering inflation.

Economic Growth and Employment

The strength of an economy influences interest rate decisions. Central banks monitor GDP growth and employment levels to determine whether the economy is expanding too quickly or stagnating.

Strong Economic Growth: Central banks may raise interest rates to prevent overheating and speculative bubbles.

Weak Economic Growth or High Unemployment: Lowering interest rates encourages borrowing, job creation, and investment.

In response to the 2008 Global Financial Crisis, central banks worldwide slashed interest rates to near-zero levels to stimulate economic recovery and prevent a deeper recession.

Government Borrowing and Fiscal Policy

Governments influence interest rates through fiscal policies, including taxation and public spending. When governments run large deficits and issue more debt, interest rates may rise as they compete with private borrowers for capital.

Expansionary Fiscal Policy: Increased government spending and tax cuts can raise borrowing costs and push interest rates higher.

Austerity Measures: Cutting government debt and spending can help lower pressure on interest rates.

The UK's controversial Liz Truss mini-budget (2022) spooked investors, driving up UK gilt yields and prompting the Bank of England to intervene with bond purchases to lower the long-term interest rate on government debt.

Global Economic and Geopolitical Events

Global economic trends and geopolitical risks influence interest rates.

Wars or political instability: This can lead to capital flight into safe-haven assets, affecting bond yields and interest rates.

Oil price shocks: Higher energy costs can fuel inflation, prompting central banks to raise rates.

Pandemics or natural disasters: These disrupt economic activity, leading to emergency rate cuts.

During the COVID-19 pandemic, central banks worldwide cut interest rates and launched substantial stimulus programs to counteract the economic shock.

Supply and Demand in Bond Markets

Bond yields and interest rates are closely linked. When investors demand more bonds, yields fall, reducing borrowing costs. Conversely, when bond prices fall, yields rise, pushing up interest rates.

Increased Demand for Bonds: Lowers yields and signals expectations of lower future interest rates.

Mass Bond Sell-Offs: Pushes yields higher, indicating rising interest rate expectations.

In 2013, the Fed's announcement that it would taper its bond-buying program triggered the "Taper Tantrum," causing a spike in U.S. Treasury yields and higher borrowing costs globally.

Currency Strength and Exchange Rates

Interest rates and currency values are interconnected. Higher interest rates tend to attract foreign investment, strengthening the local currency.

Stronger Currency: Helps reduce inflation by lowering import costs, but can hurt exports.

Weaker Currency: Makes exports more competitive but may lead to higher inflation.

The U.S. dollar surged in 2022 as the Fed aggressively raised interest rates, making U.S. assets more attractive to global investors.

Why Interest Rates Matter to Traders and Investors

In conclusion, interest rates are the foundation of financial markets, shaping borrowing costs, investment returns, and economic health. Understanding what makes them move provides traders with valuable insights into:

Bond Market Trends—Rising interest rates lower bond prices, while falling rates drive bond rallies.

Stock Market Reactions—High rates slow equity markets, while lower rates boost corporate growth.

Currency Strength—Interest rate differentials influence forex markets, creating trading opportunities.

Real Estate and Mortgage Costs—Higher rates increase mortgage payments, affecting home affordability.

As central banks navigate changing economic conditions, traders anticipating interest rate movements will be best positioned to capitalize on opportunities across different asset classes.

In the next chapter, we'll explore how traders profit from interest rate movements using futures, options, and other financial instruments.

How to Trade Interest Rates Profitably

There are multiple ways to trade interest rates, ranging from simple directional bets to more complex relative-value trades.

Outright Trading of Interest Rate Futures

The most straightforward approach is trading STIR futures outright.

If you expect interest rates to rise, you can sell interest rate futures (as rates go up, bond and futures prices go down).

If you expect interest rates to fall, you can buy interest rate futures (as rates go down, bond and futures prices rise).

Example: If the Federal Reserve signals aggressive rate hikes, traders might sell SOFR futures in anticipation of higher rates, profiting as futures prices decline.

Calendar Spreads: Profiting From Interest Rate Differentials Over Time

One of the most effective ways to trade interest rates is through calendar spreads. This strategy involves trading futures contracts with different expiry dates to capitalize on changing interest rate expectations.

What is a Calendar Spread?

A calendar spread (also known as an inter-delivery spread or time spread) is a trading strategy in which you take opposite positions in two futures contracts on the same underlying asset, with different expiration dates.

In the context of interest rate futures, this means:

Buying one interest rate futures contract (long position) in a further-dated contract.

Selling another interest rate futures contract (short position) in a nearer-dated contract.

The goal is to profit from changes in the yield curve or expectations of central bank rate adjustments.

For the past twenty years, I've been trading intra-market calendar spreads for some of the world's largest proprietary trading companies. Despite this, most of the trading world remains unaware of this powerful market segment, and even fewer have had the chance to trade and profit from it.

This is about to change as retail brokers begin listing spread contracts on their platforms, opening the door for individual traders to explore and benefit from this lesser-known corner of the trading world.

Trade Study—Trading a SOFR Calendar Spread

Imagine you are trading SOFR futures (based on the US Secured Overnight Financing Rate), and the current market expectations are:

The Fed will hike rates in the next three months, starting in January.

Interest rates will stabilize six months later.

You could place a bearish calendar spread:

Sell the near-term SOFR future (e.g., March contract)—Expecting it to fall as the Fed raises rates.

Buy the longer-term SOFR future (e.g., September contract)—Expecting it to hold steady or recover.

Profit Mechanism:

If the Fed follows through with rate hikes, short-term rates will rise, pushing the near-term SOFR futures price down.

Longer-term rates may stabilize or decline, keeping the further-dated SOFR contract stable or rising.

The spread widens, allowing traders to profit from the divergence.

Yield Curve Trades

The yield curve represents the difference between short-term and long-term interest rates. Traders can take advantage of shifts in the yield curve by trading:

Steepener Trades: Buying long-term futures and selling short-term futures if they expect long-term rates to rise faster than short-term rates.

Flattener Trades: Selling long-term futures and buying short-term futures if they expect the spread between short and long-term rates to tighten.

Making Money the Interest(ing) Way

Trading interest rate markets offers opportunities across a range of strategies, from simple directional trades to more complex yield curve and calendar spread approaches. Understanding how central banks determine rates, how inflation and economic growth influence monetary policy, and how to structure trades based on these expectations is essential for success.

- Use STIR futures (SOFR, SONIA, EURIBOR) to express views on interest rates.
- Trade outright if you have a strong directional bias on rate movements.
- Use calendar spreads to profit from changes in interest rate expectations over time.
- Monitor central bank meetings, inflation data, and economic indicators closely.

Interest rate markets are some of the most dynamic and responsive in the world. With the proper knowledge and strategy, traders can capitalize on these fluctuations and profit from the ever-changing global monetary policy landscape.

4.1.4 Mastering the Holy Trinity

Understanding Fixed Income, Currency, and Interest Rate Markets provides traders with a solid foundation for success in financial markets. These three markets are closely linked, and mastering one naturally opens doors to opportunities in the others. Interest rates influence bond prices, bond yields impact currency values, and forex markets respond to central bank policy decisions, creating a cycle that continuously shapes global finance.

The common factor across these markets is the cost of money—the interest rate on a government bond, the rate set by central banks, or the yield differential influencing currency flows. If you learn to trade one of these markets effectively, you will develop a sense for the others. The knowledge and skills needed to trade bonds, currencies, and interest rate futures strongly overlap, creating a synergy that enables traders to exploit cross-market opportunities.

How Learning One Market Helps You Trade the Others

Interest Rate Trading → Fixed Income & Forex Opportunities

Understanding how interest rates fluctuate allows you to forecast bond market responses and predict currency movements. If central banks increase rates, bond values usually decline, and the local currency may strengthen as higher yields attract international investors.

Bond Market Trading → Forex & Interest Rate Strategies

Government bond yields signal expectations for future interest rate movements, influencing forex markets. A trader who understands bond yield trends can anticipate central bank actions and position accordingly in both interest rate futures and currency markets.

Currency Trading → Interest Rate & Bond Market Strategies

Interest rate differentials between countries often drive currency movements. If one country's central bank is hiking rates while another is cutting, a skilled trader can simultaneously profit from forex trends, bond spreads, and interest rate futures.

A Unified Approach to Financial Markets

Rather than viewing these as separate asset classes, experienced traders recognize them as parts of the same puzzle. A change in one often triggers a ripple effect in the others. For example:

If the Federal Reserve signals an interest rate hike →

- US bond yields rise
- The dollar strengthens against lower-yielding currencies.
- Interest rate futures price reflects higher borrowing costs.

If the European Central Bank cuts rates →

- German Bund yields decline.
- The euro weakens against the US dollar.
- Traders adjust interest rate expectations in STIR futures.

The global financial system is built upon the interactions between fixed income, currency, and interest rates. By understanding the mechanisms that drive each, traders can confidently navigate market cycles and capitalize on macroeconomic trends.

The real edge in trading comes from being able to anticipate moves before they happen, and the knowledge gained from these interconnected markets gives you that advantage.

If you master one, you will open doors to profiting from them all.

4.2 Precious Metals: The Golden Thread of Wealth and Power

Since the dawn of civilization, precious metals have fascinated humans and served as symbols of wealth, power, and security. From the golden masks of ancient pharaohs to the silver coins that powered empires, these metals have shaped history and driven numerous fortunes. Today, they remain among the most sought-after and widely traded commodities in the financial world, offering opportunities for traders to profit from price fluctuations and hedge against economic uncertainty.

In this chapter, we delve into the fascinating world of precious metals, with a particular focus on gold, silver, and copper—the pillars of the metals market. Each has its unique characteristics, price drivers, and trading opportunities.

Gold: The ultimate safe-haven asset, gold has long been a store of value during economic turmoil and inflation. Whether you're a central banker, a billionaire investor, or a retail trader, gold's allure as a hedge against risk is unmatched.

Silver: Known as "poor man's gold," silver's dual role as both an investment metal and an industrial commodity makes it highly volatile and versatile for trading.
Silver plays a critical role in our daily lives, from jewelry to solar panels.
Copper: Dubbed "Dr Copper" for its ability to diagnose the health of the global economy, this essential industrial metal is the backbone of construction, manufacturing, and infrastructure development. When the economy is booming, copper prices tend to rise.

Whether you're aiming to hedge your portfolio against inflation, capitalize on geopolitical instability, or ride the wave of global growth, understanding the precious metals markets can be your golden ticket to profitability. Let's explore their history, what makes them tick, and the strategies that can help you turn metal into money.

4.2.1 The Metal That Needs No Introduction-Gold

Gold—it's more than just a metal; it's a symbol of power, wealth, and security that has captivated civilizations for thousands of years. From ancient Egypt to contemporary financial markets, gold has played a central role in shaping economies, cultures, and fortunes. In this chapter, we'll explore the origins of gold, key historical moments, major market movements, factors that influence its price, and trading strategies that can help you unlock the potential of this precious metal.

It started as a Shiny rock in the ground
Gold's allure dates back to the earliest days of human civilization. Its scarcity, beauty, and durability have made it a prized possession and a symbol of power across cultures and millennia.

Discovery and Early Use:
Gold was first discovered in riverbeds by ancient civilizations in the Middle East around 4,000 BCE. Early humans used gold for decorative purposes, such as jewelry and religious artefacts.

Ancient Egypt:
By 2,600 BCE, the ancient Egyptians were mining gold and using it to craft elaborate jewelry, masks, and artefacts for pharaohs. The famous funerary

mask of Tutankhamun, made of solid gold, symbolizes the metal's enduring power and mystique.

Gold as Currency:
Around 700 BCE, gold coins were first minted in Lydia (modern-day Turkey), marking the start of gold's use as a standardized medium of exchange.

Roman Empire:
The Romans expanded gold mining across Europe and Africa, using the proceeds to finance military campaigns and fuel the empire's expansion.

The Gold Standard:
In the nineteenth century, the gold standard was introduced, linking currencies to gold reserves. This system dominated global finance until it was discontinued during the Great Depression.

Bretton Woods System:
In 1944, the Bretton Woods Agreement established the U.S. dollar as the world's reserve currency, backed by gold at a fixed rate of $35 per ounce. This system lasted until 1971, when President Richard Nixon ended the gold standard, allowing gold prices to float freely.

A modern history of the gold market

Throughout history, gold has experienced pivotal moments that have shaped its role in the global economy and financial markets.

California Gold Rush (1848–1855):
The California Gold Rush was one of the most transformative events in American history, sparking a massive wave of migration, economic growth, and social change. It began in early 1848 when James W. Marshall, a carpenter working for John Sutter, discovered gold at Sutter's Mill in Coloma, California. News of the discovery spread rapidly, leading to an unprecedented influx of fortune hunters known as the "forty-niners" (a reference to the peak migration year of 1849).

The Gold Rush had a lasting impact on the U.S. and globally. It accelerated westward expansion, encouraged international migration, and helped make California an economic power. The state remains one of the most prosperous and populous in the U.S. today, and the Gold Rush spirit of innovation and opportunity continues to shape its culture.

Bretton Woods Collapse (1971):
In 1944, as World War II was ending, 44 allied nations gathered in Bretton Woods, New Hampshire, to create a new global financial system aimed at promoting economic stability and avoiding the economic chaos of the interwar years.

The Bretton Woods Agreement introduced several key mechanisms:

The U.S. dollar became the world's reserve currency, pegged to gold at a fixed rate of $35 per ounce.

Other currencies were tied to the U.S. dollar, creating a stable global exchange rate system.

Institutions such as the International Monetary Fund (IMF) and the World Bank were established to promote financial stability and economic development.

Initially, the system functioned well, fostering economic growth and international trade. However, by the 1960s, emerging weaknesses became clear. Rising U.S. government expenditure—due to the Vietnam War, social welfare programs, and widening trade deficits—raised concerns about the dollar's ability to maintain its gold backing. Confidence in the system diminished, and foreign nations, led by France, began demanding gold in exchange for their U.S. dollar reserves, which drained U.S. gold reserves.

The Nixon Shock and the End of the Gold Standard
On 15 August 1971, President Richard Nixon unilaterally ended the dollar's convertibility to gold, effectively dismantling the Bretton Woods system. This move, known as the Nixon Shock, marked the transition to a fiat currency system, where money was no longer backed by gold but by government decree.

The immediate result was the free-floating of gold prices, which increased significantly over the following decade. As inflation, economic instability, and geopolitical crises developed in the 1970s, gold rose from its long-standing $35-per-ounce price to over $800 per ounce by 1980.

A New Era in Global Finance
The collapse of Bretton Woods reshaped the global economy.

The U.S. dollar remained the dominant global currency despite no longer being tied to gold.

Central banks gained greater control over monetary policy, using interest rates and adjustments to the money supply to manage economies.

The shift to a fiat* currency system introduced greater market volatility, particularly in foreign exchange and commodity markets.

While gold prices later stabilized, the end of the gold standard fundamentally changed how modern economies operate, paving the way for the financial system we know today.

**Fiat currencies*

A fiat currency is a form of money that has no intrinsic value and is not supported by a physical commodity such as gold or silver. Instead, its worth relies on government decree and public confidence in the issuing authority, usually a central bank.

Governments designate fiat currency as legal tender, which must be accepted to settle debts and conduct transactions.

Fiat currency gives governments and central banks greater control over the economy. Adjusting interest rates and money supply can influence inflation, employment, and economic growth. However, the system relies on public confidence—if trust in a currency collapses (due to hyperinflation or financial instability), its value can plummet.

The 1980 Gold Rally:

The 1980 gold rally marked one of the most dramatic price surges in history, as gold prices soared to an all-time high of $850 per ounce in January 1980. This sharp increase was driven by rising inflation, geopolitical instability, and economic uncertainty, making gold the preferred safe-haven asset for investors worldwide.

The story of the 1980 Gold Rally

High Inflation and Economic Turmoil

By the late 1970s, the U.S. economy suffered from stagflation—a rare combination of high inflation, slow economic growth, and rising unemployment.

Double-digit inflation:

In the U.S., inflation peaked at 14% in 1980, eroding the purchasing power of the U.S. dollar.

Rising energy prices:

The 1979 oil crisis (triggered by the Iranian Revolution) caused oil prices to double, contributing to wider inflation throughout the economy.

Weak monetary policy:

The Federal Reserve initially struggled to control inflation, leading investors to seek protection in gold.

Gold is traditionally viewed as a hedge against inflation, so as prices rose in the economy, demand for gold soared.

Geopolitical Tensions and Global Instability
The late 1970s were a period of intense global uncertainty, further driving investors toward gold as a safe-haven asset. Key geopolitical events included:

The Iranian Revolution (1979):
The overthrow of the Shah of Iran led to widespread instability in the Middle East and a major disruption in global oil supplies.

The Soviet Invasion of Afghanistan (December 1979):
The Cold War escalated as the Soviet Union invaded Afghanistan, prompting fears of broader global conflict and leading to economic sanctions.

The U.S.-Iran Hostage Crisis (November 1979—January 1981):
The seizure of 52 American hostages in Tehran increased tensions between the U.S. and Iran, further shaking confidence in global stability.

These events fostered a sense of worldwide uncertainty, causing investors to shift from traditional assets to gold.

A Weak U.S. Dollar and Loss of Confidence
With the collapse of the Bretton Woods system in 1971, the U.S. dollar was no longer backed by gold, making it more vulnerable to devaluation.

The dollar lost significant value against other major currencies in the 1970s.

As confidence in the dollar weakened, investors turned to gold as a store of value.

Central banks and private investors increased their gold purchases, driving up demand and prices.

All of these factors culminated in January 1980, when gold reached $850 per ounce—a level that, when adjusted for inflation, remained the highest on record until 2020. At its peak, gold had increased by over 2,300% from its fixed price of $35 per ounce in 1971.

However, this record rally did not last long; as I write this, in 2025, the gold price has hit a new all-time high!

The 2008 Financial Crisis: Gold's Rise Amid Economic Turmoil
The 2008 financial crisis was one of the most severe economic downturns in modern history, causing a global market collapse and prompting a flight to

safe-haven assets—particularly gold. As confidence in banks, financial institutions, and fiat currencies faltered, gold rose from around $700 per ounce in 2008 to over $1,900 per ounce by 2011, marking one of the most notable price increases in history.

Causes of the 2008 Financial Crisis

We've previously discussed the financial crisis in the context of market timelines. At that time, I was mainly trading bonds, stocks, oil, and short-term interest rates, but I was intrigued by the surge in gold. As reckless risk-taking, regulatory failures, and the collapse of the U.S. housing market sparked the crisis, those of us in financial services genuinely feared that the modern monetary system was on the brink of collapse. We thought we might have to revert to bartering with goods and precious metals. So, naturally, we bought gold!

Subprime Mortgage Crisis and Housing Market Collapse

Leading up to 2008, banks and financial institutions issued high-risk mortgage loans (subprime mortgages) to borrowers with low creditworthiness.

These risky loans were repackaged into mortgage-backed securities (MBS) and sold to investors, including major banks and pension funds.

When the housing bubble burst in 2007–2008, millions of homeowners defaulted on their loans, triggering massive losses across the banking sector.

Lehman Brothers Collapse and Banking Crisis

On September 15, 2008, Lehman Brothers, one of the world's largest investment banks, filed for bankruptcy.

Panic spread as investors feared further bank failures, leading to a global stock market collapse.

Governments and central banks had to intervene with bailouts and emergency liquidity injections to prevent a complete meltdown of the financial system.

Global Economic Recession

Stock markets plummeted—the S&P 500 lost over 50% of its value between 2007 and early 2009.

Businesses collapsed, unemployment soared, and governments worldwide implemented massive stimulus programs to revive their economies.

Investor confidence was shaken, leading to a surge in demand for safe-haven assets, such as gold.

Gold as a Safe Haven: The 2008-Present Day Gold Rally

Flight to Safety: Gold's Role in Crisis

A flight to safety occurs when investors transfer their funds from riskier assets (such as stocks, corporate bonds, or emerging markets) into safer, more stable investments during periods of economic uncertainty, financial crisis, or geopolitical instability.

In late 2008, gold was trading at approximately $700 per ounce. As the crisis intensified, demand increased, pushing gold to $1,000 per ounce by early 2009.

By 2011, amidst ongoing economic uncertainty, gold reached an all-time high of $1,921 per ounce in September.

Central Bank Policies and Inflation Fears

In response to the crisis, central banks—particularly the U.S. Federal Reserve—launched unprecedented monetary stimulus programs, including:

Near-zero interest rates (reducing the appeal of bonds and savings accounts).

Quantitative easing (QE) involves injecting trillions of dollars into financial markets to stabilize banks and the economy.

Massive government bailouts were used to prevent the collapse of the corporate and banking sectors.

These actions sparked fears of inflation and currency devaluation, further boosting gold's appeal as a store of value.

Sovereign Debt Crises and Market Uncertainty

Even after the initial crisis, new economic threats emerged:

The Eurozone debt crisis (2010–2012) raised concerns about the stability of European banks and governments are increasing their demand for gold.

Political instability, including the U.S. debt ceiling crisis and concerns over central bank policies, fueled uncertainty in financial markets.

Investors continued to buy gold as a hedge against systemic risks and potential economic collapse.

COVID-19 Pandemic (2020): Amid global uncertainty and massive central bank stimulus, gold prices hit a new all-time high of over $2,070 per ounce in August 2020.

The Ukraine-Russia conflict, which has been ongoing since 2022, has increased international uncertainty due to its complex nature.

The highlight here is that there's always a challenging event around the corner, which leads to a gold rally.

A Deeper Look into Key Drivers of the Gold Market

Gold is one of the most actively traded and historically significant assets, serving as a store of value, a hedge against inflation, and a safe haven during times of economic and geopolitical uncertainty. Its price movements are influenced by complex economic conditions, central bank policies, interest rates, currency fluctuations, and global events. Unlike fiat currencies, which can be devalued through monetary policy, gold has maintained its intrinsic value throughout history, making it a vital asset for investors seeking to safeguard their wealth.

From periods of high inflation and financial crises to times of market stability and economic growth, gold's role in the global financial system has developed, yet its core appeal remains constant. Whether used for portfolio diversification, speculative trading, or as a hedge against risk, gold attracts traders and investors alike due to its liquidity and sensitivity to macroeconomic trends.

Understanding the key drivers of gold prices—including inflation trends, interest rate movements, central bank reserves, geopolitical risks, and shifts in the U.S. dollar's strength—is essential for making informed, well-timed trading decisions. By analyzing these factors, traders can identify optimal entry and exit points, capitalizing on gold's price fluctuations in response to global economic developments.

Inflation and Interest Rates

Gold is widely regarded as a hedge against inflation because it retains its value, unlike fiat currencies, which tend to lose purchasing power over time. Additionally, gold becomes more attractive when real interest rates (inflation-adjusted interest rates) decline.

Case study

In the 1970s, rising inflation, driven by loose monetary policy and oil price shocks, pushed gold prices from $35 per ounce to $850 by 1980.

In contrast, during the 1980s and 1990s, high interest rates and low inflation suppressed gold prices.

Go long on gold when inflation rises, or central banks signal lower interest rates (dovish policy).

Go short on gold when interest rates rise faster than inflation, making bonds and cash more attractive than gold.

Geopolitical Tensions and Market Crises—AKA the Safe Haven Trade

Gold is a safe-haven asset, meaning it tends to appreciate during periods of global instability. Investors seek protection in gold during war, financial crises, and political uncertainty.

Case study
During the 2008 financial crisis, gold surged from $700 to over $1,900 as investors lost faith in banks and sought safety.

The Russia-Ukraine war (2022) led to a sharp rise in gold prices due to geopolitical uncertainty.

Go long on gold when there are signs of increased geopolitical risks, such as military conflicts, terrorism, or financial instability.

Go short on gold if geopolitical risks subside and market confidence returns.

U.S. Dollar Strength
Gold is quoted in U.S. dollars (USD) and generally moves inversely to the dollar's value. When the dollar strengthens, gold becomes more expensive for foreign buyers, which reduces demand. Conversely, a weaker dollar makes gold more appealing.

Case Study
In 2010–2011, a weak dollar contributed to gold's rally past $1,900 per ounce.

Between 2013 and 2015, a strengthening dollar led to a sharp decline in gold prices, which dropped to around $1,050 per ounce.

Go long on gold when the U.S. Dollar Index (DXY) declines or when the Federal Reserve adopts a dovish (low-rate) stance.

Go short on gold when the dollar strengthens due to rising U.S. interest rates or increased global demand for U.S. dollar liquidity.

Central Bank Policies and Gold Reserves
Central banks hold substantial amounts of gold as part of their reserve assets. Their buying and selling activities can influence gold prices, especially when major economies adjust their gold holdings.

Case Study
In 2019, central banks (including China and Russia) bought record amounts of gold, supporting a price rally.

In the 1990s and early 2000s, central banks (particularly in Europe) sold off large gold reserves, keeping prices low.

Go long on gold if major central banks announce plans to increase their gold holdings.

Go short on gold if central banks indicate gold sales or policy shifts that reduce gold demand.

Global Economic Data and Recession Risks

Gold rises when economic data points to weak growth, high unemployment, or declining consumer confidence. When investors anticipate a recession, gold demand increases as a hedge against financial uncertainty.

Case study

During the COVID-19 pandemic (2020), weak global economic data and aggressive stimulus measures pushed gold to all-time highs above $2,000 per ounce.

In contrast, gold often lags behind equities and riskier assets during economic booms.

Go long on gold if global economic data suggests recessionary risks or rising unemployment.

Go short on gold if economic growth is strong and stock markets are rallying.

Trading Strategies for the Gold Market

The Enduring Allure of Gold

Gold's role as a store of value, inflation hedge, and safe-haven asset has made it one of the most essential and actively traded commodities in financial markets for centuries. Revered for its rarity, durability, and intrinsic worth, gold has been a cornerstone of economies, a medium of exchange, and a symbol of wealth and power throughout human history. While its cultural and monetary significance is deeply rooted, gold's true value in modern markets lies in its ability to preserve wealth, hedge against inflation, and provide stability during times of economic uncertainty and geopolitical turmoil.

Unlike fiat currencies, which can be influenced by monetary policy decisions, inflationary pressures, and devaluation, gold remains a tangible asset with universally recognized value. A variety of factors, including interest rates, central bank policies, global economic conditions, currency fluctuations, and investor sentiment, affect its price movements. During periods of market volatility, recessions, or financial crises, gold has historically experienced increased demand as investors seek a reliable store of value and a hedge against systemic risks.

Beyond its defensive characteristics, gold also presents lucrative trading opportunities for those who understand its price dynamics. Whether used for long-term portfolio diversification, speculative short-term trades, or as a strategic hedge against macroeconomic risks, gold's liquidity and responsiveness to market conditions make it an essential asset for traders and investors alike.

By developing a clear understanding of the main factors that influence gold prices—including inflation trends, central bank actions, global monetary shifts, geopolitical tensions, and the strength of the U.S. dollar—traders can position themselves to benefit from opportunities across different market conditions. When these insights are complemented by solid technical analysis and disciplined risk management, gold's enduring appeal and stability become valuable tools for navigating modern financial markets and making more informed, strategic trading decisions.

4.2.2 Hi Ho Silver—The Poor Man's Gold

Silver has been treasured for thousands of years, not only as a store of value but also as an essential industrial metal. Known as the "poor man's gold," silver possesses a unique dual nature—it serves as both a precious metal and a vital industrial material.

Its history is characterized by economic intrigue, notable market shifts, and opportunities for traders who recognize its volatility and potential.

From ancient civilizations minting silver coins to the rise and fall of global monetary standards, silver has played a pivotal role in shaping economies and financial systems. Its affordability compared to gold has made it more accessible to the masses, yet its scarcity and demand have often driven dramatic price swings.

Beyond its monetary value, silver is vital to industries such as electronics, solar power, healthcare, and space exploration, making it one of the most adaptable commodities globally.

For traders and investors, silver presents unique opportunities. It usually follows gold during periods of economic uncertainty but can also move independently due to changes in industrial demand. Understanding the factors that impact silver prices—such as inflation, geopolitical risks, central bank policies, and technological progress—can give a strategic advantage in navigating this evolving market. Whether regarded as a hedge against inflation, a speculative asset, or an industrial necessity, silver remains a metal rooted in history yet full of potential.

The Origins of Silver

Silver has been mined and used by civilizations for over 5,000 years. Some of the earliest evidence of silver mining dates back to Anatolia (modern-day Turkey), where ancient societies first began extracting and refining the metal around 3000 BCE.

Silver played a crucial role in the economies of Mesopotamia, Egypt, Greece, and Rome, functioning both as currency and a symbol of wealth. The Roman denarius, a silver coin first struck in the third century BCE, became one of the most influential currencies of the ancient world, enabling trade across the vast Roman Empire and beyond.

During the Spanish conquest of the Americas in the sixteenth century, the discovery of vast silver deposits in Mexico, Bolivia, and Peru fundamentally transformed global trade. The Potosí mines in Bolivia, often called "the mountain that eats men," became one of the wealthiest and most notorious silver mines in history. The immense volume of silver extracted from these mines was staggering—Potosí alone supplied much of the world's silver for centuries. European markets were flooded with the metal, resulting in one of the earliest recorded instances of inflation caused by an oversupply of precious metals.

I had the chance to explore the Potosí mines during my travels across South America in my youth, and it was an experience I will never forget. The conditions were dark, cramped, and unbearably hot—a brutal reminder of the extreme hardships miners have endured for centuries. The air was thick with dust, and the narrow tunnels barely offered enough space to move. The respect I gained for the miners working in those conditions is immeasurable. Before leaving, I made sure to pay my respects to the mining gods, a tradition among miners seeking protection in the treacherous underground labyrinth.

Beyond its monetary importance, silver played a vital role in global trade networks, especially during the era of Spanish colonial rule. Much of the silver mined in the Americas was shipped to Spain, where it was minted into coins like the famed "pieces of eight." From there, it circulated into European economies and beyond, with large quantities reaching China in exchange for silk, spices, and other luxury goods. This silver trade effectively connected Europe, the Americas, and Asia in one of the earliest examples of globalization.

Today, silver remains a key asset in both investment and industry, with its legacy deeply woven into the world's economic history. Its past is marked by booms, busts, and dramatic market moves, making it a fascinating metal that continues to capture the attention of traders, investors, and historians alike.

Silver's Key Moments in History

The Comstock Lode (1859)—America's First Major Silver Rush

The discovery of the Comstock Lode in Nevada in 1859 marked a highly significant event in silver mining history, igniting a silver rush that spurred economic growth across the United States. Before the Comstock discovery, most precious metal mining in the U.S. focused on gold. However, the vast silver deposits in Nevada rapidly shifted the focus.

Thousands of prospectors flocked to the region, hoping to strike it rich. Mining towns like Virginia City sprang up almost overnight, transforming the landscape of the American West. The large volume of silver extracted from the Comstock Lode increased global supplies, making the U.S. a dominant player in the silver trade. The wealth generated helped finance the country's rapid industrialization, with silver used for coinage, trade, and industry.

The Comstock Lode also pioneered new mining technologies, including deep-shaft mining and improved ore-processing techniques. However, the boom didn't last forever. By the 1880s, the mines had declined in output, and the once-thriving mining towns became ghost towns. Yet, the Comstock Lode remains an iconic moment in silver's history, setting the stage for future silver rushes and cementing the metal's role in global finance.

The Crime of 1873—The End of Silver as Money

For much of history, silver and gold served as the foundation of global monetary systems. The U.S. operated under a bimetallic standard, with both gold and silver coins circulating as currency. However, in 1873, the U.S. government passed the Coinage Act, which effectively demonetized silver by removing it from the list of metals eligible for free coinage. This move, later criticized as "The Crime of 1873," marked a significant shift towards the gold standard.

The impact was immediate and severe for those who relied on silver. Farmers and miners, particularly in the Western U.S., suffered as silver prices plummeted. With silver no longer a legal tender for government payments, its value collapsed, causing widespread economic distress. This policy change heightened tensions between industrialists and farming communities, contributing to the rise of the Populist movement, which demanded a return to bimetallism.

Although silver saw a partial resurgence in 1896 with the rise of the Free Silver movement and William Jennings Bryan's renowned "Cross of Gold" speech, the transition towards a gold-backed monetary system was largely irreversible. The United States would eventually abolish the gold standard altogether in 1971, but the Crime of 1873 remains a pivotal moment in silver's monetary history.

The Hunt Brothers Silver Corner (1979–1980)—The Most Infamous Attempt to Control a Market

One of the most dramatic episodes in financial history took place in the late 1970s when Nelson Bunker Hunt and William Herbert Hunt, two wealthy

Texas oil magnates, tried to corner the silver market. The Hunt brothers, fearing inflation and wary of fiat currency, began amassing vast quantities of silver in the early 1970s.

By the late 1970s, their purchases, combined with rising demand for silver as an inflation hedge, drove prices soaring from $6 per ounce in early 1979 to nearly $50 per ounce by January 1980—a more than 700% increase. Their accumulation of physical silver and large leveraged positions in silver futures sparked a frenzy, with retail and institutional investors rushing into the market in fear of missing out.

However, the U.S. government and regulators viewed this as a threat to financial stability. The Commodity Futures Trading Commission (CFTC) and COMEX raised margin requirements on silver futures contracts. This compelled traders, including the Hunt brothers, to post additional collateral, causing a liquidity crunch. On March 27, 1980, known as Silver Thursday, the price of silver plummeted by over 50% in a single day. The Hunts could not meet their margin calls, leading to a financial crisis that nearly toppled several major Wall Street firms.

The collapse of silver prices caused significant losses for the Hunts, who were subsequently accused of market manipulation. This incident stands as a clear reminder that even the most daring efforts to manipulate a commodity market can result in spectacular failure.

The 2011 Silver Spike—A Modern-Day Rally Fueled by Fear and Speculation

The 2008 financial crisis and ensuing economic uncertainty sparked a fresh wave of demand for silver. Investors sought safety in precious metals, and silver, being both a safe-haven asset and an industrial metal, experienced a surge in interest. Central bank policies, including aggressive quantitative easing and low interest rates, raised inflation fears, further boosting silver's ascent.

Between 2009 and 2011, silver prices rose from about $10 per ounce to nearly $49 per ounce in April 2011, approaching the all-time high set during the Hunt brothers' attempt to corner the market in 1980.

A combination of factors drove the rally:

Rising inflation fears

A weak U.S. dollar

Increased industrial demand for silver in electronics and solar panels

A surge in retail investor demand, particularly through silver exchange-traded funds (ETFs)

However, similar to 1980, the silver rally ended suddenly. As economic conditions stabilized and the Federal Reserve signaled potential tightening of monetary policy, silver prices plummeted, falling to approximately $26 per ounce by the end of 2011. The steep decline eliminated many speculative traders who had entered the market late in the rally, further cementing silver's reputation for extreme volatility.

The 2011 silver spike remains one of the most volatile periods in modern financial history, offering both immense opportunities and significant risks. For traders, it served as a lesson in how quickly sentiment can change in the silver market and emphasized the importance of risk management when trading such an unpredictable asset.

Silver's history is marked by dramatic market fluctuations that have shaped economies and financial markets, from ancient currency to speculative booms and busts. Silver remains one of the most fascinating and volatile assets, whether it's a silver rush in the 1800s, government policies that send prices plunging, or modern-day trading frenzies. Understanding these key moments offers valuable insight into how the silver market responds to supply shocks, policy changes, and shifts in investor sentiment—an essential knowledge base for any trader navigating this unpredictable yet rewarding market.

What's moving the silver market?

A complex interplay of macroeconomic forces, industrial demand, and investor sentiment influences silver prices. Unlike gold, which is primarily a monetary asset, silver straddles both investment and industrial sectors, making it more volatile and responsive to changing economic conditions. Here are the primary factors that drive the silver market:

Inflation and Monetary Policy—Silver as a Hedge

Silver, like gold, is commonly seen as a hedge against inflation. When inflation rises, the purchasing power of fiat currencies falls, prompting investors to turn to tangible assets such as silver.

Loose Monetary Policy & Low Interest Rates: When central banks, such as the U.S. Federal Reserve, adopt policies like quantitative easing (QE) or keep interest rates low, they increase the money supply and reduce the opportunity cost of holding non-yielding assets, such as silver. This often leads to a rise in demand for silver as a store of value.

Rising Inflation: Higher inflation expectations, particularly during times of economic uncertainty or excessive money printing, make silver an appealing investment. Historically, silver has performed well in periods of high inflation, as evidenced in the 1970s and 2011.

Real Interest Rates: Silver is sensitive to real (inflation-adjusted) interest rates. Investors flock to silver and gold to preserve wealth when real rates are negative. Conversely, when real rates rise, silver demand weakens as investors move towards interest-bearing assets.

Industrial Demand—Silver as a Critical Commodity

Silver has significant industrial applications, unlike gold, which is primarily used for investment and jewelry. Industrial demand accounts for about 50% of annual silver consumption, making it a unique asset that benefits from both economic growth and investment interest.

Electronics: Silver has the highest electrical conductivity of any metal, making it vital in electronics manufacturing, including the production of semiconductors, batteries, and RFID chips.

Solar Panels (Photovoltaics): The move towards renewable energy has notably boosted demand for silver. Silver is a vital element in solar photovoltaic (PV) cells, and the increase in solar panel manufacturing—especially in China and the U.S.—has rendered silver a strategic commodity.

Medical Applications: Silver's antibacterial properties make it valuable in the medical sector, where it is utilized in surgical instruments, wound dressings, and antibacterial coatings.

5G and AI Technology: The expansion of 5G networks and artificial intelligence (AI) computing infrastructure will boost the demand for silver in advanced technological applications.

Unlike gold, where demand mainly arises from investment and jewelry, silver's industrial uses mean that manufacturing trends, economic growth, and technological progress also affect its price.

U.S. Dollar Strength—The Inverse Relationship

Like most commodities, silver is priced in U.S. dollars (USD). This means that silver generally has an inverse relationship with the dollar—when the dollar weakens, silver prices tend to rise, and vice versa.

Weaker Dollar: A declining dollar makes silver more affordable for foreign buyers, thereby boosting demand from international markets. This was evident in 2020 when a weak USD contributed to silver's rally past $28 per ounce.

Stronger Dollar: When the USD gains strength—often because of rising interest rates or increased global demand for safe-haven assets—silver prices tend to fall as they become more expensive for non-U.S. investors.

Global Currency Trends: If major economies such as China or the Eurozone face currency instability, investors may turn to silver as a hedge against currency devaluation, which could further influence its price.

Gold Prices and Market Sentiment—Silver's High Beta

Silver is often called "gold's little brother" because its price usually tracks gold's movements, though with greater volatility.

Gold-Silver Correlation: Historically, silver tends to move in the same direction as gold, but its price fluctuations are usually more pronounced. This is because silver's market size is smaller, and it serves dual roles as both an industrial and a monetary asset.

Gold-Silver Ratio: Investors monitor the gold-to-silver ratio, which indicates how many ounces of silver are needed to purchase one ounce of gold. A high ratio (above 80:1) often indicates that silver is undervalued relative to gold, prompting traders to expect a silver rally.

Safe-Haven Demand: During financial crises, silver gains from safe-haven buying. However, it often trails gold due to its lower liquidity and greater reliance on industrial use.

Speculative Interest & Retail Investors: Silver attracts both institutional and retail investors, especially through silver ETFs (Exchange-Traded Funds) and futures markets. The 2021 Reddit-driven silver squeeze, in which retail traders sought to boost silver prices, highlighted the impact of retail speculation.

Supply Constraints—The Role of Mining and Recycling

Silver's supply is relatively inelastic in the short term because it is mainly mined as a byproduct of other metals, such as copper, lead, and zinc. Fluctuations in global mining activity can significantly affect silver supply.

Silver, by nature, is a byproduct.

Production relies on base metal mining, since only about 30% of silver comes from primary silver mines. A decline in copper or zinc mining (due to lower demand or regulatory issues) can lead to silver shortages.

Geopolitical and environmental factors: Mining regulations, environmental concerns, and geopolitical instability in key silver-producing countries (such as Mexico, Peru, and China) can disrupt supply chains.

Silver Recycling: Unlike gold, which is widely recycled, a significant portion of industrial silver is lost after use. This restricts secondary supply, making mining production a vital element in silver pricing.

Additional Factors to Watch in the Silver Market

Geopolitical Risks—Wars, trade disputes, or economic sanctions can disrupt silver supply chains and influence investor sentiment.

Central Bank Reserves—Unlike gold, silver is not a major part of central bank reserves; however, changes in monetary policy can indirectly affect silver prices.

Technological Innovations—New industrial uses for silver, such as progress in green energy or medical technologies, can cause unexpected rises in demand.

Market Manipulation & Short Squeezes—Major institutional players and hedge funds have historically manipulated silver prices, as seen with the Hunt Brothers in 1980 and the 2021 retail silver squeeze.

Silver is a distinctive asset influenced by macroeconomic trends and industrial demand. Its dual role as both an investment and an industrial metal makes it more volatile than gold, with price fluctuations driven by inflation, interest rates, industrial use, and speculative sentiment. While silver can serve as a hedge against inflation and currency devaluation, it is also vulnerable to economic cycles and supply limitations. Understanding these dynamics is essential for traders and investors seeking to navigate the silver market effectively.

Trading ideas for Silver

Silver is a versatile asset with a distinctive combination of monetary and industrial value, making it an appealing choice for traders looking for volatility and opportunities.

Unlike gold, which is primarily a monetary metal, silver is strongly influenced by industrial demand, macroeconomic conditions, and investor sentiment. This allows for a range of trading strategies. Here are some of the most effective methods for trading silver.

Seasonal Trading

Silver exhibits strong seasonal tendencies, often rallying in the first half of the year, particularly between January and May. This trend is driven by factors such as industrial demand, increased investment flows, and historical price cycles.

Enter **long** positions in silver futures, ETFs, or mining stocks in early Q1.

Target an exit before the summer months, when prices have historically consolidated or pulled back.

Silver-Gold Ratio Trading

The gold-to-silver ratio measures the number of ounces of silver required to purchase one ounce of gold.

This ratio has fluctuated historically between 30 and 100, with extremes offering trading opportunities. When the ratio is above 80, silver is often considered undervalued relative to gold, and when it drops below 50, silver may be overextended.

If the ratio is above 80, go long silver and short gold to capitalize on a potential mean reversion.

If the ratio falls below 50, consider reversing the trade by shorting silver and going long gold.

Monitor historical averages and macroeconomic conditions to confirm signals.

Inflation Hedge Trades

Silver, like gold, is often used as a hedge against inflation. When inflation expectations rise, investors turn to silver as a store of value, driving prices higher. This effect is amplified when central banks pursue loose monetary policies.

Monitor key economic indicators, including CPI (Consumer Price Index) reports, interest rate decisions, and money supply data.

If inflation expectations rise or central banks signal a dovish stance, initiate long positions in silver.

Consider using silver ETFs or Futures for this type of trade.

Industrial Demand and Tech Trends

Unlike gold, silver has extensive industrial applications, particularly in electronics, solar energy, and medical technology sectors. Industrial demand accounts for approximately 50% of annual silver consumption, making it a key driver of long-term price movements.

Track industrial production reports, renewable energy policies, and semiconductor industry trends.

If demand projections for solar panels, EV batteries, or medical applications increase, take long positions in silver futures, ETFs, or silver mining stocks.

Event-Driven Trading

Silver often reacts strongly to geopolitical events, central bank announcements, and economic crises. During periods of uncertainty, investors flock to silver as a safe-haven asset, causing sharp price spikes.

Monitor the economic calendar for major risk events, including Federal Reserve meetings, elections, geopolitical tensions, and financial crises.

Position long ahead of potential volatility spikes, especially if markets are pricing in uncertainty.

Every cloud has a silver lining.

Silver is much more than just "poor man's gold." Its dual function as a monetary metal and an industrial commodity creates unique trading opportunities in various market conditions. Whether used as an inflation hedge, a seasonal trade, or an industrial growth bet, silver offers traders the chance to profit from its volatility and cyclical patterns.

Successful silver trading depends on a thorough understanding of historical trends, economic factors, and technical signals. By applying the appropriate strategy at the right moment, traders can capitalize on silver's price movements to their benefit, confidently navigating both its sharp rallies and notable pullbacks.

4.2.3 The Doctor Will See You Now: Understanding Copper

Copper has long been seen as a key economic indicator, earning it the nickname "Dr Copper" for its remarkable ability to assess the state of the global economy. As one of the most commonly used industrial metals, copper is closely linked to economic growth, infrastructure projects, and technological progress. Its price movements frequently mirror changes in global demand, making it a crucial asset for traders and investors aiming to assess economic trends.

Beyond its financial importance, copper has played a vital role in human civilization for thousands of years. From ancient tools and early coinage to electrical wiring and renewable energy systems, copper has driven progress like no other metal. Its distinctive properties—high conductivity, corrosion resistance, and malleability—have made it essential across many industries, including construction, transportation, and electronics.

This chapter explores the origins, historical significance, key factors affecting its market value, and trading strategies that enable traders to profit from its fluctuations. Whether you're an investor looking to hedge against economic cycles or a trader pursuing volatility and opportunities, understanding copper's dynamics is crucial for navigating this important commodity market.

Copper's Origins and Early Use

Copper is among the oldest metals used by humans, with evidence of its use dating back over 10,000 years. Its discovery and early utilization marked a major milestone in human history, as it was one of the first metals to be shaped and manipulated for practical purposes. The earliest known copper artefacts, such as tools and ornaments, were found in the Middle East, especially in Mesopotamia and Egypt, where ancient civilizations quickly recognized their importance. These early societies found copper in its native, metallic state, allowing them to shape and work it without requiring advanced smelting techniques.

By 3000 BCE, civilizations in the Mediterranean, China, and the Americas had developed more advanced methods for refining and alloying copper, leading to the beginning of the Bronze Age. This era was characterized by the realization that copper combined with tin produced bronze—a stronger, longer-lasting metal that transformed human society. The widespread use of bronze significantly enhanced weaponry, tools, and architectural structures, fostering the growth of more sophisticated civilizations. Empires such as the Egyptians, Sumerians, and later the Greeks and Romans depended heavily on bronze for their military strength and infrastructure, using it for everything from swords and armor to plumbing and coinage.

In the Americas, civilizations such as the Moche in Peru and the Mississippians in North America worked with copper for ceremonial and decorative purposes, often creating intricate jewelry, religious artefacts, and statues. Meanwhile, in China, copper played a central role in the production of ritual bronze vessels used in religious ceremonies and ancestor worship.

As societies advanced, the demand for copper continued to rise, leading to the development of large-scale mining operations. Ancient mines, such as those in the Timna Valley in modern-day Israel and the Michoacán region of Mexico, served as major sources of copper, driving the expansion of empires and trade networks. The metal's role in trade flourished, with vast quantities of copper being transported across continents via the Silk Road and Mediterranean trade routes, embedding it deeply into the economic and cultural fabric of ancient civilization.

Copper's lasting utility has established its ongoing importance today. Although its role has progressed beyond weapons and simple tools, its industrial and economic significance remains as vital as ever, making it an essential asset in global trade and financial markets.

Copper's journey as a precious metal

The Bronze Age (3300–1200 BCE)

The realization that copper could be alloyed with tin to produce bronze marked a revolutionary turning point in human history. Bronze was considerably harder, more durable, and more corrosion-resistant than pure copper, making it ideal for tools, weapons, and structural components. This breakthrough replaced the widespread use of stone tools, heralding the Bronze Age, a period of exceptional technological and societal progress. Civilizations such as the Sumerians, Egyptians, Minoans, and the Shang Dynasty of China mastered bronze metallurgy, using it for agricultural implements, chariots, armor, and even intricate artwork.

Trade networks thrived as societies sought access to both copper and tin, leading to the growth of mining and long-distance trade. The demand for bronze prompted some of the earliest large-scale mining operations, with regions like Cyprus, Anatolia, and the British Isles becoming vital sources of copper for the ancient world.

The Rise of Copper Mining (1500–1800 CE)

While copper remained in use throughout the Iron Age and the Middle Ages, the Age of Exploration and Naval Expansion (15th–eighteenth centuries) greatly boosted global demand. European powers, especially Spain and England, depended heavily on copper for their expanding maritime empires. One of copper's most vital uses during this period was for copper sheathing on wooden ship hulls to combat biofouling. This innovation prolonged the vessels' lifespan and increased their speed, providing European fleets with both military and commercial advantages.

During this period, major copper mines surfaced across Europe and South America. Cyprus, a significant copper source since antiquity, lent the metal its Latin name (cuprum) and continued to produce large quantities of it. Meanwhile, Spain's Rio Tinto mines and Chile's El Teniente mine, one of the oldest still operating today, became key suppliers. The discovery of South American copper deposits further expanded European control over global resources, driving the growth of colonial economies.

The Industrial Revolution (eighteenth–nineteenth Century)

The Industrial Revolution changed copper from a crucial naval material into an essential industrial metal. The rise of electricity, steam engines, and telecommunication in the nineteenth century significantly boosted global demand. Copper's remarkable conductivity and malleability made it the preferred metal for electrical wiring, telegraph cables, and electric motors, driving a worldwide surge in copper mining.

The discovery and development of vast copper deposits in the United States (Arizona, Montana, and Michigan), Chile, and Zambia helped meet surging demand. Copper became vital for railway expansion, factories, and early electrical grids, cementing its role in modern infrastructure. By the late 1800s, companies like Anaconda Copper and Phelps Dodge dominated global production, making copper one of the most actively traded industrial metals.

The China Boom (2000s–Present)

The early twenty-first century saw an unprecedented increase in copper demand, driven mainly by China's rapid industrialization and urban growth. As the world's largest consumer of copper, China needed vast quantities for its construction boom, power grid expansion, and manufacturing development. The metal became vital for the production of electrical wiring, plumbing, industrial machinery, and renewable energy systems, further emphasizing its economic significance.

China's demand was a key driver of copper prices to record levels, raising concerns about supply shortages. The country actively secured copper resources through overseas mining investments, stockpiling strategies, and strategic alliances with major producers in Chile, Peru, and Africa.

Copper's significance has only increased with advancements in green energy and technology. The rise of electric vehicles (EVs), solar panels, and wind turbines has solidified its status as an essential metal for the future. As economies transition to sustainable energy solutions, copper's role in electrification and decarbonization is expected to sustain demand for years to come.

What Moves the Copper Market?

Unlike gold or silver, which are often regarded as safe-haven assets, copper is mainly an industrial metal. Its price fluctuations are closely tied to global economic activity and infrastructure projects.

Copper's identity as an industrial metal means that a complex network of economic, geopolitical, and technological factors influences its price. Traders and investors keep a close eye on these key influences to forecast price changes and spot trading opportunities.

Global Economic Growth: The Backbone of Copper Demand

Copper is a cyclical commodity, meaning its price moves in line with the global economy. As a key material in construction, infrastructure, manufacturing, and electrical applications, copper demand increases during economic growth and declines during recessions.

Boom Times: When global GDP growth is robust, especially in major economies like the United States, China, and the Eurozone, demand for copper rises. The construction of new buildings, roads, bridges, and electrical grids all requires large quantities of metal.

Recessions and Slowdowns: During economic downturns, fewer homes and offices are constructed, factories reduce output, and infrastructure projects decelerate. This reduces copper demand, leading to lower prices.

Traders often regard copper as a key economic indicator—when copper prices increase, it generally signals that the economy is strengthening, while declining prices may indicate economic weakness.

Chinese Demand: The Dominant Force in the Copper Market

China accounts for nearly half of the world's copper consumption, making it the most influential factor in copper prices. Several key sectors drive the country's demand for copper:

Infrastructure & Urbanization: China's rapid industrialization and urban expansion have increased demand for copper in building materials, electrical wiring, and plumbing. The government's infrastructure stimulus programs can cause sudden surges in copper consumption.

Manufacturing & Exports: China is the world's largest producer of electronics, machinery, and consumer goods—each requiring copper. When Chinese factories ramp up production, global copper prices tend to rise.

Economic Policy & Growth Targets: The Chinese government's monetary easing, lending, and stimulus spending policies directly affect copper demand. When Beijing implements large-scale infrastructure projects or real estate investment programs, copper prices usually respond positively.

Due to China's significant influence on copper demand, traders closely monitor economic data releases from the country, including GDP growth, industrial production, and fixed-asset investment. Any sign of slowing demand or policy shifts can send shockwaves through the copper market.

Supply Constraints and Mining Disruptions

Copper mining is highly concentrated, with a few countries dominating global supply. Any disruption in these regions can lead to sudden shortages, driving prices higher.

Top Producers: The largest copper-producing nations are Chile, Peru, China, and the Democratic Republic of the Congo (DRC). Collectively, they account for over 50% of the world's supply.

Labour Strikes & Political Risks: Strikes at major copper mines, especially in Chile and Peru, are frequent and can temporarily halt production. Likewise, government regulations, tax increases, or threats of nationalization can affect copper availability.

Environmental Regulations: As governments implement stricter environmental policies, new copper mining projects face longer approval processes, raising production costs and restricting supply growth.

For traders, monitoring supply chain disruptions is essential, as unexpected mine closures or export restrictions can cause rapid price increases in the copper market.

The Green Energy Revolution: Copper as a Key Metal for the Future

The shift to renewable energy and electric vehicles (EVs) has driven a new surge in copper demand. Unlike traditional fossil fuel infrastructure, green energy solutions require considerably more copper per unit of energy produced or conveyed.

Solar and wind power: Renewable energy systems utilize copper in power cables, transformers, and electrical grids. Wind turbines alone contain thousands of pounds of copper in their generators and wiring.

Electric vehicles (EVs): EVs use nearly four times as much copper as internal combustion engine (ICE) cars, mainly due to their batteries, electric motors, and charging infrastructure. As global EV adoption grows, copper demand is expected to increase significantly.

Power grid expansion: The move towards electrification, including smart grids and energy storage solutions, further emphasizes copper's vital role in the energy transition.

Many analysts foresee a long-term structural bull market for copper driven by the green energy revolution, as supply struggles to keep pace with rising demand.

Inflation and Commodities Cycles: Copper as a Hard Asset

Like most commodities, copper often acts as an inflation hedge and moves in cycles driven by macroeconomic trends.

Inflation Hedge: As inflation rises, the purchasing power of fiat currencies declines, prompting investors to seek tangible assets such as copper. This effect is particularly noticeable during periods of monetary easing or substantial government spending when inflationary pressures intensify.

Commodities Supercycle: Copper is part of the larger commodities cycle, which generally follows a boom-and-bust pattern. When demand exceeds supply for a prolonged period, prices enter a long-term upward trend (a Supercycle). Conversely, when supply catches up or demand slows, prices decline.

Interest Rates & Monetary Policy: Since copper is priced in U.S. dollars, the Federal Reserve's policies are crucial. When interest rates increase, the dollar strengthens, making copper more expensive for foreign buyers and exerting downward pressure on prices. Conversely, lower interest rates and a weaker dollar usually boost copper prices.

Moving from market theory to trading ideas

Copper is a highly dynamic and economically sensitive commodity, affected by global growth cycles, geopolitical events, and green energy trends. Grasping these key market drivers is essential for traders managing copper's volatility.

By monitoring economic growth trends, Chinese demand, mining disruptions, green energy adoption, and inflationary pressures, traders can position themselves to capitalize on copper's price movements. Whether you're trading futures, mining stocks, or ETFs, keeping an eye on these fundamental drivers will help you stay ahead in the copper market.

Trading Ideas for 'Dr Copper'

Economic cycles, supply disruptions, industrial demand, and macroeconomic indicators influence copper prices. Traders can utilize various strategies to capitalize on price trends, short-term fluctuations, and long-term structural shifts in demand.

Copper is recognized as "Dr Copper" because it is frequently used as an indicator of economic well-being. Since copper is widely used in construction, manufacturing, and the electrical industry, its price generally increases during economic growth and decreases during downturns.

Monitor key economic indicators:

GDP growth rates: Strong economic expansion supports higher copper prices.

Manufacturing PMI (Purchasing Managers' Index): Readings above 50 indicate growth, boosting copper demand.

Infrastructure spending and construction data: Increased government investment in infrastructure leads to higher demand.

Entry & Exit:

Go long on copper when GDP growth accelerates, and PMIs exceed 50.

Short copper when leading indicators suggest a slowdown or recession.

Watch for sudden changes in interest rates or monetary policy, as higher borrowing costs can slow economic growth and reduce demand for copper.

Supply Disruption Trades

Copper mining is heavily concentrated in a few key regions, especially Chile, Peru, and China. Any disruption—such as strikes, government interventions, or environmental regulations—can lead to supply shortages and sharp price increases.

Track news and geopolitical risks in major copper-producing countries:

Mining strikes in Chile or Peru can cause immediate price surges.

Export bans or government policies limiting production can reduce supply.

Environmental regulations that slow down new mining projects can create long-term bullish trends.

Go long on copper futures or mining stocks when credible reports of supply disruptions emerge.

Exit or take profits once supply constraints ease and production resumes.

Green Energy and EV Demand Plays

The global shift towards renewable energy and electric vehicles (EVs) has led to a structural rise in copper demand. Solar panels, wind turbines, and EVs require considerably more copper than traditional energy sources and combustion-engine vehicles.

Monitor long-term trends in clean energy investment and EV adoption.

Renewable energy policies (e.g., the US Inflation Reduction Act and the EU Green Deal) boost copper demand.

EV sales and production forecasts—automakers increasing EV output will drive demand for copper wiring and batteries.

Government infrastructure spending on electric grids and charging networks supports higher copper prices.

Entry & Exit:

Go long on copper when renewable energy projects or EV adoption are accelerating.

Consider long-term investments in copper mining stocks, ETFs, or physical copper exposure.

Be aware of technological advancements—new battery technologies or alternative materials may reduce the role of copper in EVs.

Monitor short-term price corrections, as copper demand growth is a long-term trend rather than an immediate one.

Copper-Gold Ratio Trading

The copper-to-gold ratio is a financial indicator that compares the price of copper (an industrial metal) to that of gold (a safe-haven asset). It is utilized to assess economic strength and risk sentiment across global markets.

Why Does This Ratio Matter?

Copper is widely used in construction, manufacturing, and electrical industries. As a result, rising copper prices often signal economic growth and strong demand for industrial goods.

Gold is mainly a store of value and a safe-haven asset. Investors purchase gold during times of economic uncertainty, inflation, or geopolitical risk, which usually causes its price to rise when confidence in economic growth wanes.

The ratio is calculated as follows: the price of Copper per pound divided by the Price of Gold per ounce.

Monitor the copper-to-gold ratio:

Rising ratio → Bullish for copper, bearish for gold.
Falling ratio → Bearish for copper, bullish for gold.

Entry & Exit:

If the ratio rises, long copper trades and short gold will be favored.

If the ratio falls, shift to defensive assets, such as gold, and avoid copper trades.

Be cautious of sudden macroeconomic shifts (e.g., Federal Reserve rate hikes or geopolitical crises), as they can disrupt the relationship between copper and gold.

Avoid employing this strategy during highly volatile periods, when both metals can fluctuate unpredictably.

Seasonal Trading

Copper prices tend to follow seasonal patterns, influenced by industrial activity, construction demand, and weather conditions. Historically, copper has performed well in Q1 and Q2 due to increased industrial production and the expansion of construction projects.

Q1 and Q2: Strong demand as construction projects and manufacturing restart after winter.

Q3: Moderate demand but the potential for price dips due to summer slowdowns.

Q4: Demand may decline due to colder weather and lower industrial activity.

Entry & Exit:

Go long in early Q1 and hold through Q2 when demand is high.

Exit before peak summer slowdowns or consider short trades in Q3 if demand weakens.

Watch for unexpected economic slowdowns or policy changes that may override seasonal trends.

Use historical price data and seasonal analysis tools to refine entry points.

The surgery is closed.

Copper offers traders a wide range of opportunities across different time horizons, from short-term plays on economic cycles, supply disruptions, and seasonality to longer-term positioning around the global electrification and green-energy transition. Macro-focused traders can also rely on tools such as the copper-to-gold ratio to gauge broader risk sentiment. By blending technical analysis with the fundamental drivers shaping supply and demand, traders can build a resilient and adaptable copper strategy suited to changing market conditions.

Beyond its role as a traded commodity, copper stands as one of the most reliable barometers of global economic health. Its influence stretches from ancient civilizations to modern technology and renewable infrastructure, making it central to both industrial activity and future growth themes. Understanding its price drivers and market dynamics not only unlocks tactical opportunities but also positions traders to benefit from the long-term forces propelling demand. For those who appreciate copper's strategic importance, it remains a market rich with volatility, direction, and opportunity.

Tales from the Trading floor.—Mr Copper

The Rise and Fall of Yasuo Hamanaka—The Copper King

The Rise: Sumitomo's Copper Dominance

In the 1980s and early 1990s, Yasuo Hamanaka, a trader at Sumitomo Corporation, one of Japan's largest trading firms, became the dominant force in the copper market. Hamanaka aggressively built positions in copper futures, using both Sumitomo's balance sheet and secret off-the-books transactions to amass huge long positions.

By the early 1990s, Sumitomo owned up to 5% of the world's annual copper supply, giving it immense influence over prices. This dominance enabled Hamanaka to manipulate the market, squeezing shorts and driving prices higher, earning him the nickname "Mr Copper."

The Fall: The 1996 Copper Market Scandal

Hamanaka's strategy was successful for years, but by the mid-1990s, copper demand declined, making it difficult to maintain high prices. In June 1996, his positions collapsed dramatically, revealing that he had engaged in unauthorized trading over a decade, resulting in losses of $2.6 billion.

When the scandal was exposed, the London Metal Exchange (LME) copper price plummeted, prompting Sumitomo to liquidate its positions. The fallout rocked the commodities industry, resulting in lawsuits, stricter regulations, and tighter risk controls in metal trading.

Lessons from the Copper Crash

Yasuo Hamanaka was sentenced to 8 years in prison for fraud and unauthorized trading.

The case revealed how a single trader could manipulate a global market if risk controls were weak.

Copper prices remained volatile for years as market confidence in fair pricing mechanisms was shaken.

This story remains one of the most infamous cases of rogue trading in commodities history, illustrating the power and dangers of controlling a significant portion of a market.

4.2.4 Platinum and Palladium: The Smaller Precious Metals With Big Potential

While gold and silver dominate the precious metals market, platinum and palladium are often overlooked despite their vital roles in industry and investment. These two metals share certain characteristics with gold and silver, but have distinct supply-and-demand drivers that make them appealing to traders and investors. This chapter examines their history, main market influences, and trading strategies.

Origins and Historical Significance

Platinum: The Metal of Kings
Platinum was first used by ancient South American civilizations as early as 1200 BCE, although it was not widely recognized in Europe until the eighteenth century. Spanish conquistadors discovered platinum deposits in Colombia during the 1500s, but at the time, it was regarded as an impurity in gold mining. It was only in the 1700s that platinum was identified as a distinct metal with unique properties, including extreme resistance to corrosion and a high melting point. By the 19th and twentieth centuries, platinum became highly sought after for jewelry, industrial applications, and catalytic converters.

Palladium: The Newcomer
Discovered in 1803 by British chemist William Hyde Wollaston, palladium is a relatively recent precious metal compared to gold, silver, and platinum. Named after the asteroid Pallas, palladium remained a niche metal for decades until the automobile industry recognized its value in catalytic converters, where it helps to reduce vehicle emissions. Today, palladium is often more valuable than platinum due to its scarcity and rising industrial demand.

Market Drivers for Platinum and Palladium

Automotive Industry Demand

Both platinum and palladium are essential for catalytic converters, which reduce emissions in petrol and diesel engines. However, their demand varies:

Palladium is mainly used in petrol-powered vehicles (widely employed in the U.S. and China).

Platinum is used in diesel engines (common in Europe and heavy-duty vehicles).

As regulations on vehicle emissions tighten globally, the demand for both metals remains strong, although shifts in automotive trends (such as the rise of electric vehicles) could influence future demand.

Supply Constraints and Geopolitical Risks

Unlike gold and silver, which are mined globally, the supply of platinum and palladium is highly concentrated:

South Africa produces nearly 70% of the world's platinum.

Russia is the dominant supplier of palladium, accounting for about 40% of global production.

Any supply disruptions, such as strikes, political instability, or sanctions, can cause price spikes.

Investment and Safe-Haven Demand

While platinum and palladium are mainly industrial metals, they are occasionally used as alternative investments to gold and silver, especially during periods of inflation or economic instability. Platinum has a reputation as a "prestige" metal, often trading at a premium to gold, although in recent years, palladium has outperformed both due to supply shortages.

Green Energy and Hydrogen Economy

Platinum is essential for hydrogen fuel cells, a vital technology in clean energy solutions. As hydrogen-powered vehicles and energy storage systems become more popular, the demand for platinum is expected to increase considerably. Palladium also supports advanced industrial applications, including electronics and chemical processing.

Trading Strategies for Platinum and Palladium

Supply Disruption Trades

Owing to the geographic concentration of platinum and palladium mining, geopolitical developments and labor strikes can greatly influence prices.

Trade Setup: Keep an eye on news from South Africa (for platinum) and Russia (for palladium). If disruptions occur, consider long positions.

Auto Industry Cycles

Car sales and emissions regulations directly influence the demand for these metals.

Trade Setup: Monitor global car sales, especially in China, the U.S., and Europe. If demand for petrol vehicles increases, palladium prices generally rise; if diesel or hydrogen technology gains popularity, platinum demand may grow.

Platinum-to-Gold and Palladium-to-Gold Ratios

Historically, platinum has often traded at a premium to gold, but it has been undervalued in recent years.

Trade setup: If platinum is significantly cheaper than gold, some traders view it as a potential long-term value play. Similarly, the palladium-to-gold ratio can indicate whether palladium is overbought or oversold.

Seasonal Trends

Platinum and palladium tend to see higher demand in the first half of the year due to industrial production cycles.

Trade Setup: Consider taking long positions in early Q1 as industrial orders rise and exit before summer slowdowns.

Speculative and Safe-Haven Plays

During periods of economic uncertainty, platinum can serve as an alternative store of value.

Trade Setup: If inflation expectations rise or financial instability grows, traders may consider platinum, like gold and silver, as a hedge against uncertainty.

Mining for profits

Although often overshadowed by gold, copper, and silver, platinum and palladium present unique trading and investment opportunities. Their industrial uses, supply limitations, and macroeconomic factors generate price volatility that traders can exploit. Whether following automotive industry trends, geopolitical risks, or safe-haven demand, traders who grasp the subtleties of these metals can uncover lucrative opportunities in the smaller but highly valuable precious metals market.

Heavy Metal

Metals have played a crucial role in human civilization, ranging from ancient tools to contemporary financial markets. Gold and silver have long been valued for their monetary and investment worth, while copper, due to its extensive industrial use, acts as a vital economic indicator. Meanwhile, platinum and palladium, though less well-known, are essential to industries such as automotive manufacturing and renewable energy.

For traders, these metals present a variety of opportunities, from trend and seasonal trading to supply-driven speculation. Economic cycles, industrial demand, geopolitical risks, and inflation expectations influence their prices. Understanding these factors enables traders to capitalize on market movements effectively.

Gold, silver, copper, platinum, and palladium are actively traded on the COMEX exchange, which is part of the CME Group. COMEX offers futures contracts that provide liquidity, transparency, and effective price discovery, making it the primary marketplace for metals traders worldwide. Whether hedging risk, speculating on price trends, or diversifying your portfolio, the metals markets present a wealth of opportunities for those willing to navigate their complexities.

4.3 The Stock Market—The Market Everyone has Heard About

When people ask me what I have done for years, I tell them I am a futures trader. This usually elicits a blank stare, so I provide a bit more explanation. Eventually, they nod and say, "Oh, like stocks and shares?"

Unlike some lesser-known markets, the stock market is something almost everyone has heard of. The world and their dog know about stocks—whether it's through headlines about the FTSE rising, the latest tech IPO, or a friend who "got in early" on Tesla. Stock markets are woven into the fabric of everyday financial discussions in a way that commodities, bonds, and currency futures aren't.

While futures trading and stock investing share some similarities—both involve speculation, analysis, and risk management—the reality is that they are fundamentally different entities. Most people think of the stock market in terms of individual companies buying shares and holding them for dividends or long-term appreciation. However, for traders, there is a much greater opportunity in trading stock indices than in trading individual companies.

That's why this chapter will concentrate on trading stock indices—what they are, how they work, and how to trade them effectively.

But first, I will offer a sprinkle of my own approach to trading shares.

4.3.1 Investing in Stocks Vs. Trading Stock Indices

Over a thousand books have been written on how to trade the stock market—specifically, individual company stocks. From the 1923 classic 'Reminiscences of a Stock Operator' to Benjamin Graham's 'The Intelligent Investor', traders and investors have long sought to master the art of stock selection. While these books offer invaluable lessons, this chapter won't delve too deeply into individual stocks. Instead, I'll share my approach to investing in stocks—not through day trading, but by following Warren Buffett's legendary strategy: value investing.

The way of the master stock picker.
Value investing involves purchasing stocks that are undervalued relative to their intrinsic value. Instead of following momentum or short-term market trends, value investors focus on companies with strong fundamentals—profitable firms that have competitive advantages, robust balance sheets, and steady earnings. The concept is straightforward: buy good companies when they are trading at a discount, hold them for the long term, and let compounding do the work.

Buffett himself summed it up best: "The stock market is designed to transfer money from the active to the patient."

More opportunities than you could catch.
While individual stock picking is one way to invest, another effective approach is trading stock indices. A stock index acts as a benchmark that tracks the performance of a group of stocks representing a specific market or sector. Instead of focusing on a single company's fortunes, indices offer a broader view of the economy or a particular industry. Using futures, ETFs, or CFDs, traders and investors can access a range of global stock markets.

Indices enable traders to invest in the overall market rather than individual stocks. They allow them to speculate on macroeconomic trends, sector performance, and broader financial conditions. We will cover the top 10 further in the book.

Single Stocks or indices?
Trading indices rather than individual stocks provides inherent diversification, reducing the risk of a single company's failure while capturing broader

market trends. With high liquidity, indices are easily traded, ensuring smooth execution. They also tend to exhibit lower volatility compared to individual stocks, leading to more stable price movements. Most importantly, indices enable traders to capitalize on macroeconomic trends by responding to overall market shifts rather than on unpredictable company-specific events.

What the professionals look at.
I'm not claiming there aren't professional single-stock traders—there are thousands of them. But even they keep an eye on the indices, using them as a gauge for the overall market while timing their entries and exits in individual stocks.

Instead of focusing solely on picking stocks, this chapter will concentrate on successfully trading stock indices. We'll analyze key strategies, the factors that influence the markets, and how to trade indices using futures, although the same principles also apply to ETFs and CFDs. Whether you're aiming to capitalize on short-term swings or follow long-term trends, becoming adept at trading stock indices can be a real game-changer in market navigation.

4.3.2 All you Need to Know About a Stock Index

A stock index is a benchmark that tracks the performance of a group of stocks, typically representing a specific market, sector, or economy. Instead of purchasing individual stocks, traders and investors can use indices to gain exposure to a wider market. Indices offer a snapshot of market health, reflecting investor sentiment and economic conditions.

How Stock Indices Are Weighted
Stock indices are often calculated using different weighting methods:

Price-weighted—Higher-priced stocks have more influence (e.g., Dow Jones Industrial Average).

Market-cap weighted—Larger companies have more influence (e.g., S&P 500, FTSE 100).

Equal-weighted—Each stock has the same impact (less common but used in some ETFs).

Top 10 Global Stock Indices

Index	Country	Exchange	Composition	Weighting Method
S&P 500 (SPX)	USA	NYSE	500 largest U.S. companies, across all sectors	Market-cap weighted
Dow Jones Industrial Average (DJIA)	USA	NYSE	30 blue-chip U.S. companies	Price-weighted
NASDAQ-100 (NDX)	USA	NASDAQ	100 largest non-financial companies, tech-heavy	Market-cap weighted
FTSE 100 (UKX)	UK	London Stock Exchange (LSE)	100 largest UK-listed companies	Market-cap weighted
DAX 40 (DAX)	Germany	Frankfurt Stock Exchange	The 40 largest German companies	Market-cap weighted
CAC 40 (CAC)	France	Euronext Paris	40 major French companies	Market-cap weighted
Nikkei 225 (N225)	Japan	Tokyo Stock Exchange	225 major Japanese companies, price-weighted	Price-weighted
Hang Seng Index (HSI)	Hong Kong	Hong Kong Stock Exchange	80 large Hong Kong-listed firms, heavy on finance & tech	Free-float market-cap weighted
Shanghai Composite (SSE)	China	Shanghai Stock Exchange	All A-shares & B-shares on the exchange	Market-cap weighted
Sensex (BSE 30)	India	Bombay Stock Exchange (BSE)	The 30 biggest companies in India	Free-float market-cap weighted

Why Understanding Index Weighting Matters

Understanding how a stock index is weighted is crucial for traders and investors, as it influences the index's behavior, drives its movements, and informs their approach to trading or investing in it. Here's why it's useful:

Identifying Market Drivers

Large companies dominate in a market-cap-weighted index (e.g., S&P 500, FTSE 100). Major players like Apple, Microsoft, or Tesla in the S&P 500 can significantly influence the index's movement, even if smaller companies perform differently.

In a price-weighted index (e.g., the Dow Jones or Nikkei 225), the stocks with the highest prices exert the greatest influence on the index, regardless of the company's actual size or market value. A high-priced stock can disproportionately affect the index.

Understanding Volatility and Risk
Market-cap and free-float market-cap indices tend to respond more to fluctuations in the largest companies, potentially causing high volatility when these firms announce earnings or make significant disclosures.

Price-weighted indices may be less representative of the wider economy because a few high-priced stocks can distort the index's performance.

Trading and Investment Strategy
Passive Investors: Those who invest in ETFs or index funds tracking an index should understand its weighting to see which stocks will most influence their returns.

Active Traders: Traders monitoring short-term movements need to know if an index is heavily influenced by a few stocks, which can cause exaggerated price swings.

Hedging Strategies: If a portfolio has exposure to a sector that dominates an index, traders can hedge using index futures or options, considering how the sector's weighting affects price movements.

Sector Bias and Economic Insight
A tech-heavy index like the NASDAQ-100 (market-cap-weighted) is more responsive to technological trends and interest-rate fluctuations.

A financially-heavy index like the Hang Seng (free-float market-cap-weighted) reacts more to developments in the banking and property sectors.

Understanding index weighting helps traders and investors make better decisions, predict market movements, and design their portfolios effectively. Whether monitoring economic health, developing a trading strategy, or managing risk, knowing how an index is weighted provides an advantage in interpreting market behavior.

A Brief History of Stock Markets and Indices

The Evolution of Stock Markets
Stock markets date back to the seventeenth century, with the Amsterdam Stock Exchange, founded in 1602, being the first official market where investors could buy and sell shares of the Dutch East India Company. This

model of trading company shares soon spread across Europe, fostering the development of major financial centers.

London Stock Exchange (LSE)—Formed in 1801, it became a global financial hub.

Paris Bourse—Established in 1724, it played a key role in European finance.

New York Stock Exchange (NYSE)—Founded in 1792, it is now one of the world's largest stock exchanges.

As stock markets expanded in size and complexity, the need for a dependable method to measure market performance prompted the creation of stock indices—benchmarks that monitor the overall movement of groups of stocks.

The Birth of Stock Indices

Stock indices emerged to provide investors with a snapshot of how the broader market was performing:

Dow Jones Industrial Average (DJIA)—1896

The first major U.S. index, created by financial journalist Charles Dow, initially tracked 12 industrial stocks before expanding to 30.

S&P 500–1957

A more diversified U.S. index covering 500 leading companies is now the primary benchmark for investors.

FTSE 100–1984

It represents the 100 largest companies listed on the London Stock Exchange and serves as a key indicator of the UK stock market's performance.

DAX 40–1988

Germany's main stock index, the DAX, tracks the top 40 companies listed on the Frankfurt Stock Exchange.

These indices became crucial for traders and investors, helping them gauge market sentiment and track long-term trends.

Big moments in the stock market timeline.

Stock markets have experienced massive booms and devastating crashes, shaping the financial landscape and influencing economic policy worldwide. I bet that everyone reading these pages will remember at least one bust. Some of the most notable events include:

1929—The Great Depression: The Stock Market Crash That Changed the World

The Great Depression was one of the most devastating economic crises in modern history, and it all started with the Wall Street Crash of 1929. The stock market had been thriving throughout the Roaring Twenties, driven by rapid industrial growth, technological progress, and speculative investment. However, beneath the surface, cracks had already begun to appear.

The Boom Before the Bust

During the 1920s, stock prices soared as an increasing number of Americans began investing, many using borrowed funds (margin trading). The widespread belief was that stock prices would keep rising indefinitely, and banks were keen to lend money for speculation. Companies inflated their valuations, and inexperienced investors entered the market, pushing prices to unsustainable levels.

By 1929, the stock market was in a full-blown bubble, with many stocks trading at prices well above their intrinsic value. The market was driven not by company performance but by speculation and excessive optimism.

The Crash Begins: Black Thursday & Black Tuesday

The bubble finally burst in October 1929, when investors began to lose confidence. A wave of selling began, leading to:

Black Thursday (24 October 1929)—The market crashed, with almost 13 million shares traded—more than triple the normal daily volume. Panic spread as brokers issued margin calls, forcing investors to sell their holdings to cover debts.

Black Monday (28 October 1929)—The market dropped nearly 13% in a single day, sparking further panic.

Black Tuesday (29 October 1929)—A record 16 million shares were traded, and the Dow Jones fell by a further 12%. Within weeks, the market had lost nearly half its value.

By mid-November, the Dow Jones had dropped nearly 50% from its peak in September. Yet, this was only the start. The market continued to fall for years, ultimately losing almost 90% of its value by 1932.

The Ripple Effect: A Global Economic Catastrophe

The crash had a profound effect on Wall Street and the global economy, triggering a chain reaction that culminated in a worldwide economic crisis.

Bank Failures:
As stock prices plummeted, banks that had lent money to investors also faced heavy losses. Unable to recover their loans, thousands of banks across the U.S. failed, erasing the life savings of millions.

Mass Unemployment:
As businesses lost access to credit and consumer demand plummeted, companies laid off a large number of workers. By 1933, unemployment in the U.S. had soared to 25%, with millions struggling to survive.

The Dust Bowl & Agricultural Collapse:
The crisis worsened in rural regions as farmers, already coping with declining crop prices, faced harsh droughts in the Dust Bowl. Many lost their land and were compelled to migrate in search of work.

Deflation and Reduced Consumer Spending:
Prices of goods and services plummeted, but with wages cut and unemployment rising sharply, people couldn't afford to spend. This further worsened the economic downturn.

International Impact:
The collapse had a major impact on economies worldwide, as the U.S. was a key global lender. Countries like Germany, already burdened by post-WWI reparations, experienced banking crises and economic chaos, which contributed to the growth of political extremism.

The Road to Recovery
It wasn't until President Franklin D. Roosevelt's New Deal programs in the mid-1930s that the U.S. economy started to show signs of recovery. Government expenditure on public works, banking reforms, and financial regulations helped stabilize the system. However, it wasn't until World War II, when mass government spending on military production increased significantly, that the global economy truly recovered.

Lessons from the 1929 Crash
The Great Depression profoundly transformed the financial world, prompting major reforms in stock market regulation, banking practices, and economic policy, including:

The Glass-Steagall Act (1933): Separated commercial and investment banking to prevent excessive speculation.

The Securities and Exchange Act (1934): Established the Securities and Exchange Commission (SEC) to oversee financial markets.

Deposit Insurance (FDIC): Guarantees bank deposits to prevent widespread bank failures.

Why It Still Matters Today

The 1929 crash remains one of the most significant events in financial history. It highlighted the perils of speculation, excessive risk-taking, and inadequate financial regulation. Many of its lessons were echoed in later financial crises, from the Dot-Com Bubble (2000) to the Global Financial Crisis (2008).

For traders and investors, understanding the 1929 crash isn't just about history; it's about recognizing warning signs of market bubbles, managing risk, and maintaining financial discipline to avoid repeating past mistakes.

1987—Black Monday: The Day Global Markets Collapsed

Black Monday, 19 October 1987, remains one of the most shocking days in financial history. Stock markets worldwide experienced a sudden and severe crash. The Dow Jones Industrial Average (DJIA) dropped 22.6% in a single day, marking the largest one-day percentage decline ever recorded. Unlike previous crashes associated with prolonged economic downturns, Black Monday happened without warning, leaving traders, investors, and economists scrambling for answers.

The Lead-Up: The Market Boom of the 1980s

Throughout the mid-1980s, stock markets experienced a historic bull run. Several factors contributed to the rally:

Economic Expansion:

The U.S. economy grew rapidly, fueled by tax cuts under President Ronald Reagan and increased consumer and corporate spending.

Mergers & Acquisitions:

The 1980s saw a wave of corporate takeovers and leveraged buyouts (LBOs), in which companies borrowed heavily to acquire other companies, boosting stock prices.

Foreign Investment:

Japanese and European investors poured money into U.S. stocks, driving higher valuations.

The Rise of Program Trading:

Computer-driven trading strategies were becoming more common, with institutional investors using automated systems to buy and sell stocks based on pre-defined conditions. This marks the beginning of a new era in the markets; the 'Algo' was born.

By the summer of 1987, the Dow Jones had risen over 40% in less than a year, reaching a peak of 2,722 in. August. However, this rapid increase raised growing concerns about whether stocks had become overvalued.

A Global Meltdown

On 14 October 1987, the stock market started to show signs of weakness, with the Dow dropping 3.8%, its largest single-day decline since 1986. Rising interest rates and concerns over a growing U.S. trade deficit began to undermine investor confidence.

The situation escalated over the next few days, and on Monday, October 19, panic set in:

Dow Jones Industrial Average: Dropped 508 points (−22.6%), wiping out nearly $500 billion in market value.

S&P 500: Dropped 20.4%, its worst single-day performance ever.

Global Contagion: The panic wasn't limited to the U.S.—stock markets worldwide experienced similar collapses:

The UK's FTSE 100 plunged over 10%.

Hong Kong's Hang Seng Index lost 45% over the next few days.

Australia's All Ordinaries Index fell by over 40% in the weeks following the crash.

Markets in Canada, Japan, and Germany also suffered double-digit losses.

What happened!?

A single event didn't cause Black Monday; rather, a mixture of factors created the perfect storm.

Overvaluation and Investor Anxiety—The market had grown too rapidly, making valuations harder to justify. Worries about increasing interest rates and inflation heightened the tension.

Program Trading & Portfolio Insurance—Institutional investors have started using computerized trading programs to sell stocks automatically if markets fall.

These algorithms, known as portfolio insurance, were designed to protect portfolios but instead accelerated the sell-off as computers dumped shares in large volumes.

Illiquidity and Market Panic—With numerous sell orders flooding the market, few buyers were willing to step in, causing prices to plummet even further.

Global Interconnectivity—Markets were becoming progressively more globalized, and financial shocks spread swiftly from one country to another.

The Aftermath

The severity of the crash shook investor confidence, but unlike the 1929 crash, it did not result in a prolonged economic depression. Instead, markets recovered surprisingly quickly.

By 1988, the Dow had largely recovered from its losses, and the bull market of the late 1980s continued.

The U.S. Federal Reserve, led by Alan Greenspan, acted quickly to ensure liquidity in the financial system by reducing interest rates and backing banks.

The introduction of circuit breakers—To prevent future extreme sell-offs, stock exchanges implemented "circuit breakers", which automatically halt trading when markets fall too sharply in a short period. These mechanisms remain in place today and have been triggered during later market panics, such as in 2008 and 2020.

Lessons from Black Monday

Black Monday highlighted the risks of automated trading, liquidity shortages, and high leverage. It remains a crucial case study in market structure and risk management, shaping the way financial markets operate today.

For traders and investors, the lessons are clear:

Market sentiment can change rapidly, and even strong rallies can reverse overnight.

Automated trading systems, if not adequately controlled, can accelerate market crashes.

Liquidity matters—during times of panic, buyers disappear, leading to extreme price swings.

Although Black Monday was a frightening day for investors, its swift recovery demonstrated that even severe market crashes do not necessarily result in economic collapse.

Nonetheless, it served as a stark reminder that financial markets are vulnerable to unexpected shocks—and that risk management is crucial in trading.

2000—the Dot-Com Bubble: The Rise and Fall of Internet Mania

The Dot-Com Bubble was one of the most dramatic financial booms and busts in modern history, and I remember it vividly. I was in my early teens when the hype cycle began. I recall part-time workers at market stalls with very little money, trying to figure out how they could get their hands on some of these golden stocks. This was my first experience of a bubble inflating.

In the late 1990s, investors became captivated by the internet's potential, pouring money into technology stocks at an unprecedented pace. However, when reality failed to meet expectations, the market crashed, eroding wealth and transforming the tech industry for years to come.

The Boom: The Internet Gold Rush

The mid-to-late 1990s saw the rapid rise of the Internet, and investors were eager to capitalize on what they believed was a revolutionary new economy. Several factors fueled the tech stock frenzy:

Explosive Growth of the Internet

The World Wide Web became mainstream, and companies rushed to establish an online presence.

The number of internet users skyrocketed, and businesses sought to capitalize on the growing digital economy.

Speculative Investment & Irrational Exuberance

Investors and venture capitalists poured money into any company with a ".com" in its name, regardless of its profitability or business model.

The belief was that "eyeballs" mattered more than earnings—companies focused on attracting users rather than making profits.

Traditional valuation metrics were ignored, and stock prices were based on **hype** rather than fundamentals. This cycle is not too dissimilar to the Crypto market, which we will examine.

While writing this, I spoke with my father to see if he remembered any of the stocks that dominated conversations at the time—he immediately mentioned Lastminute.com.

Founded in 1998, Lastminute.com became one of the UK's most talked-about dot-com startups, promising to revolutionize online travel bookings. Its IPO in 2000 was massively oversubscribed, and the stock initially surged as investors piled in, caught up in the frenzy.

Within months, the hype shifted to panic as concerns about profitability arose, sending the stock plummeting by more than 90%. Although it eventually recovered and was acquired by Travelocity for £577 million in 2005, this was only a small fraction of its dot-com era valuation. At the peak of the mania, everyone was talking about it—yet for some investors, it cost them dearly.

Easy Access to Capital
The Federal Reserve kept interest rates low, making borrowing cheap and fueling speculative investments.

Initial Public Offerings (IPOs) exploded, with many internet companies going public at sky-high valuations.

Retail investors flooded the market, eager to cash in on the "new economy."

Media Hype & Fear of Missing Out (FOMO)
Financial media contributed to inflating the bubble by continually hyping internet stocks. Having had business channels on in my office for the past 20 years, I can tell you they haven't ceased with the hype, one way or another.

The fear of missing out (FOMO) prompted more investors to invest, driving stock prices up.

By early 2000, the NASDAQ Composite Index, which was heavily weighted towards tech stocks, had surged over 500% in just five years, peaking at 5,048 in. March 2000.

When Reality Hits
Despite the euphoria, many dot-com companies were unprofitable and burning through cash at unsustainable rates. Cracks started to show:

Rising Interest Rates
In early 2000, the Federal Reserve raised interest rates to cool down the overheated economy.

Higher borrowing costs put pressure on speculative companies, many of which relied on cheap capital to survive.

Profitability Became a Concern
Investors started to doubt whether Internet companies could truly turn a profit.

Many dot-com firms had no viable business models and spent millions on marketing without generating revenue.

Companies with weak fundamentals began collapsing.

The Bubble Bursts—NASDAQ Collapse
As investor confidence faltered, panic selling took hold, causing the NASDAQ to plummet from its March 2000 high of 5,048 to just 1,114 by October 2002 —a nearly 80% collapse that wiped out trillions in investor wealth.

The Dot-Com Crash's Lasting Impact

The Dot-Com Crash had widespread effects, with hundreds of internet companies, such as Pets.com, Webvan, and eToys, going bankrupt. Even giants like Amazon and eBay saw their share prices plummet by over 80% before bouncing back. Tech giants Cisco, Intel, and Microsoft lost billions in market value.

However, the crash transformed the industry, compelling companies to focus on profitability rather than hype—a lesson that aided later success stories like Google and Facebook in developing sustainable business models.

Regulatory Changes & Stricter Accounting Rules

The Sarbanes-Oxley Act (2002) introduced tougher regulations on corporate accounting and financial reporting.

Investors became more skeptical of speculative startups.

Lessons Learned for Future Bubbles

The Dot-Com Bubble served as a clear warning about the risks of irrational exuberance and speculation. It showed how markets can become completely detached from reality, but in the end, fundamentals still matter.

However, the Dot-Com Crash wasn't the end of technology or the bursting of bubbles. While the collapse was painful, it didn't prevent technology from reshaping the world, even if not in the way investors had originally envisaged.

Companies like Amazon, Google, and Apple not only survived but also became stronger, leading the next phase of the digital revolution. The NASDAQ, which had been decimated, eventually recovered and surpassed its 2000 peak in 2015, 15 years later.

The Internet economy proved to be real, but success required patience, strong business models, and sustainable growth. The Dot-Com Bubble remains a textbook example of market mania, where speculation ran far ahead of reality. Yet, some of today's biggest companies were born from its ashes, proving that while bubbles burst, innovation never stops, and another bubble is always waiting to form.

2008—The Global Financial Crisis

The 2008 financial crisis was one of the most devastating economic events in recent history, nearly causing the global financial system to collapse. At that time, I had just established my first trading floor and began hiring traders, only to witness what felt like the end of the financial world as we knew it. Although the crisis was triggered by the fall of Lehman Brothers, a major

Wall Street investment bank, its foundations had been laid long before, built on years of reckless lending, excessive risk-taking, and an unsustainable housing bubble that was destined to burst.

A House of Cards

During the early 2000s, banks and financial institutions aggressively issued subprime mortgages—home loans given to borrowers with poor credit histories. These loans were bundled into mortgage-backed securities (MBS) and collateralized debt obligations (CDOs), which were sold to investors worldwide under the false assumption that they were low-risk.

At the same time, banks and hedge funds employed extreme leverage, borrowing large sums to invest in these securities. When U.S. housing prices started to decline in 2006–2007, mortgage defaults increased, revealing the fragility of the entire system.

Lehman's Fall & Market Panic

On 15 September 2008, Lehman Brothers filed for bankruptcy, marking the largest collapse of a financial institution in U.S. history. Confidence in the banking system vanished overnight, triggering a chain reaction of panic and sell-offs.

Stock markets worldwide tanked—the Dow Jones dropped nearly 34% in just one month, while the FTSE 100 lost almost half its value during the crisis. Credit markets froze, banks stopped lending to each other, and financial institutions faced insolvency.

Government Bailouts & Economic Turmoil

Governments and central banks intervened with unprecedented bailout packages to prevent a total economic collapse. The U.S. government approved the $700 billion Troubled Asset Relief Programme (TARP), while the UK government intervened to rescue major banks, including RBS and Lloyds. The Federal Reserve and other central banks slashed interest rates to near zero and launched quantitative easing programs to inject liquidity into the markets.

This was when I first learned that the Plunge Protection Team (PPT) is the nickname for a Working Group on Financial Markets, a body formed by U.S. President Ronald Reagan in 1988 after the 1987 Black Monday crash. Its official aim is to sustain market stability and prevent financial crises. However, conspiracy theories claim that the PPT has a more active, behind-the-scenes role in supporting stock markets during times of extreme volatility.

Rumors claim that the PPT secretly intervenes by coordinating large-scale buying of equities or index futures to prevent sharp declines. Allegedly, it includes top officials from the U.S. Treasury, the Federal Reserve, the SEC, and the CFTC, who work with major banks and financial institutions to inject liquidity into markets when needed.

During the 2008 financial crisis, whispers about the PPT grew louder, with some traders convinced that sudden market rebounds were not organic but engineered interventions to prevent a total collapse. While no concrete evidence confirms these theories, the idea that authorities discreetly support markets during times of turmoil remains a widely debated topic in financial circles.

Despite these efforts, the damage was already done. The global economy entered a severe recession, with millions losing their jobs, businesses closing down, and household wealth vanishing. The crisis also triggered a sovereign debt crisis in Europe, forcing countries such as Greece, Ireland, and Spain to seek financial assistance.

Regulation & Lessons Learned

The crisis prompted significant financial reforms, especially the Dodd-Frank Act in the U.S., which implemented stricter controls on banks and financial institutions. Regulators in the UK and Europe enforced tighter capital requirements to minimize risk-taking.

Although markets eventually recovered, the crisis left enduring scars—from a distrust of banks to widening wealth inequality. It also permanently transformed central banking, as low interest rates and extensive government intervention became the new standard in economic policy.

The 2008 financial crisis served as a wake-up call for financial markets, highlighting the devastating consequences of unchecked speculation, excessive risk-taking, and inadequate regulation. Yet, as history has shown, markets have a short memory, and new bubbles continue to form, driven by the same forces of greed, fear, and the search for ever-higher returns.

2020—COVID-19 Crash & Recovery

Still fresh in our memories, the COVID-19 pandemic triggered one of the most severe stock market crashes in financial history, with global stock indices falling by more than 30% in just a few weeks.

As the virus spread rapidly across the world in early 2020, governments implemented lockdowns, shutting down entire economies. Investors panicked, fearing a severe global recession as businesses closed, supply chains broke down, and unemployment reached record levels. The Dow Jones

Industrial Average experienced its worst single-day point drop ever, while the S&P 500 and Nasdaq fell into bear market territory at an unprecedented speed.

However, just as rapidly as markets collapsed, they recovered with remarkable speed. Central banks and governments unleashed an unprecedented wave of stimulus—trillions of dollars in liquidity, near-zero interest rates, and aggressive asset purchases by the Federal Reserve and other central banks. The U.S. government injected $5 trillion into the economy through stimulus checks, business relief programs, and bond-buying initiatives. This flood of liquidity sparked a historic rally, with the S&P 500 rebounding to pre-pandemic levels within just five months and reaching all-time highs by the end of 2020.

Although the recovery appeared miraculous, it raised serious concerns about inflation, debt levels, and market distortions. The excess stimulus and easy money policies fueled speculative bubbles in assets such as tech stocks, cryptocurrencies, and housing.

By 2021, inflation was rising at its fastest rate in decades, prompting central banks to tighten policies and sparking another wave of volatility in 2022. Each of these major historical events—from the Great Depression to the COVID-19 crash—has shaped how markets function today. Regulatory policies, risk management strategies, and trading techniques have evolved in response to past crises, providing valuable lessons for traders.

What is notably clear from all these significant market movements is that they are almost always followed by policy interventions aimed at correcting the situation in the medium and long term. This pattern has become a defining feature of modern economics and forms the backbone of one of the most popular trading strategies: "buy the dip."

The reality is that too much depends on the stock market's success for policymakers to permit a complete collapse. The stock market isn't just a place where traders speculate; it is a vital pillar of economic growth and financial stability. Governments and central banks understand that when markets crash, economies suffer, so intervention—whether through interest rate cuts, stimulus packages, or bailouts—has become an anticipated response to major downturns.

Beyond this, the stock market is closely connected to everyday financial well-being. The top-performing companies spur economic growth, creating jobs, innovation, and wealth. Pension funds, which manage trillions in assets, depend on stock market growth to ensure retirees have financial security after a lifetime of work. A prolonged market slump threatens these long-term investments, making financial market stability a priority for policymakers.

And then there's the army of wealth managers, financial advisors, and investment firms constantly promoting stocks, ETFs, and funds as the best way to "secure your financial future." The financial industry thrives on market participation, ensuring that capital continues to flow into equities, reinforcing the cycle of market corrections followed by recoveries.

This is a valuable insight for traders—understanding that market downturns are often met with intervention opens up trading opportunities. The strategy of buying the dip relies on the historical resilience of stock markets, recognizing that in modern finance, the system is designed to recover—because there is too much at stake for it not to.

As Warren Buffett famously reminds us, "Be fearful when others are greedy, and greedy when others are fearful." This mindset underpins the "buy the dip" strategy and the idea that the best opportunities come when panic seizes the market.

Or, to put it even more bluntly, "When there is blood in the streets, that's the time to buy." Market crashes, sell-offs, and corrections generate fear and uncertainty. Still, history has shown that these moments often present some of the greatest buying opportunities for those with the courage and discipline to act.

When panic arises, fundamentals are disregarded, valuations drop to irrational lows, and assets sell off well below their intrinsic value. This is when experienced investors step in—while retail traders rush for the exits, the savvy money is grabbing bargains.

Of course, this doesn't mean buying blindly every time the market dips. It means having the patience to wait for the right moment, ensuring that structural market conditions remain intact, and developing a strategy to ride the recovery wave when policymakers step in to stabilize the financial system.

Whether it's the Great Depression, Black Monday, the Dot-Com Bust, the 2008 Financial Crisis, or the COVID-19 crash, history has demonstrated that markets recover, and those who buy at the right moment are often greatly rewarded.

What Influences the Stock Markets

Stock index prices are constantly fluctuating due to a complex interplay of economic forces, corporate performance, investor sentiment, and external events. Understanding these key drivers is crucial for traders looking to anticipate market movements and capitalize on opportunities.

Economic Data—The Pulse of the Market

Stock indices react sharply to economic indicators that offer insights into the general health of an economy. Key reports that influence index values include:

Gross Domestic Product (GDP) Growth—A robust GDP indicates economic expansion, boosting investor confidence and raising stock indices. A slowdown or contraction in GDP can trigger selloffs as recession fears rise.

Employment Numbers—High job creation and low unemployment rates indicate economic strength, which can encourage market rallies. Conversely, rising unemployment signals economic distress, often leading to market declines.

Inflation Data—Moderate inflation is normal, but excessive inflation erodes purchasing power and increases borrowing costs, negatively impacting stock markets. Conversely, deflation signals weak demand and economic stagnation, which can also weigh on indices.

Consumer Spending & Retail Sales—Since consumer spending fuels economic growth, positive retail sales data indicate strong demand, which boosts stock prices. Weak spending signals economic strain, reducing investor confidence.

Trade Study: The 2016 U.S. Election & Market Rebound
In November 2016, market uncertainty surrounding the U.S. presidential election triggered a sharp overnight sell-off in stock index futures, with Dow Jones Industrial Average futures dropping over 800 points when it became evident that Donald Trump would win. However, instead of falling further, markets reversed dramatically, rallying in the following weeks as investors anticipated corporate tax cuts, deregulation, and infrastructure expenditure under the new administration.

The S&P 500 and Dow Jones reached record highs in the following months, with traders who capitalized on the panic-driven dip and bought into the fiscal stimulus narrative making substantial gains. Those who remained short, expecting extended uncertainty, were caught off guard by the sharp rebound.

Interest Rates—The Cost of Money
Stock indices are highly sensitive to central bank policies, especially interest rate decisions. Central banks such as the Federal Reserve (USA), the European Central Bank (ECB), and the Bank of England (BoE) set interest rates to manage inflation and to either encourage or slow economic growth.

Lower Interest Rates = Bullish for Stocks
Cheap borrowing encourages businesses to invest and expand.

Consumers have more disposable income, fueling corporate profits.

Investors move capital from bonds (low returns) into stocks, pushing indices higher.

Higher Interest Rates = Bearish for Stocks
As borrowing becomes more expensive, business expansion and consumer spending slow, bond yields rise, reducing the attractiveness of equities relative to fixed-income investments, and market volatility increases as investors reassess their risk exposure.

Trade Study: Federal Reserve Rate Hike Cycle (2022)
In response to soaring inflation, the Federal Reserve aggressively raised interest rates throughout 2022, causing a sharp decline in stock indices. The S&P 500 and NASDAQ fell by more than 20%, entering bear-market territory. Traders who shorted index futures or moved into defensive sectors (utilities, consumer staples) capitalized on the downturn. Those who waited for the eventual pause in rate hikes in late 2023 positioned themselves well for the next bull cycle.

Corporate Earnings—The Fuel for Market Growth
Stock indices represent a basket of individual companies, so their performance is directly linked to those companies' earnings. If companies report strong revenue and profit growth, indices tend to rise. Weak earnings, on the other hand, trigger sell-offs.

Earnings Season:
Companies report their financial results every quarter. Strong reports can lift entire indices, while disappointing results drag markets down.
Investors closely watch profit margins, revenue growth, guidance for future performance, and management commentary.

Tech Giants and Market Influence:
Some indices, such as the NASDAQ-100 and S&P 500, are heavily weighted towards large-cap tech stocks (e.g., Apple, Microsoft, Amazon, Tesla).
A significant move in these companies can influence the entire index.

Trade Study: Tech Earnings & NASDAQ Rally (2023)
In 2023, AI-related stocks soared, led by NVIDIA, Microsoft, and Alphabet, pushing the NASDAQ to new heights. Traders who recognized the strong earnings momentum in semiconductor and AI sectors benefited from the trend, while those who shorted struggling sectors (such as traditional retail) capitalized on relative weakness.

Political & Geopolitical Events—Market Disruptors
Stock indices are not just driven by financial data—politics and global events can trigger massive market movements.

Elections & Policy Changes:
U.S. presidential elections often cause volatility as investors evaluate potential policy changes in taxes, regulations, and trade agreements.
New economic policies, such as corporate tax cuts or increased infrastructure spending, can strengthen market confidence. Conversely, additional regulations or higher taxes can weigh down on stock prices.

Trade Wars & International Conflicts:
Trade tensions (e.g., the U.S.-China trade war) can disrupt global supply chains, leading to market uncertainty and price swings.
Wars, terrorist attacks, and geopolitical crises often trigger a risk-off sentiment, prompting investors to seek safe-haven assets such as gold, bonds, and the U.S. dollar.

Regulatory Changes:
Government intervention in key sectors, such as Big Tech regulations, environmental policies, and shifts in monetary policy, can influence stock indices.

Trade Study: Brexit & UK Stock Market Volatility (2016–2020)
When the UK voted to leave the European Union in 2016, the FTSE 100 initially plummeted but then rebounded sharply as the British pound weakened, making UK exports more competitive.
Over the following years, continued Brexit uncertainty kept markets volatile, presenting trading opportunities in FTSE 100 index futures and currency hedging strategies.

Market Sentiment & Liquidity—The Psychology of Trading
Stock indices are ultimately influenced by investor psychology, with fear and greed guiding short-term price changes.
Bull markets are driven by optimism, strong corporate results, and economic growth, leading to ongoing buying and rising stock indices.
Bear Markets: Panic, economic downturns, or financial crises cause sell-offs, dragging indices lower.

Liquidity & Institutional Flows:

Hedge funds, mutual funds, and central banks substantially influence market movements.

Corporate stock buybacks can boost indices, while forced liquidations (e.g., margin calls) can hasten selloffs.

Trade Study: The 2021 Retail Trading Frenzy & The Hype Cycle
In early 2021, retail traders, mainly using commission-free platforms like Robinhood and pooling on Reddit's WallStreetBets, triggered an unprecedented wave of short squeezes in heavily shorted stocks such as GameStop (GME), AMC Entertainment (AMC), and other so-called "meme stocks." What started as a coordinated effort to challenge hedge funds shorting these stocks quickly developed into one of the most extreme instances of the market hype cycle—a phenomenon we've seen before in the Dot-Com Bubble and repeatedly in cryptocurrency markets.

The Hype Cycle in Markets
Markets often follow a predictable pattern during speculative manias:

- Innovation or Catalyst—A new trend or narrative captures investor attention.
- Early Adoption & Acceleration—Early movers pile in, and prices rise quickly.
- Media Frenzy & Public Euphoria—Retail traders rush in, fueling extreme price moves.
- Reality Check & Blow-Off Top—Prices peak as fundamentals struggle to justify valuations.
- Crash & Consolidation—The bubble bursts, and only the strongest investments survive.

The Reddit-driven short squeezes fit this cycle perfectly. As GME soared from $20 to over $480 per share in just weeks, institutional traders found themselves in a liquidity trap. Hedge funds that had heavily shorted GME, expecting it to fall, were compelled to buy back shares at inflated prices, fueling a vicious feedback loop known as a short squeeze.

Impact on the Broader Market & VIX Futures
The retail-driven volatility not only affected meme stocks; it also spread into broader markets. As hedge funds sold other positions to cover their losses, the S&P 500 and NASDAQ experienced sharp intraday swings. This increased uncertainty caused a surge in trading volume in VIX futures—a popular instrument used to hedge against market volatility.

A Little introduction to the VIX.
The VIX (Volatility Index), also called the "Fear Gauge," measures expected volatility in the S&P 500 over the next 30 days. When markets face increased uncertainty, VIX futures usually spike as traders look to protect themselves against possible declines.

During the GameStop short squeeze, the VIX rose above 30 as traders flocked to volatility-based trades. Some traders took advantage of these spikes by going long on VIX futures, anticipating further market chaos. Others capitalized on the inevitable collapse of retail-driven euphoria, shorting overbought stocks and profiting as meme stocks retraced their gains.

Lessons from the 2021 Retail Frenzy
The hype cycle observed in meme stocks is nothing new. It reflects past manias, from the Dot-Com Bubble in 2000 to Bitcoin's rapid rise and fall in 2017 and 2021.

Understanding market cycles, crowd psychology, and risk management is vital in speculative environments. Those who recognized the signs of unsustainable euphoria and acted accordingly—whether by shorting overvalued stocks or trading volatility—managed to profit. Meanwhile, those who chased the hype at its peak suffered a harsh lesson in market dynamics.

Win or Learn

Stock indices fluctuate due to a mix of fundamental, macroeconomic, and psychological factors. Recognizing economic data, central bank policies, earnings reports, political events, and investor sentiment can help traders anticipate market trends and get ready for success.

As with all our markets, it is essential to understand the underlying theory behind market movements. When we hear about an event that we know will influence the market and, more importantly, how it will do so, we gain an advantage over most of the world and a better chance to profit.

How to Make Money Trading Stock Indices

Stock indices are among the most popular markets for traders, offering broad market exposure while reducing the risks associated with individual company stocks. Their high liquidity, nearly 24-hour trading, and responsiveness to macroeconomic events make them an ideal choice for those aiming to profit from market movements.

Before exploring strategies, it's important to understand why stock indices are such a popular trading instrument:

Diversification—Instead of betting on a single company, you gain exposure to an entire market.

Liquidity—Indices possess deep, highly active markets, facilitating easy entry and exit from positions.

Leverage Opportunities—Futures and CFDs enable traders to manage large positions with a comparatively small capital investment.

Macro Trading—Indices respond to economic trends, making them well-suited for trading broad market themes.

With these benefits in mind, let's look at some of the most effective methods of trading stock indices, concentrating on market fundamentals, economic cycles, and event-driven strategies.

Trading Economic Cycles

Stock indices are closely linked to the economy. Understanding our position in the economic cycle helps traders prepare for long-term trends.

This adopts a longer-term perspective on the market, but it is very important for those of us who trade intraday to understand.

The Four Market Cycles and Their Impact on Indices

Expansion (Bullish for Indices)

GDP growth is strong

Corporate earnings rise

Central banks keep interest rates low

Consumer confidence is high

Go long on indices like the S&P 500 or Nasdaq during periods of strong economic growth.

Focus on indices with high exposure to growth sectors, such as the tech-heavy NASDAQ 100.

Peak (Caution Phase—Volatility Increases)

The economy overheats, and inflation increases. Central banks signal interest rate hikes. Markets become more volatile.

Reduce exposure to long positions. Search for hedging opportunities in safe-haven assets such as bonds or gold. Keep a close eye on central bank policies for potential changes.

Contraction (Bearish for Indices)

Growth slows, recession fears increase.

Corporate earnings fall

Interest rates are raised to combat inflation
Consumer spending weakens

Short stock index futures.
Buy defensive indices, such as the Dow Jones Industrial Average (DJIA), which holds safer, dividend-paying stocks.
Monitor job data and GDP reports to assess the potential depth of the slowdown.

Recovery (Bullish for Indices)
Central banks cut rates.
Economic stimulus measures are introduced.
Business sentiment improves

Buy indices when rate cuts are announced or stimulus packages are introduced.
Look for "Buy the Dip" opportunities after sharp market corrections.

Trade Study: The 2011 U.S. Debt Ceiling Crisis & Market Sell-Off
In the summer of 2011, political deadlock in the U.S. over raising the debt ceiling caused widespread market panic. Investors feared a potential government default, which led to a sharp sell-off in stock markets. The S&P 500 fell almost 17% within a few weeks, while the VIX (Volatility Index) surged above 40, indicating extreme uncertainty.

Adding to the chaos, Standard & Poor's downgraded the U.S. credit rating for the first time in history, further speeding up the decline. However, as negotiations eventually led to a resolution and the Federal Reserve reassured markets with supportive monetary policies, indices bounced back strongly.

Traders who recognized the crisis's temporary nature and went long on indices at oversold levels saw notable gains as the S&P 500 fully recovered by early 2012. Those who hedged with volatility products also capitalized on the short-term panic.

Trading Market Events
Although economic cycles unfold over months or years, short-term events can present trading opportunities in stock indices. We explore this more thoroughly in the book, as data drives the global economy, but here is a taster nonetheless.

Critical Market Moving Events

Central Bank Decisions (Interest Rate Changes & QE)

Stock indices react sharply to monetary policy decisions. Rate hikes weigh on equities while cuts fuel rallies.

If the Federal Reserve signals an unexpected rate move, indices such as the S&P 500 and the NASDAQ 100 often respond positively.

Corporate Earnings Seasons

Stock indices reflect the collective performance of their constituent companies. Strong earnings seasons drive indices higher, while weak earnings create selloffs.

Trade Idea: If major companies (Apple, Amazon, Microsoft) report strong earnings, NASDAQ 100 futures often rally in response. A sign to get long!

Geopolitical Risks & Market Shocks

Wars, trade conflicts, and political instability create market volatility.

Trade idea: During uncertain geopolitical times, traders often turn to defensive indices like the Dow Jones Industrial Average (DJIA), which includes blue-chip, dividend-paying stocks. If you act quickly on the news, you can short the major indices and aim to buy the dip once details become clearer.

Trading the Spread Between Global Stock Indices

Stock indices from various countries respond differently to economic cycles, monetary policies, and geopolitical events. Traders can exploit relative strength and weakness between indices by trading spreads across international markets.

The benefit of trading Index spreads.

Diverging Central Bank Policies:

If one country's central bank tightens policy while another eases, their respective indices will probably diverge.

Economic Growth Disparities:

Faster-growing economies usually display stronger index performance than those facing recessions.

Sector Composition:

Some indices are technology-focused (NASDAQ 100), while others tend towards financials, industrials, or commodities (FTSE 100, ASX 200).

Index Pairing Examples
S&P 500 vs. Euro Stoxx 50 → U.S. markets often recover faster from downturns than European markets.

Nikkei 225 vs. Hang Seng Index → Japan's economy and stock market react differently to China's policies and trade conditions.

DAX 40 vs. FTSE 100 → The German index is more industrially driven, while the UK's FTSE 100 benefits from global commodity exposure.

If the Federal Reserve raises interest rates while the European Central Bank remains accommodative, the S&P 500 may underperform the Euro Stoxx 50. Traders might short the S&P 500 while going long on the Euro Stoxx 50, capitalizing on Europe's relative strength.

Trade Study: U.S. versus European Market Divergence (2023)
In 2023, while the Federal Reserve signaled rate hikes to combat inflation, the European Central Bank adopted a more cautious approach. As a result, U.S. stocks, especially tech-heavy indices like the NASDAQ 100, struggled amid higher borrowing costs, whereas European indices outperformed. Traders who shorted the S&P 500 while going long on the Euro Stoxx 50 capitalized on this divergence, profiting as European markets outpaced U.S. growth during the period.

Mastering Stock Index Trading
Stock indices enable traders to observe broad market trends without analyzing individual companies, providing exposure to entire economies and allowing them to respond directly to macroeconomic forces. Whether trading via futures, CFDs, or ETFs, indices offer an efficient way to capitalize on large-scale movements driven by economic cycles, central bank policy shifts, and global events. With the global accessibility of stock index futures on the CME Group's Globex platform, traders can engage with major benchmarks such as the S&P 500, NASDAQ-100, and Dow Jones nearly around the clock, reacting instantly to data releases and geopolitical developments.

Successful index trading relies on a few key principles: aligning positions with the broader economic cycle, monitoring market-moving events, and understanding how sector rotation affects different indices during bull and bear phases. Traders must also select the appropriate instrument for their goals—futures for leverage and short-term speculation, ETFs for longer-term exposure. Applying these principles enables traders to navigate index markets confidently, manage risk effectively, and seize opportunities in various conditions.

Stock indices, however, represent only one avenue for trading macro trends. The next chapter focuses on one of the most disruptive and rapidly evolving markets of the modern era: cryptocurrencies. From Bitcoin's emergence as "digital gold" to the rise of DeFi, NFTs, and blockchain innovation, crypto has transformed the financial landscape. Understanding what drives this volatile market is vital for traders seeking to capitalize on price swings, adoption trends, and changing regulatory environments. Let's explore how crypto markets operate, what influences them, and the strategies traders can use to navigate their unique challenges.

4.4 The Rise of Crypto: The Future of Money?

Cryptocurrencies

My business partner, on my very first trading floor, once stood up, pulled out his wallet stuffed with banknotes, and declared to one of our junior traders:

> "I'd rather keep hold of my real money, not a few dodgy bits of code."

This was around 2009, and the junior trader in question had just suggested investing in Bitcoin, which was trading at about $1 per coin at the time. He was met with laughter—after all, the idea of an unregulated digital currency, backed by nothing but computer algorithms, seemed absurd to most seasoned traders then.

Fast-forward over a decade, and let me tell you—that quote has been repeated to him more times than I can count.

Bitcoin has transformed from being dismissed as an obscure experiment for tech enthusiasts to becoming a multi-trillion-pound asset class, now adopted by institutions, hedge funds, and even governments. Alongside it, thousands of other cryptocurrencies have appeared, creating a completely new financial ecosystem that challenges traditional banking, monetary policy, and even the very notion of money itself.

Whether you believe in crypto's revolutionary potential or are skeptical of its volatility, one thing is certain. This market is here to stay, and it moves in a way unlike anything traders have seen before.

4.4.1 The Evolution of Crypto: From Niche to Mainstream

From Bitcoin's early days on cryptography forums to the rise of Ethereum and smart contracts, the crypto market has experienced rapid growth, creating unique trading opportunities.

But with great opportunity comes great risk. Prices can increase by hundreds of per cent over weeks, only to plummet just as quickly. Crypto has seen booms, busts, regulatory battles, exchange failures, and outright scams, yet it continues to develop, attracting new participants and capital year after year.

This chapter will break down:

The origins and history of crypto—How Bitcoin and blockchain came to be.

Key moments in crypto history—The major booms, busts, and market shifts.

What moves the crypto markets—The forces that drive Bitcoin, Ethereum, and altcoins.

Trading strategies for crypto—How traders navigate volatility and profit from this new asset class.

Whether you're aiming to trade Bitcoin's boom-and-bust cycles, Ethereum's role in DeFi, or altcoin mania, understanding how this market works is vital to riding the waves instead of being overwhelmed by them.

Let's get started.

Bitcoin & Ethereum

Cryptocurrencies have revolutionized the financial landscape, introducing a decentralized, trustless system for transferring value without intermediaries. While thousands of digital assets exist today, Bitcoin (BTC) and Ethereum (ETH) remain the two most influential forces in the space.

Bitcoin is digital gold—a scarce, decentralized store of value built to resist inflation. Ethereum, meanwhile, is the world's decentralized computer—a platform for smart contracts and decentralized applications (dApps) that broaden blockchain technology's use cases beyond currency.

To grasp the importance of these two assets, we need first to examine their origins, the issues they seek to address, and their development over time.

4.4.2 Bitcoin: The Birth of Decentralized Money

The Problem: Trust in Money and Centralized Banking

Throughout history, money has shifted from bartering to gold, paper currency, and now digital transactions. Still, one constant remains: trust in a central authority. Governments and central banks control traditional fiat money, printing more whenever needed, which causes inflation and economic instability.

Bitcoin was created as a direct response to the 2008 global financial crisis, during which excessive risk-taking by banks and reckless monetary policies led to catastrophic economic failure. The idea was simple: eliminate the need for trusted third parties and establish a financial system that allows people to transact peer-to-peer without banks or intermediaries.

In October 2008, an anonymous figure (or group) under the pseudonym Satoshi Nakamoto released the whitepaper titled:

"Bitcoin: A Peer-to-Peer Electronic Cash System."

This document introduces blockchain technology—a decentralized ledger that records transactions transparently and permanently. Instead of relying on banks to verify transactions, Bitcoin utilizes a network of miners who validate and secure the system through a proof-of-work (PoW) mechanism.

Innovations of Bitcoin

Decentralization—No single entity controls Bitcoin; a global network of participants secures it.

Fixed Supply—Unlike fiat currencies, Bitcoin has a hard cap of 21 million coins, making it deflationary.

Proof-of-Work—Transactions are validated through mining, where computers solve complex puzzles to confirm transactions and secure the network.

Transparency & Security—Every Bitcoin transaction is recorded on a public blockchain, ensuring immutability and preventing fraud.

Early Adoption & Key Events in Bitcoin History

Genesis Block (2009): The Birth of Bitcoin and Its Hidden Message.

On 3 January 2009, an anonymous entity known as Satoshi Nakamoto mined the first-ever Bitcoin block, called the Genesis Block (Block 0). This marked the official launch of Bitcoin, the world's first decentralized digital currency.

Embedded within this historic block was a hidden message, forever etched into Bitcoin's blockchain:

"The Times 03/Jan/2009 Chancellor on brink of second bailout for banks."

This message referred to a headline in The Times on the same day, alluding to the ongoing financial crisis and the UK government's impending bailout of failing banks.

The inclusion of this particular newspaper headline was deliberate. Satoshi Nakamoto was making a clear statement about the failures of the traditional banking system and the centralized control of money. Bitcoin was designed as a decentralized alternative to fiat currencies, free from government manipulation, excessive money printing, and reliance on financial institutions that had proven themselves fragile during the 2008 financial meltdown.

This moment symbolized Bitcoin's core ethos:

A direct critique of central banks and their role in economic instability.
A call for a decentralized, trustless financial system.
A historic turning point—the beginning of a financial revolution.

Genesis Block Anomalies: Why It Can Never Be Spent

Unlike every other block in the Bitcoin blockchain, the Genesis Block's 50 BTC mining reward can never be spent. Whether this was intentional or a technical quirk, it adds a sense of mystique to Bitcoin's origins.

Some believe it acts as a monument to Bitcoin's origin, permanently sealing away the first BTC to prevent its use. Others speculate that Nakamoto designed it this way to strengthen Bitcoin's role as a long-term store of value, not merely a digital asset for transactions.

The mining of the Genesis Block was more than just a technical milestone—it was the first step in a decentralized movement that would go on to challenge traditional finance, reshape monetary policy debates, and spark an entirely new asset class.

From a hidden message criticizing the banking system to the development of a borderless, censorship-resistant currency, Bitcoin's creation was a direct response to the financial excesses and failures of the past.

It marked the beginning of a new era—one in which financial sovereignty became accessible to anyone, anywhere in the world.

First Bitcoin Transaction (2010): The Most Expensive Pizzas in History
On 22 May 2010, a Florida-based programmer named Laszlo Hanyecz made history by completing the first-ever real-world Bitcoin transaction. His purchase? Two large pizzas from Papa John's, paid for with 10,000 BTC.

At that time, Bitcoin was still in its early stages, worth only a fraction of a penny. The transaction was not just a milestone for Bitcoin's practicality but also a defining moment that demonstrated digital currencies could serve as a medium of exchange for tangible goods and services.

How the Transaction Happened
Hanyecz, an early Bitcoin miner and enthusiast, posted an offer on a Bitcoin forum:

"I'll pay 10,000 bitcoins for a couple of pizzas . . . maybe two large ones, so I have some left over for the next day. If you're interested, let me know, and we can work out a deal."

A fellow forum member from the UK, Jeremy Sturdivant (username: "jercos"), accepted the deal. He ordered two pizzas from a local Papa John's in Florida and had them delivered to Hanyecz—securing the first-ever recorded commercial Bitcoin transaction.

The Value of Those 10,000 BTC Today
At the time of the transaction, Bitcoin was trading at around $0.0025 per coin, making 10,000 BTC worth just $25—a fair exchange for two pizzas.

However, as Bitcoin's price skyrocketed over the years, the value of those same 10,000 BTC has reached astronomical levels:

2011 (BTC = $1) → $10,000 worth of pizza
2013 (BTC = $100) → $1,000,000 worth of pizza
2017 (BTC = $20,000) → $200,000,000 worth of pizza
2021 (BTC = $69,000) → $690,000,000 worth of pizza
Today (BTC fluctuating between $80,000–$100,000) → Over $800,000,000 worth of pizza

The transaction has since become a cautionary tale of early adoption, highlighting the significant rise in Bitcoin's value over time.

Laszlo Hanyecz: The Man Who Spent Millions on Pizza
Although Hanyecz spent what would later be worth hundreds of millions of dollars on pizza, he has no regrets. In interviews, he stated that he was experimenting with Bitcoin and had no way of knowing how valuable it would become.

"It wasn't like Bitcoin had any value back then, so the idea of trading them for a pizza was incredibly cool. Nobody knew it would turn into what it is today."

Hanyecz continued to mine and use Bitcoin, making similar purchases in the early days. His story is now legendary in the crypto world, and May 22 is celebrated annually as "Bitcoin Pizza Day"—a tribute to Bitcoin's first real-world use case.

At a time when Bitcoin was largely viewed as an experimental technology, this transaction demonstrated that BTC could be utilized for real-world payments, not just as an abstract digital asset traded among enthusiasts.

First real-world Bitcoin purchase—It set the precedent for Bitcoin's use as a currency.

Proved Bitcoin's functionality—Showed that people were willing to exchange BTC for goods and services.

Marked Bitcoin's transition from experiment to real economy—A step toward mainstream adoption.

The Ultimate HODL (Hold on for Dear Life) Lesson

While Laszlo Hanyecz's story is often told with amusement and disbelief, it serves as a powerful lesson for traders and investors. The true value of an asset isn't always clear at the time, and what seems like a fair deal today could turn into a fortune—or a painful hindsight moment—years down the line.

For all the Bitcoin investors who have stayed the course through volatility, the Pizza Day story is the ultimate example of why patience and long-term vision in crypto can be incredibly rewarding.

The Mt. Gox Hack (2014): The First Major Bitcoin Exchange Collapse

In early 2014, the cryptocurrency world was shaken to its core when Mt. Gox, the world's largest Bitcoin exchange at the time, collapsed following a massive hack. Around 850,000 BTC—worth over $450 million at the time—was stolen, making it the largest Bitcoin heist in history. The incident significantly undermined confidence in cryptocurrency security and exposed the risks associated with centralized exchanges.

Mt. Gox (short for "Magic: The Gathering Online Exchange") began as a trading platform for Magic: The Gathering game cards in 2006 but was later converted into a Bitcoin exchange by Jed McCaleb in 2010. At its height, Mt. Gox managed over 70% of all Bitcoin transactions worldwide, making it the most dominant and influential exchange in the early crypto market.

How the Hack Happened

Mt. Gox's problems started long before its eventual collapse. Security issues, mismanagement, and weak internal controls troubled the exchange. The 2014 hack was not an isolated incident—hackers had allegedly been siphoning BTC from the exchange's wallets for years, without Mt. Gox executives realizing it.

In 2011, a hacker used stolen credentials to access the Mt. Gox exchange and artificially plummeted Bitcoin's price from $17 to $0within minutes.

Later, funds mysteriously vanished from Mt. Gox wallets over several years, but the problem went unnoticed due to poor bookkeeping.

The Final Blow (2014):

In February 2014, customers started experiencing delayed withdrawals and issues accessing their funds.

On February 7, 2014, Mt. Gox suspended all Bitcoin withdrawals, citing "technical issues."

By February 24, the exchange went completely offline, leaving users locked out of their accounts.

Shortly after, it was revealed that 850,000 BTC had been stolen—worth approximately $450 million at the time and over $100 billion at Bitcoin's 2024 peak.

Impact of the Mt. Gox Hack

The collapse of Mt. Gox sent shockwaves through the crypto industry, causing a massive sell-off in Bitcoin and fueling skepticism about cryptocurrency security.

Before the hack, Bitcoin was trading at nearly $1,100.

After the news broke, BTC fell to around $400, wiping out billions in market value.

Many early investors lost their entire Bitcoin holdings, leading to a loss of faith in centralized exchanges.

Governments and regulators started taking a closer look at crypto security and regulation.

The hack reinforced the importance of personal wallet security, prompting traders to adopt hardware wallets and self-custody solutions instead of leaving funds on exchanges.

Exchanges began implementing Proof of Reserves and better security protocols to avoid a repeat of Mt. Gox.

The Aftermath & Mt. Gox's Legal Battles
Following its collapse, Mt. Gox CEO Mark Karpelès was arrested in Japan and charged with embezzlement and data manipulation. However, he denied any involvement in the theft and was later acquitted of most charges, though he served time for falsifying financial records.

The legal battles surrounding Mt. Gox dragged on for years, with creditors and former customers waiting over a decade for reimbursement.

In 2021, a long-awaited civil rehabilitation plan was approved, allowing creditors to recover a portion of their lost Bitcoin holdings.

As of 2024, Mt. Gox plans to return billions of dollars' worth of Bitcoin to former users, though some assert the payouts remain uncertain.

The Mt. Gox disaster served as a wake-up call for the cryptocurrency industry, exposing the dangers of weak security and poor exchange management.

"Not Your Keys, Not Your Coins"

One of the biggest lessons from Mt. Gox is that leaving large amounts of crypto on centralized exchanges is a risk.

Many investors now favor hardware wallets (Ledger, Trezor) or self-custody solutions.

Modern cryptocurrency exchanges offer enhanced security, cold storage, and insurance policies; however, users should still thoroughly vet platforms before depositing funds.

Regulation & Oversight Have Improved

The Mt. Gox collapse paved the way for improved regulatory oversight, though crypto remains largely unregulated in many jurisdictions.

The Mt. Gox Legacy
The Mt. Gox hack was a crucial moment in Bitcoin's early history, influencing how exchanges operate today. It served as a tough yet vital lesson, resulting in stronger security protocols and greater awareness of self-custody and risk management.

Although the early investors who lost their BTC at Mt. Gox may never fully recover their funds, the incident helped build a more secure and resilient cryptocurrency ecosystem that continues to evolve with each market cycle.

Bitcoin Halving Events (2012, 2016, 2020, 2024): The Catalyst for Crypto Bull Runs

One of the most significant and widely awaited events in Bitcoin's economic framework is the Bitcoin Halving—a scheduled decrease in the rate at which new Bitcoins are produced. Taking place roughly every four years, the halving cuts the block reward that miners receive for validating transactions by 50%, reducing the supply of new BTC entering the market.

The halving is a crucial part of Bitcoin's deflationary design, aimed at restricting supply and boosting scarcity, often sparking substantial bull runs as demand exceeds new issuance.

Bitcoin operates on a fixed supply model, with a maximum of 21 million BTC. Unlike fiat currencies that central banks can print endlessly, Bitcoin follows a strict issuance schedule.

Every ten minutes, miners compete to validate transactions and add new blocks to the Bitcoin blockchain.

As a reward, they receive a set amount of newly minted BTC.

However, this reward is halved every 210,000 blocks (roughly every four years), an event known as Bitcoin Halving.

This reduction means fewer new Bitcoins enter circulation over time, creating a supply shock that has historically driven price increases.

History of Bitcoin Halving & Its Market Impact

Each Bitcoin Halving has profoundly impacted price action, market sentiment, and miner economics.

Halving Date	Block Reward Before	Block Reward After	Bitcoin Price Before	Bitcoin Price 1 Year After
Nov 28, 2012	50 BTC	25 BTC	$12	$1,000 (+8,200%)
July 9, 2016	25 BTC	12.5 BTC	$650	$2,500 (+285%)
May 11, 2020	12.5 BTC	6.25 BTC	$8,600	$55,000 (+540%)
April 2024	6.25 BTC	3.125 BTC	$58,000	$75,000 (+29%)

The First Bitcoin Halving (2012)—Bitcoin's First Bull Run

Date: November 28, 2012
Block Reward Cut: 50 BTC → 25 BTC
Bitcoin Price Before: $12
Bitcoin Price One Year Later: $1,000

The first-ever Bitcoin Halving largely went unnoticed outside early crypto circles. At that time, Bitcoin remained a niche asset, and few institutional investors participated. However, as the supply of new BTC was halved, a supply shock ensued—demand for Bitcoin continued to rise while new issuance slowed.

What followed was Bitcoin's first parabolic bull run, pushing BTC from $12 to $1,000 in. just over a year, an 8,200% increase. This event cemented Bitcoin's status as a legitimate asset class and laid the groundwork for future halvings.

The Second Bitcoin Halving (2016)—The Rise of Institutional Interest

Date: July 9, 2016
Block Reward Cut: 25 BTC → 12.5 BTC
Bitcoin Price Before: $650
Bitcoin Price One Year Later: $2,500

By 2016, Bitcoin was no longer just a fringe technology—it had attracted mainstream media attention, and early institutional investors were beginning to take notice. With the halving reducing new supply, Bitcoin started another bull run, eventually reaching $20,000 by December 2017.

Nevertheless, this cycle also signaled the ICO (Initial Coin Offering) craze, when thousands of new cryptocurrencies were introduced, many of which later failed. Despite the boom and bust, Bitcoin established itself as a store of value, drawing parallels to gold.

The Third Bitcoin Halving (2020)—The Institutional Adoption Era

Date: May 11, 2020
Block Reward Cut: 12.5 BTC → 6.25 BTC
Bitcoin Price Before: $8,600
Bitcoin Price One Year Later: $55,000

The 2020 halving was unlike any that had occurred before. COVID-19 had triggered a global financial crisis, causing central banks to print trillions of dollars in stimulus funds. Bitcoin, which had once been regarded as a speculative asset, was now seen as an inflation hedge—a digital alternative to gold.

Market Trends Post-Halving:

Massive institutional adoption—Tesla, MicroStrategy, and hedge funds started buying Bitcoin.

Inflation fears drove demand—Governments were printing money at an unprecedented rate.

Bitcoin reached new all-time highs—BTC hit $69,000 in. November 2021, marking the peak of the bull run.

This halving reinforced Bitcoin's role as "digital gold" and attracted major financial players into the space.

The Fourth Bitcoin Halving (2024)

Date: April 2024
Block Reward Cut: 6.25 BTC → 3.125 BTC
Bitcoin Price Before: $58,000
Bitcoin Price One Year Later: $75,000

Will the cycle continue?
With the next halving set for April 2028, speculation is already mounting about what will happen next. Based on previous halvings, traders expect:

Another supply shock reduced new Bitcoin issuance to just 450 BTC per day.

Increased institutional interest, especially as ETFs and financial products integrate Bitcoin.

Potential for new all-time highs if demand continues to grow.

If past cycles are any indication, Bitcoin could be gearing up for another significant rally in 2028–2029. Time will tell.

The importance of the halving.
Scarcity Drives Value—Bitcoin's fixed supply (21 million BTC) makes it inherently deflationary. Every halving event reduces new supply, increasing scarcity.

Market Cycles Follow Halving—Historically, bull runs have followed each halving, as reduced supply meets rising demand.

Miners Adjust to Lower Rewards—With fewer new BTC to earn, miners must operate more efficiently, which can impact network security and mining difficulty.

Institutional Awareness Increases—Each halving brings more mainstream attention to Bitcoin, driving further adoption.

Unlike fiat currencies, Bitcoin has a transparent, predictable monetary policy. Every four years, its supply issuance slows down, reinforcing its role as "hard money".

Understanding Bitcoin's halving is crucial for traders and investors, as it enables them to time market cycles effectively. While past performance doesn't guarantee future results, history suggests that each halving event has set the stage for Bitcoin's largest bull runs—and 2025 may be no different.

Institutional Adoption of Bitcoin (2021-present): The Evolution From Fringe Asset to Financial Mainstream

Bitcoin's rise from an experimental digital currency to a mainstream financial asset accelerated significantly in 2021, with institutional investors, corporations, and even governments beginning to take it seriously. What was once dismissed as a speculative craze evolved into an asset class capable of competing with gold, shares, and fiat currencies as a store of value.

The Institutional Shift: From Skepticism to Acceptance

For most of its early history, Bitcoin was seen as a niche product for retail traders, tech enthusiasts, and libertarians skeptical of the traditional financial system. However, by 2021, concerns about inflation, monetary expansion, and digital finance innovations had compelled major financial players to reconsider their stance.

Companies such as Tesla and MicroStrategy included Bitcoin on their balance sheets, treating it as a reserve asset.

Wall Street hedge funds and institutional investors began accumulating Bitcoin, viewing it as a hedge against fiat devaluation.

Major banks and payment companies have integrated Bitcoin-related services, including JPMorgan, Goldman Sachs, and PayPal.

Bitcoin was no longer just an idea—it had become a recognized asset class, compelling the financial world to re-evaluate traditional investment strategies.

Major Institutional Players in Bitcoin

Tesla—Bitcoin on the Balance Sheet

In February 2021, Tesla announced a $1.5 billion investment in Bitcoin, citing its potential as a hedge against inflation and currency devaluation.

The company briefly accepted Bitcoin as payment for Tesla vehicles but later suspended it, citing environmental concerns.

Elon Musk's public influence over the crypto market has been undeniable, with tweets moving Bitcoin prices significantly.

Despite Tesla later selling a portion of its holdings, this move signaled corporate confidence in Bitcoin as a treasury asset.

MicroStrategy—The Bitcoin-Backed Public Company

Business intelligence firm MicroStrategy, led by Michael Saylor, has become the most aggressive corporate buyer of Bitcoin.

The company converted billions of dollars of cash reserves into BTC, believing it to be a superior store of value.

As of 2024, MicroStrategy holds over 190,000 BTC, making it the largest publicly traded holder of Bitcoin.

Saylor's conviction in Bitcoin reshaped corporate treasury strategies, inspiring other firms to consider Bitcoin as a long-term reserve asset.

Hedge Funds & Institutional Investors Enter the Market

Historically, hedge funds viewed Bitcoin as a high-risk speculative asset, but by 2021, attitudes had changed.

Paul Tudor Jones—One of the first major hedge fund managers to allocate a portion of his portfolio to Bitcoin, citing concerns over monetary inflation.

Stanley Druckenmiller—A legendary investor who acknowledged Bitcoin as a store of value comparable to gold.

Fidelity Investments—One of the first major asset managers to offer Bitcoin custody services to institutional clients.

As hedge funds increasingly allocated capital into Bitcoin, Wall Street was forced to recognize crypto as a legitimate asset class.

Bitcoin's Integration Into Traditional Finance—TradFi to the Crypto Community.

Although Bitcoin was initially seen as a challenge to traditional finance, it has become deeply embedded within mainstream financial infrastructure in recent years. The introduction of regulated investment vehicles, such as Bitcoin ETFs and Futures, has enabled institutional investors to gain exposure without directly holding crypto assets.

Bitcoin Futures—Bringing Crypto to Wall Street

Bitcoin futures contracts first launched on the CME (Chicago Mercantile Exchange) in December 2017.

These futures allow traders and institutions to speculate on Bitcoin's price without owning the asset.

Futures contracts also introduced Bitcoin to institutional-grade risk management tools, such as hedging strategies.

Since then, Bitcoin futures trading volume has surged, allowing institutional players to trade Bitcoin within regulated markets.

Bitcoin ETFs—A Milestone for Institutional Adoption

A significant breakthrough came with the launch of Bitcoin ETFs (Exchange-Traded Funds), which allow investors to gain exposure to Bitcoin without directly holding the asset.

The first U.S. Bitcoin Futures ETF, the ProShares Bitcoin Strategy ETF (BITO), launched in October 2021, marking a turning point for crypto adoption.

Spot Bitcoin ETFs were approved in January 2024, allowing institutions to hold Bitcoin directly rather than through futures contracts.

Grayscale Bitcoin Trust (GBTC) was one of the largest pre-ETF institutional products, holding billions in BTC.

These ETFs opened the floodgates for traditional investors who couldn't previously invest in Bitcoin due to regulatory or risk constraints, such as pension funds, which have access to trillions of dollars of cash.

Central Bank Digital Currencies (Cbdcs)

As Bitcoin and decentralized finance gained traction, central banks worldwide started exploring their own digital currencies, known as central bank digital currencies (CBDCs).

China's Digital Yuan—The first major CBDC pilot was launched, with the Chinese government testing digital yuan transactions in multiple cities.

European Central Bank (ECB) Digital Euro—The ECB is developing a - digital euro to modernize payments and counter private-sector cryptocurrencies.

U.S. Federal Reserve's Digital Dollar Discussion—The Fed has considered launching a digital dollar but has yet to finalize plans.

CBDCs are centralized, issued and controlled by governments.

Bitcoin is decentralized, with no single entity controlling supply or transactions.

CBDCs could enable financial surveillance, whereas Bitcoin allows for permissionless transactions.

While CBDCs offer efficiency and financial inclusion, Bitcoin remains an alternative monetary system that operates outside government control.

A New Monetary Paradigm

Bitcoin's rise from an obscure internet experiment to a legitimate global asset has reshaped the financial world.

Governments and institutions now recognize Bitcoin's role in modern finance.

Regulated investment products like ETFs and futures have opened the doors for mainstream investors.

The battle between decentralized crypto and centralized digital currencies will define the future of money.

As Bitcoin continues to develop, its role in the financial system remains one of the most exciting and transformative trends in modern investing. The question is no longer "Is Bitcoin legitimate?" but instead "How large will it grow?"

4.4.3 Ethereum: The Birth of Smart Contracts

Bitcoin revolutionized digital money, but it was created mainly as a store of value and a medium of exchange. However, it could not perform complex transactions and applications without relying on intermediaries.

Enter Ethereum—a programmable blockchain that could support decentralized applications, automated agreements, and new financial systems.

At just 19 years old, Vitalik Buterin proposed Ethereum as a blockchain capable of running self-executing contracts, known as smart contracts. These digital contracts could automatically execute actions when predefined conditions were met, removing the need for intermediaries such as banks, lawyers, and escrow services.

Ethereum was officially launched in 2015 to build a decentralized internet where applications could operate without centralized control.

Innovations of Ethereum

Smart Contracts—Self-executing agreements that eliminate the need for third parties.

Decentralized Finance (DeFi)—A financial system enabling borrowing, lending, and trading without banks.

NFTs (Non-Fungible Tokens)—Unique digital assets stored on the blockchain, revolutionizing art, gaming, and collectables.

Ethereum Virtual Machine (EVM)—Allows developers to build decentralized apps (dApps) on Ethereum's blockchain.

Transition to Proof-of-Stake (PoS)—Ethereum's Merge in 2022 replaced mining with staking, resulting in an over 99% reduction in energy consumption.

Big Moments in Ethereum History

Ethereum ICO (2014): The Birth of Smart Contracts & the DeFi Revolution

Ethereum's launch signified a paradigm shift in the cryptocurrency scene. Unlike Bitcoin, which was primarily created as a store of value and a medium of exchange, Ethereum introduced programmable smart contracts, allowing developers to build decentralized applications (DApps) on a blockchain.

Vitalik Buterin, the founder of Ethereum, required funding to realize his vision. In July 2014, Ethereum launched an Initial Coin Offering (ICO) that raised $18 million, marking it as one of the earliest and most notable crowdfunding successes in crypto history.

But before the ICO, Vitalik Buterin gained support from influential figures, including Peter Thiel, the billionaire co-founder of PayPal and an early investor in Facebook. In 2014, Buterin received a $100,000 Thiel Fellowship, which allowed him to drop out of university and devote himself entirely to developing Ethereum.

Thiel's fellowship, designed to support young visionaries working on groundbreaking ideas, helped Buterin speed up Ethereum's development, cementing its place in crypto history.

With Thiel's early backing and a network of key crypto pioneers, Ethereum's ICO became a massive success, propelling it beyond a simple altcoin into a full-scale decentralized ecosystem.

The ICO Boom: How Ethereum Changed Fundraising Forever

Ethereum's ICO model became the blueprint for a significant wave of token-based fundraising, sparking the ICO boom of 2017–2018.

The ICO (Initial Coin Offering)—Crypto's answer to TradFi's IPO

An ICO is a fundraising method where new blockchain projects sell tokens to investors in exchange for Bitcoin or Ethereum. This enables startups to raise capital without depending on traditional venture capital or banks.

Ethereum provided the infrastructure (ERC-20 tokens) that enabled thousands of new blockchain projects to launch their own ICOs. Some became massive successes, while others proved fraudulent or unsustainable.

The Biggest ICOs Following Ethereum

Ethereum's success inspired some of the largest ICOs in history, many of which raised hundreds of millions (or even billions) in funding. Here are the top five biggest ICOs that followed Ethereum's lead.

EOS ($4.2 Billion—2018)

EOS launched the largest ICO in history, raising a staggering $4.2 billion over a year.

Marketed as an "Ethereum killer", EOS promised faster and more scalable smart contract capabilities.

Despite its massive funding, EOS struggled with centralization concerns and governance issues, leading to a decline in adoption.

Telegram (TON)—$1.7 Billion (2018)

Telegram, the popular messaging platform, planned to launch its own blockchain, the Telegram Open Network (TON), through a private ICO.

Raised $1.7 billion from private investors before being shut down by the SEC (Securities and Exchange Commission) over regulatory concerns.

The community later revived the TON blockchain, but it never achieved its original vision.

Tezos (XTZ)—$232 Million (2017)
Tezos promised to improve on Ethereum by offering self-amending smart contracts and an on-chain governance system.

Raised $232 million, making it one of the largest ICOs at the time.

Faced internal legal disputes and leadership conflicts, delaying its launch, but later gained traction in the NFT space.

Filecoin (FIL)—$257 Million (2017)
Filecoin introduced decentralized cloud storage, allowing users to rent out unused hard drive space.

Raised $257 million in a highly anticipated ICO backed by major investors.

Became one of the most successful ICO projects, with real-world adoption in decentralized data storage.

Bancor (BNT)—$153 Million (2017)
Bancor pioneered automated market makers (AMMs), allowing decentralized token swaps without traditional order books.

Raised $153 million, helping kickstart the DeFi movement.

Despite early success, newer AMM models, such as Uniswap and Curve, later surpassed Bancor in popularity.

There is (digital) gold in those mountains.
During the peak of the cycle, around 2021, the ICO market saw substantial gains; here is a selection of the top 10. A small investment before launch would have resulted in a life-changing return.

Golden tickets—Top 10 ICO investments up to 2025

Rank	Cryptocurrency	ICO Price ($)	ATH Price ($)	ROI (%)	ROI (Multiplier)
1	NXT	0.0000168	2.16	12,857,100%	128,571x
2	Ethereum (ETH)	0.311	4,362.35	1,402,600%	14,026.8x
3	IOTA	0.000434	5.69	1,311,000%	13,110x
4	Spectrecoin	0.001	6.74	674,000%	6,740x

(continued)

(continued)

Rank	Cryptocurrency	ICO Price ($)	ATH Price ($)	ROI (%)	ROI (Multiplier)
5	NEO (Antshares)	0.032	196.85	615,150%	6,151.5x
6	NEM (XEM)	0.0002	1.87	935,000%	9,350x
7	Stratis	0.007	22.66	323,714%	3,237.14x
8	Ark	0.01	10.91	109,000%	1,090x
9	Lisk	0.076	39.31	51,600%	516x
10	Qtum	0.3	100.22	33,307%	333x

The gains made by those who invested during the pre-ICO stage to help the project succeed would have been well rewarded for their trust in the founders, and those who rode the wave to the all-time high would also have done very well.

It's easy in hindsight, as we will discuss when examining the trading process, to identify where you could have made money and what you should have bought or sold. This book aims to bring you closer to becoming one of those successful traders in any market.

While the ICO boom was happening and billions of dollars were being invested, the traditional finance (TradFi) world was mostly unaware. Fear or a lack of knowledge has prevented many baby boomers—who hold most senior roles in investment banks and funds—from investing in the internet gold rush. I was lucky to be an early adopter in the space and have since advised blockchain start-ups on their journey to the ICO stage. Every Ethereum ICO has faced thousands of failures before and after. It feels like a mirror image of the Dot-Com boom-and-bust cycle.

Ethereum's Lasting Impact on Crypto and DeFi

Ethereum's crowdfunding success demonstrated that blockchain technology could finance projects in a decentralized manner, bypassing traditional finance. However, the ICO boom also exposed the dangers of an unregulated market, resulting in high-profile scams and regulatory crackdowns.

Despite competition from newer blockchains such as Solana, Avalanche, and Polkadot, Ethereum remains the backbone of DeFi, NFTs, and tokenized assets.

It facilitated the growth of decentralized finance, enabling individuals to trade, borrow, lend, and earn yields without banks.

Pioneered the NFT (Non-Fungible Token) market, enabling artists and creators to tokenize digital assets. NFTs built on Ethereum's ERC-721 standard drew mainstream attention, with digital art and collectables selling for millions.

Introduced smart contracts, which are now an essential part of blockchain technology. Ethereum transitioned from Proof-of-Work (PoW) to Proof-of-Stake (PoS), improving sustainability and paving the way for future scalability.

With Ethereum 2.0 moving to proof-of-stake, its scalability, efficiency, and environmental impact are being addressed, ensuring it remains at the center of blockchain innovation for years to come.

Ethereum's ICO was not only a fundraising triumph—it transformed the crypto industry. By launching a programmable blockchain that enabled developers to build upon it, Ethereum established an entirely new financial ecosystem, boosting the development of DeFi, NFTs, and Web3 applications.

With early support from figures such as Peter Thiel and the Ethereum co-founders, it evolved from an ambitious idea into the world's second-largest cryptocurrency.

While the ICO boom led to both innovation and excess, Ethereum established itself as the foundation of decentralized applications, finance, and digital assets. Its influence continues to shape the future of blockchain technology, proving that it was more than just an ICO—it marked the start of a financial revolution.

Bitcoin vs. Ethereum: Different Purposes, Same Revolution

Feature	Bitcoin (BTC)	Ethereum (ETH)
Purpose	Digital Gold, Store of Value	Smart Contracts, dApps, DeFi
Supply Cap	21 Million (Fixed)	No Fixed Cap (Deflationary Mechanisms)
Consensus Mechanism	Proof-of-Work (PoW) → PoS (Future)	Proof-of-Stake (PoS)
Speed	~ 10 minutes per block	~ 15 seconds per block
Use Case	Money, Inflation Hedge	Programmable Contracts, DeFi, NFTs

Both Bitcoin and Ethereum serve unique yet complementary roles in the crypto ecosystem. Bitcoin is the strongest form of decentralized money, while Ethereum is the foundation for decentralized applications and digital innovation.

4.4.4 Decentralized Finance (Defi): The New Financial Frontier

The development of Ethereum was a game-changer, forming an entire industry built on cryptocurrency. Decentralized finance—DeFi—was established and has continued to expand rapidly, transforming how people engage with money, investments, and financial services.

From altcoins and meme coins to yield farming, staking, looping, NFTs, and market manipulation tactics like pump-and-dumps, the DeFi ecosystem has grown rapidly. Some of these innovations will endure, while others will disappear as fleeting hype cycles.

I'll concentrate on the aspects of DeFi that traders and investors can utilize to spot genuine opportunities, rather than getting lost in the vast sea of speculative projects.

Let's start with an overview of DeFi—what it is, how it works, and why it matters.

Decentralized Finance

At its core, DeFi is an open, permissionless financial system built on blockchain technology that removes banks, brokers, and traditional financial intermediaries from the equation.

Instead of relying on centralized institutions, DeFi uses smart contracts—self-executing agreements written into code—to facilitate financial transactions such as borrowing, lending, trading, and earning interest.

Decentralization—No single entity controls DeFi platforms; they run on public blockchains like Ethereum, Solana, and Binance Smart Chain.

Transparency—All transactions are recorded on the blockchain and can be verified in real time by anyone.

Accessibility—Anyone with an internet connection can use DeFi—no bank account, credit score, or government approval required.

Programmability—Smart contracts allow for automated financial services, reducing the need for human intervention.

Non-Custodial: Users own and control their assets, removing counterparty risk associated with banks or traditional finance.

Think of DeFi as the "Wild West" of finance—remarkable opportunities but high risks for the unprepared. If traditional finance is a walled garden with rules and regulations, DeFi is a permissionless open jungle where anything goes.

Components of DeFi

DeFi is a vast ecosystem comprising various applications and protocols, each serving a distinct financial purpose.

Decentralized Exchanges (Dexs)—the Unregulated Trading Floors

Decentralized Exchanges (DEXs) allow users to trade cryptocurrencies directly with one another—without intermediaries or centralized control.

Unlike traditional crypto exchanges like Binance or Coinbase, which require identity verification and hold users' funds in custody, DEXs allow users to trade directly from their wallets, retaining full control over their assets.

Popular DEXs:
Uniswap (Ethereum)—The first major DEX, known for its automated market maker (AMM) model.
SushiSwap (Ethereum, BSC, Polygon)—A fork of Uniswap with additional yield farming incentives.
PancakeSwap (Binance Smart Chain)—The go–to DEX for low-fee trading on BSC.
Curve Finance (Ethereum & others)—Specializes in stablecoin swaps with low slippage.

How Traders Use DEXs:
Swap tokens without relying on centralized exchanges.
Provide liquidity to earn trading fees and yield.
Front-run hype cycles in new altcoins and meme coins.

Trade Study: Uniswap & the Rise of DEXs (2020–2021)
During the DeFi Summer of 2020, Uniswap became the leading DEX, with daily trading volume in the billions. Early traders who recognized the potential of decentralized trading exploited yield farming, governance tokens, and token launch trends, making substantial profits before the hype subsided.

Lending & Borrowing—Earning Interest Without Banks
DeFi facilitates a peer-to-peer lending system that lets users borrow and lend crypto without relying on a bank. Instead of credit scores, these platforms employ collateral-based lending, meaning you must deposit crypto as security before borrowing assets.

Popular DeFi Lending Platforms:
Aave (Ethereum & Polygon)—Allows users to lend and borrow crypto with dynamic interest rates.
Compound (Ethereum)—One of the first DeFi lending protocols.
MakerDAO (Ethereum)—Lets users mint DAI stablecoins by locking up Ethereum as collateral.

How Traders Use DeFi Lending:
Earn passive income by lending crypto and collecting interest.

Borrow against holdings instead of selling assets (great for avoiding taxes on capital gains).

Leverage trading positions by borrowing additional funds.

Trade Study: Aave Flash Loans (2021–2022)
Aave introduced flash loans, enabling users to borrow unlimited funds without collateral—so long as they repay within the same transaction. This fostered inventive arbitrage strategies but also led to manipulative exploits, demonstrating that innovation in DeFi brings both great opportunity and substantial risk.

Yield Farming & Staking—Earning Passive Crypto
Yield farming is the crypto equivalent of depositing money in a high-interest savings account—but with considerably more risk and reward.

Instead of earning a few percentage points at a bank, DeFi platforms offer double, triple, or even four-digit APYs (Annual Percentage Yields) for providing liquidity to protocols.

Methods of Yield Farming:
Liquidity Mining—Provide liquidity to a pool and earn rewards.
Staking—Lock up crypto in a protocol to earn passive income.
LP Tokens—Earn fees by staking LP (Liquidity Provider) tokens from DEX trading pairs.

Popular Yield Farming & Staking Platforms:
Yearn Finance (Ethereum)—Automates yield farming strategies.
PancakeSwap (BSC)—Offers high APY staking pools.
Convex Finance (Ethereum)—Optimizes rewards from Curve Finance liquidity pools.

Trade Study: The DeFi Yield Boom (2020–2021)
Early adopters of DeFi farming achieved remarkable returns, with some protocols offering over 1000% APY to liquidity providers. However, as with any gold rush, many of these yields proved unsustainable, and those who did not manage their risks lost fortunes when the DeFi bubble burst.

Stablecoins—The Backbone of DeFi
Since crypto is highly volatile, stablecoins provide a way to store value without exiting the ecosystem.

Types of Stablecoins:
Fiat-backed (e.g., USDC, USDT)—Pegged 1:1 to fiat currencies like the U.S. dollar.
Crypto-backed (e.g., DAI)—Pegged to crypto collateral but decentralized.
Algorithmic (e.g., UST—now failed)—Uses smart contracts to maintain a peg (high risk).

Trade Study: The UST & LUNA Collapse (2022)
Terra's UST stablecoin lost its peg, triggering a $40 billion crypto crash that wiped out investors unaware of the risks of algorithmic stablecoins. A clear example of DeFi's potential—both for massive gains and severe losses.

Enter the United States of America—Genius Act
The United States has recently taken a decisive step towards integrating digital assets into the mainstream financial system with the passage of the GENIUS Act. In simple terms, this legislation establishes a clear legal framework that permits regulated, dollar-backed stablecoins to be recognized as a legitimate form of digital currency. This marks a significant transition. For the first time, the world's largest capital market explicitly acknowledges that blockchain-based settlement can coexist alongside traditional banking infrastructure rather than remain on the periphery. For traders, this is a development far beyond crypto hype.

Faster settlement, reduced counterparty risk, and the merging of on-chain liquidity with traditional markets all alter the fundamental infrastructure of our trades. As with every major market evolution, those who understand the mechanics early will be better equipped to adapt, while those who overlook it risk trading with yesterday's market and yesterday's assumptions.

Navigating DeFi as a Trader
DeFi offers incredible opportunities but requires serious research. Projects can make people millionaires overnight—or leave them with worthless tokens.

Speaking from experience, it's important you:

Learn the fundamentals before diving in.
Never chase unsustainable yield—if it seems too good to be true, it probably is.
Stay ahead of trends—DeFi evolves fast.
Use risk management—don't put all your capital in one DeFi protocol.
DeFi is a financial revolution, but only those who understand it can truly profit from it.

4.4.5 The Future of Crypto

Bitcoin and Ethereum have transformed the way the world perceives money, finance, and technology. While Bitcoin seeks to replace gold, Ethereum is building a new financial and digital ecosystem. Both assets have endured market cycles, technological upgrades, and regulatory challenges—yet they continue to prosper.

The question is no longer "Will crypto survive?" but rather "How big will it become?"

As we move forward, traders and investors should keep an eye on:

Bitcoin adoption by institutions and nations
Ethereum's scalability upgrades and DeFi expansion
The evolving regulatory landscape

The next chapter will explore the key drivers of the crypto market—what moves Bitcoin, Ethereum, and the broader altcoin space. Understanding these forces is crucial for navigating and profiting from the dynamic world of cryptocurrency trading.

Who is driving this ship?

Cryptocurrency markets are known—or perhaps notorious—for their dramatic and sometimes confusing price fluctuations. Watching values soar and plummet within days, weeks, or months can leave even experienced investors puzzled. At its heart, crypto grew from a strong sentiment: a deep mistrust of traditional financial systems and a genuine desire for a decentralized store of wealth, exemplified by Bitcoin. Its limited supply, combined with steadily increasing demand, has historically driven its price upward.

However, beyond the basic explanations of supply and demand lies a captivating web of reasons behind crypto market volatility. We identify patterns and trends that reveal significant opportunities by exploring these underlying forces—regulatory changes, technological advances, institutional movements, emotional trading, and macroeconomic factors. Understanding the unseen currents shaping these unpredictable markets can turn what appears irrational into a landscape full of potential.

Hype Cycle

Cryptocurrencies often experience major price swings driven by waves of enthusiasm and speculation, commonly called the hype cycle. This cycle involves rapid adoption, spurred by media attention and investor excitement, leading to inflated valuations. Eventually, reality catches up, causing sharp corrections as expectations are adjusted. Recognizing and predicting these hype-driven cycles can provide strategic entry and exit points for investors.

Trade Example: Navigating the Crypto Hype Cycle
Cryptocurrency markets regularly undergo hype cycles driven by speculative interests, extensive media coverage, and widespread excitement. These cycles offer clear trading opportunities, marked by rapid price increases followed by sharp declines. SHIBU Inu

In early October 2021, rumors about Shiba Inu (SHIB)—another playful, dog-themed crypto riding on the coattails of DOGE's popularity—began to circulate on Twitter, Reddit, and Telegram. Soon, these rumors transformed into a roaring chorus, amplified by enthusiastic media headlines and a frenzy of speculative trading. Investors who recognized this growing trend bought in at modest levels of $0.000007–$0.000008, riding the upward wave as SHIB quickly gained listings on major exchanges. However, just as excitement reached $0.000088, astute traders observed warning signs—declining volume, overly optimistic chatter—and realized it was time to step back before the wave inevitably crashed.

Traders who skillfully identified the early signs of market hype and exited positions at the peak of investor euphoria reaped substantial profits. In contrast, investors who remained invested beyond peak sentiment faced severe losses during the inevitable correction—highlighting the critical importance of accurately recognizing the stages of the hype cycle, from initial excitement through media frenzy to ultimate decline, by using sentiment analysis tools and volume indicators, combined with disciplined risk management, swift execution, and a keen awareness of behavioral shifts to capitalize on fleeting market opportunities effectively.

Industry Adoption
Widespread industry adoption enhances the legitimacy and practical usefulness of cryptocurrencies, significantly shaping their long-term value. As businesses and traditional institutions increasingly adopt crypto solutions—from integrating cryptocurrency payment gateways to implementing blockchain-based supply chain management systems—it indicates growing confidence and stability, often leading to sustained upward price movements.

In February 2021, traders worldwide woke to a headline that shook both the crypto and traditional financial sectors: Tesla had purchased a substantial £1.5 billion in Bitcoin and announced plans to accept BTC as payment for its iconic electric vehicles. This wasn't merely another corporate announcement; it was an industry-changing moment, instantly elevating Bitcoin from a speculative curiosity to a mainstream asset.

The news broke with Bitcoin trading between £38,000 and £42,000, offering a prime entry point for traders who recognized the significance of Tesla's endorsement. The announcement wasn't merely about one company's gamble—it signaled legitimacy, trust, and mainstream acceptance, attracting fresh waves of institutional and retail investors eager to ride Bitcoin's rise.

And rise it did. Momentum surged quickly, pushing Bitcoin to a record high near $64,000 by April 2021. Traders who rapidly took positions upon the announcement and carefully held and scaled out during periods of heightened sentiment reaped significant profits.

The Tesla-Bitcoin moment wasn't just another trading event—it was a masterclass in recognizing high-impact industry adoption. It demonstrated to traders the powerful rewards of remaining vigilant, acting swiftly, and leveraging major market shifts to turn news into profits.

Regulation

Regulatory developments have significant impacts on crypto markets. Positive regulatory frameworks can enhance confidence, attract institutional investment, and stabilize prices, whereas restrictive or uncertain regulations may lead to sudden declines due to fears of reduced accessibility or usage restrictions. Staying alert to regulatory changes allows investors to manage market volatility more effectively.

China's Crypto Crackdown (May 2021)

In May 2021, crypto traders worldwide received a sudden wake-up call as news broke that China was tightening its crackdown on cryptocurrencies, banning financial institutions and payment companies from offering services linked to crypto. Initially dismissed by some as just another routine clampdown, the seriousness of the situation soon became clear—this was no ordinary regulatory tightening.

Bitcoin, which had been soaring above $50,000, quickly started to fall as uncertainty took hold of the market. Investors who recognized the warning signs early and acted swiftly—selling short, exiting long positions, or hedging their exposure—protected substantial profits or avoided significant losses. Within weeks, Bitcoin dropped sharply, briefly falling below $30,000 by July, wiping out billions in market value and shattering investor confidence worldwide.

But, as always in markets, volatility created opportunities. Savvy traders who understood that markets often overreact to initial shocks waited patiently, buying the panic-induced dips once selling pressure eased and stabilization became clear.

This regulation-driven event highlights the strong link between crypto prices and the speed of regulation. Traders who stay alert to regulatory changes and can quickly grasp their potential effects turned volatility into opportunity—showing that, in crypto, understanding regulatory landscapes isn't just clever; it's crucial.

KOLs: Trump and Elon

Key opinion leaders (KOLs), such as President Donald Trump and entrepreneur Elon Musk (whose names come up frequently when discussing crypto), wield considerable influence over crypto market sentiment. Their public statements or tweets can trigger rapid market reactions, either positive or negative.

Understanding this influence helps investors anticipate short-term volatility driven by sentiment rather than fundamental factors.

Trade Study -Elon Musk Sends DOGE to the Moon (2021)

In early 2021, Dogecoin (DOGE)—initially created as a joke—became one of the most discussed cryptocurrencies, and no figure boosted its popularity more than Elon Musk. Known for his influential tweets, Musk regularly shared humorous and bullish commentary on DOGE, referring to himself as the "Dogefather" and tweeting memes suggesting Dogecoin could become "the future currency of Earth."

One particularly memorable moment happened on 8 May 2021, when Musk hosted Saturday Night Live (SNL). Anticipation was extremely high, and retail traders feverishly speculated that he might further endorse DOGE on live television. In the weeks leading up to his SNL appearance, Dogecoin surged from about $0.06 in. early April to an all-time high near $0.74 just before the show—an astonishing increase of over 1,100% in a single month.

However, traders who understood the classic "buy the rumour, sell the news" dynamic took profits as hype peaked just before the event. Indeed, when Musk jokingly called DOGE "a hustle" during the broadcast, sentiment turned sharply negative, and prices plummeted nearly 40% overnight.

This trade study demonstrates how influential opinion leaders can significantly impact crypto markets—often beyond the scope of fundamental analysis. Traders who carefully monitored Musk's influence patterns and the crowd-driven sentiment before his SNL appearance were well-positioned to capitalize on DOGE's meteoric rise and exit swiftly as hype reached its peak, highlighting the importance of staying ahead of sentiment-driven volatility.

Trust

Trust is essential in the cryptocurrency world, especially given its decentralized nature and recent rise. Events such as hacks, scams, or the collapse of well-known platforms undermine confidence and cause rapid price declines. Conversely, transparency, security improvements, and reputable governance enhance trust, supporting long-term value growth.

Trade Study—SBF and the collapse of FTX

In November 2022, the crypto industry faced one of its greatest trust crises with the dramatic fall of FTX, once the world's second-largest cryptocurrency exchange, founded by billionaire Sam Bankman-Fried. Initially regarded as a credible and innovative platform, FTX had attracted support from elite investors, celebrities, and institutions, making its sudden collapse a huge shock to the sector.

The collapse unfolded quickly: leaked documents revealed dubious financial practices and concealed debts at FTX, prompting a surge in withdrawals as panicked users rushed to withdraw their funds. Within days, FTX declared bankruptcy, leaving billions of dollars of customer assets stranded. In a dramatic turn of events, founder Sam Bankman-Fried was arrested, charged with fraud, money laundering, and conspiracy, and subsequently imprisoned, further undermining public confidence.

The consequences rippled through the crypto markets. Bitcoin fell from around $21,000 to below $16,000 in. a week, and Ethereum similarly dropped by almost 30%, pulling the wider market sharply lower. Investors swiftly withdrew liquidity, unsure which platforms could be trusted, and sentiment hit a new low.

Nevertheless, traders closely watching the unfolding events saw an opportunity amid the turmoil. As regulators acted quickly, promising greater oversight, major exchanges proactively issued "proof-of-reserves" to regain trust. Sharp investors started buying fundamentally strong cryptocurrencies at notable discounts.

Within months, as transparency increased, reputable exchanges gained market share, and prices stabilized. Traders who recognized the restoration of trust early and bought high-quality crypto assets at significantly depressed prices profited substantially when markets rebounded.

This event emphasizes the vital role trust has in crypto markets. A swift loss of confidence can devastate prices, but proactive improvements in transparency, security, and regulatory clarity can also support sustained recoveries. For traders, staying attuned to trust dynamics is crucial, enabling them to position themselves effectively when market fear creates exceptional opportunities.

TradFi Adoption

Traditional finance (TradFi) institutions adopting crypto assets is a significant sign of maturity and stability in the market. As established financial entities such as banks, asset managers, and hedge funds incorporate cryptocurrencies into their portfolios, it indicates mainstream acceptance, increased liquidity, and reduced volatility over time. Recognizing TradFi's adoption journey can highlight stable, long-term investment opportunities.

Trade Study: BlackRock's Crypto Breakthrough—A TradFi Turning Point

In June 2023, a crucial moment occurred in the history of cryptocurrency. BlackRock, the world's largest asset manager with over $9 trillion in assets under management, has officially submitted an application for a spot Bitcoin ETF with the U.S. Securities and Exchange Commission (SEC). This action was significant—a traditional finance giant endorsing Bitcoin in theory and through tangible investment products aimed at mainstream investors.

The market reaction was swift and electrifying. Bitcoin jumped nearly 20%, rising from about £25,000 to over £30,000 in. just a few days. Investors, sensing the seismic shift, flocked into Bitcoin and other crypto assets, expecting similar moves from other financial giants.

Indeed, BlackRock's action opened the floodgates of institutional confidence. Fidelity, WisdomTree, and Invesco quickly followed suit, submitting their own Bitcoin ETF proposals. This wave of applications significantly shifted market sentiment, sending a strong signal to both retail and institutional investors that crypto was now firmly integrated within traditional finance.

Traders who recognized the importance of BlackRock's endorsement acted quickly, positioning themselves early and reaping the benefits of the initial surge. Additionally, investors who viewed the filings as part of a broader TradFi shift rather than a fleeting market boost held on for longer-term gains as regulatory approval approached, supporting prices and reducing volatility.

This case highlights the influence of TradFi adoption as a strong market driver. Spotting early signals from respected institutions provides traders and investors with opportunities for short-term gains and long-term stability. As traditional finance increasingly embraces cryptocurrencies, astute traders will continue to use these signals to benefit from the growing link between digital assets and global finance.

Macroeconomic Performance

Global economic conditions significantly influence cryptocurrency markets. During times of economic uncertainty, inflation, or currency devaluation, cryptocurrencies—especially Bitcoin—can serve as alternative stores of value or hedges. Conversely, strong economic growth and favorable monetary policies can shift investor focus towards traditional financial markets, possibly decreasing inflows into the crypto sector. Monitoring macroeconomic indicators enables investors to anticipate broader market trends and make well-informed investment choices.

Trade Study: Bitcoin's Inflation Rally—Crypto as Digital Gold

In late 2020, as global economies struggled due to the COVID-19 pandemic and central banks printed money at unprecedented rates, fears of inflation began to take center stage. Investors looked for safe havens, worried about the erosion of their wealth as currencies devalued. In previous generations, gold had been the traditional hedge—but this time, Bitcoin moved into the spotlight, earning recognition as "digital gold."

As governments across the globe implemented substantial stimulus packages and central banks reduced interest rates, macroeconomic uncertainty increased. Bitcoin, then trading around $10,000 in. October 2020, attracted the attention of institutional investors, hedge funds, and retail traders who recognized its potential as a hedge against inflation and currency fluctuations.

By December 2020, Bitcoin had surpassed its previous 2017 peak of $20,000, driven by increasing demand from institutional investors—including MicroStrategy and MassMutual—who publicly announced their Bitcoin acquisitions. This institutional backing affirmed Bitcoin's status as a macroeconomic hedge, sparking a surge of new inflows.

Momentum carried on into early 2021, and by April, Bitcoin had surged to nearly $64,000—an impressive 540% rise in just six months. Traders and investors who had carefully tracked macroeconomic indicators, observing rising inflation expectations and the central bank's loose monetary policies, positioned themselves early, reaping considerable profits.

However, those who failed to recognize Bitcoin's role in the macroeconomic landscape or underestimated how investor preferences shift during economic uncertainty missed one of history's most significant crypto rallies.

This trade story clearly demonstrates the importance of staying aware of macroeconomic performance. Recognizing the link between global economic conditions and crypto markets is essential, enabling informed traders and investors to seize timely opportunities amid major financial shifts.

It seemed like a good idea at the time!

Altcoins & DeFi: Capturing the Next Big Thing in Web 3.0

Beyond Bitcoin and Ethereum, the broader altcoin and decentralized finance market is mainly driven by ideas, community support, and market buzz. Thousands of new tokens and coins have emerged, each promising innovative solutions tailored to the emerging Web 3.0 landscape.

Web 3.0, often called the next stage of the Internet, signifies a decentralized online environment driven by blockchain technology. In this setting, users retain control over their data, digital identities, and transactions, without depending on traditional intermediaries such as banks or tech giants.

Start-ups and developers in this field frequently produce detailed white-papers—comprehensive documents outlining a project's vision, goals, technical specifics, and roadmap. These whitepapers act as essential marketing tools to attract initial funding from venture capitalists eager to find the next groundbreaking crypto asset, such as NXT, Solana, or Avalanche.

Many projects within the Web 3.0 ecosystem also utilize concepts such as the Internet of Things (IoT)—a network of interconnected physical devices, such as sensors, appliances, and vehicles, that can exchange data seamlessly and interact autonomously. Altcoins often aim to enable secure, efficient micropayments and transactions within IoT ecosystems, removing barriers to innovation and encouraging frictionless connectivity.

Initially, these projects secure seed funding, allowing them to launch their tokens or coins into the market. Nonetheless, genuine success starts after launch, when these companies must attract the attention and enthusiasm of the wider crypto community—roughly 400 million users globally. Successful projects in the competitive DeFi and altcoin markets combine visionary ideas, strategic marketing, and tangible utility to foster adoption and boost their value.

Tokens that strike this balance effectively often experience explosive growth—or "moon," as crypto traders enthusiastically say—offering significant opportunities for early investors and informed traders.

Understanding and navigating this ecosystem for savvy market participants involves staying attuned to emerging trends, critically evaluating white papers, gauging community sentiment, and anticipating genuine innovations that deliver lasting value beyond short-lived hype.

MEME Coin mania

MEME coins showcase one of the more outrageous yet fascinating aspects of the crypto and blockchain scene. Usually hosted on inexpensive blockchains, these tokens emerge quickly, inspired by viral trends, internet jokes, or social media sensations. Essentially, meme coins are digital tokens driven by hype, community support, and often little else in terms of fundamentals. Their lifespan can resemble a financial fireworks display, with extreme surges and collapses within just hours, as early adopters rush in and out, aiming to cash out at many times their original investment.

One of the most well-known examples of meme coin success is Dogecoin (DOGE). Created in 2013 by software engineers Billy Markus and Jackson Palmer as a playful parody of Bitcoin, Dogecoin features the Shiba Inu dog from the "Doge" meme as its logo. Although it started as a joke, Dogecoin developed a surprisingly passionate community and widespread adoption, significantly boosted by the vocal support of billionaire Elon Musk. Musk's tweets and playful endorsements caused dramatic price increases, famously pushing DOGE to an incredible $88 billion market cap at its peak in 2021.

Another fascinating, yet cautionary, tale of meme coin mania involved singer-songwriter and TikTok star Haliey Welch, who spontaneously created a meme token named "GIRL" following an impulsive social media post. The coin rapidly gained popularity, attracting thousands of speculators eager to ride the wave of hype. Almost overnight, GIRL became a viral sensation, showing how easily tokens can gain traction through celebrity influence and social media momentum.

However, as swiftly as it rose, GIRL's price inevitably crashed, highlighting the rapid volatility and speculative nature typical of meme coins.

These examples demonstrate meme coins' dual nature—both as potentially profitable opportunities for quick traders and cautionary tales highlighting the risk of speculative bubbles driven by internet trends and celebrity endorsements.

To the Moon

Cryptocurrency markets are influenced by a variety of interconnected forces, ranging from the seriously impactful—such as regulatory crackdowns—to the truly ridiculous—such as viral memes and humorous internet images. Add in traditional macroeconomic factors, celebrity tweets, and unpredictable market sentiment, and any combination can instantly send prices soaring 'to the moon' or plunging straight to the bottom of the ocean, leaving investors thoroughly 'rekt'. Navigating these uncertain waters requires understanding all these variables, giving blockchain enthusiasts and traders the insight needed to prosper in this volatile yet exciting new financial landscape that's certainly here to stay.

With a solid understanding of the factors that influence crypto markets, it's now time to focus on the art and science of trading in this volatile landscape. Let's explore tried-and-true strategies, practical techniques, and actionable insights to help you identify opportunities, manage risks, and—most importantly—consistently profit from trading cryptocurrencies.

Trading Strategies and Ideas to Make Money in Cryptocurrencies

Trading cryptocurrencies can be both exciting and profitable—provided you have a clear plan, disciplined execution, and the flexibility to adapt quickly. Crypto markets are notoriously volatile, but volatility is exactly what traders thrive on. In this chapter, we'll explore some practical strategies and actionable ideas to help you confidently navigate crypto markets and capitalize on opportunities as they arise.

The Buy-and-Hold Strategy ("HODLing")

A large group of dedicated crypto enthusiasts firmly believe that the financial landscape will soon change, making digital assets the primary means of transacting and storing value. These individuals are the original HODLers—those committed to "Holding On for Dear Life." They argue that crypto prices, supported by limited supply and rising demand, will inevitably climb as the wider world adapts to this digital transition.

If you feel connected to this vision, even in a more cautious way, you might think of yourself as a practical HODLer—someone who values a long-term buy-and-hold approach without getting distracted by daily price fluctuations.

One of the simplest yet most effective cryptocurrency strategies is to choose fundamentally strong digital assets and hold them long-term, regardless of short-term volatility.

Identify sound cryptocurrencies: Focus on established assets with proven utility, security, and community support, such as Bitcoin (BTC) and Ethereum (ETH).

Purchase strategically: Take advantage of market corrections or dips to accumulate your chosen cryptocurrencies at discounted prices.

Hold through volatility: Remain steady during market fluctuations, keeping a clear eye on long-term appreciation potential rather than short-term noise.

Adopting the HODLing mindset enables investors to capitalize on cryptocurrencies' overall growth trajectory, offering a simple route through the often-volatile crypto markets.

Event-Driven Trading

As we discussed in our section on "What Moves the Crypto Market," cryptocurrency prices can fluctuate quickly due to news and events. The key to making a profit from event-driven trading is distinguishing between bullish news (which pushes prices up) and bearish news (which pushes prices down). Once you grasp these catalysts, you can position yourself proactively.

Below is a quick-reference table highlighting key market drivers and their typical market impact:

Market Driver	Impact on Crypto Prices
Positive Regulatory Developments	Bullish
Restrictive Regulations (e.g., bans)	Bearish
Institutional Adoption (TradFi involvement)	Bullish
High-Profile Hacks/Exchange Failures	Bearish
Major Technological Upgrades	Bullish
Negative KOL (Influencer) Statements	Bearish
Positive KOL (Influencer) Statements	Bullish
Inflation & Economic Uncertainty	Bullish (for Bitcoin, ETH)
Strong Economic Performance (TradFi growth)	Bearish (as capital flows to traditional markets)
Meme & Hype Cycles (early stage)	Bullish (initially)
Meme & Hype Cycles (late stage)	Bearish (eventually)

Mastering this event-driven, fundamental approach gives traders a strong advantage. It allows us to navigate crypto's notorious volatility with confidence and identify significant opportunities. In the next section of the book, we'll explore more practical strategies and actionable insights for trading based on fundamentals.

Trading the Crypto Hype Cycle

You could argue that almost all markets in the fiat world revolve around hype cycles—my personal favorites include the ongoing fear of running out of oil and the recurring panic that humanity might revert to trading physical gold if the financial system collapses. However, these hype cycles can occur in crypto at lightning speed, sometimes lasting mere hours. While they can offer spectacular rewards, they're just as capable of leaving traders badly burned.

Here's a structured approach to navigating crypto's volatile hype cycles:

Identify Trends Early:

Look for emerging narratives or themes gaining initial traction (NFTs, Metaverse, AI tokens, meme coins).

Early Entry:

Enter positions before mainstream attention peaks, capitalizing on early enthusiasm.

Sell the Excitement:

Exit positions as hype reaches a frenzy before sentiment inevitably cools and reality sets in.

Gauge Sentiment:

Use social media activity, sentiment analysis tools, and volume indicators to pinpoint optimal exit timing.

By mastering the art of timing these cycles, traders can seize explosive opportunities while carefully managing the significant risks involved. Given the high potential rewards, there is fierce competition to become the next Ethereum.

Arbitrage Trading

Arbitrage is often discussed in the crypto trading scene because, especially in the early years of adoption, it offered highly profitable opportunities. As numerous exchanges competed to establish themselves and gain market share, discrepancies in cryptocurrency prices appeared, enabling traders to profit by essentially trading the same crypto asset against itself.

Although automated, algorithm-driven traders have largely dominated this space, occasional gaps still remain for keen-eyed human traders.

The Arb-Line (as the crypto bros call it)

Crypto arbitrage involves exploiting price differences for the same asset across multiple exchanges.

Identify Opportunities:

Monitor real-time prices across several exchanges to detect significant price discrepancies.

Execute Simultaneously:

Quickly buy the cryptocurrency at the lower-priced exchange while simultaneously selling it at the higher-priced exchange.

Automate Where Possible:

Using automated arbitrage bots or software to identify and execute trades rapidly maximizes efficiency and speed.

While arbitrage trading has become more challenging due to advanced automated competition, opportunities still arise during times of extreme volatility or rapid market shifts, providing disciplined traders with the chance to profit from market inefficiencies.

Altcoin Trading & DeFi Opportunities

Two key attributes that have consistently driven my trading success are curiosity and a willingness to embrace calculated risk-taking. Developed over a lifetime and showing no signs of waning, these traits have naturally led me into the dynamic, ever-evolving world of altcoin trading and DeFi.

In crypto markets, these opportunities offer a blend of technological innovation, rapid growth potential, and considerable risk—a combination I've found irresistible and rewarding.

Emerging altcoins and DeFi projects offer high-risk, high-reward opportunities driven by innovative technology, promising use cases, and community-led adoption. Here's how I approach these opportunities:

Identify Promising Projects:

Dive into project whitepapers, scrutinize the experience and credibility of founding teams, check the reputation of early backers, and assess genuine (crypto) real-world utility.

Early Entry Points:

Enter early, preferably during initial coin offerings (ICOs), initial exchange offerings (IEOs), or at first market listings, to secure attractive entry prices before mainstream attention arrives.

Active Profit-Taking:

Lock in profits regularly as valuations rise. Given crypto's volatile nature, gains can evaporate quickly, making disciplined profit-taking crucial.

Risk Awareness and Management:

Always stay alert to the possibility of sudden, sharp market downturns. Remaining flexible and prepared to exit positions quickly helps protect gains and reduce potential losses.

By cultivating my natural curiosity and carefully managed risk-taking, altcoin and DeFi trading have become among my most rewarding and exciting pursuits in the broader crypto landscape. As the market becomes more saturated, this may change, and I will need to adapt as well.

Successfully trading cryptocurrencies demands discipline, risk management, and a clear grasp of market dynamics. Whether you're trading macroeconomic trends, riding the hype cycle, or taking advantage of institutional moves, having a structured strategy will help you turn volatility into profit. As always, understand your risks, manage them carefully, and enjoy the journey in one of today's most exciting trading markets.

4.5 Energy—The Means to Get Anything Done!

The upcoming chapters will examine the markets that stem from the energy we depend on to power modern civilization. From heating our homes to fueling transport and even intergalactic space travel, energy markets constitute the core of the global economy. These markets are volatile, continually changing, and highly sensitive to geopolitical developments, supply limitations, and fluctuations in demand.

While numerous energy derivatives are available for trading, we will concentrate on the two dominant forces in the sector: oil and natural gas. These commodities serve as the backbone of industrial production, transportation, and global trade, making them some of the most actively traded markets in the world. Their price fluctuations create significant opportunities for traders who understand the factors that drive supply and demand.

In the coming chapters, we will examine how these markets operate, what influences their movements, and, most importantly, how traders can profit from their volatility. Whether you are new to energy trading or aiming to refine your strategy, this section will offer the insights needed to navigate one of the most exciting and impactful areas of financial markets.

4.5.1 Black Gold (Oil)

Oil is one of the world's most influential and actively traded commodities. It powers industries, fuels transport, and is a key driver of economic and geopolitical stability. The oil market is extensive and intricate, influenced by supply and demand, geopolitical events, production policies, and financial speculation.

To understand how the oil market operates, we must first examine its origins, significant historical moments, the role of major players, and the organizations that influence its prices. Oil trading presents substantial profit opportunities for those who grasp these dynamics, and in this chapter, we will unpack the fundamentals of this constantly changing market.

The Origins of the Oil Market

The modern oil industry traces its roots back to the mid-nineteenth century, but oil has been used for thousands of years. Ancient civilizations, including the Mesopotamians and the Chinese, used crude oil for medicinal purposes and as a waterproofing agent. However, oil as a global commodity began with the first modern commercial oil well:

1859—The Birth of the Modern Oil Industry: Edwin Drake drilled the first successful commercial oil well in Titusville, Pennsylvania, USA. This discovery sparked an oil boom and led to the rise of the modern petroleum industry.

Early twentieth Century—The Rise of Oil Giants: As automobiles and industrialization expanded, oil became a crucial energy source. Companies like Standard Oil (founded by John D. Rockefeller) emerged as dominant forces in the global oil market.

World Wars I & II—Oil as a Strategic Resource: The wars highlighted the significance of oil as a military asset. Control over oil fields became a key strategic goal, further embedding oil into global economic and political affairs.

Post-War Boom & The Middle East's Dominance: As oil demand soared, the Middle East emerged as the primary supplier. Countries such as Saudi Arabia, Iraq, Iran, Kuwait, and the UAE became dominant players due to their vast reserves.

Big Moves in recent history

The oil market has experienced several key events that have shaped its current structure. Understanding these moments provides insight into how oil prices react to supply disruptions, geopolitical shifts, and policy changes.

The 1973 Oil Crisis—The First Major Shock

In response to US support for Israel in the Yom Kippur War, the Organisation of the Petroleum Exporting Countries (OPEC) imposed an oil embargo against the United States and its allies.

Oil prices quadrupled in a matter of months, leading to economic turmoil and stagflation in Western economies.

The 1979 Iranian Revolution—Another Supply Shock

The Iranian Revolution caused a significant disruption in the global oil supply as production in Iran collapsed.

Oil prices doubled, further exacerbating inflation and economic instability worldwide.

The 1980s Oil Glut—A Price Collapse

OPEC attempted to maintain high oil prices by reducing production, but non-OPEC producers, such as the US and North Sea producers, increased supply.

Oil prices crashed by over 50%, leading to economic hardship in oil-dependent nations.

The 1991 Gulf War—Temporary Disruption
Iraq invaded Kuwait, threatening global oil supplies. The US-led Operation Desert Storm quickly intervened, and the market stabilized.

Oil prices initially surged but later stabilized as supply concerns eased.

The 2008 Financial Crisis—Demand Shock
Oil prices reached a record high of $147 per barrel in mid-2008 due to speculative demand and weakness of the US dollar.

The financial crisis caused a global economic slowdown, leading to a collapse in oil demand and a rapid price drop below $40 per barrel.

The 2014 Oil Price Crash—Oversupply & OPEC's Shift
A surge in US shale oil production led to a global oil oversupply.

OPEC, led by Saudi Arabia, refused to cut production, causing prices to plummet from $110 to $30 per barrel. Neither the US nor Saudi Arabia benefited from low oil prices, and it led to a war of attrition.

The 2020 COVID-19 Crash—Unprecedented Demand Destruction
The pandemic caused a historic collapse in oil demand as global travel and industry shut down.

Oil prices fell into negative territory (-$37 per barrel) for the first time in history, reflecting a lack of storage capacity and extreme market panic.

4.5.2 OPEC: The World's Most Powerful Cartel

What Is OPEC?
The Organisation of the Petroleum Exporting Countries (OPEC) was founded in 1960 to coordinate oil production and pricing among major oil-producing nations. By adjusting production levels, OPEC aims to stabilize oil markets and influence global prices.

OPEC is often called a cartel because it is a group of producers that collectively controls the oil supply to influence its price. Unlike a free market, where supply and demand determine price movements, OPEC sets production quotas among its members to keep oil prices at profitable levels.

How OPEC Controls Oil Prices:

Production Quotas: OPEC sets limits on the amount of oil each member can produce.

By restricting supply, they attempt to maintain higher prices.

Cutting Supply During Price Drops: If oil prices fall too low, OPEC members agree to cut production to raise prices.

Flooding the Market:

At times, OPEC has increased production to push prices lower, often to drive competitors (such as US shale producers) out of business.

OPEC decisions are not solely driven by supply and demand fundamentals; they are often politically motivated and crafted to serve the interests of member states and influence the economic landscape of oil-importing nations. By managing oil production and, consequently, global oil prices, OPEC can apply financial pressure on countries that depend heavily on imported energy. These actions carry significant geopolitical implications, affecting everything from inflation rates to trade balances and even foreign policy choices.

Oil as a Political Tool

Pressuring Economic Rivals—OPEC can raise oil prices by reducing production, which puts financial pressure on countries heavily reliant on oil imports. Conversely, they may flood the market with cheap oil to harm competitors or deter investment in alternative energy.

Influencing Inflation and Growth—Oil price increases can drive inflation in energy-dependent economies, prompting central banks to hike interest rates and potentially slow economic growth.

Responding to Geopolitical Conflicts—OPEC can utilize oil production as a bargaining tool in international negotiations, rewarding allies with lower prices or penalizing adversaries with higher costs.

OPEC Members (As of 2025):

Country	Region	Year Joined
Saudi Arabia	Middle East	1960
Iraq	Middle East	1960
Iran	Middle East	1960
Kuwait	Middle East	1960
Venezuela	South America	1960
United Arab Emirates	Middle East	1967
Algeria	North Africa	1969

(continued)

(continued)

Country	Region	Year Joined
Nigeria	West Africa	1971
Libya	North Africa	1962
Angola	Central Africa	2007
Equatorial Guinea	Central Africa	2017
Republic of the Congo	Central Africa	2018

OPEC +

In 2016, OPEC expanded its influence by forming OPEC +, which includes Russia, Kazakhstan, Mexico, and other oil producers. OPEC + coordinates production decisions to stabilize prices, making it a powerful force in the global oil market.

OPEC Vs Russia—the 2020 Oil Price War

OPEC has historically maintained its dominance in the oil market through coordinated production cuts among its members. However, tensions occasionally arise when non-OPEC producers, particularly Russia, fail to comply with agreed-upon production reductions. One of the most significant examples occurred in March 2020, triggering an oil price war that sent global crude prices into a tailspin.

As the COVID-19 pandemic began to spread globally in early 2020, economies shut down, and oil demand plummeted. Airlines grounded fleets, factories shut down, and transportation activity dropped to historic lows. Given the collapsing demand, OPEC proposed deep production cuts to stabilize oil prices and prevent a market oversupply that would drive prices even lower.

At an emergency meeting in Vienna in March 2020, OPEC proposed cutting oil production by 1.5 million barrels per day (bpd) to offset the sharp drop in demand. Russia, a key OPEC + member, was expected to support the plan.

However, Russia refused to comply, stating it was unwilling to sacrifice market share, primarily while US shale oil production remained high. Russian officials argued that if OPEC + cut output, they would give up ground to US shale producers, who would continue pumping oil and taking a larger share of the global market.

This refusal surprised OPEC, especially Saudi Arabia, which had expected Russia to cooperate. Lacking a consensus, Saudi Arabia reacted strongly by initiating a price war.

Angered by Russia's refusal to cut, Saudi Arabia slashed its official selling prices (OSP) for crude oil and announced plans to increase production to over 12 million barrels per day—a massive jump from its previous levels. This was a direct move to flood the market with cheap oil, putting pressure on Russia and US shale producers.

The consequences were catastrophic for oil prices:

Brent crude, the international benchmark, plunged from $50 per barrel in early March to below $20 per barrel by April 2020.

West Texas Intermediate (WTI), the US benchmark, suffered an unprecedented collapse, briefly trading at -$37 per barrel on April 20, 2020, as storage capacity filled up and traders rushed to offload contracts.

A Forced Agreement

As oil prices plummeted, Russia and Saudi Arabia recognized the extent of the damage they had caused—not just to each other but also to their economies. With oil prices well below the level needed to sustain government budgets, both sides were compelled to return to the negotiation table.

In April 2020, a historic deal was struck between OPEC, Russia, and other OPEC + members to cut production by 9.7 million barrels per day—the largest oil production cut in history. The agreement helped stabilize the market, and oil prices gradually recovered in the following months.

Lessons from the 2020 Oil Price War

OPEC's Influence Has Limits—While OPEC can coordinate production among its core members, it relies on compliance from external partners like Russia. When major producers refuse to cooperate, OPEC's control over the market weakens.

Oil Markets Can Collapse Without Coordination—The breakdown in cooperation between Saudi Arabia and Russia led to an oversupplied market and historic price crashes, proving that a lack of coordination can be disastrous.

Politics and Market Share Can Drive Policy—Russia's refusal to cut production was not purely economic; it was also a strategic move to challenge US shale producers. This highlights the role of geopolitics in oil market decisions.

OPEC + remains fragile—Although OPEC + agreements offer stability, they are continually under pressure. Members frequently priorities their own interests, making adherence an ongoing challenge.

The Power Struggles Within OPEC +

The 2020 oil price war demonstrated that although OPEC wields significant influence in oil markets, its ability to set prices is limited when major non-OPEC producers, like Russia, refuse to cooperate. This event also exposed the fragility of alliances within OPEC + and how quickly oil markets can spiral out of control when key players pursue their own interests rather than collaborate.

Although OPEC has traditionally wielded significant influence over the global oil market, the landscape is continually changing as new economic and geopolitical factors emerge. A notable example of this was in October 2022, when OPEC + announced a production cut of 2 million barrels per day, despite high global inflation and energy shortages caused by the Russia-Ukraine conflict.

OPEC + vs. The West: A Political Standoff

Western nations, led by the US, urged OPEC to boost production to ease inflationary pressures and reduce energy prices, which had surged due to sanctions on Russian oil.

OPEC +, led by Saudi Arabia and Russia, refused and instead reduced production, keeping prices high.

This move guaranteed higher revenues for oil-exporting nations, especially Russia, which was facing economic sanctions and relied on oil income to sustain its economy and war efforts.

Many analysts viewed this as a strategic alignment between OPEC and Russia, undermining Western sanctions and economic policies aimed at reducing Moscow's oil revenue.

Strained US-Saudi Relations

This decision heightened tensions between Saudi Arabia and the US, with Washington accusing OPEC of intentionally impairing global economic recovery. Some US officials even proposed retaliatory measures, including:

Releasing oil from the US Strategic Petroleum Reserve to offset OPEC's cuts.

Legislative actions (such as the NOPEC bill) challenge OPEC's capacity to coordinate supply decisions.

Reevaluating the long-standing US-Saudi alliance, which had traditionally centered on energy and security cooperation.

However, Saudi Arabia and OPEC defended their actions, arguing that oil markets require stability and that political interference should not determine production policy.

A Shifting Power Balance?

This event marked a turning point in OPEC's role in global energy politics, highlighting that:

OPEC is willing to prioritize its own economic and political interests over traditional alliances with Western nations.

Geopolitical partnerships between Saudi Arabia and Russia are becoming increasingly significant in shaping oil market dynamics.

The West's ability to influence oil prices through diplomatic pressure on OPEC is weakening.

As the energy landscape evolves, traders and policymakers must recognize that OPEC's decision-making is not just about supply and demand—it is deeply tied to shifting geopolitical alliances and economic power struggles. Understanding these underlying motives is key to predicting future oil market movements and potential investment opportunities.

The oil market is as much about politics and power as it is about supply and demand. Understanding these dynamics is crucial for traders looking to capitalize on oil price fluctuations.

4.5.3 A Tale of Two Oils: Light Sweet Crude Vs. Brent Crude

Oil is often called "black gold," but not all oil is the same. Two of the most widely traded crude oil benchmarks globally are West Texas Intermediate (WTI), often known as Light Sweet Crude, and Brent Crude. These two types of oil set the global pricing standard for energy markets and serve as reference prices for millions of barrels traded daily.

Although both are crude oils, meaning they are unrefined petroleum products, WTI and Brent have different characteristics, origins, and pricing behaviors that distinguish them. Recognizing these differences is essential for traders, investors, and businesses affected by oil prices.

What Defines Light Sweet Crude and Brent Crude?

West Texas Intermediate (WTI)—Light Sweet Crude

Origin: WTI is sourced primarily from the Permian Basin and other oil fields in the United States, particularly in Texas, Oklahoma, and North Dakota.

API Gravity: 39.6 (light crude, meaning it flows more easily and is less dense).

Sulphur Content: 0.24% (low sulphur, making it "sweet").

Primary Trading Hub: Delivered at Cushing, Oklahoma, a central oil storage and pipeline hub.

Uses: Preferred by US refineries due to its low sulphur content, which makes it easier to refine into gasoline and diesel.

Brent Crude

Origin: Brent is extracted from oil fields in the North Sea, mainly in the UK and Norway, and is also used as a benchmark for Middle East oil.

API Gravity: 38 (also light, but slightly heavier than WTI).

Sulphur Content: 0.37% (still classified as sweet, but slightly higher sulphur content than WTI).

Primary Trading Hub: Delivered at various North Sea terminals and traded internationally.

Uses: Brent is more widely consumed in Europe, Africa, and Asia due to its flexibility for global shipping.

Both crudes are light and sweet, making them highly desirable for refining into fuels like gasoline and jet fuel. However, their pricing varies due to factors such as geography, refining demand, and market infrastructure.

Why Is There a Price Disparity? WTI vs. Brent Spread, Also Known as 'The Arb'

While WTI and Brent are both benchmark oils, Brent typically trades at a premium to WTI—a difference known as the WTI-Brent spread. Several key factors contribute to this price divergence:

Geographic Location and Transportation Costs

Brent is a seaborne crude, making it easier to transport globally via oil tankers.

WTI is landlocked, meaning its transportation depends on pipelines and storage facilities within the US. If pipeline capacity is limited, excess WTI supply can accumulate in Cushing, Oklahoma, causing WTI prices to fall relative to Brent.

Global vs. Regional Pricing Dynamics

Brent is the global benchmark for oil, influencing around 75% of the world's traded crude. This makes it more susceptible to international geopolitical events, supply disruptions, and OPEC decisions. WTI better reflects US supply and demand fundamentals. The growth of US shale oil production has increased WTI supply, exacerbating the price discount relative to Brent.

Supply and Demand Factors
Brent crude production has been gradually declining as North Sea oil fields mature, keeping supply relatively tight.

WTI production has surged in recent years due to the US shale revolution, leading to periodic oversupply, which pressures prices downward.

Refinery Preferences
Brent's slightly higher sulphur content makes it less attractive for US refiners, who prefer WTI for gasoline production.

Brent is better suited for European and Asian refineries, making it more in demand outside the US.

Geopolitical Risks and OPEC Influence
Brent crude is more susceptible to geopolitical risks, especially in the Middle East, Africa, and Russia, since it is priced based on global supply chains.

WTI is less affected by global tensions, as the US is essentially energy self-sufficient.

Historical WTI-Brent Price Differences
The price gap between WTI and Brent has fluctuated over time, reflecting changes in US oil production, global demand, and transportation constraints. Some key moments:

2011–2015: WTI traded at a steep discount (as much as $25 per barrel) as US shale oil production surged, but pipeline infrastructure couldn't keep up, leading to storage bottlenecks in Cushing.

2016–2019: The gap narrowed as pipeline expansions improved transportation from Cushing to Gulf Coast refineries.

2020 (COVID-19 Crash): WTI briefly traded negatively (-$37 per barrel) due to storage shortages, while Brent remained in positive territory, highlighting the impact of logistical constraints.

2022 (Russia-Ukraine War): Brent rose above WTI due to European energy shortages, widening the spread as global buyers rushed to buy non-Russian oil.

WTI and Brent crude oil are the two most influential global oil benchmarks, determining the price for trillions of dollars' worth of oil contracts each year. Although both are classified as light sweet crude, they differ significantly in their supply chains, transportation methods, refinery preferences, and global influence.

Brent crude plays a crucial role as the benchmark for Middle Eastern and African oil prices, linking it directly to OPEC pricing strategies.

The price spread between WTI and Brent reflects regional supply-demand dynamics, logistical constraints, and geopolitical factors. While WTI depends more on US infrastructure and production levels, Brent remains the world's preferred benchmark for globally traded oil.

Understanding these differences is essential for anyone involved in the oil markets, whether as a producer, refiner, or investor. The energy landscape is constantly evolving, and as new challenges and opportunities emerge, the relationship between WTI and Brent will remain a key indicator of global economic health and energy demand.

What Moves the Oil Markets?

We have established that oil is the lifeblood of the global economy, powering everything from transportation and industrial production to petrochemicals and electricity generation. Even with the worldwide push towards renewable energy and a reduced dependency on fossil fuels, history shows that energy consumption has never decreased—only increased as economies develop, populations grow, and new technologies generate additional energy demand.

The oil market is one of the most heavily traded and strategically important markets worldwide. It is not merely a commodity; it serves as a geopolitical tool, a catalyst for inflation, and a crucial factor in economic stability. The price of oil can determine the fate of nations, influencing government policies, corporate earnings, and consumer purchasing power. Due to its significance, the oil market is highly volatile, responding to a broad, interconnected range of influences.

To successfully trade oil, invest in energy markets, or understand how price movements influence the broader economy, you need to grasp key supply-and-demand factors, geopolitical risks, economic cycles, technological advancements, market speculation, and the influence of OPEC and other major producers.

In this chapter, we will break down the main drivers of oil prices, why they fluctuate so much, and what causes significant shifts in the Brent-WTI spread.

Supply and Demand Fundamentals

Like any market, oil prices are fundamentally determined by supply and demand. When supply exceeds demand, prices fall. When demand outstrips supply, prices rise. However, oil's unique role as a strategic and non-renewable resource means that these fluctuations are often exaggerated. Let's break this down further:

Global Supply Factors

Production Levels: The world's largest oil producers—including OPEC members, the US, Russia, and Canada—control most of the global supply. Any unexpected increase or decrease in production can cause prices to fluctuate significantly.

OPEC Production Decisions:

As a cartel, OPEC + (OPEC plus Russia and allies) can influence oil prices by controlling supply. When OPEC cuts production, oil prices typically increase.

Conversely, when output rises, prices usually fall.

US Shale Oil Production:

The US, particularly through shale oil, has become one of the world's leading swing producers. Unlike OPEC, which adjusts output collectively, shale production is prompted by market-driven investment decisions.

Geopolitical Supply Disruptions:

Wars, sanctions, and natural disasters can disrupt supply chains, limit available oil and push prices higher.

Strategic Reserves Releases:

Governments, particularly the US Strategic Petroleum Reserve (SPR), sometimes release oil to stabilize prices during crises.

Global Demand Factors

Economic Growth:

The stronger the global economy, the more energy is consumed. Booming economies drive higher oil demand, while recessions reduce it.

Industrial and Transportation Demand:

The transportation sector accounts for roughly 60% of global oil consumption, while industry and petrochemicals also drive significant demand.

Seasonality:

Winter heating demand, summer travel season, and hurricane season in the Gulf of Mexico can all cause seasonal price fluctuations.

Technological Advancements:

Innovations in energy efficiency, electric vehicles, and alternative fuels can reduce long-term demand growth.

Trade Study: The 2020 Oil Price Crash and How London Traders Made Millions Using TAS

One of the most dramatic moments in oil trading history occurred on 20 April 2020, when West Texas Intermediate (WTI) crude oil futures dipped into negative territory for the first time, settling at -£37.63 per barrel. This event was unprecedented and caught many market participants off guard. Nonetheless, a handful of shrewd traders in London managed to capitalize on the chaos, making millions using TAS (Trade-at-Settlement) orders.

The Perfect Storm Leading to Negative Oil Prices

In early 2020, the COVID-19 pandemic crippled the global economy. With widespread lockdowns, travel restrictions, and factory shutdowns, oil demand plummeted almost overnight. Airlines were grounded, cars remained parked, and industrial activity nearly came to a halt, leading to a significant oversupply of oil.

At the same time, the OPEC + price war between Saudi Arabia and Russia led to a surge in oil production just as demand collapsed. The result? Global storage tanks were filling rapidly, and there was nowhere left to store excess crude oil.

The main issue was in Cushing, Oklahoma, the delivery hub for WTI crude oil futures. The available storage was almost full, and traders who still held long positions in the May WTI futures contract—due to expire the next day—had nowhere to take physical delivery. As desperation grew, holders of the contracts began paying buyers to take the oil off their hands, causing prices to go deeply negative for the first time in history.

How Traders in London Profited From the Move Using TAS Orders

While many traders and funds experienced significant losses, a small group of sophisticated traders in London recognized an extraordinary opportunity. They implemented their strategy using Trade-at-Settlement (TAS) orders, a mechanism in futures trading that enables traders to enter or exit a position at the settlement price.

Anticipating the Storage Crisis—These traders foresaw the inevitable storage shortage and recognized that WTI crude oil futures could fall sharply as the contract expiry date drew near.

Using TAS Orders to Lock in Settlement Prices—Instead of taking outright speculative directional positions, they placed TAS orders to buy at settlement, ensuring they would receive the final closing price of the day, regardless of how low it went. Then they bought back their WTI shorts when the price plummeted.

Profiting from Forced Liquidation—As desperate traders still holding the May WTI contract desperately tried to offload their positions before expiry, selling pressure surged sharply in the final trading hours. With no storage options available, traders were willing to pay to dispose of contracts, pushing prices deeply into negative territory.

The result was a series of extraordinary payouts. By shorting WTI futures and simultaneously buying TAS contracts near zero, these traders locked in the spread between their short sale prices and the eventual settlement. No one in the market anticipated such a historic collapse into negative pricing—not even the London traders who captured it. When WTI settled at—$37.63, the TAS buys effectively crystallized a gain of $37.63 per barrel. Those who had positioned aggressively reportedly made tens of millions of pounds in a single session, marking one of the most remarkable trading outcomes in modern market history.

Why This Event Was Historic

For the first time in history, crude oil traded negatively: A sign of extreme market dysfunction.

Exposed flaws in oil futures contract structure: Cushing storage constraints meant physical traders couldn't take delivery.

Highlighted the role of algorithmic traders and arbitrageurs: London's TAS traders understood market structure well enough to exploit the forced liquidation scenario.

Lessons from the 2020 Oil Crash

Understanding Market Structure Matters—Unlike stock markets, Oil futures have physical delivery constraints. A contract's expiry can force traders into liquidation if they don't have the means to take delivery.

Liquidity Can Disappear Instantly—just because a market is liquid today doesn't guarantee it will be tomorrow. The swift exit of buyers turned a $10 oil contract into a -$37.63 in a matter of hours.

Trade-at-Settlement (TAS) Strategies Can Be Powerful—This event showcased the potential for TAS orders to create asymmetric profit opportunities, especially during extreme volatility.

The 2020 oil price crash was one of the most extraordinary trading events in financial history. While many suffered significant losses, a select group of traders in London turned the chaos into profit by exploiting weaknesses in market structures. Their ability to anticipate storage constraints, contract expiry effects, and forced liquidations enabled them to execute one of the most profitable TAS trades ever recorded.

This event acts as a clear reminder that understanding futures market mechanics can open up substantial trading opportunities, particularly during periods of extreme stress.

4.5.4 Oil Futures and Derivatives You Can Trade

Beyond Brent and WTI crude oil futures, traders utilize several oil-related derivatives to speculate, hedge, or arbitrage price differences in refined products and alternative crude grades. Below is a table of the most actively traded oil derivatives futures and the exchanges where they are listed.

Oil Derivative	Symbol	Exchange	Description
WTI Crude Oil	CL	NYMEX (CME)	Benchmark for US oil
Brent Crude Oil	BZ or BRN	ICE Futures Europe	Benchmark for Middle East/Europe oil
RBOB Gasoline	RB	NYMEX (CME)	Gasoline blend stock futures
Ultra Low Sulfur Diesel (Heating Oil)	HO	NYMEX (CME)	Diesel and heating fuel futures
Gasoil	GO	ICE Futures Europe	European diesel benchmark
WTI Midland Crude	WTC	ICE Futures US	Light sweet crude from Texas
Dubai Crude	DC	DME (Dubai Mercantile Exchange)	Middle Eastern crude oil futures
Oman Crude	OQD	ICE Futures Europe	Gulf-region crude benchmark
Fuel Oil 3.5% FOB Rotterdam	FU	ICE Futures Europe	Fuel oil used in shipping and power
Jet Fuel	JET	NYMEX (CME)	Aviation fuel pricing benchmark

By diversifying into these markets, traders can hedge crude oil positions, speculate on refined product prices, or capitalize on spread opportunities between different oil products.

How to Make Money Trading Oil Futures

Oil remains one of the world's most speculative and actively traded markets. A complex interplay of supply and demand fundamentals, geopolitics, and market speculation drives its price movements. As the lifeblood of the global economy, oil plays a crucial role in fueling transportation and industrial production and even shaping global politics, underscoring its immense significance.

As a result, the oil market offers significant opportunities for traders, especially in the futures sector. Crude oil prices can fluctuate by several dollars daily, and during major geopolitical events or supply disruptions, movements of over $10 are common. This volatility provides countless opportunities for traders who understand the market's structure and price behavior.

Unlike traditional investors who might own physical barrels of oil, traders speculate solely on price movements without ever taking delivery. Whether oil is rallying or crashing, as long as you're on the right side of the trend, there's money to be made.

This chapter will break down how to profit from trading oil futures, key strategies used by professionals, and how oil derivatives expand trading opportunities beyond WTI Crude and Brent Crude.

The Foundations of the Oil Futures Markets

Before diving into strategies, let's quickly recap the key oil futures markets:

WTI Crude Oil (West Texas Intermediate)
Symbol: CL
Exchange: CME (NYMEX)

Description: WTI is the US benchmark crude oil, primarily sourced from Texas and surrounding states.

Characteristics: Light, sweet crude (low sulphur), ideal for gasoline refining.

Key Factors: US production, storage levels, pipeline constraints, and geopolitical risks affecting North America.

Brent Crude Oil
Symbol: BZ or BRN
Exchange: ICE Futures Europe

Description: Brent is the global oil benchmark used for pricing two-thirds of the world's oil contracts.

Characteristics: Slightly heavier than WTI but still considered high-quality crude.

Key Factors: OPEC policies, European and Middle Eastern production, geopolitical tensions, and global demand trends.

These two crude oil benchmarks underpin global oil pricing, and their price spread—the Brent-WTI spread—can also be traded.

Beyond these, the oil market extends to refined products and regional crude grades (as shown in the earlier table), creating even more opportunities.

What do the Pros do?

I enjoy trading the two oil contracts—WTI Crude and Brent Crude. The fundamental dynamics of the oil market are genuinely captivating. Imagine a group of countries with questionable morals and contrasting belief systems, holding a bountiful supply of black gold pouring out from the ground. These nations use their fortunate position to increase their power, influence, and collection of gold-plated cars, leveraging their resources to compete for global recognition and dominance.

The oil market is more than just a financial transaction—it's a dynamic saga filled with villains and heroes. Sadly, when the story unfolds, the repercussions for humanity can be dire. Disputes over oil have sparked wars, economic downturns, and political turmoil, with ordinary people bearing the brunt of the cost.

As a trader, you must accept that these events are beyond your control. While you may sympathize with those affected by war, terrorism, and economic hardship, your job is to trade these events as efficiently as possible. This is the role you have chosen as a market participant—one that demands objectivity, discipline, and the ability to filter news for profitable opportunities.

The greatest opportunities in oil trading almost always stem from some form of conflict, whether verbal or military. In my 20 years of trading oil, I can't recall a single year that passed without a war, terrorist attack, or political standoff causing the market to fluctuate dramatically. The only exception might have been during the COVID-19 pandemic, and, ironically, that period felt far more frightening than any war—for a moment, we all feared that civilization as we knew it could be wiped out by a virus.

This is why it is crucial to follow global news and connect it to the oil market. The ability to interpret geopolitical developments and evaluate their effect on oil supply and demand distinguishes professionals from amateurs.

The professionals understand:

- Who the biggest producers are.
- Who the biggest consumers are.
- What's happening in these key locations geopolitically.
- How global political tensions are affecting the production and transportation of oil.
- How much physical oil is currently "floating"—in times of low crude prices, physical producers often hire VLCCs and store the oil offshore until prices increase before delivering to refineries to maximize profits.

When I've taught junior traders or coached more advanced market participants, understanding these elements is essential to have a chance of beating the market.

Just as with trading currencies, bonds, and STIRs, oil trading is heavily influenced by supply-and-demand fundamentals. Understanding these fundamentals helps professionals anticipate market movements and position themselves ahead of the herd.

The oil market is one of the world's most volatile and strategically important markets.

Professional traders stay ahead of the game by tracking these key factors:

1. OPEC Strategies: Supply cuts, quota adjustments, and political leverage.
2. Supply & Demand Shifts: Inventory data, infrastructure damage, and economic trends.
3. Regulatory Changes: Government interventions affecting production and consumption.
4. Geopolitical Risks: Wars, sanctions, and terrorist threats.

By understanding these drivers, traders can position themselves in advance of major market moves, ensuring they profit from oil price fluctuations rather than reacting after the event.

Why the Oil Market Favors the Upside—a Bull's Tale

Apart from the pandemic, most major price movements in the oil market—driven by breaking news—tend to push prices up rather than down. This has led to a strong presence of long-only traders and funds whose main goal is to profit from rising oil prices.

The reason behind this bias is simple: market dynamics structurally favor higher prices.

The Role of OPEC and Supply Manipulation

One of the main reasons oil tends to rise is that it operates in a semi-controlled market. Unlike many commodities, which fluctuate solely on supply and demand, oil prices are actively managed by a cartel—OPEC—that aims to influence prices in its favor.

OPEC manages about 40% of worldwide oil output and frequently adjusts quotas to keep prices steady or push them higher.

Production cuts are among the most common tools used to tighten supply, often causing artificially high price spikes.

Unlike other markets, where oversupply can lead to prolonged price declines, oil producers can choose to produce less to keep prices stable.

Trade Study: OPEC Production Cuts (2022)

In October 2022, OPEC + announced a 2 million-barrel-per-day production cut, despite Western pleas to increase output. This move immediately pushed oil prices higher, reinforcing the cartel's power to control supply and sustain higher price levels.

The "Crisis Premium" in Oil

Unlike stocks or bonds, oil prices react disproportionately to geopolitical instability.

Wars, conflicts, and supply chain disruptions typically cause prices to surge because the market fears supply shortages.

Unlike other financial assets, where uncertainty can cause panic selling, oil thrives on uncertainty—traders tend to buy crude in anticipation of higher prices.

Trade Study: Saudi Aramco Attack (2019)

In September 2019, drone strikes on Saudi Arabia's Abqaiq oil facility temporarily took out 5% of the world's crude supply. Oil prices jumped 15% overnight, marking the largest one-day increase in oil history.

The Nature of Demand: Oil is Essential

Oil is one of the few markets where demand is almost non-negotiable.

Unlike luxury goods or discretionary purchases, energy is an absolute necessity for economic function.

Even during recessions, industries, transportation networks, and households require oil, ensuring that demand rarely collapses completely.

The global shift towards green energy is happening, but history shows that total energy consumption of a resource has never shrunk—only increased.

Trade Study: Oil Demand Resilience Post-COVID

After the pandemic-induced collapse in April 2020, when oil briefly traded at negative prices, demand rebounded sharply in 2021–2022. As economies reopened, crude prices surged past $100 per barrel.

The Presence of Long-Only Funds

The oil market has historically attracted institutional and retail funds that are structurally long.

Many funds only take long positions, expecting oil prices to rise over time.

This has created a persistent buying bias in the market, where dips are frequently met with aggressive buying.

Large financial players, including pension and hedge funds, allocate capital to oil as a hedge against inflation and global uncertainty.

Trade Study: Inflation and Oil as a Hedge (2022)

As global inflation surged in 2022, institutional investors flocked to oil as a hedge, further pushing prices higher.

So . . . Should You Only Buy Oil?

I'm not saying that you need to buy oil, but if timed correctly, going long can be one of the most profitable trades available.

When you combine:

1. OPEC's structural manipulation to support prices
2. The market's tendency to rally on geopolitical tensions
3. The fact that demand rarely collapses completely
4. The presence of long-only funds backing the market

. . . it becomes clear why oil has historically favored the upside.

As a trader, your job is to identify the right moments to get long, whether that's during a crisis, after an OPEC decision, or when technical levels align with bullish fundamentals.

4.5.5 Arbitraging the Brent-WTI Spread

A popular trade among professional oil traders is Brent-WTI crude oil arbitrage. This spread trade capitalizes on the relative price differences between the two major oil benchmarks, which can become exaggerated during times of crisis, offering compelling counter-trend opportunities.

Although both Brent and WTI crude oil serve as global benchmarks, they differ in terms of geography, supply chains, and pricing mechanisms:

Brent Crude – The global benchmark used for pricing Middle Eastern, European, and African oil and is heavily influenced by geopolitical risks.

WTI Crude – Primarily tied to North American production and logistics, with its price driven more by US domestic factors.

Because Brent is more exposed to international shipping disruptions, OPEC policies, and geopolitical risks, it often trades at a premium to WTI. However, at times, this spread expands or contracts excessively, presenting profitable trading opportunities.

Although I have traded the Brent-WTI spread less frequently over my career, I have been inclined to intervene when it reaches extreme highs or lows, presenting clear arbitrage opportunities.

My Approach to Trading the Spread:

Buy WTI & Sell Brent when the spread is too wide, expecting it to narrow.

Sell WTI & Buy Brent when the spread is too tight, expecting it to widen.

This strategy is based on the principle of relative value trading, which states that two related assets should maintain a predictable price relationship over time.

When an asset's price deviates significantly from its historical or fundamental value relative to another asset, traders anticipate that market forces will eventually correct the imbalance, bringing the prices back into alignment. This can occur if there is extreme weather in the US but not in the EU, and vice versa.

In the case of Brent and WTI:

If Brent becomes excessively expensive relative to WTI, it suggests that geopolitical concerns or temporary supply disruptions have inflated Brent's price beyond its fundamental value. Traders will expect it to fall back in line.

If WTI trades at an unusually tight discount to Brent, it may indicate that US oil supply bottlenecks or refinery issues have artificially suppressed WTI prices. The expectation is that once these short-term disruptions clear, the spread will widen again.

This type of trading is often used in professional markets, where traders seek more than just directional moves: they aim for assets to revert to their typical pricing relationships. The key to trading Brent-WTI successfully is understanding the historical range of the spread, seasonal patterns, recognizing the forces causing the deviation, and knowing when those forces are likely to diminish.

Crack Spreads and Their Role in Oil Trading

The most experienced oil traders I know always have a clear understanding of where the crack spreads are trading. Although I have never traded them extensively myself, I have always recognized their significance and their ability to influence oil markets. Having a good grasp of refining margins is essential for any trader operating within the energy sector.

The crack spread is one of the most commonly used indicators of refining profitability. It measures the difference between the cost of crude oil and the market prices of refined petroleum products such as petrol, diesel, and heating oil. This spread serves as a vital gauge for refiners, as it directly influences their margins and decision-making.

Since oil refiners buy crude oil and sell refined products, they are effectively long refined products and short crude oil. The crack spread provides a means to hedge against fluctuations in refining margins. For traders, it presents opportunities to speculate on changes in supply, demand, and seasonal refinery trends.

Understanding the Crack Spread

The crack spread is quoted as the difference in price between crude oil and refined products. Refining a barrel of crude generally produces a mix of products, including petrol, diesel, jet fuel, and heating oil. Since refineries operate on fixed margins, monitoring these spreads helps decide whether it is more profitable to refine crude or keep it in storage.

The wider the crack spread, the more profitable refining oil becomes. A narrower crack spread indicates lower margins for refiners, which could lead to reduced refinery activity or, in severe cases, shutdowns.

Key Crack Spread Ratios and Their Uses

3:2:1 Crack Spread (Most Commonly Used)

Formula:

Buy 3 barrels of crude oil

Sell 2 barrels of gasoline

Sell 1 barrel of distillate (diesel or heating oil)

This spread is the industry benchmark, particularly in the US, where refineries typically produce two parts gasoline to one part distillate from a barrel of WTI crude oil.

If gasoline and distillate prices rise faster than crude oil, the crack spread widens, benefiting refiners.

If gasoline and distillate prices fall relative to crude oil, the spread narrows, making refining less profitable.

Trade Study:

During the summer US driving season, gasoline demand surges, often widening the 3:2:1 crack spread.

Traders anticipating this might go long on gasoline futures and short crude oil futures to profit from the seasonal increase in refining margins.

2:1:1 Crack Spread (Balanced Refining Model)
Formula:

Buy 2 barrels of crude oil
Sell 1 barrel of gasoline
Sell 1 barrel of distillate

Represents a more balanced refinery output, where diesel demand is expected to be stronger than gasoline.

This is more significant in Europe and Asia, where diesel and heating oil are used more than petrol.

Trade Study:

If distillate prices rise faster than gasoline, traders might prefer the 2:1:1 crack spread over the 3:2:1.

5:3:2 Crack Spread (European Refinery Model)
Formula:

Buy 5 barrels of crude oil
Sell 3 barrels of gasoline
Sell 2 barrels of distillate

Popular in Europe, where Diesel consumption is higher relative to gasoline than in the US.

Reflects the refining dynamics of Brent crude oil rather than WTI.

Additional Spreads in Oil Trading

Gasoline vs. Distillate Spreads (Heat Crack & RBOB Crack)

Refiners and traders compare the profitability of gasoline vs. diesel or heating oil.

Trade study. Ahead of winter, heating oil demand spikes, widening the heating oil crack spread relative to gasoline.

A trader expecting this might go long heating oil futures and short gasoline futures.

Jet Fuel vs. Diesel Arbitrage
If jet fuel prices rise faster than diesel, traders may go long jet fuel futures and short diesel futures to take advantage of demand shifts.

Trade study. After the pandemic recovery, air travel demand rebounded, pushing jet fuel prices above diesel prices.

How Traders and Refiners Profit from Crack Spreads
Refiners Hedging Their Margins

Oil refiners hedge their future margins by locking in crack spreads to secure profitability.

If a refiner expects lower margins, they may hedge by selling crude futures and buying gasoline/diesel futures.

Speculators Trading Crack Spreads

Traders buy or sell crack spreads based on seasonal demand, supply disruptions, and refining trends.

If refiners are operating at full capacity due to high demand, crack spreads typically widen, creating trading opportunities.

Arbitrage Crack Spreads in Different Regions
Spreads between US, European, and Asian refining margins can create arbitrage opportunities.

If gasoline prices are higher in Asia than in the US, traders may buy gasoline in the US and sell it in Asian markets.

Why Crack Spreads Matter to Traders?

Predicting Refinery Profitability: Helps anticipate refinery shutdowns or production shifts.

Understanding Seasonal Trends: Gasoline spreads widen in summer, and heating oil spreads widen in winter.

Identifying Arbitrage Trades: Regional Spreads Create Global Opportunities.
For serious oil traders, keeping an eye on crack spreads is essential, whether or not they trade them directly. They provide key insights into the profitability of refining and the broader oil-market supply-and-demand balance.

A lot to take in at first glance, but throughout a healthy trading career, I'm sure you will get time to investigate these trading opportunities. You 100% won't if I don't tell you about them.

Key Fundamentals That Move Oil Prices
All market participants rely on a handful of high-impact reports that give insights into global supply and demand conditions:

EIA Weekly Crude Oil Inventory Report (Wednesdays)
Published by the US Energy Information Administration (EIA), this report shows changes in US crude oil stockpiles.

A bigger-than-expected inventory draw signals stronger demand → Oil prices rise.

A larger-than-expected inventory build suggests oversupply → Oil prices fall.

As a side note, something I picked up over the years is that a private analytics firm regularly flies drones over the Cushing storage hub in Oklahoma, providing early estimates of inventory levels. Their data is delivered to clients on a Monday—a full two days before the official EIA release—giving those subscribers a noticeable informational edge in a market where storage shifts can move prices sharply.

OPEC Monthly Oil Market Report
Released by the Organisation of the Petroleum Exporting Countries (OPEC), this report provides details on oil production levels, demand forecasts, and policy direction.

If OPEC announces production cuts, it signals tighter supply → oil prices rise.

If OPEC increases output, it suggests oversupply → oil prices fall.

US Rig Count (Baker Hughes Report—Fridays)
Tracks the number of active oil rigs in the US, providing insights into future US crude production.

A rising rig count signals increased future production. → Oil prices could decline.

A declining rig count suggests a potential supply squeeze → Oil prices could rise.

IEA (International Energy Agency) Reports
The IEA Oil Market Report provides a global outlook on supply and demand trends.

Changes in global energy demand forecasts impact trader sentiment, particularly for long-term positioning.

Chinese Crude Imports Data
As China is one of the largest oil consumers, any changes in its oil imports impact global prices.

Higher-than-expected crude imports → Oil demand is strong, and prices increase.

Lower-than-expected imports → Demand concerns, prices fall.

Trade Study: How Inventory Data Moves the Market

One of the most consistent drivers of short-term price movements in the oil market is the release of inventory data, especially the EIA Weekly Crude Oil Inventory Report. Professional traders vigilantly monitor these figures, which offer real-time insights into supply and demand imbalances in the US, the world's largest oil consumer and producer.

Trade Scenario: A Surprise Draw in US Crude Inventories

Market Expectations: Traders expect a build in crude stockpiles, indicating more supply than demand, which would typically weaken oil prices.

Data Release: When the EIA report is published, it instead shows a larger-than-expected drawdown in inventories, indicating that demand is outpacing supply.

Market Reaction: As a result, WTI crude oil surges by $2 per barrel within minutes as traders scramble to adjust their positions.

4.5.6 Anticipation Vs. Reaction in Fundamental Trading

As with all fundamental trading, anticipation and reaction are absolutely crucial in successfully trading oil markets.

Anticipation:
A professional trader who analyzed market conditions beforehand and anticipated an inventory drawdown could have taken a long position before the data release.

If their forecast proved correct, they would have captured the entire price movement as oil surged on the unexpected supply shortfall, resulting in substantial profits.

This strategy involves greater risk—if the data released differed from expectations, the market could have moved against the position.

Reaction:
An alternative strategy is to wait for the actual data release and then enter a trade based on the market's reaction.

Once the inventory report confirmed a drawdown, traders who quickly bought oil contracts could have ridden the move's momentum as prices surged.

This approach is generally lower risk, as the trade is executed with confirmation of the fundamental catalyst. However, it may capture a smaller share of the price move than anticipation-based trades.

Both anticipation and reaction-based trading can be highly effective. The best traders master analyzing the fundamental setup in advance while remaining flexible enough to respond to market data as it unfolds.

We will explore the finer details of trading fundamentals later in the book when we fully cover the trade process, as we look into how to use them and where to find the information needed to make thoughtful and profitable trading decisions.

4.6 Natural Gas: The Market Fueled by Mother Nature

Natural gas is one of the most volatile markets in the world—perhaps the most volatile I have ever traded. Unlike crude oil, which is influenced by geopolitical events and supply factors, natural gas prices can be driven by as unpredictable a factor as the weather. A sudden cold snap or an unexpected hurricane can cause prices to surge, while mild winter forecasts or oversupply can lead to sharp declines. This volatility makes it an exciting yet challenging market to trade, attracting speculators, hedge funds, and even giants like Mark Zuckerberg and Ray Dalio, as we'll explore in case studies later in the chapter.

Natural gas is a fossil fuel primarily composed of methane, found in underground reservoirs. It is utilized for generating electricity, heating, and as an industrial feedstock. Due to its essential role in energy production, natural gas is extensively traded in futures markets and forms a vital part of the global energy system.

The most actively traded natural gas futures contract is the Henry Hub Natural Gas (NG) contract, listed on the New York Mercantile Exchange (NYMEX) and part of the CME Group. Henry Hub, located in Louisiana, is the benchmark for US natural gas prices. Other major natural gas markets include:

TTF (Title Transfer Facility)—Europe's benchmark (traded on ICE Europe)

NBP (National Balancing Point)—UK benchmark (traded on ICE)

JKM (Japan-Korea Marker)—Asian LNG benchmark (used for liquefied natural gas pricing)

These benchmarks provide regional pricing references; however, the Henry Hub contract dominates global speculative trading, and it remains the primary focus for professional traders throughout the chapter.

The Story of Natural Gas: A Historical Perspective

Natural gas has been utilized for centuries, but its role in global markets has experienced significant development.

Some of the key milestones in the commodity's history.

500 BCE—The First Known Use: The Chinese used bamboo pipelines to transport natural gas from seeps to fuel stoves and lanterns.

1821—First Commercial Well: In the United States, William Hart drilled the first natural gas well in Fredonia, New York.

1950s—Expansion of Pipelines: The development of large-scale pipeline infrastructure in the U.S. and Europe enabled widespread use and trade.

1990s—Birth of Natural Gas Futures: NYMEX launched the Henry Hub Natural Gas Futures contract, which became the global benchmark for pricing.

2000s—The Shale Revolution: Advances in hydraulic fracturing (fracking) unlocked large natural gas reserves, leading to increased supply and lower prices. This revolution greatly benefited the U.S., transforming it into a major energy exporter, reducing dependence on foreign oil, boosting its economy, and lowering domestic energy costs.

2022—Russia-Ukraine War: A significant geopolitical shock that triggered an energy crisis in Europe, driving up TTF gas prices. The crisis revealed Europe's heavy dependence on Russian gas, with countries such as Germany, Italy, and Austria being among the most reliant. This reliance intensified the effects of supply disruptions, leading to sharp price increases.

Major Price Moves in Natural Gas

Natural gas is notorious for its price fluctuations. Unlike crude oil, where supply disruptions and OPEC policies affect prices, natural gas is highly weather-dependent. Many of the most extreme price changes are caused by this and other factors.

2000–2001—California Energy Crisis: Supply shortages and market manipulation (notably by Enron and other energy companies) led to a massive price spike.

2005—Hurricane Katrina: Major disruptions to Gulf Coast production led to a surge in prices.

2008—The Financial Crisis: Prices hit an all-time high of $13.69/MMBtu before collapsing amid plummeting demand.

2021—Texas Freeze (Winter Storm Uri): A sudden deep freeze led to power outages, sending natural gas prices surging by more than 1,000% in some regions.

2022—Russia-Ukraine War & European Energy Crisis: European natural gas (TTF) prices soared to over €300/MWh, five times their normal level, as Russia cut supplies to the continent.

Factors That Move Natural Gas Prices

Weather Patterns

Winter Cold: Increases heating demand, pushing prices higher.

Summer Heat: Drives power demand for air conditioning, boosting natural gas consumption.

Hurricanes: Can disrupt Gulf of Mexico production, leading to price spikes.

Storage Levels & Inventory Data

EIA Natural Gas Storage Report (Thursdays): Monitors the amount of gas stored underground. A larger-than-expected draw indicates strong demand, increasing prices.

LNG Exports

The U.S. is now a leading LNG exporter, meaning global events (e.g., demand in Asia or Europe) can impact U.S. natural gas prices.

Production & Supply Chain Constraints

Pipeline disruptions, regulatory policies, and drilling activity all affect supply levels.

Speculation & Algorithmic Trading

Natural gas futures are heavily traded by hedge funds and algorithmic traders, contributing to exaggerated price swings.

Taken together, these factors make natural gas one of the most dynamic and reactive markets globally. Prices seldom move for a single reason; instead, it is the constant interaction between weather, storage, exports, production, and speculative flows that causes the sharp swings traders are all too familiar with. Understanding how each element influences the others is what differentiates guesswork from informed decision-making. For professionals, the aim is not to predict every twist, but to recognize the conditions that shift the odds—and to position accordingly.

How Professional Traders Approach Natural Gas Markets

Case Study: Mark Zuckerberg's Natural Gas Trade

Mark Zuckerberg, best known for founding Facebook, has an intriguing link to the natural gas market. Before establishing Facebook, he reportedly traded natural gas contracts during his university years, gaining early experience in financial markets.

In 2022, Zuckerberg made headlines for a $100 million wager on natural gas markets through Meta Platforms' corporate treasury.

With energy prices rising sharply due to the Russia-Ukraine conflict, Zuckerberg's team used derivatives to hedge Meta's energy costs, effectively profiting from higher gas prices. This dual story—from his early personal trades to his corporate market activity—illustrates how both large companies and individuals can use commodities to manage risk and generate returns.

Case Study: Ray Dalio's Macro Bet on Energy
Ray Dalio, founder of Bridgewater Associates and one of the most successful fund managers ever, started trading natural gas from his garage before founding Bridgewater. This early experience laid the foundation for his macro investment philosophy, which later contributed to Bridgewater's success. During the 2022 energy crisis, Bridgewater was heavily invested in European natural gas and U.S. LNG, benefiting from rising prices. Dalio's approach shows how natural gas plays a vital role in the broader macroeconomic landscape, often acting as a hedge against inflation and geopolitical risks.

What You Need to Know to Trade Natural Gas Successfully
Monitor Weather & Storage Reports—Unexpected cold snaps or storage drawdowns can send prices soaring.

Track LNG Exports & Global Demand—European and Asian demand can affect Henry Hub prices.

Understand Seasonal Trends—Winter contracts are often more volatile than summer contracts.

Use Technical Analysis—Natural gas frequently respects support/resistance levels and reacts sharply to moving averages.

Control Risk—Due to extreme volatility, position sizing and stop-losses are crucial.

The Wild Ride of Natural Gas Trading
Natural gas is one of the most volatile markets worldwide, influenced by unpredictable factors such as weather patterns and geopolitical tensions. This volatility presents both opportunities and challenges, attracting speculators and major investors like Mark Zuckerberg and Ray Dalio.

In this chapter, we have explored the complexities of natural gas trading, including its market structure and historical price fluctuations, and presented case studies demonstrating professional methods for profit from this dynamic commodity.

Like all chapters on markets, I aim to highlight some unknowns that deepen your understanding of energy markets and help you profit from trading them.

The energy markets have expanded every year and show no signs of slowing. As populations grow and societies become more developed, global demand for fuel and food continues to increase.

This leads us to our next group of markets: Food.

4.7 Hungry for the Markets—Food

Moving from Money and Energy to the Markets That Feed the World
Having examined money, which sustains economies, and energy, which powers industry, we now focus on markets that support life: soft commodities and agricultural markets. If money is the heartbeat of the global economy and energy its lifeblood, then food is its nourishment—feeding populations, fostering commerce, and shaping societies.

Soft commodities are among the oldest traded assets, with roots dating back to ancient marketplaces. Today, they remain essential to the global economy, providing traders with opportunities to capitalize on the cyclical nature of planting, harvesting, and consumption.

From staples like wheat, corn, and soybeans to soft commodities such as coffee, cocoa, and sugar, these markets are lively and deeply affected by natural forces, economic cycles, and geopolitical events.

Unlike financial or energy markets, soft commodities are highly vulnerable to weather patterns, seasonal trends, and shifts in consumer demand. A drought in the U.S. Midwest can cause corn prices to spike, while a bumper coffee harvest in Brazil may lead to multi-year lows.

Furthermore, government policies, tariffs, and subsidies significantly impact these markets as nations emphasize food security and agricultural stability. Navigating these complexities demands an understanding of supply and demand fundamentals and the wider geopolitical landscape.

Despite their challenges, agricultural markets present abundant opportunities. Their seasonal cycles, price fluctuations, and sharp reactions to fundamental news make them suitable for traders who can understand their patterns.

In the chapters ahead, we'll explore:

Key soft commodities and agricultural products that dominate global trade.

Price drivers, from crop forecasts to climate patterns.

Trading strategies, including seasonal patterns, supply-demand imbalances, and hedging techniques.

As with currencies, bonds, and energy markets, success lies in knowledge. Understanding agricultural markets not only opens new trading opportunities but also reveals the deep interconnection of the global economy.

Now, let's move from powering the world to feeding it—exploring how traders profit from the grains, fibers, and crops that sustain humanity and drive economies.

Soft Commodities

Coffee, sugar, and cocoa are familiar ingredients for your barista, but even more intriguing for traders. These crops form the backbone of global indulgences, from creamy Frappuccinos to decadent salted caramel desserts. While they tempt our taste buds, they also offer unique opportunities for traders due to their high demand, limited growing regions, and price volatility driven by unpredictable factors such as weather, geopolitics, and supply disruptions.

This trio of soft commodities has been especially profitable for the trading group I once co-owned and me. Around 2010, at our peak, we became the largest-volume trader on the NYBOT Exchange—briefly surpassing even Citadel, the giant hedge fund—providing me with a wealth of experience to share with you on your trading journey.

4.7.1 The Sugar Market: Sweet Opportunities in Soft Commodities

Sugar is one of the most widely traded soft commodities, playing a vital role in the global food supply chain. Apart from sweetening beverages and desserts, sugar is a key ingredient for ethanol production, pharmaceuticals, and various industrial processes. Every day, people across the world consume over 500,000 tons of sugar—an astonishing figure that highlights the market's size and significance. As a trader, understanding the sugar market provides an opportunity to capitalize on one of the oldest and most actively traded agricultural products.

The Origins and Historical Milestones of the Sugar Market

The global sugar market has a rich and captivating history, rooted in humanity's enduring love for sweetness. From its ancient beginnings in tropical Asia to its evolution into a globally traded commodity, sugar has shaped economies, spurred colonial expansion, and caused notable price fluctuations. Understanding the historical background of the sugar market offers traders valuable insights into its price movements and the factors that can lead to extreme volatility.

Early Beginnings: From Grass to Gold

Ancient Origins (6,000 BCE): Sugarcane, the main source of sugar, was first cultivated in Southeast Asia, especially in modern-day Papua New Guinea and India. Early societies chewed the cane to extract its natural sweetness long before any refining techniques were developed.

Indian Innovation (500 CE): Indian communities learned to crystallize sugar, making it easier to transport and store. The Sanskrit word "sharkara," meaning "ground or candied sugar," became the root for sugar in many languages.

Persian and Arab Expansion (600–1000 CE): Knowledge of sugar refining spread from Persia to the Arab world. As Islamic empires expanded across the Mediterranean, sugar plantations were established in North Africa and southern Spain.

The Rise of the European Sugar Trade

The Crusades (11th-thirteenth centuries): Crusaders returning from the Middle East introduced Europeans to sugar, which was initially a luxury for the wealthy.

The Age of Exploration (15th-sixteenth centuries): European powers sought tropical colonies suitable for sugarcane cultivation. Portugal established plantations in Brazil, while Spain introduced sugarcane to the Caribbean.

The Transatlantic Slave Trade (17th-eighteenth centuries): Sugar plantations in the Caribbean, particularly in Jamaica, Barbados, and Saint-Domingue (now Haiti), became dependent on enslaved labor. Sugar became Britain's most profitable commodity during this period.

Industrial Revolution and Mass Production

Beet Sugar Discovery (1747): German chemist Andreas Marggraf identified sugar beet as a viable sugar source, reducing dependency on tropical sugarcane.

Napoleonic Wars (1803–1815): A British blockade of French ports forced Napoleon to promote beet sugar production, catalyzing Europe's beet sugar industry.

Industrialization (nineteenth century): Technological advancements in milling and refining made sugar more affordable, and consumption soared across Europe and North America.

Defining Moments in Sugar's History

The Sugar Act (1764)
Britain imposed a tax on sugar imports to its American colonies, contributing to the colonial unrest that led to the American Revolution.

The Haitian Revolution (1791–1804)
Haiti was the world's largest sugar producer until enslaved people overthrew French rule, halving global sugar production and causing a significant price spike.

The Abolition of Slavery (1833–1865)
The abolition of slavery in the British Empire (1833) and the US (1865) disrupted labor supplies in sugar-producing regions, reducing output and temporarily raising prices.

The Cuban Boom (1850s–1900s)
Cuba became the world's dominant sugar exporter following the collapse of Haiti's sugar industry, bolstered by US investment and modernized mills.

World War I (1914–1918)
Disruptions to global shipping and the redirection of resources to war efforts led to sugar shortages and price surges in Europe.

The Great Depression (1929–1939)
The economic downturn decreased global demand, leading to a sharp fall in sugar prices. Countries implemented quotas to safeguard their local producers.

World War II (1939–1945)
Sugar was rationed in many countries, including the US and the UK. After the war, demand surged as economies recovered.

The 1970s Sugar Crisis
In the early 1970s, global sugar prices skyrocketed due to a combination of factors:

Poor Harvests: Adverse weather in key producing regions.
OPEC Oil Crisis (1973): Rising oil prices increased production costs and encouraged Brazil to convert more sugarcane into ethanol.
Speculative Frenzy: Speculators flooded the sugar market, driving prices to an all-time high of 66 cents per pound in 1974.

The 1980s Market Collapse
Following the 1970s boom, sugar prices collapsed due to:

Overproduction: Countries expanded their output to cash in on high prices.
Weak Demand Growth: Economic stagnation in key consumer markets.
Price Drop: By 1985, sugar prices fell below 4 cents per pound, devastating producers.

The 2000s Brazilian Ethanol Boom
Brazil's ethanol industry boomed in the 2000s as oil prices surged. Sugar prices rose sharply as more sugarcane was diverted to ethanol production, notably when oil prices exceeded $100 per barrel.

The 2010 Sugar Rally
Global sugar prices spiked to 36 cents per pound in 2010 due to:

Drought in Brazil: Reduced output from the world's largest exporter.
Floods in Australia: Damaged crops and restricted exports.
Strong Asian Demand: Rapid growth in India and China increased global competition for available supply.

The 2022 Sugar Volatility
Sugar prices saw significant volatility in 2022 due to:

Pandemic Aftershocks: Disrupted supply chains and labor shortages.
Energy Market Impact: Rising oil prices encouraged Brazilian producers to shift more sugarcane into ethanol production.
Indian Export Restrictions: The Indian government limited sugar exports to control domestic inflation, tightening global supply.

Like all agricultural commodities, sugar responds to natural cycles, human innovation, and economic forces. Understanding the historical factors that have shaped this market helps traders anticipate potential future developments and seize trading opportunities when history repeats itself, as it often does.

Soft Commodities Dominating Global Trade
Sugar is part of a broader category of soft commodities and agricultural products that drive the global economy. Alongside coffee, cocoa, and cotton, sugar is a staple of the commodities markets.

The most traded types of sugar are:

Raw Sugar (#11 Contract—ICE Futures): The global benchmark for raw cane sugar.

White Sugar (#5 Contract—ICE Futures Europe): Refined sugar, predominantly traded in Europe.

The largest producers (supply) of sugar are Brazil, India, Thailand, and China. Brazil dominates global exports due to its vast sugarcane plantations and efficient production methods. While primarily a consumer, India has rapidly increased its production in recent years. Thailand benefits from its strategic location for exports to Asia, and China remains significant despite rising domestic demand.

Major consumers (demand) include India, China, the European Union, and the United States, with India leading the world in per capita sugar consumption.

Price Drivers in the Sugar Market

Supply and Demand Dynamics

Production Levels: Weather patterns, crop diseases, and agricultural policies directly influence sugar output. For example, prolonged droughts in Brazil, the world's largest sugar producer, have historically reduced production and caused price spikes. Conversely, favorable growing conditions can lead to bumper crops, resulting in lower prices.

Consumption Trends: Increasing demand for sugar in food products, beverages, and ethanol influences global prices. This demand is driven by population growth, evolving dietary habits, and the rising consumption of processed foods worldwide. For example, the average person consumes around 24 kilograms of sugar each year, with countries such as India and Brazil experiencing even higher per capita intake. Additionally, the growing availability of low-sugar and sugar-free alternatives presents both challenges and opportunities within the sugar market.

Weather and Climate Patterns

Monsoons in India and Rainfall in Brazil: Significant disruptions to the growing season can lead to price spikes. India's sugarcane growing season runs from June to September, with harvesting from October to March. Brazil's growing season runs from September to March, with harvesting from April to November. Understanding these cycles helps traders anticipate potential weather impacts on supply and price movements.

Hurricanes and Droughts: Severe weather events can destroy crops and disrupt supply chains. These events often follow seasonal patterns, such as the Atlantic hurricane season from June to November, which regularly threatens sugar-producing regions in the Caribbean and southern United States.

Ethanol Market Link

Ethanol, derived from sugarcane, serves multiple purposes: it is blended with petrol to reduce carbon emissions, used as a renewable biofuel in the transport sector, and employed in various industrial applications, such as solvents and plastics. In Brazil, when oil prices rise, producers often divert more sugarcane towards ethanol production, reducing sugar availability and pushing sugar prices higher.

Government Policies and Trade Tariffs

Subsidies, export bans, and import tariffs can significantly influence the global sugar supply and prices.

Notably, India's sugar export policies are carefully watched as they can influence global supply levels. India frequently adjusts its export quotas based on domestic supply situations and international market trends. For instance, during periods of domestic inflation, the government might impose export restrictions to keep local prices low. Such political actions can lead to global supply shortages and price rises, making Indian policy decisions a key focus for sugar traders worldwide.

Currency Movements

Sugar prices are quoted in US dollars, meaning currency exchange rates greatly influence the market. Specifically, the Brazilian Real is especially important because Brazil is the world's largest producer and exporter of sugar. When the real weakens against the dollar, Brazilian sugar becomes more affordable for international buyers, increasing exports and possibly boosting global supply. Conversely, a stronger real can make Brazilian sugar more expensive, reducing exports and tightening global supply, which often causes sugar prices to rise.

Trading Strategies in the Sugar Market

Sugar's seasonality and sensitivity to supply-demand imbalances create opportunities for various trading approaches:

Seasonal Patterns Trading

Sugar prices generally follow a seasonal cycle aligned with planting, growing, and harvesting periods. We can examine past harvest cycles, compare them with the current year, and spot any recurring patterns.

India's Monsoon Season (June-September): Traders carefully watch rainfall forecasts for potential price signals.

Brazil's Harvest Season (April-November): Increased supply during harvest often causes price fluctuations and dips.

Supply-Demand Imbalance Trading

Weather Shocks: Severe droughts or storms often cause sharp price spikes.

Production Reports: Regular updates from key producers (e.g., Brazil's UNICA report) can influence market sentiment.

Spread Trading

Traders frequently utilize the Raw versus White Sugar Spread to profit from price differences between raw and refined sugar. The price gap between the two contracts arises from variations in processing costs, transportation logistics, and regional demand. Raw sugar, being unrefined, is cheaper but requires refining, while white sugar involves additional production costs and market-specific demand factors.

Trade study: Going long on raw sugar futures and short on white sugar futures if the spread widens beyond historical norms, anticipating a return to relative value.

Hedging Strategies

Sugar producers and food manufacturers frequently hedge their exposure to price fluctuations through futures contracts. Some of the largest companies that hedge positions include global food giants such as Coca-Cola, Nestlé, and Mondelez International, as well as major sugar producers like Cosan, Tereos, and Wilmar International.

At the foundation of the futures market is a simple and powerful idea: the transfer of risk. A sugar producer, for example, may sell futures contracts to lock in a price before the harvest is complete. By doing so, they remove the uncertainty of future price fluctuations from their business and pass that risk to another market participant—typically a speculator—who is willing to accept the potential profit or loss in exchange for the opportunity. This exchange of risk is what creates liquidity and, in turn, trading opportunities for those who can accurately assess supply, demand, and price behavior.

Variations of this arrangement are believed to have existed hundreds of years ago, notably among rice farmers, where early forms of futures contracts allowed producers to stabilize (hedge) their income while others assumed price risk. What began as a practical solution to an agricultural problem has since evolved into a global, multi-billion-dollar marketplace spanning commodities, interest rates, currencies, and financial indices—yet the core principle remains unchanged. Someone seeks certainty; someone else accepts risk.

Trading on Ethanol-Sugar Arbitrage
Given the link between sugar and ethanol in Brazil, traders monitor oil prices for potential impacts on sugar production decisions.

Trade study: Rising oil prices could shift sugarcane use towards ethanol, leading to a tighter sugar supply and higher prices. This is a common trade, as a sugar rally typically follows a significant increase in the oil market.

Sweet Profits in Sugar Trading
The sugar market is a vibrant and highly liquid segment of the soft commodities sector, offering traders opportunities to profit from seasonal shifts, geopolitical developments, and energy market links. Understanding the key factors influencing sugar prices and applying sound trading strategies can help you navigate this lively market effectively. As with all commodities, success relies on thorough research, risk management, and remaining alert to market-moving news.

4.7.2 The Cocoa Market: I Mean, Who Doesn't Like Chocolate!

Cocoa, the essential ingredient in chocolate, is among the most widely consumed and culturally significant soft commodities worldwide. From luxurious truffles to mass-produced chocolate bars, global demand for cocoa remains robust despite economic fluctuations. Each year, over 4.5 million tons of cocoa beans are consumed, supporting an industry valued at over $150 billion. For traders, cocoa offers a dynamic, volatile market with opportunities shaped by weather conditions, geopolitical developments, and evolving consumer preferences.

The Origins and Historical Milestones of the Cocoa Market
The cocoa market has a rich and fascinating history that spans thousands of years. From ancient Mesoamerican civilizations to the bustling futures

exchanges of London and New York, cocoa has evolved into a global commodity with deep cultural and economic significance.

Early Beginnings: The Sacred Bean

1500 BCE—Olmec Civilization (Mexico): Archaeological evidence suggests that the Olmecs were the first to cultivate cacao plants and consume cocoa as a bitter, fermented drink, often used in religious ceremonies.

600 CE—Mayans: Cocoa became central to Mayan culture, used in social rituals, religious practices, and even as currency.

1400s—Aztecs: The Aztecs valued cocoa beans so highly that they used them as currency. Montezuma II was said to consume large quantities of cocoa daily, believing it had energizing and aphrodisiac properties, which some people still believe today.

European Discovery and Expansion

1502—Columbus Encounter: Christopher Columbus came across cocoa beans during his fourth voyage, but didn't realize their importance—talk about missing a great trade. We've all been there, Chris!

1528—Hernán Cortés: Cortés introduced cocoa to Spain, where it was sweetened with sugar and became a luxury beverage. Known for his unwavering determination, Cortés famously burned his ships upon arriving in Mexico, removing any chance of retreat and forcing his men to commit fully to the conquest. Like a successful trader, he had no Plan B—just conviction in his strategy, which ultimately led to the fall of the Aztec Empire and his rich rewards.

1600s—European Popularity: Cocoa spread across Europe, especially in Spain, Italy, and France, becoming the preferred drink of the aristocracy. I mean, who doesn't enjoy a cup of hot chocolate on a cold day?

Industrialization and Global Expansion

1828—Cocoa Press Invented: Dutch chemist Coenraad Johannes van Houten developed the cocoa press, enabling mass production of cocoa powder and paving the way for modern chocolate manufacture.

1875—Milk Chocolate Invented: Swiss chocolatier Daniel Peter created milk chocolate by adding condensed milk, expanding cocoa's appeal to mass markets.

Late 1800s—African Plantations: European colonial powers established large cocoa plantations in West Africa, particularly in Ghana, Côte d'Ivoire, and Nigeria, due to the region's ideal growing conditions—high humidity, consistent rainfall, and warm temperatures. Furthermore, access to colonial infrastructure and cheap labor made these countries prime locations for mass cocoa production.

World War II (1939–1945)
The global cocoa trade was severely disrupted as shipping routes were blocked and plantations were neglected. Cocoa prices soared due to scarcity.

The Ghanaian Cocoa Crisis (1960s)
Once the world's leading cocoa producer, Ghana saw output plummet due to government mismanagement, political instability, and disease outbreaks.

Government Mismanagement: The Ghana Cocoa Marketing Board (CMB) set artificially low prices for cocoa farmers to stabilize domestic markets and boost government revenues. This price control discouraged production, as farmers received little reward for their labor compared to the international market.

Political Instability: The country experienced several military coups during the 1960s and 1970s, including the overthrow of President Kwame Nkrumah in 1966. The lack of consistent agricultural policies, combined with corruption and poor governance, created uncertainty for cocoa producers.

Disease Outbreaks: Cocoa Swollen Shoot Virus Disease (CSSVD) devastated plantations across Ghana, greatly reducing yields. The government struggled to implement effective disease-control measures, further worsening the decline in production.

The 1977 Cocoa Rally
Cocoa prices surged to record highs as production shortfalls in Ghana and political instability in Nigeria reduced global supply.

The 2002 Côte d'Ivoire Civil War
Côte d'Ivoire, the world's top cocoa producer, was engulfed in civil war. The conflict disrupted production and exports, driving up cocoa prices.

The 2020 COVID-19 Pandemic
Lockdowns and supply chain disruptions affected cocoa production and demand. Prices initially declined as chocolate consumption decreased in commercial sectors, but later rebounded as home consumption increased.

The 2023 Supply Crisis and Price Rally
In 2023, cocoa prices surged sharply due to a combination of poor harvests in West Africa, supply chain disruptions, and rising global demand.

West African Crop Failures: Unfavorable weather conditions and disease outbreaks, such as black pod and swollen shoot virus, significantly decreased output in Côte d'Ivoire and Ghana.

Export Restrictions: Ghana and Côte d'Ivoire imposed temporary restrictions to secure their domestic supply, further tightening the global market.

Speculative Buying: Traders and funds capitalized on the reduced supply, pushing prices higher as they anticipated prolonged shortages.

The 2023 rally underscored the fragility of cocoa supply chains and the ongoing importance of monitoring West African production levels.

Key Cocoa-Producing Regions and Global Trade

Cocoa is grown in tropical regions within 20° of the equator, where warm temperatures, rainfall, and humid conditions create the ideal environment for cacao trees.

Country	Region	Annual Production (Tons)	Global Market Share
Côte d'Ivoire	West Africa	2,100,000	40%
Ghana	West Africa	900,000	18%
Indonesia	Southeast Asia	700,000	14%
Ecuador	South America	330,000	6%
Nigeria	West Africa	300,000	5%

West Africa: The Cocoa Heartland

Côte d'Ivoire and Ghana together produce nearly 60% of the world's cocoa beans. Both countries rely heavily on cocoa exports, making them susceptible to fluctuations in global cocoa prices and weather patterns.

Côte d'Ivoire is known for its robust infrastructure and high productivity.

Ghana: Recognized for premium-quality beans used in high-end chocolate products.

Emerging Producers

Indonesia: Primarily supplies Asian markets, with production declining due to ageing plantations.

Ecuador: Renowned for its fine-flavored cocoa varieties.

Nigeria continues to expand its production despite infrastructure challenges.

Factors That Drive Cocoa Prices

Weather and Climate

Rainfall Patterns: Cocoa trees are susceptible to rainfall levels. Inconsistent rainfall or drought conditions in West Africa can significantly reduce yields.

Harmattan Winds: The dry, dusty Harmattan winds from the Sahara often cause crop stress in Ghana and Côte d'Ivoire, leading to supply shortages.

Political and Social Instability

Cocoa-producing countries, particularly in West Africa, have experienced political instability, which has impacted production and exports.

Trade Study: In 2011, post-election violence in Côte d'Ivoire halted cocoa exports for several months, causing a 30% spike in global cocoa prices.

Demand for Chocolate Products

Rising middle-class populations in Asia, particularly in China and India, have driven increased chocolate consumption.

Seasonal demand surges during holidays such as Easter, Christmas, and Valentine's Day.

Currency Movements

Cocoa is traded in US dollars. Fluctuations in the Ghanaian cedi and the Ivorian franc against the dollar can affect production costs and export volumes.

Government Intervention and Price Floors

The introduction of the $400/ton Living Income Differential (LID) by Ghana and Côte d'Ivoire in 2019 aimed to enhance farmer incomes amid historically low cocoa prices. However, the initiative inadvertently caused significant market distortions.

The governments of both countries, which together produce about 60% of the world's cocoa, have historically used futures contracts to fix prices before harvests. The LID aimed to guarantee a minimum income for farmers. However, it also caused tension with international buyers who were hesitant to pay the premium, especially during times of global oversupply.

The real challenge emerged in 2023 when cocoa futures prices surged amid adverse weather, disease, and other crop issues that significantly reduced yields. The futures contracts the governments had previously sold—based on lower expected prices and the LID—became problematic. Farmers, faced with a fixed farmgate price and rising market prices, were incentivized to smuggle their cocoa to neighboring countries or sell on the black market to make higher profits. As a result, the governments found it difficult to deliver the cocoa they had already sold through futures contracts, exposing their hedging strategies to considerable risk.

This scenario highlights the delicate balance governments face when intervening in commodity markets. While the LID was a well-meaning attempt to improve livelihoods, it also showed how misaligned incentives, combined with external shocks such as poor harvests, can undermine both market stability and policy aims.

Trading Strategies in the Cocoa Market

Seasonal Patterns Trading

Long/Short Decision:

Go Short: Ahead of the main crop harvest (October to March), when supply is expected to increase, putting downward pressure on prices.

Go Long: Leading into the mid-crop harvest (May to July) if early indicators (e.g., poor weather or pest issues) suggest a potential supply shortfall.

Trade Study:

In Q4 2016, cocoa prices fell from approximately $3,000 to $2,000 per ton as West Africa experienced a bountiful main crop harvest. Traders who shorted cocoa ahead of the harvest, expecting this supply increase, made significant profits.

Conversely, taking a long position in mid-2015, when early reports indicated that mid-crop yields might underperform, also proved lucrative.

Weather Event Trading

Long/Short Decision:

Go Long: When droughts, excessive rainfall, or Harmattan winds threaten yields.

Go Short: If favorable weather conditions point to above-average production.

Trade Study:

In 2015, a severe El Niño event triggered extensive droughts in Côte d'Ivoire and Ghana, significantly reducing crop yields. Cocoa prices rose by over 20%, reaching $3,400 per ton. Traders who went long based on early meteorological reports and historical El Niño patterns made substantial profits.

Indicators to Watch:

- West African rainfall patterns
- Temperature deviations
- Harmattan wind intensity reports

Cocoa-Butter Ratio and Processing Margins
Long/Short Decision:

Go Long on Cocoa Beans: If the cocoa-butter ratio increases, it signals higher processing demand.

Go Short on Cocoa Beans: If margins shrink due to higher bean costs or declining chocolate consumption.

Trade Study:

In 2014, cocoa prices rose due to strong demand for cocoa butter, driven by increased processing activity in Europe and Asia. Traders who tracked the cocoa-butter ratio and went long on beans as margins widened saw returns as cocoa hit $3,200 per ton.

Key Ratios:

Cocoa-Butter Ratio > 3.0—bullish for cocoa prices.

Cocoa-Butter Ratio < 2.5—bearish signal.

Spread Trading
Calendar Spreads (Intra-Market)

Long/Short Decision:

Go Long (buy near-month/sell far-month): If supply shortages are expected.

Go Short (sell near-month/buy far-month): When harvest surpluses or stockpile buildups are forecast.

Trade Study:

In early 2023, West Africa's poor main crop resulted in a tightening of short-term supply. The March–May calendar spread on ICE New York widened considerably, benefiting traders who bought the near-month contract and sold the deferred contract.

Inter-Market Spreads (ICE London vs. ICE New York)
Long/Short Decision:

Go Long London/Short New York: If GBP weakens or European demand strengthens.

Go Short London/Long New York: When USD strengthens, or U.S. processing demand rises.

Trade Study:

In 2016, a sharp post-Brexit devaluation of GBP made London cocoa contracts relatively cheaper. Traders who went long London cocoa while shorting New York cocoa captured gains as the spread corrected.

Producer and Consumer Hedging

Long/Short Decision:

Go Short: Producers (e.g., Ghana Cocoa Board) hedge by selling futures to lock in current prices and protect against future declines.

Go Long: Chocolate manufacturers go long on futures to secure future supply at current costs.

Trade Study:

In 2020, amid COVID-19 disruptions, chocolate manufacturers such as Mars and Lindt increased their futures purchases (going long) to secure raw materials at lower pandemic-driven prices. When cocoa prices recovered as demand rebounded, their hedge positions proved highly profitable.

The Bittersweet Nature of Cocoa Trading

In summary, trading cocoa successfully involves closely monitoring the entire supply chain—including the hedging behavior of major producers and processors, whose actions often reveal early hints about tightening or loosening conditions. The best strategies usually combine seasonality, weather risks, processing margins, and spread dynamics into one clear view. Ultimately, success depends on aligning with the structural shifts in supply and demand and adjusting your positions as those pressures change, rather than trying to predict short-term fluctuations.

The cocoa market's unique blend of weather-driven supply challenges, strong consumer demand, and geopolitical influences makes it an exciting space for traders. Success requires staying informed about global production trends, seasonal patterns, and policy changes in key producing regions. By mastering the interplay of these factors, traders can navigate the volatility of cocoa markets and seize sweet opportunities when they arise.

4.7.3 Coffee, the Original Energy Drink

Coffee is the second-most traded commodity in the world, after crude oil, with billions of cups consumed daily around the globe. From the morning ritual of an espresso in Italy to a caramel latte in New York, coffee is an essential part of modern life. This huge demand fuels a dynamic, volatile, and globally linked market that offers many opportunities for traders.

With supply chains extending from tropical farms in Latin America, Africa, and Asia to roasters and cafés around the world, a complex network of agricultural, economic, and geopolitical factors greatly influences the coffee market. In this chapter, we will explore the history of coffee, the factors affecting its price, the key market players, and the strategies that professionals use to trade it profitably.

The Origins and Historical Milestones of the Coffee Market

Coffee's journey from an Ethiopian hillside to becoming a multi-billion-dollar global market is steeped in myth, exploration, and commerce. Understanding its origins and development provides context for the market dynamics we trade today.

Early Beginnings: From Goat Herds to Global Markets

800 CE—Ethiopian Discovery: Legend has it that a goat herder named Kaldi discovered coffee when his goats became unusually energetic after eating berries from a particular shrub. Kaldi shared his discovery with local monks, who used the berries to stay awake during prayers.

1000 CE—Arabian Peninsula: Coffee cultivation and consumption spread to Yemen, where Sufi monks brewed "qahwa" to aid religious devotion.

1500s—Coffee in the Middle East: Coffeehouses, known as "qahveh khaneh," appeared in Mecca and Constantinople, becoming hubs of social and intellectual exchange. The original Starbucks was born.

European Adoption and Global Expansion

1615—Coffee Reaches Europe: Venetian merchants introduced coffee to Europe, where it rapidly gained popularity.

1652—London's First Coffeehouse: The first coffeehouse opened in London, followed by hundreds more, becoming the preferred meeting place for merchants and traders.

Bizarre trading fact: Lloyd's of London, originally a coffeehouse where merchants and shipowners gathered to discuss insurance and trade, has developed into a globally renowned insurance and reinsurance marketplace. It offers a platform for insurance underwriters to share and distribute risks across various industries and regions. Recent estimates suggest that Lloyd's is worth over £50 billion and has a worldwide presence in more than 200 countries. Its modern role includes insuring assets such as ships, aircraft, and cyber risks, as well as covering natural disasters, demonstrating how its modest coffeehouse beginnings laid the groundwork for one of the world's most innovative financial institutions.

1700s—Colonial Expansion: European powers introduced coffee to their colonies across the Caribbean, South America, and Asia, transforming it into a lucrative global commodity.

Industrialization and Market Growth

1880s—Coffee Exchanges Established: The New York Coffee Exchange was founded in 1882 and later became part of ICE Futures U.S., which formalized coffee futures trading under the NYBOT exchange.

1930s—Brazil's dominance in global coffee production, accounting for nearly 80% of the world's coffee exports at its peak, can be attributed to several key factors:

Favorable Climate and Geography:

Brazil's extensive size and varied climate create excellent growing conditions for coffee, especially in states like Minas Gerais, São Paulo, and Espírito Santo. The country's tropical and subtropical regions offer optimal conditions for Arabica and Robusta coffee varieties, providing a balanced combination of rainfall, temperature, and elevation.

Large-Scale Plantations and Infrastructure:

By the late 19th and early twentieth centuries, Brazil had established large coffee plantations, known as fazendas, which adopted more mechanized and efficient farming techniques than other producers. These economies of scale enabled Brazil to produce coffee more cost-effectively.

Government Support and Infrastructure Development:

The Brazilian government invested significantly in infrastructure, such as railways and ports, to facilitate the transport and export of coffee. Policies like the Valorization Scheme also helped stabilize coffee prices and shield the industry from market volatility.

Labour Supply and Historical Context:

During the coffee boom, Brazil relied on enslaved labor until abolition in 1888. Afterwards, waves of European immigrants, particularly from Italy, filled the labor gap, ensuring continued productivity.

Proximity to Major Markets:

Brazil's strategic position and extensive shipping routes enable it to supply growing coffee markets in North America and Europe efficiently.

Soil Fertility and Land Availability:

Brazil has vast areas of fertile land suitable for coffee cultivation, enabling the ongoing expansion of plantations as global demand rises.

Market Adaptability and Product Diversity:

Brazil produces Arabica and Robusta beans, making them versatile and adaptable to shifts in consumer preferences and industrial demand (e.g., instant coffee production).

1962—International Coffee Agreement (ICA): This agreement introduced export quotas to stabilize coffee prices, which remained in effect until 1989, an early attempt to mirror what OPEC were doing in the Oil market to control prices.

Market moves in modern times.

The Great Frost of Brazil (1975)

In July 1975, a severe and unexpected frost hit Brazil's coffee-growing regions, particularly in Paraná and São Paulo. Temperatures plummeted below freezing for several hours, killing young coffee trees, severely damaging mature ones, and destroying nearly 65% of the country's coffee crop, with some plantations losing their entire harvest. Within months, prices surged from $0.50 to over $3.00 per pound.

A new player in town (2001–2003)

Oversupply from Vietnam and declining global demand drove coffee prices below $0.50 per pound, devastating farmers in Latin America.

Vietnam went from being a minor producer to becoming the world's second-largest coffee producer within a decade. By the early 2000s, its output surged, flooding the global market with Robusta beans (used primarily for instant coffee and blends).

2021 Brazilian Coffee Crisis

Brazil, the world's largest coffee producer, faced an unprecedented one-two punch of climate-related disasters:

Drought:

From 2020 into early 2021, Brazil experienced one of its worst droughts in decades. Key coffee-growing regions like Minas Gerais, São Paulo, and Espírito Santo received significantly below-average rainfall, weakening trees and reducing their ability to produce cherries.

Severe Frost (July 2021):

Three successive frost events hit just as the weakened trees entered their crucial flowering phase. These were the most severe frosts since 1994, damaging coffee blossoms, killing young plants, and reducing yields for multiple seasons due to the long recovery time required for coffee trees.

In mid-2020, Arabica coffee traded at around $1.20 per pound. Still, by July 2021, following severe frost events, prices had surged past $2.40 per pound as the futures market reflected concerns that the damage would impact both the immediate harvest and future yields.

2024/5 prices hitting record highs

As of February 2025, Arabica coffee prices have experienced significant volatility due to adverse weather conditions, supply chain disruptions, and market dynamics.

Early 2024: Arabica coffee futures were trading around $1.20 per pound.

Late 2024: Prices surged to approximately $3.26 per pound, marking a 70% increase for the year.

February 2025: Prices reached an all-time high, exceeding $4.00 per pound.

Brazil: The world's largest coffee producer faced severe droughts in 2024, leading to a 4.4% decline in coffee bean production.

Vietnam and Indonesia: Extreme weather, including heatwaves and heavy rains, adversely affected robusta bean production, further tightening global coffee supplies.

Important Coffee-Producing Regions and Global Trade

Coffee grows in tropical regions along the so-called "Coffee Belt" between the Tropics of Cancer and Capricorn. Two primary coffee species dominate global production: Arabica and Robusta.

Country	Region	Annual Production (Tons)	Global Market Share
Brazil	South America	3,800,000	35%
Vietnam	Southeast Asia	1,800,000	16%
Colombia	South America	800,000	7%
Indonesia	Southeast Asia	700,000	6%
Ethiopia	Africa	400,000	4%

Insights into Regional Production

Brazil: The World's largest producer, particularly of Arabica beans. Its harvest cycles and weather patterns significantly influence global prices.

Vietnam: Specializes in Robusta coffee, which is cheaper and primarily used in instant coffee production.

Colombia: Known for high-quality Arabica, it has mountainous terrain that provides ideal growing conditions.

Indonesia: A significant Robusta producer, Sumatra's coffee is known for its earthy flavors.

Ethiopia is coffee's birthplace, producing uniquely flavored Arabica beans prized by specialty roasters.

After a thorough exploration of the coffee market, you should now be better equipped to capitalize on market movements. Let's analyze the price drivers and scenarios where we can profit from trading coffee futures.

Price drivers and trading strategies for the international Coffee market

Understanding what drives prices and the strategies to profit from them is simple in theory. However, the real secret to successful trading is obtaining the right information and acting on it promptly. The following insights will help you develop a sharp eye for event-driven price movements in the world's favorite hot drink, giving you the advantage needed to trade coffee markets effectively.

Weather and Climate

Coffee plants, particularly Arabica, are vulnerable to weather extremes like frost, drought, and irregular rainfall.

Trade Ideas:

Go Long on Arabica Futures Before a Predicted Weather Event:

In 2021, Brazil experienced severe frost, which decimated a significant portion of its Arabica crop. Traders who went long on ICE Arabica futures after the first frost event saw prices surge from around $1.20 to over $2.40 per pound.

Trigger: Early meteorological reports of cold fronts or prolonged droughts in Brazil or Colombia.

Entry: Buy Arabica contracts (ICE Coffee "C") when weather anomalies are forecasted.

Exit: Take profits as damage reports confirm yield reductions.

Use Calendar Spreads to Hedge Weather Volatility:

During uncertain growing seasons, the near-month contract might spike on fears of immediate supply shortages while later contracts lag. Going long on near-month contracts and short on far-month contracts can profit from temporary weather-driven disruptions.

Example: In July 2021, the March-May spread widened significantly due to frost fears.

Supply Chain and Logistics

Logistics disruptions, such as port strikes, container shortages, or transport delays, can cause delivery delays and price spikes.

Trade Ideas:

Go Long on Robusta When Vietnam Faces Shipping Issues:

In 2023, Vietnam, the world's largest Robusta producer, faced container shortages and port congestion, causing supply delays. Robusta prices surged from $1,800 to $2,400 per ton.

Trigger: Reports of port congestion, strikes, or container shortages in Southeast Asia.

Entry: When logistics disruptions are reported, buy Robusta contracts (ICE London).

Exit: As logistical bottlenecks ease or alternative shipping routes are established.

Short Coffee Futures After Supply Chain Resolutions:

When port strikes in Brazil were resolved in 2021, supply quickly returned to normal, pushing prices downward.

Trigger: Announcements of labor agreements or resumed port operations.

Entry: Short Arabica contracts once normal shipping activity resumes.

Currency Fluctuations

Coffee is traded in USD, but major producers like Brazil, Colombia, and Vietnam price labor and local costs in their domestic currencies. A weaker currency (e.g., the Brazilian real) generally lowers coffee prices as exports become more affordable.

Trade Ideas:

Short Arabica When the Brazilian Real Depreciates:

In 2020, the Brazilian real weakened significantly against the USD, coinciding with a drop in coffee prices.

Trigger: Central Bank policy changes or political uncertainty weakening the BRL.

Entry: Short Arabica on ICE when the BRL/USD moves significantly downward.

Hedge: Go long USD/BRL simultaneously to hedge currency risk.

Long Arabica When BRL Strengthens:

In 2021, when the Brazilian real recovered, coffee prices surged.

Trigger: Political stability, increased commodity demand, or favorable macroeconomic policies.

Entry: Buy Arabica when BRL appreciates significantly against USD.

Monitor: Decisions on the Brazilian Central Bank interest rate. Movements in the USD/BRL exchange rate.

Political and Social Factors

Political unrest, labor strikes, and evolving regulations can disrupt coffee production and distribution.

Trade Ideas:

Long Coffee Futures During Political Unrest:

In 2021, Colombia faced nationwide protests that disrupted coffee exports. Prices for Colombian differentials rose substantially during the unrest.

Trigger: Reports of labor strikes, political instability, or new restrictive regulations in producing nations.

Entry: Buy Arabica futures when protests or unrest affect major exporters like Colombia or Ethiopia.

Short Coffee When Regulatory Pressure Eases:

In 2023, easing EU regulations on coffee imports briefly pressured prices downward.

Trigger: Changes in labor or environmental regulations.

Entry: Short coffee futures upon regulatory announcements promoting easier export processes.

Political Events to Monitor:

Colombian protests.

Brazilian labor strikes.

African geopolitical situation developments.

Demand Dynamics

Global coffee consumption patterns are shifting, with increased demand for specialty and premium coffee in developed markets.

Trade Ideas:

Go Long on Arabica Futures in Anticipation of Specialty Demand Surges:

The U.S. and Europe have seen growing demand for specialty coffee. Arabica beans, preferred for higher-quality blends, are more sensitive to these shifts.

Trigger: Reports of increased café openings, higher specialty coffee sales, or emerging market demand (e.g., China).

Entry: Buy Arabica contracts ahead of seasonal or cultural events that boost coffee consumption (e.g., winter holidays in Western markets).

Long Robusta When Demand for Instant Coffee Rises:

During the pandemic, demand for instant coffee surged, driving up Robusta prices.

Trigger: Economic downturns or increased demand for cost-effective coffee options.

Entry: Buy Robusta futures when consumer trends shift toward convenience and cost savings.

Seasonal Patterns and Crop Cycles

Coffee follows well-established seasonal patterns tied to harvest cycles.

Trade Ideas:

Short Arabica Ahead of Brazil's Main Harvest (May–September):

Historically, Arabica prices tend to soften as Brazil's harvest season begins, increasing supply.

Trigger: Reports of normal or above-average yields during Brazil's main crop harvest.

Entry: Short Arabica futures in April or early May.

Long Colombian Coffee Before the Mitaca Harvest:

Colombia's secondary harvest (Mitaca) provides a mid-year supply boost. If the main harvest underperforms, traders sometimes go long before this period.

Trigger: Reports of low yields from the main harvest.

Entry: Buy Colombian coffee differentials in March or early April.

A Percolating Market for Profits

The coffee market offers unique opportunities due to its global reach, weather sensitivity, and evolving consumption trends. Traders who stay informed about production cycles, weather patterns, and macroeconomic factors are best placed to capitalize on profitable prospects in this dynamic, continuously evolving market.

Field to Fork—via the Futures Markets

The agricultural and livestock markets are some of the world's most essential and actively traded futures markets. From the cornfields of the Midwest to the cattle ranches of Texas, these commodities form the backbone of the global food supply chain. Their prices are driven by supply and demand fundamentals, weather patterns, government policies, and speculative interest, making them highly dynamic markets with ample trading opportunities.

This chapter will examine key agricultural and livestock futures, their origins, important historical milestones, factors influencing these markets, and trading strategies to help you capitalize on price movements.

4.7.4 Mastering Corn Trading

The A-maize-ing crop
Corn (Maize to many people around the world) has been cultivated for over 10,000 years, originating in Mesoamerica, where civilizations such as the Aztecs and Mayans relied on it as a staple crop. Over time, it spread globally, becoming one of the world's most important agricultural commodities.

The leading corn-producing nations include the United States, which is the largest producer and exporter, accounting for over 35% of global output. Iowa, Illinois, Nebraska, and Minnesota are key cultivation regions, motivated by strong domestic demand for livestock feed and ethanol.

China, the second-largest producer, contributes around 23% of global corn output, primarily for domestic livestock feed, and relies on imports from the U.S. and Brazil.

Brazil, a rapidly growing exporter, produces 10% of the world's corn and has become a key supplier to China, particularly after the 2022 U.S.-China trade tensions, making it the second-largest exporter after the U.S.

Argentina, another major exporter, produces 5–6% of global corn and exports over 70% of its production, making it a key competitor to the U.S. in international markets.

Ukraine, historically a top-four exporter, primarily supplies Europe, China, and the Middle East. Although it remains a significant player, the Russia-Ukraine war has disrupted its role.

Lastly, a smaller but growing producer, India, focuses primarily on domestic animal feed and food processing, with a limited but increasing role in global trade.

Brazil is hot on its heels.

Modern-day market moves

1973—U.S.-Soviet Grain Deal.
In 1973, the U.S. finalized a significant grain deal with the Soviet Union, selling over 10 million metric tons of corn and wheat at subsidized prices. This unexpected increase in demand caused a global grain shortage, leading to sharp price increases for corn, wheat, and soybeans.

The deal, later known as the Great Grain Robbery, caught the market by surprise as the Soviet Union had been experiencing poor harvests and secretly stockpiled U.S. grain to rebuild its reserves. This event highlighted the vulnerability of global grain markets to geopolitical deals and revealed flaws in U.S. export monitoring systems. It prompted reforms in grain trade transparency and market oversight to prevent future supply shocks.

2005—Rise of Ethanol Demand.

The Renewable Fuel Standard (RFS), enacted in 2005 as part of the Energy Policy Act, mandated a gradual increase in biofuel production, requiring refiners to blend a certain percentage of renewable fuels, primarily ethanol, into petrol. Since corn is the primary feedstock for ethanol in the U.S., this policy significantly boosted corn demand, leading to higher prices and changing long-term market dynamics.

By 2010, the mandate had expanded under the Energy Independence and Security Act (EISA), setting a target of 36 billion gallons of renewable fuel production by 2022. This change caused a structural shift in the corn market, linking its price more closely to crude oil and energy markets.

The increased competition between ethanol producers and livestock feed users also caused volatility, as farmers had to allocate more land to corn for fuel production, reducing supplies of food and animal feed. Over time, the RFS shifted corn from mainly an agricultural commodity to an important part of the global energy market, making its price changes more responsive to oil prices, government policies, and environmental regulations.

2012—U.S. Drought Crisis

The 2012 U.S. drought, one of the most severe on record, devastated the Corn Belt, with over 80% of U.S. farmland experiencing drought conditions at its peak. The extreme heat and lack of rainfall severely reduced corn yields, with the USDA estimating a 27% decline in production compared to early-season forecasts. States such as Iowa, Illinois, and Indiana, which usually produce the majority of U.S. corn, experienced widespread crop failures, forcing farmers to abandon fields or harvest significantly lower-quality grain.

As supply concerns grew, speculative buying increased, and corn futures on the Chicago Board of Trade (CBOT) reached a record high of $8.31 per bushel in August 2012, showing a more than 50% rise in just a few months. This price surge highlighted corn's vulnerability to extreme weather, especially as global demand remained strong, driven by its use in livestock feed, ethanol production, and exports to major buyers such as China and Mexico.

The crisis also reignited debates over crop insurance, climate resilience, and reliance on corn-based ethanol, as some policymakers questioned whether ethanol mandates worsened food price inflation during supply shortages.

What moves the corn market, and how can we profit from the moves?
Corn is one of the most actively traded agricultural commodities. Supply and demand fundamentals, government policies, energy markets, and speculative trading influence its price. Understanding what moves the corn market can help traders position themselves ahead of major price shifts, capitalizing on the volatility that often follows unexpected events.

Weather Conditions: The Make-or-Break Factor
Corn is very sensitive to weather conditions, with droughts, floods, unexpected frosts, and even the timing of rainfall during the growing season all critically influencing supply. The annual corn-growing cycle is a delicate process—one bad weather event at the wrong time can ruin yields.

Key Weather Events to Watch:

Droughts: Prolonged dry spells can reduce crop size, leading to lower supply and higher prices.

Excessive Rainfall & Flooding: Delayed planting and waterlogged fields can impact yields, leading to smaller harvests.

Temperature Extremes: Early or late frosts can damage crops, while extreme heat can stunt growth.

Trade Study: The 2012 U.S. Drought

In 2012, the U.S. experienced one of its worst droughts in history, severely impacting the Corn Belt. With over 50% of corn-growing regions suffering from extreme drought, supply collapsed, and prices soared past £8 per bushel—an all-time high at the time. Traders who anticipated the drought and took long positions in corn futures made significant profits.

Weather is an ever-present risk, and tracking forecasts, soil moisture levels, and seasonal climate patterns is essential for trading corn successfully.

Strategy Overview:

Droughts & heatwaves reduce yields, pushing prices higher.

Excess rainfall or floods damage crops, supporting bullish bets.

Trade Setup:

Go long on Corn Futures (CME) in early summer if NOAA drought forecasts predict reduced rainfall.

Exit once the drought peak is confirmed, and global supply shifts rebalance the market.

Ethanol Demand: The Energy-Corn Connection

Corn isn't just food—it's fuel. A large portion of U.S. corn production is used to produce ethanol, a biofuel blended with petrol. This establishes a direct link between corn prices and energy markets. When oil prices rise, demand for ethanol increases, which consequently raises corn prices.

Higher Crude Oil Prices → Increased Ethanol Demand → Higher Corn Prices.

Lower Oil Prices → Less Ethanol Demand → Lower Corn Prices.

Trade Study: The 2008 Oil Boom

In 2008, crude oil surged to $140 per barrel, prompting an increase in ethanol production. Consequently, corn prices reached record levels, exceeding $7 per bushel. Traders who recognized the link between rising oil and corn capitalized on this by going long on corn futures.

Corn traders must monitor the energy markets. Big moves in crude oil often have a knock-on effect on corn demand.

Strategy Overview:

Since corn is a key ingredient in ethanol, corn prices often move in step with crude oil prices.

Higher oil prices → Higher ethanol demand → Bullish for corn.

Trade Setup:

Go Long Corn when oil prices break above key resistance levels ($100 + per barrel).

Monitor ethanol production reports to confirm increasing demand.

Global Trade & Export Demand

Corn is a globally traded commodity, and the actions of major importers can significantly influence prices. China, Mexico, Japan, and South Korea are the largest purchasers of U.S. corn.

How Exports Move Prices:

Increased Purchases from Major Buyers → Tighter Supply → Higher Prices.

Export Restrictions or Trade Wars → Lower Demand → Lower Prices.

Trade Study: China's 2020 Corn Buying Spree

In 2020, China made historic purchases of U.S. corn, acquiring over 26 million tons—more than twice its previous record. The sudden increase in demand caused corn prices to jump above $7 per bushel for the first time in nearly ten years. Traders who monitored U.S. export reports and observed the rise in Chinese demand benefited from the rally.

Monitoring export sales reports and geopolitical developments—especially with China—is essential for successfully trading corn.

USDA Reports: The Market-Moving Data Releases

The United States Department of Agriculture (USDA) releases key reports that provide updated information on global supply, demand, and stockpiles. The monthly WASDE (World Agricultural Supply and Demand Estimates) Report is the most important for corn traders.

Why the WASDE Reports Matter to Traders:

Yield Revisions: Prices may spike if the USDA reduces expected yields due to poor weather.

Stockpile Data: Larger-than-expected stockpiles can push prices down, while smaller stockpiles can cause them to rise.

Export Forecasts: If global demand increases, the USDA will revise its estimates, which will affect trader sentiment.

Trade Study: The Bullish WASDE Reports of 2021

In 2021, the USDA repeatedly downgraded U.S. corn production due to severe droughts in the Midwest. Each new report confirmed tighter supplies, and corn prices rose sharply over several months. Traders who anticipated these bullish revisions and positioned themselves long before the reports were published saw significant gains.

WASDE release days are among the most volatile in the agricultural markets—savvy traders plan their positions accordingly by anticipating trends before the release or reacting quickly to the data as it emerges.

WASDE Trade Setup:

Go Long in March-April when USDA planting projections indicate lower acreage.

Exit in May-June before the market shifts its focus to summer weather.

Speculation and Managed Money: The Hedge Fund Factor

Beyond its fundamentals, corn also constitutes a highly speculative market, attracting hedge funds, institutional investors, and commodity trading advisors (CTAs). These major players utilize futures contracts to hedge risk, manage exposure, or simply speculate on price movements.

How Speculators Influence Prices:

Heavy Buying by Funds → Bullish Momentum → Higher Prices.

Large Liquidations by Funds → Bearish Momentum → Lower Prices.

Trade Study: The 2010–2011 Corn Rally

As global food prices rose sharply in 2010, hedge funds aggressively purchased agricultural commodities, including corn. Their buying spree intensified an already bullish market, driving corn prices from $3.50 per bushel to nearly $8 within a year.

Traders who followed Commitment of Traders (COT) reports, which track fund positions, were able to anticipate the rally and profit from speculative buying.

Watching fund positioning and market sentiment can provide key trading signals, especially when speculative money aggressively enters or exits the market.

Trading Corn Successfully

The corn market is constantly evolving, driven by a combination of fundamental supply and demand factors, macroeconomic influences, and speculative activity. Successful traders don't just respond to price movements—they forecast them by monitoring the key elements discussed in this chapter.

Keeping eyes open for the Next Opportunity?

Watch for U.S. Weather Patterns: Any sign of a 2012-style drought could send prices soaring.

Follow USDA Reports Closely: Yield surprises create instant trade opportunities.

Monitor Energy Markets: High oil prices = higher ethanol demand = bullish corn.

Be Ready to Short Post-Harvest: October-November is often a low point in the season.

4.7.5 Wheat, Give us our Daily Bread

Wheat has been a staple crop for over 8,000 years, originating in the Fertile Crescent, an area covering parts of modern-day Iraq, Syria, Turkey, and Iran. As one of the earliest crops cultivated by ancient civilizations, wheat played a vital role in the development of settled agricultural societies, supporting population growth and the rise of major civilizations such as the Mesopotamians, Egyptians, and Romans.

Today, wheat remains one of the most vital food sources globally, supplying 20% of the world's calories and serving as a dietary mainstay in numerous cultures. Its versatility goes beyond mere food, with wheat derivatives used in biofuels, animal feed, and industrial products.

Global Producers and Their Influence

Modern wheat production is concentrated in a few key regions, each of which influences the global market.

United States—A leading exporter, particularly of hard red winter wheat and soft red wheat, heavily influencing global pricing through the Chicago Board of Trade (CBOT).

Russia—The largest wheat exporter, known for its Black Sea wheat, with geopolitical factors often influencing supply chains.

Canada is a major producer of high-protein wheat, supplying premium-grade exports to milling markets worldwide.

European Union—A powerhouse in soft wheat production, heavily impacting global prices due to France, Germany, and Poland's strong export capacities.

Australia—A key supplier to Asia and the Middle East, specializing in drought-resistant wheat varieties.

Argentina—An emerging exporter, competing with Australia for South American and Asian markets.

Wheat Markets Matter

Wheat prices serve as an indicator for global food security. Weather conditions, geopolitical tensions, export policies, and supply chain logistics influence market fluctuations. Understanding these factors is vital for traders aiming to capitalize on price movements and reduce risk in a commodity that sustains billions worldwide.

In the following sections, we will examine the main price drivers, trading strategies, and historical market shifts that have shaped the wheat industry, equipping you to trade wheat effectively.

Big market moves in Wheat.

2007–2008—Global Food Crisis

During the 2007–2008 period, the world faced a severe global food crisis, characterized by record-high wheat prices driven by a series of poor global harvests, high oil prices (which increased transportation and production costs), and surging demand from emerging economies.

The crisis was especially devastating for developing nations, as rising food costs sparked food riots in over 30 countries, including Egypt, Haiti, and Bangladesh.

Governments responded by imposing export bans and trade restrictions, which further worsened price volatility. This period served as a stark reminder of the interconnectedness of commodity markets and global food security, emphasizing the importance of supply chain resilience and strategic stockpiling.

2022—Russia-Ukraine War & Global Wheat Shock
Ukraine, often called the "breadbasket of Europe," is one of the world's largest wheat exporters, supplying significant amounts to Africa, the Middle East, and Europe. However, the outbreak of the Russia-Ukraine war in 2022 severely disrupted global wheat supply chains.

With ports blocked, infrastructure damaged, and farming activities hindered, Ukraine's wheat exports dropped sharply, causing a major supply shock in global markets. Sanctions on Russian grain exports further worsened the situation, reducing overall supply.

As a result, wheat futures soared to record highs above $12 per bushel, and concerns about food security worldwide increased. This event highlighted how geopolitical risks can affect agricultural markets, prompting countries to reassess their food supply dependencies and diversify their grain sourcing strategies.

Price Drivers in the Wheat Market

Weather Conditions

If you've ever seen a farmer nervously checking the weather forecast, you'll understand how much Mother Nature controls the wheat market. Droughts, excessive rainfall, and temperature extremes can make or break a harvest, causing prices to fluctuate wildly. Too little rain? Yields decrease. Too much rain? Crops drown. Sudden frost? That's game over.

Trade Study—2012 U.S. Drought: The worst drought in decades decimated the Corn Belt, slashing output and skyrocketing wheat prices. Traders who positioned long early in the summer capitalized on the supply shock; likewise, those who jumped on the extended move in the following days.

Global Trade & Export Demand

The wheat market depends not only on U.S. events but also on global demand. Countries such as China, Mexico, and Japan are among the top purchasers of U.S. wheat, and any change in their buying patterns can dramatically affect the market overnight. Trade restrictions, tariffs, or geopolitical tensions can disrupt major export routes, causing volatility.

Trade Study—2020 China Wheat Surge: As China rapidly increased its wheat imports, U.S. wheat prices rose sharply, rewarding traders who anticipated the surge in demand early.

Geopolitical Risks—War, Sanctions, and Export Controls

Wheat markets are highly sensitive to political and military conflicts, as major producers like Russia and Ukraine supply significant global volumes.

Trade Study: During the 2022 Russia-Ukraine War, Ukraine, one of the world's largest wheat exporters, saw its exports plummet as the war disrupted supply chains, driving wheat futures above $12 per bushel. This emphasized that oil is not the only commodity affected by conflict; Ukraine is nicknamed the 'breadbasket' of Europe because of its wheat production.

USDA Reports
Every month, the USDA's WASDE (World Agricultural Supply and Demand Estimates) Report strikes like a bomb on the wheat market. These reports update traders on supply, demand, stockpile levels, and yield forecasts, with any unexpected changes causing futures prices to fluctuate.

Trade Study—2021 Bullish WASDE Report: In early 2021, the USDA lowered its expected wheat stocks, triggering a multi-month rally in wheat futures that pushed prices up by over 40%.

Pro Tip: Always keep an eye on USDA report release dates and position yourself accordingly—an unexpected revision can be a straightforward opportunity to make money!

With those price drivers and trade studies highlighted, the following is an easily digestible trading opportunity guide for the Wheat market.

Wheat Market Trading Opportunity Ideas

Seasonal Trends Trading—Capitalizing on Wheat's Annual Price Cycles
Post-Harvest Decline (July–September): Prices typically drop as fresh supply floods the market.

Winter Wheat Planting Season (October–December): Uncertainty over weather and acreage can support prices.

Pre-Harvest Rally (March–June): Weather risks and global demand drive potential price spikes.

Trade Setup:

Go long in February-April if supply concerns emerge from weather disruptions or geopolitical tensions.

Exit in May-June, before harvest, when price pressure is lower.

Weather-Based Trading—Reacting to Droughts, Rains & Frosts
Droughts in key wheat-producing regions (U.S., Russia, Australia) reduce yields and push prices higher.

Excessive rain or frost during harvest can damage quality and restrict supply.

Trade Setup:

Go long on Wheat Futures when prolonged droughts are forecasted in major producing regions (U.S., Russia, Australia).

Monitor government policies (e.g., export bans) to confirm momentum continuation.

Geopolitical Supply Disruptions—Trading Wheat's Role in Global Food Security
Wheat is a staple food, so wars, sanctions, and trade embargoes can lead to significant price shocks.

The Russia-Ukraine conflict demonstrated how quickly global supply constraints can lead to price spikes.

Trade Setup:

Go long on Wheat when geopolitical risks threaten key producing/exporting nations (Russia, Ukraine, the U.S., Australia).

Watch for trade embargoes or export bans, as these can further exacerbate supply shocks.

USDA Report Trading—Positioning Before Market-Moving Announcements
Monthly WASDE Reports provide updated forecasts on global wheat supply and demand.

Unexpected revisions to yield forecasts, exports, or stockpiles can lead to immediate price fluctuations.

Trade Setup:

Go long a few days before the WASDE Report if preliminary data suggests a bullish surprise (lower production or higher demand).

Go Short if USDA signals record-high stockpiles, anticipating a selloff.

Wheat-Corn Spread Trading—Exploiting Price Correlations
Wheat and corn compete in the livestock feed market, so their prices are often correlated.

If wheat becomes too expensive relative to corn, demand shifts to corn, which in turn lowers wheat prices.

Trade Setup:

Go Long Wheat/Short Corn when wheat is undervalued relative to historical norms.

Go Short Wheat/Long Corn if wheat becomes too expensive relative to corn.

Managed Money & Fund Positioning—Trading Large Speculator Activity

Hedge funds and institutional money often drive wheat price trends.

When managed money holds extreme long or short positions, a reversal may be imminent.

Trade Setup:

Go Long Wheat when funds are excessively short, anticipating a short squeeze.

Go Short when funds are extremely long, expecting profit-taking.

Seizing Wheat Market Opportunities

The wheat market offers a wealth of trading opportunities through fundamental, geopolitical, and spread-based strategies. By monitoring key price drivers—such as weather patterns, global trade disruptions, and USDA reports—traders can improve their chances of capitalizing on wheat's volatility.

4.7.6 Soybeans and Soy-based Products

Ancient Beginnings and Global Expansion

Soybeans have been cultivated for over 3,000 years, originating in China, where they were a staple crop used for food, medicine, and soil enrichment. The Chinese recognized the crop's ability to replenish soil nitrogen, making it an essential part of sustainable farming practices.

By the eighteenth century, European explorers and traders introduced soybeans to the Western world, but it wasn't until the 19th and early twentieth centuries that the crop gained widespread attention in North America.

In the 1920s and 1930s, American agricultural scientists—most notably George Washington Carver—advocated for soybeans as a high-protein, versatile crop. Their research emphasized soybeans' potential for livestock feed, industrial applications, and oil production. This encouraged increased cultivation in the United States, particularly in the Midwest, where climate and soil conditions proved ideal.

The twentieth Century: Industrialization and Market Growth

The United States quickly became the world's largest soybean producer during the twentieth century, driven by technological advances in agriculture and increasing global demand for plant-based protein and vegetable oils. Key historical moments shaped the soybean market's development into a worldwide power:

1973—The U.S. Soybean Export Ban

Global food markets were in chaos during the early 1970s. The Soviet Union, facing poor domestic crop yields, made large-scale purchases of grain and soybeans from the U.S., causing shortages at home and driving up prices.

In response, the U.S. government under President Richard Nixon temporarily banned soybean exports to curb inflation and stabilize domestic prices.

The ban shocked international buyers, particularly those from Japan and European countries, who had become heavily reliant on U.S. soybean imports.

It accelerated soybean production in Brazil and Argentina, creating an opportunity for them to compete with the U.S. as alternative suppliers.

The event highlighted the geopolitical risks to food security, emphasizing the need for long-term trade agreements to prevent sudden disruptions.

To this day, the 1973 U.S. soybean export ban is considered a major turning point in the history of global agricultural trade. It shifted the power balance, allowing South America to become a dominant force in soybean production.

1996—The Introduction of GMO Soybeans

The biotechnology revolution of the 1990s transformed global agriculture, and soybeans were at the forefront. In 1996, Monsanto introduced the first genetically modified (GMO) soybeans, Roundup Ready soybeans.

These GMO soybeans were engineered to resist herbicides, allowing farmers to control weeds more effectively without damaging crops. The introduction of genetically modified soybeans revolutionized farming practices and became one of the most significant innovations in modern agriculture.

This led to the following advancements.

Increased Yields: GMO soybeans enabled higher productivity per acre, enhancing global supply.

Lower Production Costs: Farmers cut weed-control costs and increased efficiency in farming operations.

Rapid Global Adoption: By 2010, over 90% of soybeans grown in the U.S. were genetically modified.

Trade Tensions: Some countries, particularly in Europe, have resisted the use of GMO soybeans, leading to fragmented global trade policies.

As a result, today, genetically modified soybeans dominate global markets, particularly in the U.S., Argentina, and Brazil, contributing to record-breaking production levels.

2018–2019—The U.S.-China Trade War
Soybeans became a political weapon during the U.S.-China trade war, one of the most significant trade disputes in modern history.

In 2018, President Donald Trump imposed tariffs on Chinese goods, citing unfair trade practices. In response, China retaliated with tariffs on U.S. agricultural exports, especially soybeans, as a strategic move against a politically influential sector in the U.S.

Significant Drop in U.S. Exports: China previously purchased over 60% of U.S. soybean exports before the trade war. Tariffs led to a steep decline in demand, prompting U.S. farmers to seek alternative buyers.

Soybean Prices Collapsed: China's sudden loss of a major buyer sent prices from $10.50 per bushel in early 2018 to below $8.50 per bushel by mid-2019.

Brazil and Argentina benefited: As China shifted its sourcing strategy, South American soybean producers gained market share, further reducing U.S. dominance in global soybean exports.

U.S. Government Bailouts: The U.S. government provided billions in subsidies and direct payments under the Market Facilitation Program (MFP) to support struggling farmers.

By early 2020, a Phase One trade deal was agreed between the U.S. and China, partially restoring soybean trade. However, the trade war fundamentally changed global soybean supply chains, strengthening South America's position as a major competitor to the U.S.

This shift is unlikely to reverse quickly. Even with occasional efforts to restore free-trade agreements, the structural realignment caused by the trade war has altered buyer preferences, investment flows, and long-term supply commitments. South America's increased role is now integrated into the global system, making regional rivalry—rather than smooth free trade—the key theme for the soybean market in the coming years.

The Modern Soybean Market
Today, soybeans are one of the most important agricultural commodities in the world. They are a vital component of global food production, serving as:

A primary protein source for livestock feed (pigs, poultry, and cattle).
A key ingredient in vegetable oils used in cooking and processed foods.
A significant input in biofuels, particularly in the U.S. and Brazil.

Current Major Soybean Producers & Exporters

Country	Annual Production (Million Tons)	Global Market Share
Brazil	155	37%
United States	120	29%
Argentina	45	10%
China	19	4%
India	12	3%

From their origins in ancient China to their current role as a staple of global agriculture, soybeans have experienced significant changes driven by technological progress, trade policies, and geopolitical tensions.

They are more than merely a commodity—they are central to food security, trade policy, and renewable energy. For traders, understanding historical shifts and predicting future supply-demand trends is crucial for navigating this constantly changing market.

Soybeans offer diverse trading opportunities in an increasingly interconnected world, whether through seasonal patterns, geopolitical developments, or weather-related supply issues and shocks.

What's moving the Soyabean market

Soybeans are among the most dynamic and widely traded agricultural commodities. A mix of fundamental supply-demand factors, geopolitical tensions, and macroeconomic trends influences their price. Understanding these drivers helps traders to anticipate major market movements and prepare for profitable trades.

Chinese Demand

China is the world's largest importer of soybeans, buying over 60% of the globally traded soybeans. The country's demand is mainly driven by its large livestock industry, especially pork and poultry production, which depends on soybean meal as a vital feed ingredient.

Since China does not produce enough soybeans domestically to satisfy its needs, it relies heavily on imports from Brazil, the U.S., and Argentina. Any change in Chinese demand—whether due to policy shifts, trade agreements, or disease outbreaks—can significantly affect global soybean prices.

Trade Study: 2020 China's Buying Surge

In early 2020, China was recovering from the African Swine Fever (ASF) outbreak, which had devastated its pig population in 2018 and 2019.

The government launched vigorous livestock rebuilding efforts, boosting demand for soybean meal to feed the new hog herds. Meanwhile, the Phase One U.S.-China trade deal was signed, committing China to purchasing record amounts of U.S. agricultural products, including soybeans.

In April 2020, soybeans traded around $8.50 per bushel amid cautious markets.

By October 2020, with China increasing its imports, soybean prices had surged to $12 per bushel, representing a 40% rise in just six months.

Traders who anticipated China's soybean demand resurgence and went long on soybean futures in early 2020 enjoyed one of the biggest agricultural rallies of the decade.

Trade Setup

Go Long on Soybeans when:

China increases soybean import quotas or signs large purchase agreements.

China's hog population is expanding, driving up demand for soybean meal.

Go Short on Soybeans when:

China imposes import restrictions or diverts purchases to alternative suppliers (e.g., Brazil over the U.S.).

Disease outbreaks, such as African Swine Fever, reduce China's livestock population, weakening demand.

Weather Events—The Critical U.S. Midwest Factor

Soybeans are highly sensitive to weather, and adverse conditions during critical growth stages can significantly affect yields. The most important weather periods to monitor are:

Planting Season (April—June) → Wet conditions or delayed planting can affect acreage.

Pollination & Pod Filling (July—August) → Droughts or excessive heat can reduce soybean pod formation and yield.

Harvest Season (September—October) → Heavy rains can damage quality and delay transportation.

Although Brazil and Argentina are major soybean exporters, the U.S. Midwest remains a vital production area, and weather disruptions in this region tend to cause the greatest immediate impact on soybean futures prices.

Trade Study: The 2012 U.S. Midwest Drought

In spring 2012, NOAA weather forecasts warned of below-average rainfall and high temperatures in the U.S. Corn Belt and Midwest.

As the summer unfolded, July 2012 became one of the hottest and driest on record, severely reducing soybean yield potential.

Soybeans were trading near $13 per bushel in May 2012.

By July 2012, as drought conditions worsened, soybean prices exploded to $17.50 per bushel—an all-time high.

Traders who monitored early drought forecasts and went long ahead of the crop stress period made massive gains.

Trade Setup

Go Long on Soybeans when:

NOAA forecasts below-average rainfall and high temperatures in the U.S. Midwest during critical growing stages.

La Niña events (which tend to bring dry weather to South America) emerge during Brazil's growing season.

Go **Short** on Soybeans when:

Favorable weather conditions lead to higher-than-expected yields in the U.S. or Brazil.

El Niño patterns (which typically bring excess rain) improve crop conditions and boost production expectations.

The Soybean Crush Spread—Profiting from Processing Margins

Soybeans are not merely consumed as a raw commodity—they are processed into two main products:

Soybean Meal—Used mainly as livestock feed.

Soybean Oil—Used in cooking, biofuels, and industrial applications.

The Soybean Crush Spread measures the profitability of crushing soybeans into these two products. If soybean meal and oil prices rise faster than raw soybeans, crushers profit more, incentivizing increased production and boosting demand for soybeans.

Trade Study: 2016 Crush Spread Expansion

In early 2016, global livestock production was expanding, increasing demand for soybean meal.

At the same time, crude oil prices rebounded, boosting demand for soybean oil in biodiesel production.

This led to a surge in soybean meal and oil prices, significantly widening the crush spread.

Soybean futures traded around $8.75 per bushel in January 2016.

By July 2016, soybean prices had climbed to over $11.50 per bushel, fueled mainly by rising demand for crushed products.

Traders who monitored the expanding crush margins and went long on soybeans positioned themselves ahead of the bullish move.

Trade Setup

Go Long on Soybeans when:

The soybean crush spread is widening, indicating strong demand for soybean meal and oil.

Livestock expansion (especially in China and the U.S.) increases demand for soybean meal as feed.

Rising crude oil prices support higher demand for soybean oil in biodiesel production.

Go Short on Soybeans when:

The crush spread narrows, signaling weak demand for soybean meal and oil.

Feed demand decreases due to livestock culls or economic downturns, resulting in lower meat consumption.

Crude oil prices fall, weakening demand for soybean oil biofuels.

By understanding these key price drivers and applying proven historical trade setups, traders can start to anticipate significant moves in the soybean market. I know niche agricultural traders who have built very successful careers by specializing in these markets—deeply understanding the fundamentals, seasonality, and trading strategies outlined here. That competitive edge comes from focus and repetition, and now you have access to the same framework and mindset they use.

4.7.7 Lean Hogs: The Market that Sizzles with Opportunity

Lean hog futures may not be the most glamorous markets, but they have long been a crucial part of commodity trading, especially in the UK and the U.S., where pork production is a multi-billion-pound industry. If you've seen the 1983 classic Trading Places, you might recall the famous scene where pork bellies—alongside orange juice futures—are discussed as key components of the financial markets. Although pork bellies (which once had a dedicated futures contract for bacon production) are no longer traded, lean hog futures remain a highly liquid, volatile market with many opportunities for traders.

Pork is one of the world's most widely eaten meats, especially in China, the U.S., and Europe, and lean hog futures enable producers, packers, and traders to hedge against price fluctuations caused by supply and demand imbalances, disease outbreaks, and geopolitical trade issues. Let's examine the history, key market factors, and strategies traders use to profit in the lean hog market.

Origins and Key Historical Moments in the Lean Hog Market

Hog production has been a vital part of human agriculture for thousands of years, with pigs being domesticated as early as 5,000 BCE in China and the Middle East.

However, it was not until the twentieth century that the modern pork industry and lean-hog commodity trading genuinely developed.

The Evolution of the Pork Market

Pre-twentieth Century: Pork was primarily produced and consumed locally due to the lack of refrigeration and modern transportation.

The 1860s—Chicago: The Hog Butchery Capital of the World: The expansion of the railroads and stockyards made Chicago the epicenter of pork production in the U.S.

1966—The Introduction of Lean Hog Futures: The Chicago Mercantile Exchange (CME) introduced lean hog futures to allow pork producers and processors to hedge price risk and create stability in an often-volatile market.

1983—Pork Bellies Become Famous: The film Trading Places popularized the concept of trading in pork bellies. At the time, pork belly futures were actively traded, as demand for frozen bacon was high.

2011—The End of Pork Belly Futures: Due to changing consumer preferences and industry shifts, pork belly futures were removed from the CME, but lean hog futures continued to lead pork trading.

Events That Shaped the Lean Hog Market

2013—Porcine Epidemic Diarrhoea Virus (PEDv) Outbreak

A devastating virus spread across the U.S. hog population, killing millions of piglets and reducing pork supply.

Market Impact: The severe supply shortage drove lean hog prices up by more than 60%, reaching record highs.

2018—African Swine Fever (ASF) in China

ASF wiped out nearly half of China's pig population, causing a severe pork shortage in the world's largest pork-consuming country. Market Impact:

China was forced to import large quantities of pork from the U.S., Brazil, and the EU, driving up global pork prices.

2020—COVID-19 and Processing Plant Shutdowns
The pandemic disrupted slaughterhouses and pork-processing plants, leading to a backlog of hogs on farms.

Market Impact: Prices initially collapsed due to an oversupply of live hogs, but rebounded when processing plants reopened, spurring a surge in consumer demand.

Trade ideas for big market movements in Lean Hogs
Like all agricultural markets, lean hog prices are influenced by basic supply and demand, but they also exhibit unique seasonal trends and risk factors that make them highly volatile.

Disease Outbreaks—The Most Devastating Market Movers
Pork production is highly vulnerable to disease outbreaks, which can wipe out millions of pigs in a short period, disrupting supply chains and driving prices skyrocketing.

Trade Study: African Swine Fever (ASF) in China (2018)

ASF decimated nearly 40% of China's pig herd, forcing the country to import record amounts of pork.

Lean hog futures surged over 100% between 2018 and 2019 as global supplies tightened.

Trade Setup:

Go long on Lean Hogs if a major hog disease outbreak reduces supply in the U.S., China, or the EU.

Go short on Lean Hogs if disease outbreaks subside or a vaccine is found and supply levels normalize.

Seasonal Cycles—Hogs Follow a Predictable Price Pattern
The lean hog market follows a well-established seasonal cycle driven by breeding and production patterns:

Key Seasonal Patterns:

Spring (April—June): Prices tend to rally as pork demand increases heading into the summer grilling season.

Summer (July—September): Peak pork demand increases prices.

Fall/Winter (October—February): Prices decrease as production increases and demand weakens.

Trade Setup:
Go Long in April-May ahead of peak summer demand.
Go Short in October-November when supply increases post-harvest.

Feed Costs—Corn and Soybean Prices Influence Hog Prices
Since hogs are grain-fed, changes in the cost of corn and soybeans directly impact production costs. When feed prices rise, hog farmers reduce herd sizes, leading to lower supply and higher pork prices.

Trade Study: The 2012 Drought and High Feed Costs

A severe drought in the U.S. Corn Belt led to a surge in corn and soybean prices.

Farmers reduced hog production due to the high cost of feed, causing lean hog prices to spike by 30%.

Trade Setup:
Go long on Lean Hogs when corn and soybean prices increase significantly.
Go Short on Lean Hogs when feed prices decline, leading to higher pork production.

U.S.-China Trade Relations—The Largest Pork Trade Flows
China is the world's largest pork consumer, and U.S. exports play a critical role in balancing the global supply. Trade tariffs, sanctions, and trade agreements significantly impact lean hog prices.

Trade Study: 2018 U.S.-China Trade War

China imposed tariffs on U.S. pork, reducing exports and causing lean hog prices to collapse by nearly 40%.

As the trade war eased in 2020, China ramped up pork purchases, leading to a major price recovery.

Trade Setup:
Go long on Lean Hogs when China increases pork imports from the U.S.
Go short on Lean Hogs if trade tensions escalate and tariffs are imposed.

Keeping your snout in the trough.
To all vegetarians out there, trading lean hogs might not match your ethical views—I completely understand. I haven't eaten meat for years, but as a trader, my main goal is to outperform the market, not to change it (yet). Trading isn't about personal beliefs; it's about spotting opportunities and making the most of them.

Lean hogs may not be as commonly followed as crude oil or gold, but they present some of the most explosive trading opportunities in the agricultural commodity market. Disease outbreaks, seasonal patterns, and global trade flows generate substantial price swings that can be highly profitable for traders who understand the market.

From ancient pig farming in China to modern futures contracts on the CME, pork remains a vital global commodity. With the right strategy and understanding of key market drivers, trading lean hogs can be just as rewarding as capitalizing on a major move in crude oil—or, for some, enjoying a perfectly cooked bacon sandwich!

4.7.8 Feeder and Live Cattle: Trading the Meat Markets

Cattle have been a cornerstone of human civilization for thousands of years, providing food, labor, and materials. In modern markets, feeder and live cattle futures serve as vital tools for ranchers, meatpackers, and traders to hedge against price fluctuations. These markets are highly cyclical, influenced by weather conditions, feed costs, and consumer demand, creating trading opportunities for those who understand market dynamics.

Although feeder and live cattle futures may lack the widespread appeal of crude oil or gold, they have been fundamental to agricultural trading for many decades. Whether you're an experienced trader or new to commodities, understanding what influences these markets is vital for capitalizing on price movements.

Origins and Key Historical Moments in the Cattle Market

Cattle farming has a history spanning thousands of years, but modern futures trading in feeder and live cattle originated from the growth of the U.S. cattle industry and the need for price stability.

The Birth of the Cattle Trade

Ancient Domestication (10,000 BCE): Early humans domesticated cattle for milk, meat, and labor in Mesopotamia and the Indus Valley.

Spanish Introduction to the Americas (1500s): Spanish explorers brought cattle to the Americas, laying the foundation for the U.S. cattle industry.

U.S. Cattle Drives (1800s): Cowboys drove cattle across the Great Plains, supplying beef to booming cities in the East.

The Evolution of Cattle Futures

1964—Live Cattle Futures Introduced: The Chicago Mercantile Exchange (CME) launched live cattle futures to provide ranchers and processors with a way to hedge against price volatility.

1971—Feeder Cattle Futures Added: As feedlots expanded, the need for a futures contract that reflected younger cattle before they were fattened for slaughter led to the introduction of feeder cattle contracts.

Pivotal market moments in the cattle market
The cattle market has experienced significant price fluctuations, driven by disease outbreaks, droughts, and shifting consumer pRefs.

2003—Mad Cow Disease (Bovine Spongiform Encephalopathy, BSE)
The discovery of BSE in a U.S. cow led to an immediate ban on exports to key beef buyers, including Japan and South Korea.

Prices plummeted, with live cattle futures dropping over 20% in the following months.

It took years for U.S. beef exports to recover as countries slowly lifted restrictions.

2014–2015—Record Cattle Prices Due to Drought
A severe drought in the U.S. Midwest and Texas led to a significant decline in cattle herd sizes.

With fewer cattle available for slaughter, live cattle prices reached record highs, exceeding $170 per hundredweight (cwt). The limited supply pushed up beef prices, causing ripple effects throughout the food industry.

2019–2020—COVID-19 Supply Chain Disruptions
Meatpacking plant closures due to worker shortages led to massive cattle backlogs.

With fewer slaughterhouses processing cattle, feeder cattle prices fell as ranchers struggled to offload livestock.

Live cattle futures also saw extreme volatility, with prices briefly crashing before rebounding as processing plants reopened.

Trade ideas and market-moving events
Like all agricultural markets, the prices of live cattle and feeder cattle are influenced by fundamental supply and demand factors. However, feed costs, weather conditions, consumer demand, and global trade create distinct price fluctuations that traders can exploit.

Feed Costs—Corn & Soymeal Prices Impact Cattle Production
Cattle are grain-fed, meaning fluctuations in corn and soybean meal prices directly affect production costs.

Higher Feed Prices → Increased Production Costs → Smaller Herds → Higher Future Cattle Prices

Lower Feed Prices → Reduced Costs → Herd Expansion → Lower Cattle Prices

Trade Study: The 2012 Drought and High Corn Prices

A historic U.S. drought in 2012 caused corn prices to soar past $8 per bushel. Ranchers sold off herds early to avoid high feeding costs, temporarily lowering cattle prices. However, by 2013–2014, reduced herd sizes caused a significant supply shortage, pushing live cattle prices to record highs.

Trade Setup:

Go long on Live Cattle Futures when feed costs rise, expecting herd liquidations and future supply shortages.

Go short on Live Cattle Futures when corn and soybean meal prices drop, anticipating herd expansion and increased supply.

Seasonal Cycles—Cattle Prices Follow a Predictable Annual Pattern

Cattle markets have well-defined seasonal price trends, primarily driven by breeding cycles and consumer demand.

Key Seasonal Patterns:

Spring (March-May): Feeder cattle prices rise as ranchers prepare for summer grazing.

Summer (June—August): Live cattle prices peak due to high grilling season demand.

Fall (September—November): Live cattle prices decline as slaughter numbers increase post-summer.

Winter (December—February): Prices often remain weaker due to reduced demand for premium beef cuts.

Trade Setup:

Go long on Feeder Cattle in March-April, anticipating rising demand from ranchers.

Go long on Live Cattle in June-July ahead of peak summer beef consumption.

Go short on Live Cattle in October-November, expecting seasonal slaughter-driven price drops.

Weather Conditions—Droughts & Harsh Winters Disrupt Cattle Supply

Extreme weather can affect cattle production, impacting pasture conditions, herd sizes, and transportation logistics.

Droughts = Poor Grazing Land → Ranchers Sell Cattle Early → Short-Term Supply Surge → Long-Term Supply Shortage.

Winter Storms = Delayed Slaughter & Transport Disruptions → Short-Term Price Spikes

Trade Study: The Texas Drought (2011–2013)

A prolonged drought in Texas and the Midwest caused pasture shortages, forcing ranchers to liquidate herds early. Cattle prices initially fell, but by 2014–2015, the scarcity of available cattle led to record-breaking price rallies.

Trade Setup:

Go long on Live Cattle if NOAA forecasts drought, anticipating future supply shortages.

Go long on Live Cattle if winter storms disrupt slaughterhouse operations, expecting short-term price spikes.

Consumer Demand & Beef Prices—The Steak vs. Fast-Food Effect

Live cattle prices are heavily influenced by consumer demand for beef, particularly in steakhouses, grocery stores, and fast-food chains.

Economic Growth = Higher Demand for Steak = Higher Cattle Prices

Recessions = Weaker Premium Beef Demand = Lower Cattle Prices

Fast Food Demand = Consistent Base-Level Beef Consumption

Trade Study: The 2008 Financial Crisis

During the 2008 recession, expensive steak cuts experienced lower demand, leading to weaker prices for live cattle. However, demand for fast-food beef products remained stable, preventing a total price collapse.

Trade Setup:

Go long on Live Cattle if consumer confidence and disposable income rise, leading to higher beef demand.

Go short on Live Cattle if a recession or economic downturn weakens steak and grocery store beef consumption.

Global Trade & Export Demand—The China & Japan Factor

The U.S. is a top beef exporter, with major buyers including China, Japan, and South Korea. Trade policies, tariffs, and disease outbreaks can cause sharp price movements.

Trade Study: China's U.S. Beef Import Ban Lifted (2017)

In 2017, China ended a 14-year ban on U.S. beef imports, leading to a 15% rally in live cattle futures as traders anticipated higher demand.

Trade Setup:

Go long on Live Cattle when China or Japan increase U.S. beef imports.

Go short on Live Cattle if export bans or tariffs restrict U.S. beef sales abroad.

Profiting From the Cattle Market's Cycles

The live cattle and feeder cattle markets display some of the most predictable price cycles in the agricultural commodity sector. Whether you're analyzing seasonal patterns, macroeconomic developments, or spread opportunities, the key to success is understanding how weather, feed costs, consumer demand, and exports influence price movements.

While non-professional traders may overlook these food-based markets unless they are at their local grocery store, their predictability, interconnected dynamics, and volatility create year-round opportunities that give traders FOOD for thought!

4.7.9 Understanding the Importance of COT and WASDE Reports in Agricultural Markets

When trading agricultural markets such as corn, wheat, soybeans, and livestock, two essential reports can greatly influence market prices and offer valuable insights for traders: the Commitments of Traders (COT) Report and the World Agricultural Supply and Demand Estimates (WASDE) Report.

Understanding these reports, knowing when they are published, and interpreting the information they provide can help traders identify market trends, sentiment shifts, and potential trading opportunities.

Commitments of Traders (COT) Report

The COT report, released weekly by the U.S. Commodity Futures Trading Commission (CFTC), provides a breakdown of positions held by various types of traders in the futures markets, including agricultural commodities. It offers insights into market sentiment and positioning, helping traders understand what the "smart money" is doing.

The COT report is published every Friday at 3:30 PM ET, reflecting data as of the previous Tuesday.

It covers a range of commodities, including corn, wheat, soybeans, live cattle, and lean hogs.

Types of Traders in the COT Report

Commercial Traders (Hedgers)

These producers and end-users mitigate their exposure to price risks through the futures markets.

For example, a grain farmer would be hedging against a future fall in wheat prices.

Non-Commercial Traders (Speculators)
These include large traders, such as hedge funds and commodity trading advisors (CTAs), who aim to profit from price movements.

Speculative positions are often a good indicator of market sentiment.

Non-Reportable Traders (Retail Traders)
Smaller traders who do not meet the reporting thresholds.

How to Interpret the COT Report
Net Long/Short Positions: If non-commercial traders are significantly net long, it suggests a bullish sentiment; if they are net short, it suggests a bearish sentiment.

Position Changes: Sharp increases or decreases in positions can indicate a potential trend reversal or breakout.

Commercial vs. Speculator Divergence: When commercial traders are heavily long while speculators are heavily short (or vice versa), it often signals a potential shift in the market.

Potential Trading Ideas Using the COT Report
Trend Reversal Setup: If speculators hold an extreme net short position while commercials are net long, consider going long, expecting a short squeeze or trend reversal.

Momentum Play: If speculators are increasing net long positions, consider following the trend with a momentum-based strategy.

Basically, the COT report gives traders insight into where the main players are positioned and how sentiment is changing beneath the surface. It is not a standalone indicator, but when combined with solid technical and fundamental analysis, it becomes a powerful tool for spotting turning points, confirming trends, and understanding the wider forces influencing a market.

World Agricultural Supply and Demand Estimates (WASDE) Report
The WASDE report, published monthly by the U.S. Department of Agriculture (USDA), provides a detailed overview of supply and demand forecasts for key agricultural commodities. It includes data on production, consumption, exports, and ending stocks, making it one of the most influential reports in agricultural markets.

The WASDE report is released on or around the 10th of each month at noon ET.

It covers major agricultural commodities, such as corn, wheat, soybeans, and livestock.

Important Sections of the WASDE Report

Production Estimates
Forecasts for crop yields and livestock production.

Impact: Lower-than-expected production can lead to higher prices, while higher production can lead to price declines.

Consumption and Export Projections
Estimates of domestic consumption and international exports.

Impact: Strong export demand can be bullish, while weak demand can be bearish.

Ending Stocks
The projected amount of a commodity left over at the end of the marketing year.

Impact: Lower ending stocks are bullish, indicating tight supply; higher ending stocks are bearish, indicating ample supply.

Price Projections
The USDA's projection of average farm prices for key commodities.

Impact: These projections can influence market sentiment.

How to Interpret the WASDE Report
Bullish Signals: Lower-than-expected production, higher export demand, or lower ending stocks.

Bearish Signals: Higher-than-expected production, weaker export demand, or higher ending stocks.

Neutral Signals: Data in line with market expectations.

Potential Trading Ideas Using the WASDE Report

Breakout Setup: If the WASDE report reveals bullish news (e.g., lower production or stocks), consider going long on futures contracts, anticipating a price breakout.

Fade the Move: If the market initially reacts strongly but overextends, consider fading the move (shorting after a bullish spike or buying after a bearish drop).

Combining COT and WASDE Insights for Trading Strategies

Pre-WASDE Positioning Using the COT Report

Strategy: Utilize the COT report to assess market sentiment and positioning before the WASDE release.

Example: If speculators are net long in soybeans ahead of the WASDE report and it is bullish, the move could be amplified.

Trend Confirmation Using COT and WASDE

Strategy: If the COT report shows increasing long positions in corn and the WASDE confirms lower production or strong exports, consider going long for a trend-following trade.

Contrarian Play

Strategy: If the COT report shows extreme speculative positioning and the WASDE contradicts market expectations, consider a contrarian trade (e.g., shorting after a rally).

Timing Considerations for COT and WASDE Reports

Fridays (COT Report): Ideal for planning trades for the following week based on shifts in positioning.

Mid-Month (WASDE Report): Ideal for anticipating major market moves based on fundamental supply and demand data.

Traders analyzing the COT and WASDE reports can gain a valuable advantage in agricultural markets. These reports provide insights into market sentiment, positioning, and fundamental supply and demand dynamics, allowing traders to make better-informed decisions and capitalize on market-moving events.

Preparation doesn't stop here.

This first section of the book has been deliberately meaty. Preparation is not the most exciting part of trading, but it is the part that determines who lasts long enough to succeed. For that reason, this section has been designed as a reference you can return to long after finishing the book.

We started by immersing you in the language of the markets—learning how traders speak, think, and interpret information—so that it becomes familiar rather than daunting. From there, we concentrated on developing the trader mindset: goal-setting, motivation, and managing the psychological forces that damage performance. Fear, greed, and overconfidence are not only problems for beginners; they are challenges faced throughout a career, and I still encounter them in my own trading.

We then established the fundamentals of how markets truly operate: supply and demand, the circular flow of income, efficient markets, and the central role of monetary policy in the modern economy. Without this knowledge, traders often respond to price movements without understanding what is actually driving them.

From there, we examined the markets themselves, categorized into three practical groups. Money markets—currencies, interest rates, equities, precious metals, and digital assets. Energy markets—oil and natural gas—drive economic activity. And agricultural markets—the food sector that supports daily life, from sugar and grains to soybeans and livestock. Each market has its own drivers, reports, and cycles, all of which will become increasingly important as you use fundamental analysis later in the book.

The markets discussed here are not random choices. They are highly liquid markets I have personally traded, and the same markets where many traders in my network—including several earning seven figures annually—continue to succeed. There are many others to explore. I've traded nearly a hundred over my career, and my advice is straightforward: start with what genuinely interests you, develop your competence, and gradually expand as your confidence builds.

This level of preparation is crucial. Successful trading requires much more analysis and planning than just execution. The best traders understand their markets, know their goals, and trade with purpose before making a move.

With that foundation established, you're prepared to advance. The following section transforms preparation into action.

Welcome to the trading process.

Part II

Process

5

The Professional Trading Process

5.1 Moving from Preparation to Process

An old but powerful saying in trading is: "Fail to prepare, prepare to fail." Preparation sets the stage for your trading journey, equipping you with the right mindset and foundational market knowledge. Before you step into active trading, it's vital to clearly understand why you're trading and which markets genuinely excite and align with your personal goals.

By now, you will have a solid grasp of the following, providing a strong foundation as you progress to the next phase of your trading journey:

Developing a Professional Trader's Mindset: Focusing on critical mental attributes such as discipline, resilience, patience, and setting realistic goals. These traits form the backbone of consistent trading success.

Understanding Mental Toughness: Embracing the reality of trading and preparing yourself to manage and thrive during inevitable highs and lows. Mental toughness transforms setbacks into stepping stones.

Grasping Core Market Concepts: Building your foundational understanding of essential market dynamics, including supply and demand, macroeconomic influences, market efficiency, and your role within the broader financial ecosystem.

Exploring Asset Classes: Delving into various markets such as forex, commodities, stocks, crypto, energy, and bonds. Identifying which markets naturally align with your interests, strengths, and financial ambitions.

Simplifying Key Trading Terms: Familiarizing yourself with essential trading vocabulary through a clear, beginner-friendly glossary. Demystifying

S. Warner-Baker, *Learn to Trade Like a Professional*,
https://doi.org/10.1007/978-3-032-20125-6_5

complex jargon ensures you engage confidently and competently in market discussions.

Thoroughly covering these areas equips you with both the mental clarity and market knowledge required to trade confidently. This preparation enables you to make informed decisions, manage risks effectively, and seize profitable trading opportunities.

With solid preparation complete, you are now perfectly positioned to transition seamlessly into the book's Sect. 5.1: the Trade Process.

5.1.1 Origin and Evolution of the Professional Trading Process

'I'm sure you'll figure it out, you're a smart guy ... That was the advice I received from the owner of the trading floor where I'd just landed a job. He was referring to trading short-term interest rates around the world, a product I had never even heard of before walking through those doors.

He was a veteran of the LIFFE trading floor, a world with little to no computer interaction. Truth be told, I believe he was somewhat hesitant around the machines, which is probably why he left me to it. The LIFFE floor had closed down a couple of years earlier, and I was part of a new era—one characterized by digital screens, electronic markets, and a steep learning curve with no handrails.

His assumption proved to be correct. I did figure it out—not before wiping out six months of profits in a single day and earning myself a stern talk and a final warning. I never said the path to success was easy.

The method I was taught was straightforward: sink or swim. For the first six months, I was trying to stay afloat. My technical analysis training came from someone who, I later discovered, was an actor—never traded a day in his life. The rest of my early education involved two exchange visits, where they explained what their markets were—but not how to profit from them.

So we learned the hard way: through trial and error. Twelve hours a day, five days a week, staring at screens and trying to crack the markets' puzzle with the traders around me. That sense of community and camaraderie was like gold dust. A few of those traders I sat shoulder to shoulder with back then are still some of my closest friends today.

Among us, fresh-faced juniors dreamed of Porsches and Rolexes, rubbing shoulders with seasoned veterans from the old trading pits. Those guys were bursting with wisdom and experience, and the cost of learning from them? Usually just a cup of tea–or six each day.

It was a unique environment, but it worked. It equipped us with the skills we needed to survive and, for a fortunate few, to thrive. I was one of those lucky ones. I made a profit in my first year—something only 1% of traders in the company had achieved in its entire history.

That first year taught me something that no chart, mentor, or course ever could—success in trading isn't about being right all the time. It's about having a repeatable, reliable process. One that keeps you grounded when you're riding high, and stops you bleeding out when you're taking hits.

Back then, my approach was instinct, repetition, and lessons written in red on a P&L screen. It was reactive, not refined. But gradually, through testing, tracking, and tweaking, I began to develop a framework I could rely on—one that adapted across different market conditions and product types.

Fail fast, learn the lesson, move on. That became my mantra. Every day, over and over again. And it shaped my trading career.

Fast-forward ten years, and I found myself in my own office with space for over a hundred traders. I recruited from top institutions, mentored a new generation of traders, and lectured at a top-ten business school.

But something wasn't right.

The junior traders weren't achieving the same results. The success rate had fallen. The game had evolved, and our training hadn't kept pace. Something had to give—and the area most within my control was training and mentoring these individuals.

So I stepped back and took a proper look. Not just at my own office, but at the entire group, now comprising 15 offices worldwide. Hundreds of traders. And I realized something fundamental:

It was time for an overhaul.

The way we trained traders had to evolve. Because if there's one thing the markets teach you, it's that what worked yesterday won't always work tomorrow. Adapt or be left behind.

Evolution

During this period of reflection, the company appointed a new Head of Markets, Mike Shirley, in the UK, and he was the first to ask how he could genuinely assist me; prior to that, I had to figure out new markets with the support of my expanding team of traders. I was already familiar with this individual—he used to run a similar-sized office on the other side of the country, and, in a curious twist of fate, his wife and I attended the same university in the same year.

My only wish was to access performance data from over 500 traders in the group. I aimed to identify what was lacking in our training—what distinguished good traders from elite performers.

Over the next three years, I studied the data sets diligently. I retrospectively analyzed winning trades across various markets, interviewed as many top performers as possible, and tested every insight on my own trading account before implementing it more broadly.

The outcome of that investigation and knowledge hunt was the trading process that laid the foundation for the professional trainee trader program for the traders in my office, and later for the hundreds of new, eager professional market participants employed through the international trading academy I helped establish for the group.

A comprehensive, proven methodology became the gold standard of trader training for Europe's largest proprietary trading company. One that I am now sharing with you in the hope that it will help change your life as much as it has changed mine and many others.

5.1.2 Enter the Trading Process

Most new traders begin by chasing trades—jumping between markets, grabbing at setups, hoping something will work. There's no strategy, no consistency, just a frantic rush to be 'in the market'. It's noisy, reactive, and tiring. That's why so many fail.

In the UK, it's estimated that over 75% of retail traders lose money. That's not a trivial statistic—it's a reality check for this industry. Look a little deeper, and you'll find the main reason for failure isn't a lack of intelligence or effort. It's the absence of a clear vision and solid process.

This statistic inspired me to combine my coaching, education, and trading skills and share them with as many people as possible to help bridge that gap.

Professionals don't trade noise. They operate from clarity.
They start with a clear approach. Yes, they analyze multiple markets using various strategies. However, everything they do is based on a structured, repeatable process—a mindset and a method that enable them to focus on high-probability opportunities and avoid the emotional pitfalls that trap many.

This chapter focuses on that initial step in the process: finding a trade. Because you can't manage or evaluate something you never had a reason to pursue.

We're not relying on guesswork. We're creating a clear vision, and that begins with understanding what you're seeking and why.

6

Identifying a Trade

When I sit down at my trading screens, I have a strange little habit—I talk to the market.

Not out loud (most of the time), but in my mind. I see the market as a living, breathing entity—one that, if I'm present, focused, and respectful, will reveal the opportunities I need to reach my goals.

Each day begins with a quiet ritual.

I ask the market: "Show me what I need to do today."

This is how I begin to move forward in my process.

Step one is always exploration—identifying the trades.

We accomplish this using technical analysis, fundamental analysis, seasonality, and price action—four potent tools that can operate independently or together to offer a complete overview.

In this chapter, we'll examine the techniques professionals use to spot opportunities that can make—or even transform—your trading day.

First up, Technical Analysis.

6.1 What Does the Chart Say?

I was first introduced to technical analysis in the early 2000s.

An "expert" came in to guide us junior traders through the basics over a couple of days. He confidently pointed to charts and, in hindsight, demonstrated how obvious certain market moves had been because of the formations that had appeared.

S. Warner-Baker, *Learn to Trade Like a Professional*,
https://doi.org/10.1007/978-3-032-20125-6_6

The problem?

I never saw him do it live. Not once.

A few years later, I heard he had left the trading world entirely ... to become an actor. No joke. This was also the same bloke who proudly told us about the £1,000 coffee machine he had just bought while being paid to show us this fantasy world of pretty colored charts.

To say I was skeptical of technical analysis after that would be a serious understatement.

You're telling me that after three years at university studying business and finance, after all the models, theories, and macroeconomic frameworks, the world's trillion-dollar markets are being driven by patterns on a chart?

Come on. You've got to be kidding.

Fast-forward over a decade, and I'm standing before a full university lecture hall, delivering my first talk on technical analysis.

I tell the students the truth—the same truth I wish someone had told me when I first learned about candlestick patterns and chart formations.

Technical analysis is a pseudoscience.

It exists—and functions—because enough people believe in it.

It's not based on rigorous economic theory or Nobel Prize-winning models. It's not even attempting to be.

What it is, however, is a shared language—a visual framework that helps traders, from retail speculators to institutional professionals, make sense of price behavior, human emotion, and collective psychology.

When you examine a chart, you're not merely observing data. You're witnessing belief, fear, greed, and momentum.

You're observing everyone else's decisions, opinions, and hesitations reflected in the price.

Because many people watch the same charts—and often the same patterns, levels, and indicators—those patterns tend to become self-fulfilling.

Support and resistance exist not because they're magical, but because enough traders believe they are significant ... and act accordingly.

So yes, technical analysis isn't about being "right" in a scientific sense.

It's about understanding what everyone else sees—and then using that understanding to position yourself ahead of the crowd.

And after nearly two decades of trading, I can tell you this:

It may not be science ... but it works.

Let's be clear—the aim of this book isn't to become the go–to encyclopedia on technical analysis.

There are already shelves full of those.

What I am going to do is provide you with an honest, professional view on how traders use charts in real-world situations—not in theory, but in practice—to help them move closer to profitability.

As a trader, when I look at a chart, I really only care about two things:

Which direction is this market heading?
Where might it turn around?

That's it.

That's the lens I use. That's the focus I want you to develop, too.

This section will cover a core set of technical indicators and the basic psychology behind them. There will be no fluff or overcomplication—just what works.

Because here's the truth: technical analysis is a rabbit hole, filled with opinion, sorcery, and endless debate.

You'll get lost if you don't anchor yourself with simplicity and clarity.

I live by the mantra: Keep it simple.

And by the end of this chapter, you'll understand why.

6.1.1 The Basics of Technical Analysis

I always operate under the assumption that anyone I am training or teaching has never seen a candlestick chart before—and that you don't yet know what one is. If I explain things from the very beginning, I can ensure we don't lose you as we explore the deeper aspects of technical analysis.

So, let's start right there.

98% of the trading world uses a candlestick chart to analyze a market. This chart resembles the one below.

Why does everyone use these charts? Two key reasons:

Clarity—Color quickly shows market direction (typically green for up, red for down).
Depth—Each candle gives you four essential data points:
Open—where the market started that session.
High—the highest price traded.
Low—the lowest price traded.
Close—where it finished.

This makes candlestick charts far more informative than a simple line chart, which only shows closing prices.

Time runs along the X-axis on any chart, and market price runs up and down the Y-axis.

Each candlestick represents what happened during a specific time period, and that time period is your first adjustable variable when conducting technical analysis.

Common time frames include:

Daily charts—each candle shows a full day of market activity.
Hourly charts—each candle represents one hour.
10-minute charts—each candle gives a snapshot of the most recent price action.

These three time frames—daily, hourly, and 10-minute—are the ones we will focus on throughout this book. I describe them as examining the market from a:

Long-term view (daily),
Medium-term view (hourly),
Short-term view (10-minute).

They'll become the backbone of our TA exploration in the coming chapters.

Once you're confident with your own technical analysis, you can select the time frames that best suit your trading style. For now, however, we'll establish your foundation with these three—simple, structured, and highly effective.

Each candle tells a story—and once you know how to read that story, the market starts to reveal its rhythm.

Here's a visual to help you see exactly what each part of the candlestick represents:

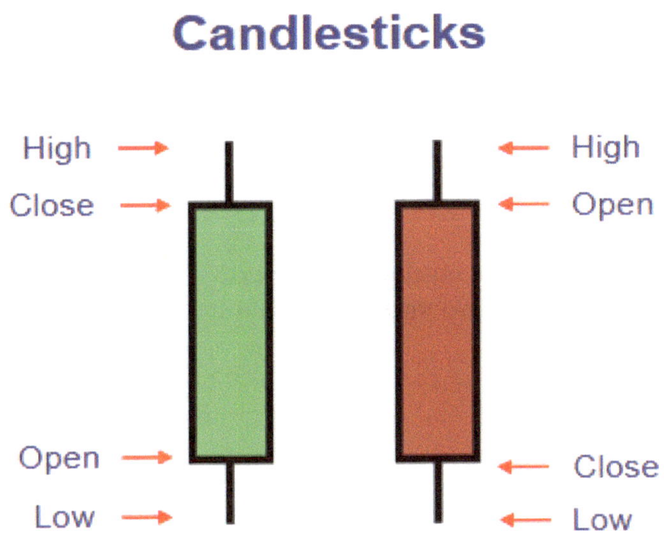

Remember—Green = up and Red = down. Simple (so far)

The Birth of the Candlestick Chart

The candlestick chart dates back to the eighteenth century in Japan.

It was developed by a legendary rice trader named Munehisa Homma, often referred to as the "God of Markets."

Homma observed that although supply and demand influenced rice prices, emotions and psychology also played a crucial role. Therefore, he started monitoring price movements—not just the market trends, but how traders responded to them.

He developed a system using visual "candles" to record the open, high, low, and close for each trading day. This provided him with a clearer view of market structure and trader sentiment.

Homma reportedly accumulated a fortune in the rice markets, and his charting methods ultimately laid the groundwork for what is now recognized as candlestick analysis.

The method remained a well-kept Japanese secret until the 1980s, when Steve Nison introduced it to the Western world in his book Japanese Candlestick Charting Techniques, a timeless classic that is well worth a look if TA becomes your thing. It is full of a multitude of technical candlestick signals, in my opinion, too many to implement them all successfully in your trading.

Today, nearly every trader worldwide uses candlestick charts.

What are we looking for?

Just like the late, great Munehisa Homma, we're not just looking at charts for the sake of it—we're looking to identify winning trades.

More specifically, we're asking two critical questions as mentioned before, but need repeating:

Which direction is the market going next?
Where is it likely to stop and turn around?

These two questions form the foundation of our use of technical analysis. They keep our focus sharp and our process grounded.

For many years, every time I open a new chart, I come back to a quiet mantra I've repeated for years:

"Show me where you want to go."

Because the market will tell you—if you know how to listen.

6.1.2 "The Trend Is Your Friend." Identifying a Market Direction

Yes—it's the most overused rhyme in trading. But clichés stick around for a reason: there's truth in them.

And that's exactly where we're headed next—learning how to locate market direction.

When you strip it all back, a market can only move in one of three ways:

Bullish—the market is going up.
Bearish—the market is going down.
Sideways/Rangebound—the market is moving without a clear direction, stuck in a range.

This third type can trip up many traders when a market is rangebound. However, it's just as important as recognizing a strong uptrend or downtrend, and it will help us when we focus on identifying counter-trend opportunities.

Before we get ahead of ourselves, I would like to share my tried-and-true top three techniques, which consistently deliver clear results and a repeatable format that can be applied across any market.

6.1.3 My Three Core Techniques for Spotting a Market Direction

Number 1—Higher Highs and Higher Lows / Lower Highs and Lower Lows
This is the most natural way to assess a trend—by reading the price structure itself.

If the market is consistently making higher highs and higher lows, it's in an uptrend.

If the market is making lower highs and lower lows, you're looking at a downtrend.

If there's no clear structure and the price is chopping sideways, you're likely in a range-bound or consolidating market.

You don't need an indicator for this—just your eyes, a clear chart, and some focus. A strong series of green candles signals that the market is trending upward, while red candles indicate the opposite. You need to put on your detective's cap and examine the minute details of each candle's open/close and high/low.

Example—Bullish uptrend

This chart shows a higher number of green candles, indicating a bullish (up) market. Upon closer inspection, most candles close higher each time; if they don't, the low is higher than the previous candle's low.

Example—Bearish downtrend

You can observe a slow, gradual downtrend forming to the left of the chart, characterized by lower lows and lower highs. The chart appears to flatten in the middle and is trending sideways. Afterwards, the price action shifts back to a bearish trend with a steep decline, again with lower lows and lower highs.

Example—When the market goes sideways. Rangebound

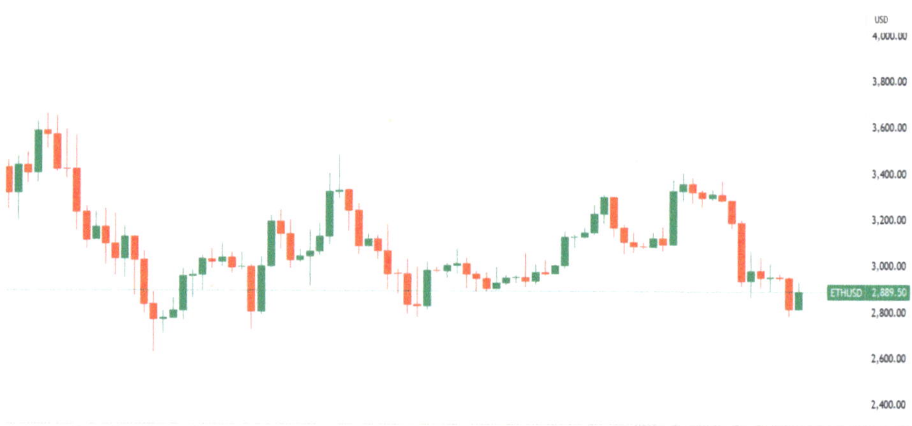

In a range-bound market, the price tends to bounce between a clear low and a clear high, levels that are relatively close together compared to a trending environment.

You'll often notice this when the market lacks clear direction. It's caught in indecision. Buyers and sellers are evenly matched, and the market is essentially pausing to catch its breath.

Markets rarely remain in a range forever. There is almost always a catalyst nearby—a data release, a geopolitical event, or simply a shift in sentiment. History repeatedly demonstrates that sideways markets eventually break into directional moves.

Our role as traders is to be prepared for that breakout if we aim to trade in that direction, and to remain patient until it occurs.

Number 2—Trendlines

This is, without question, the most-used piece of technical analysis in my entire trading career. Trendlines have helped me locate thousands of trades over the years—and I keep returning to them for one simple reason: they work.

They're easy to use.

They cut through the noise.

And when drawn correctly, they offer powerful insights into the market's current direction, momentum, and potential turning points.

At its core, a trendline is a straight line drawn on a chart to help you identify the direction of the market's movement. It connects two or more key price points—usually swing highs or lows—and helps you quickly assess whether the market is trending up, down, or sideways.

It's simple, visual, and one of the first tools I use when analyzing a market. But before we delve into some real examples of trendlines in action, it naturally leads us to one of the most important principles in all of technical analysis:

Support and Resistance—the two sides in the ongoing battle for market supremacy between the bulls and the bears.

This is where price meets decision.

Where buyers and sellers fight for dominance.

Where direction is either confirmed or reversed.

Understanding support and resistance is like learning to read the terrain of a battlefield—it provides context, clarity, and the ability to anticipate what might happen next.

Support and Resistance—where the bulls and bears clash

If trendlines give you a sense of direction, then support and resistance show you where the fight takes place.

These levels are the battlegrounds between buyers and sellers, where momentum can pause, reverse, or surge depending on who gains the upper hand.

They're also among the most commonly observed levels in technical analysis.

Why?

Because, like trendlines, they work—not through magic, but because everyone sees them.

Support and resistance are powerful because they're shared.

When thousands of traders watch the same levels, waiting for the same reaction, those levels start to matter. They become self-fulfilling.

This is the art, science, and mythology of technical analysis—

a self-fulfilling prophecy in motion.

It's not about whether the level is "real" in some economic sense—it's about belief.

If enough people believe in the level, suddenly, it becomes real in the only way that counts: the market price responds.

That's the edge we're looking for.

***Support**—Protecting the Bulls*

Support is a price level at which buyers step in to prevent the market from falling further.

It's often formed at previous lows or after a sharp sell-off, when the market finds a floor and bounces.

When price approaches a support level, you're essentially asking the market:

"Are buyers strong enough to defend this line?"

If the answer is yes, price bounces, and support holds.

If the answer is no, support breaks, and we often see a sharp move lower as stop-losses are triggered and sellers take control. There will be more on this later!

***Resistance**—Saving the Bears*

Resistance is the opposite—it's where sellers emerge to halt upward momentum.

It generally forms around previous highs or levels where rallies have failed.

When the price approaches a resistance level, the question becomes:

"Are sellers strong enough to push the price back down?"

A bounce lower from resistance can indicate a potential shorting opportunity.

A break above can signal that the bulls have taken control and might even lead to a new trend.

Trendline Support—example

Whenever I demonstrate this live, whether in a classroom or a training session, I can almost guarantee the first question someone asks is:

"Why did you choose those points to connect?"

So, I'll answer that now because I suspect you might have whispered the same question while reading. This explanation will help build a stronger foundation as we progress further into chart work.

The points I choose—whether for a trendline or to mark support and resistance—are always clear, significant market turning points.

They're not subtle. They're not hidden. They're the moments where price clearly reacted—either reversing direction or stalling with force.

You're looking for places where the market made a decision.

These are the levels traders remember—and those memories shape future price action.

When in doubt, zoom out.

If it stands out on the chart, it's probably important.

We specialize in price discovery, and charts reveal exactly where those moments have occurred—where larger market forces entered, where value was established, and where the direction shifted.

Looking at the chart's left side is essential for identifying these key moments.

Then, work your way forward to the present.

This is how you begin to build context—and see the story the market is trying to tell.

In the case of the example we are using, I highlighted the most recent low point on the chart, where the bulls stepped in strongly and triggered a clear uptrend. This became the base of my trendline—Point A.

Point B was chosen from a smaller pullback—a brief sell-off led by the bears—that once again ended with a strong rally.

Both are significant turning points: the market found support and then pushed higher. These are the types of moments we look for when building the foundations of a trendline.

Once these two points are connected, a clear bullish trendline forms, indicating that the market respects a rising structure.

And here's the beauty of it:

When we extend that line into the future, it becomes more than just a visual aid.

It now serves as a support level for the bulls—and, conversely, as a barrier that the bears must break if they wish to reverse the trend.

It's important to remember that drawing a trendline is always a trader's choice.

There is no fixed formula, and there is no guarantee it will work every time or that the market will respect it. You can use any time frame you prefer, connect any points you choose, or even use the bottom of the wick or the low of the candle to draw your lines. I will offer you the benefit of my many years of drawing and trading them on these pages.

Trendlines offer a framework—an uncomplicated, visual guide that helps us make better-informed decisions about the market's direction. They're not predictive instruments; they're tools for context.

You're not trying to be perfect.

You're trying to give yourself the best possible read on momentum, direction, and potential turning points—and a well-drawn trendline can do exactly that.

Trendline Resistance—Example

In this case, my resistance line has a clean, downward slope to the right—a clear indication that sellers have been in control.

I began the line from the high of a candle that marked the start of the downtrend. It stood out like a sore thumb—a clear turning point where the bulls lost momentum, and the bears took over.

The second point I noted was the peak of a near-term rally that seemed promising for the bulls but was ultimately rejected as sellers reasserted control, driving the market back down.

Both of these points matter because they indicate clear reactions, not only on the chart but also in market psychology.

By connecting them, I've created a descending resistance line that helps define the downtrend and offers context for future price action.

This line now acts as a sort of ceiling—a barrier the bulls must break if they wish to change the narrative.

Until then, the trend remains bearish.

This chart gives me a great opportunity to demonstrate a subtle but important point:

You can draw a technical line using either the wick or the body of a candlestick, and both can be valid, depending on what you're trying to observe.

In this case, Line A and Line B both start from the same candle, but they differ in what part of that candle I used:

For Line A, I used the top of the wick—the high of that market move.
For Line B, I used the top of the candle body.

It gets interesting with the second point I chose for Line B.

Because I was concentrating on the candles' bodies, I linked the second point to a steep sell-off in April, when the price closed sharply lower.

Once I extended that line forward, it provided a clear technical level—and sure enough, that trendline acted as resistance in mid-May, halting a bullish rally in its tracks.

It eventually broke, and that breakout formed the high from which I used the second point for Line A, when the bears took back control.

Same chart. Same starting candle. Two different lines.

Both are meaningful, but each tells a slightly different version of the market's story.

This is where technical analysis becomes an art form.

It's about understanding the story behind the candles—and recognizing when to zoom in, when to zoom out, and when a level might be more significant than it first seems.

The channel—Trendline bonus

You can draw as many trendlines on your chart as you like, across as many timeframes as you want. There's no rulebook.

But in my discipline, I keep it simple.

I tend to have no more than four trendlines on my chart at any one time—and more often than not, I stick to just one support and one resistance line.

The key isn't how many lines you have—whether they're meaningful enough to trade from.

If I've got one good support line and one solid resistance line, something miraculous can happen:

A trend channel forms.

And trend channels are powerful.

They provide a clear visual corridor that indicates where the market is likely to move and where other traders are also watching.

You gain structure when price respects both lines, bouncing between support and resistance.

And when the price finally breaks out of that channel, the movement is often dramatic.

Because once the pattern breaks, it indicates that something has changed, and that change can act as a catalyst for a much larger directional shift.

Channel example—Bullish

I've drawn my support and resistance trendlines on the same chart, and together, they have formed what we call a trend channel.

In this case, it's a bullish channel because the trend is moving higher.

Each successful test of either line enhances credibility and strength, increasing the chances that other traders will notice and respond to it in the future.

Channel Example—Bearish

Just like with our bullish channel, you can also form a bearish channel by drawing two trendlines on the same chart—one acting as support to catch any counter-trend buying from the bulls, and one serving as resistance to guide the bears.

Together, they form a clear downward-sloping range—a structure market participants will closely watch.

It's the same principle in reverse:

As long as the price stays within the channel, we expect it to move between those boundaries.

Any break below the channel confirms the bears' dominance—a sign that sellers have taken control and the market may accelerate lower.

On the other hand, a break above the upper trendline would signal a potential shift in sentiment, setting a new precedent for the market. Such a breakout could signal the start of a bullish trend, as buyers step in with conviction and shorts are forced to cover, driving the price even higher.

In both cases, the channel gives us context.

It tells us: "If we're still inside, respect the range. If we break out, pay attention—something's changing."

A key point in all our technical analysis, above any line we draw—bullish, below that line, bearish.

Number 3—Simple Moving Averages SMAs

When I was first getting to grips with candlesticks, trendlines, and market structure, I kept hearing the senior traders around me casually drop comments like:

"We're still above the 30-day ..."
"Watch out—the 200-day's just been broken."

To me, at the time, this sounded like some secret code—as if they were seeing something I couldn't. It was only when I started reading Clive Lambert's daily research as a Master Technician that it finally made sense.

They were talking about simple moving averages.

Once I understood what they were actually referencing, it unlocked a whole new level of clarity in my trading.

To keep it simple (pun fully intended):

A simple moving average is the average of the closing prices over a specified number of periods.

Each new closing price shifts the average forward, creating a smooth, flowing line on your chart that helps reveal the market's underlying direction.

Example:

A 30-day Simple Moving Average (SMA) indicates the average closing price over the last 30 days, offering a short- to medium-term view of market momentum.

A 200-day Simple Moving Average (SMA) offers a much longer-term perspective—one that many funds, banks, and institutional traders closely monitor.

Simple moving averages help filter out short-term noise, providing a clean, objective snapshot of the market's current trend.

It is one of the most widely used tools by professional traders, making it an essential part of your technical analysis.

How I Use SMAs to Spot Market Direction

The Slope

SMA pointing upwards? Market trending up.
SMA pointing downwards? Market trending down.
Flat SMA? Market consolidating.

Price vs. SMA

Price above the SMA? Bullish bias.
Price below the SMA? Bearish bias.

SMA Stacking

I often layer short-, medium-, and long-term SMAs (such as 10, 30, and 200) to see how momentum shifts across different timeframes.

When the shorter averages are above the longer ones, it suggests strength. When they flip, it can be an early warning of weakness.

What Moving Averages Are—and Are Not

Many newer traders make the mistake of treating SMA crossovers as automatic buy or sell signals. This isn't how professionals employ them.

I regard SMAs as a contextual tool:

They don't predict turning points.
They don't guarantee anything.

Simple moving averages give me an objective way to see where the market stands relative to its recent history. They cut out the noise, reduce emotional fluctuations, and keep me focused on what truly matters: the actual direction of prices.

This helps me avoid one of the biggest mistakes traders make—fighting the market.

When in doubt, zoom out and check your moving averages.

They simplify complex markets, cut out the emotional noise, and offer me a professional-level anchor for framing trades with the trend, not against it.

Bullish Simple Moving Average example—30 Day

The slope to the right of the chart clearly points upwards, emphasizing that we are in a bullish trend. The market also trades above the line, providing further confirmation of the direction.

Bearish Simple Moving Average example—30 Day

We have a clear example of a 30-day Simple Moving Average (SMA); the market remains below it, except for a brief moment when it briefly moves above, then returns to the right side of the chart—indicating a clear bearish trend with the slope continuing to decline.

Layering the SMAs. 10/30/200 Example

In this example, I have layered a 10-, 30-, and 200-day simple moving average to display a range of time scales. The shorter 10-day Simple Moving Average (SMA) (yellow line) closely follows the market price, as expected, and acts as an excellent guide to market direction. Since the market price is above all three SMAs, it clearly signals a bullish trend.

Flat SMA Example

The main sign of the sideways market here is that the 200-day SMA in red is nearly a straight line, while the 10 and 30-day SMAs zig-zag above and below the market price, failing to show any clear trend. Not suited for a directional trade—yet!

By combining these three simple yet powerful tools—Higher Highs and Higher Lows, Trendlines, and Simple Moving Averages—you create a clear, structured framework for confidently identifying market direction.

The price structure indicates whether buyers or sellers are consistently in control.

The trendlines help you visually map the market's momentum and key decision points.

The moving averages filter out the noise and keep you grounded in the broader trend.

When used together, they strip away emotion, eliminate second-guessing, and offer you an objective lens through which to analyze any market, on any timeframe.

However, as every trader knows, markets do not move in straight lines indefinitely.

Even the strongest trends eventually change. And when they do, new opportunities—and new risks—arise.

In the next chapter, we'll explore how to recognize when a market is changing direction so you aren't caught on the wrong side of a shift and can position yourself early as momentum begins to turn.

6.1.4 How to Spot the Market Turn—Counter-Trending or Mean Reversion

"It always comes back."

This has been a battle cry in nearly every office I've traded in, managed, or owned.

It's the tell-tale calling sign of the counter-trend trader—the one stepping in against market direction, looking for a turn back to a place of relative value.

In truth, around 80% of my trading career over the past 20 years has been built on this exact approach.

6.1.5 Counter-Trend Technical Trading Ideas

Much of what I teach traders to watch for are points on a chart where the market seems to have exhausted itself—areas where price has historically acted as a turning point or may have moved too far, too quickly.

At first glance, this might appear to contradict the principle we've just covered—the trend is your friend. After all, why would anyone deliberately trade against a moving market? Isn't that financial suicide?

But here's the reality:

The market is very often wrong—or at least temporarily overextended.

Momentum overshoots. Emotions take control. Herd mentality pushes prices past fair value. When that occurs, it creates some of the most compelling trading opportunities you'll encounter.

In fact, some of the most consistently profitable setups happen when you learn to identify exhaustion, where buyers or sellers have overextended themselves, and the price is ready for a reversal.

Range-bound markets, in particular, can present multiple clear opportunities to buy near lows and sell near highs well before any sustained trend takes hold.

In line with our principle of simplicity, I will share the three most relied-upon counter-trend technical signals—tools I've used thousands of times to identify, frame, and execute high-probability reversal trades.

Allow me to introduce the Double/Triple Top or Bottom, the Hammer and Shooting Star, and finally, the Overextension.

Double or Triple Top or Bottom

No—this isn't a high score in a game of darts.

But it is one of the most tried-and-tested and reliable methods for identifying where a market may find strong support or resistance—and potentially reverse.

At the core, these are simple price patterns that highlight market exhaustion:

Double Top: The market reaches a high, pulls back, then attempts to break through the high again but fails. Sellers dominate buyers at the same level for a second time. This often signals a strong bearish reversal.

Triple Top: The market tests the same high three times, failing to break through each time. Each unsuccessful attempt strengthens the level of resistance. If sellers continue to intervene at the same level, buyers will eventually lose momentum.

Double Bottom: The opposite of a double top. The market falls to a low, bounces, and retests the same low. If buyers successfully defend that level again, it indicates potential bullish strength and a possible reversal higher.

Triple Bottom: The market tests the same support level three times without breaking lower. This repeated defense of the lows indicates increasing buyer conviction and often leads to a rally.

These patterns work because they reflect market memory and psychology:

Buyers and sellers remember these levels.
Institutions place orders around these zones.
Each failed breakout reinforces the significance of the level.
Eventually, one side (buyers or sellers) runs out of energy.
Let's take a look at them in action.

Double top formation.

Although this is one of my most frequently used tools in technical analysis, I'll admit—it took me some time to find a genuinely textbook example to demonstrate.

In the example chart, you can see two clear wick highs at the same price level. I've connected them with a simple horizontal trendline. This price zone marked a point where the market twice rejected higher prices and quickly reversed. That failure to break higher triggered significant shifts in market sentiment and direction.

The theory behind this setup is simple: if the market reaches this level again, we should expect strong selling pressure to resurface. Historically, traders have placed a high value on selling at this price. Until proven otherwise, it remains a major resistance area and a clear reference point for spotting potential reversals.

Double Top Example

The same theory applies to the double bottom, with the lower level acting as support for the bulls and providing potential for a market reversal to the upside.

Double Bottom Example

In this clear example, you can see two candle-wick lows forming at the same price level. This indicates a strong area where buyers stepped in each time, rejecting lower prices and causing a bullish reversal in the market direction.

The result is that the market remains above this level, having been defended by buyers twice already. Going forward, traders will pay close attention to how the price acts if it revisits this zone. Will buyers defend it again? Or will the level finally break? Either way, it serves as a key reference point for future price discovery and potential trade opportunities.

Triple Top/Bottom

As we have eloquently covered the double top and bottom, it should be fairly straightforward to cover their close relatives in technical analysis, the triple top and bottom.

All we need to do is add another test of the same level as shown below.

Triple top example

Triple Bottom example

With the examples I've shown for the double and triple tops and bottoms, you may have noticed something important:

The price levels I used to draw the horizontal trendlines were already reversal points before the pattern formed.

This is no coincidence.

Markets remember. And traders remember. When the price reacts sharply at a level once, it often reacts again. These levels serve as reference points for future trades, not by magic, but because many participants are watching them.

This idea—that history leaves clues on a chart—will become even more significant as we advance into the Practice stage of your trading journey. There, we'll explore in more detail how to identify these key areas in real time and transform these patterns into executable trades with a clear edge.

The Hammer and Shooting Star formations.

Some of the strongest counter-trend signals don't originate from complex patterns or indicators—they come from a single candle.

The hammer and the shooting star are two of the most visually striking and psychologically significant candlestick patterns you'll observe on any chart. They signify market rejection—the instance when a price movement in one direction is strongly rejected and closes in the opposite zone.

These candles often form at the extremes—near market tops or bottoms—and can signify the early stages of a reversal when confirmed by other signals.

What makes them especially valuable is how they capture the battle between buyers and sellers:

The hammer indicates that sellers are driving the market lower, only for buyers to step in aggressively and close the session near the high. It's a classic bullish reversal signal.

The shooting star is the reverse: buyers push the price up, only to get overwhelmed by sellers who drag it back down before the close—a strong bearish reversal signal.

What you're observing in these candles isn't merely price—it's emotion.

Panic. Euphoria. Rejection. Hesitation.

And when those emotions show up at the right levels, they can offer high-probability setups to fade the move and trade the reversal -Let's break each one down.

Hammer Time

The hammer is among the most well-known and widely respected single-candle reversal patterns in technical analysis—and for good reason. It visually captures a moment of rejection and reversal, often found at the bottom of a downtrend.

What It Looks Like:

A small real body at the top of the candle.

A long lower wick (at least twice the length of the body).

Little to no upper wick.

The long lower shadow shows that sellers dominated most of the session, pushing prices lower. However, something shifted. Buyers entered strongly, pushing the price back up to close near the session's highs. This change in momentum suggests that selling pressure may be waning.

This is what makes the hammer such a powerful bullish reversal signal.

It must appear after a downtrend to have reversal value.

The longer the lower wick, the stronger the rejection.

Volume confirmation enhances confidence (a hammer with a volume spike is more meaningful).

It works best when combined with support levels, divergence, or oversold indicators.

In my own trading, I regard hammers as a warning shot—a possible sign that Sellers are losing control. I don't trade a hammer by itself. However, when I see a hammer form at a crucial support level—or as part of a double bottom—my interest level quickly increases.

If the next candle confirms the reversal (by closing higher), it often becomes a setup worth trading.

A hammer is the market saying:

"We tried to go lower . . . but we couldn't stay there."

And that's precisely the kind of signal I'm watching for when looking to go long against a downtrend.

Hammer Example

This one isn't your perfect textbook hammer—the candle body is a little bigger than usual—but it's such a clean example of a reversal that I had to include it.

We saw a strong move lower being completely rejected as buyers stepped in decisively, reversing the session and initiating a solid bullish correction. The message here is clear: the market tried to break down but failed. That failure triggered a shift in sentiment, and the buyers did not look back.

Twinkle, Twinkle Shooting Star

The shooting star is the mirror image of the hammer and just as powerful when it appears in the right place.

It's a single-candle formation indicating possible exhaustion at the peak of a move. The market attempts to rally, reaching for new highs, but ultimately fails to sustain the momentum. Sellers arrive forcefully, pushing the price back down, and the candle closes near the session low.

It's a visual punch in the face for the bulls.

What It Looks Like:

A small real body near the bottom of the candle.

A long upper wick—ideally twice the size of the body or more.

Little to no lower wick.

The upper shadow shows that buyers were in control early, pushing the price higher. However, by the end of the session, they had lost that control. Sellers took over and drove the market lower, often signaling the initial signs of a reversal.

It appears after an uptrend.

Rejection from a key resistance level strengthens it.

A volume spike adds significance to the rejection.

It's often seen near round numbers, recent highs, or news-driven rallies.

A shooting star is one of those candles I take seriously, especially when it forms after a prolonged rally. It's like watching the market take a big breath in . . . and then choke.

"We tried to go higher—and got smacked back down."

In my trading, I watch how the price moves around the next few candles. If there's no follow-through from the bulls and instead another bearish close or a break of support happens, that's often the signal for a counter-trend opportunity.

Shooting Star example

This is a lovely example of the shooting star pattern in action. A strong bullish rally ends with a rapid push to new highs, but then the bears intervene and take control, dragging the price straight back down.

That upper wick tells the story perfectly: the market tried to keep going, got ahead of itself, and then got hit hard.

It's a classic sign of exhaustion—and a great opportunity to fade the move and counter the market.

Both the hammer and the shooting star are straightforward, potent tools—one candle, revealing the entire story.

They do not predict the future on their own. Still, when they appear at key levels—such as previous highs or lows, major support and resistance, or after a strong trending move—they often indicate a shift in sentiment already in progress.

In counter-trend trading, that's exactly what you're seeking: a hesitation, a sign of rejection, or that initial crack in the momentum that suggests the market might be ready to reverse.

They're easy to spot.

They're rich in psychology.

And when paired with structure, they can form the foundation of a high-probability reversal setup.

The Overextension

Sometimes, a market doesn't need a candlestick pattern or a trendline to show that it's overcooked.

You can see it. You can feel it.

Price has surged too quickly, too far—well beyond what seems sensible or sustainable—and is now ready for a correction.

This is what I call overextension, and it's one of the most common setups I've used in my counter-trend trading career.

What It Looks Like:

A sharp, near-vertical price move—often driven by emotion, headlines, or herd behavior.

Multiple consecutive green (or red) candles with little to no pullback.

The price is distancing itself dramatically from the moving averages (especially the 30- or 200-day).

A parabolic curve forming on the chart—it appears as though it can't keep going ... and usually, it can't.

Markets move in waves—push and pull, expansion and contraction.

When they extend too far in one direction, they often snap back violently in the opposite direction. That's not merely a technical phenomenon—it's driven by traders taking profit, closing positions, or becoming trapped.

On the trading floor, we often said.

'It can't go one way forever'

That's the principle here. Overextended moves create fragile price structures. All it takes is a spark—a weak data point, a sentiment shift, or simply a lack of buyers or sellers—and the whole thing can unwind quickly.

Overextension setups are some of my favorites because they tend to be clear, simple, and high-probability, particularly in range-bound markets or near longer-term levels.

If I see a runaway rally or selloff heading straight into a major level, with stretched momentum, extended candles, and signs of fatigue, I'm watching closely. The market's telling me:

"This move is tired."

And tired markets are where reversals are born.

Let's examine some classic over-extensions.

Bullish Over-Extension example

In this example, we have a huge green candle that sticks out like a sore thumb when compared to the rest of the candle periods and would grab my attention in any market. Once the high had been posted, I would look to see where the sellers closed the candle and use the candle's close as a sell level. The next candle saw the selling continue and a sharp correction take place.

Bearish Over-Extension Example

This is a prime example of a bearish overextension. We observe the market breaking lower from a range and selling off aggressively.

The bears made another attempt in the following session to regain control, but the market stayed above the previous day's close. This shows strong buyer support and indicates a possible turning point.

It is a fine art to trade a market overextension solely using technical analysis. In my experience, being alerted to these moves can set off a chain reaction of analysis to determine whether the move has gone too far and needs to be countertrend traded, or whether it's a bona fide change in market sentiment and a trend is forming.

Off the Charts!

By now, you've gained a clear understanding of how to spot market directions and potential turning points using technical analysis—the structure, patterns, and psychology concealed in price.

We've covered how to:

Spot trending or range-bound markets using price structure and moving averages.

Draw meaningful trendlines and channels to frame the market's momentum.

Identify powerful reversal signals, such as double tops and bottoms, hammers, shooting stars, and overextensions.

These tools form the backbone of my daily decision-making.

They keep me focused, consistent, and objective—especially when markets are noisy and headlines are flying.

But here's the thing . . .

Charts tell you what the market is doing.

Fundamentals tell you why.

If you want to build trades with genuine conviction—the kind you can sustain through volatility—you need to go beyond the candles and understand the broader story behind the moves.

That's where fundamental analysis comes in.

It's not about predicting the future with economic jargon or making reckless guesses based on headlines. It's about understanding what genuinely influences markets beneath the surface: supply and demand, economic cycles, central banks, energy flows, corporate earnings, inflation data, and geopolitical pressure points.

In the next section, we'll explain how to use fundamental analysis in a way that's simple, practical, and trader-focused—not overly academic or theoretical.

Because when you combine solid technical analysis with sharp fundamentals, you begin to form a trading view that's difficult to challenge—and even harder to bet against.

6.2 Fundamental Analysis

The data never lies, but it could also be wrong

For me, one of the most exciting parts of trading is this: news breaks, and I get to ask, "What does this mean for the markets?" The process of connecting the dots, of tuning into the macroeconomic story unfolding in real time, is endlessly fascinating.

I love the rhythm of it—how policy decisions ripple out, how corporate earnings shift sentiment, and how political instability in one part of the world can send capital flooding into another.

It's all interconnected.

A drought in South America boosts sugar prices. A surprise cut in interest rates causes bond yields to fall sharply. An explosion in a pipeline increases oil prices overnight. These aren't just headlines—they're opportunities.

To me, the markets feel alive. They have a heartbeat, constantly shifting and reacting to new inputs. That heartbeat is driven by three core needs we all share:

- Food—the agricultural markets
- Energy—the fuel that powers the world
- Money—the exchange that keeps the system ticking

We don't trade random squiggles on a screen—we trade the price of life. And fundamental analysis is the art of interpreting that life.

Foundations of fundamental analysis

Earlier in the book, in Market Preparation, we discussed why fundamentals matter. We looked at the markets that might attract your attention, analyzing what has influenced them in the past and what could impact them in the future. We also briefly considered the Efficient Market Hypothesis—the idea that markets incorporate all available information—and its flaws. Because markets aren't perfect, they overshoot, underreact, and misprice.

And it's in those inefficiencies that the best opportunities often appear.

So, here's a simple definition:

Fundamental analysis involves studying the information that influences markets—economic data, news, policies, and events—and using that understanding to form an opinion on price movements.

It's about understanding the why behind the what.

Even if you're a purely technical trader, you need to understand why the price might break through a level or why momentum suddenly shifts. More often than not, the answer lies in the fundamentals.

We've already dipped our toes in. Now it's time to explore more deeply the two aspects of fundamental analysis.

6.2.1 Qualitative Analysis

When people think about fundamental analysis, they often picture spreadsheets, inflation numbers, and economic forecasts.

But some of the biggest market-moving events in history haven't come from hard data—they've come from humans.

A social media post.

A press conference.

A single sentence from a central banker.

A surprise decision from a politician.

Nothing is more unpredictable than human thought and action. And when ego, politics, or fear come into play, that unpredictability becomes fuel for traders like us.

This is what we call qualitative analysis—the chaotic, unpredictable side of the market that isn't based on a data release but still significantly influences prices.

Look at central bank speeches. Most are carefully prepared, cautious, and highly refined—but occasionally, someone deviates from the script. They hint at policy adjustments. They sound more "hawkish" (raising rates) or "dovish" (cutting them) than anticipated.

The market reacts immediately.

Why? Because these institutions determine the cost of money. If the tone shifts, everything from currency pairs to equity indices can change within minutes.

The same applies to unexpected geopolitical events. A surprising election result. A new war. A trade embargo. All of these fall into the qualitative category because they aren't scheduled and can't be modelled in a spreadsheet—yet they ripple through global markets quickly.

We're living in an era of extreme information.

Everyone has an opinion.

Every event has a spin.

Minds are made up—and then changed—in the space of a headline refresh.

This steady stream of news, tweets, strong opinions, and clickbait has generated something significant: both a great opportunity and great confusion.

This is because, if the market's role is to discover price based on available information—but that information is now endless, conflicting, and often emotional—how do we know what's truly driving a move?

That's where I come back to two simple anchor points when trading qualitative data:

Timing

Markets are hyper-sensitive to the context in which news arrives.

The same comment from a central banker can be overlooked one month and trigger a market tantrum the next. A politician's threat might already be factored in—or it might hit at a moment of vulnerability and cause chaos.

Timing is everything.

Always ask yourself:

Is the market already positioned for this?

Has the same message already been delivered to the market and been priced in?

Are we near a technical inflexion point that could amplify the reaction?

I still ask myself these questions each time I digest new information.

Relevance

Not all headlines deserve your attention. Most don't. The key is knowing what matters—and more importantly, what matters right now.

The market doesn't respond to noise. It reacts to credible threats, significant shifts, and unexpected information from people or institutions with the power to influence the price.

Always ask yourself:

Is the speaker or source influential? (Think central bankers, OPEC, top politicians, corporate CEOs)

Is this news directly tied to the asset you're trading?

Does it confirm or contradict a dominant market narrative?

Is it actionable—or just opinion?

For example, a press release from the ECB president days before a rate decision is highly relevant. But a social media post from a backbench MP? Probably not.

Relevance is about cutting through the drama and hype to focus on what the market genuinely cares about.

It helps you avoid trading distractions, stay focused, and align your decisions with the real drivers of price action.

When timing and relevance come together, you have a winning formula for a great market opportunity. It doesn't happen very often, but when it does, the rewards are fantastic.

On the other hand, if your timing is wrong or you overemphasize the importance of some information, you could be chopping yourself in and out of a market, wasting valuable trading energy ... and money!

6.2.2 Quantitative Analysis

Quantitative analysis involves studying hard data—the measurable numbers and statistics that influence market prices. These are the facts that can be counted, compared, and charted: employment figures, inflation rates, GDP growth, central bank decisions, inventory levels, and more. Unlike the unpredictability of human behavior, these data points offer traders a rare sense of certainty.

That certainty comes in the form of the economic calendar.

The calendar is a schedule of economic data releases and events. Most of these occur regularly each month—for instance, U.S. Non-Farm Payrolls (first Friday of every month), Eurozone CPI, or oil inventory reports. Each country has its own rhythm, and each market tends to react more to certain data than others.

But it's not just the routine numbers. The calendar also captures—or at least warns us to expect—ad hoc quantitative events:

A government spending review or emergency budget
An OPEC supply decision
An unexpected fiscal stimulus package

These planned data announcements can have just as much impact as the monthly staples—sometimes even more.

One of the advantages of quantitative analysis is that it creates opportunities for different time frames:

Short-term: The immediate reaction to the release—sharp volatility, liquidity gaps, and price spikes. Perfect for traders who thrive on speed and momentum.

Medium-term: The trend that follows as the market digests the number, often lasting hours or days as positioning adjusts.

Long-term: The broader narrative shift—how repeated data surprises reshape expectations of monetary policy, growth, or supply/demand, and how that repricing filters across asset classes over weeks or months.

The value of the economic calendar lies in its predictability. You may not know the outcome of the event—whether inflation will come in hot or cold, or whether the Fed will raise or cut rates—but you do know exactly when the number will be released.

This creates several key advantages:

Preparation

Traders can plan ahead. If you know Non-Farm Payrolls are due at 1:30 pm London time, a sudden surge in volatility does not blindside you. You're ready for it.

Risk Management

By being aware of scheduled events, you can reduce position sizes, widen stops, or even step aside completely if you don't want to be caught in the storm.

Opportunity

Some traders thrive on trading the immediate reaction to news; others wait for the dust to settle and trade the ensuing trend. Either way, the calendar gives you the structure to position accordingly.

Market Sentiment

The calendar also tells you what the market is expecting. Every major release comes with a consensus forecast. Comparing the actual number to the forecast is what drives price reaction—surprise is where the edge lives.

The market doesn't always respond to the raw number—it reacts to the gap between expectation and reality. A CPI figure of 3% may seem high, but if the market were expecting 3.3%, that would be dovish for rates and bullish for bonds.

The market doesn't trade the number—it trades the surprise. That gap between what was expected and what actually happened is where the real money is made.

The economic calendar is one of the few constants in a world full of noise. It doesn't predict what will happen in the markets, but it anchors your trading around recognized points of volatility. That's why it's often the very first thing I check at the start of a trading week.

In a trader's life, knowing when risk will arrive is half the battle, and with it, opportunity.

Sourcing the sources

Over my many years as a professional trader, one thing has remained constant: the primary sources of financial news and data. The names haven't changed much—Bloomberg, Reuters, Market News International—but their surrounding landscape has.

Major providers still charge high prices for their speed and depth, and if you are trading professionally, they are essential. However, today there are many free or affordable options: online calendars, free news feeds, Twitter/X, and forums.

At the same time, the number of commentators has surged. Social media is filled with charts, opinions, and news bots. Some are insightful. Many are just background noise. Distinguishing between the two is one of the modern trader's greatest challenges.

And the kind of news that influences markets has changed. Jobs data and rate decisions still matter—but now a president's tweet, a meme-stock frenzy, or a crypto hack can ripple across asset classes just as strongly.

That is why those same two pillars—timing and relevance—remain essential filters for your information flow.

How to Respond to News—And When Not To

On the first trading floor I ever worked on, I was thrown straight into the deep end of fundamental trading. Along with a news terminal, the firm subscribed to what we called a squawk—essentially a trader's radio.

A squawk service employed a team of researchers who monitored all the newswires. The moment they identified something market-moving, they would "squawk" it live through their microphones into hundreds of trading rooms worldwide. This allowed traders to keep their eyes fixed on the markets without having to scan endless headlines.

In those early months, I lived in constant fear of missing something. If I left my desk even for a moment, I believed the news would break, my portfolio would collapse, or I'd miss the trade of a lifetime. So I stayed glued to the screen, reacting to every squawk.

Every piece of information that hit the tape, I would immediately try to apply: Was that bullish? Bearish? What should I do now?

It was excellent practice—but in hindsight, it also led to fatigue. I was attempting to trade on a timeframe that was too short and, to be honest, I was overly eager. However, those years of overexposure taught me a vital lesson: not all news is equal.

What's Worth Listening To

Over time, I learned to filter. The key was to listen out for those with the most power to move markets:

Central banks and their members
Heads of state and government leaders
Ratings agencies
Government research facilities (like the U.S. Bureau of Labour Statistics or USDA)
Natural disasters, acts of war or terrorism

These are the announcements and events that can move markets instantly and without warning. This is where your reaction needs to be fast—and correct.

But here's the truth: you don't always need to act on the immediate reaction. If ultra–short-term trading isn't your advantage, then your task is to interpret how the new information will influence the market over the medium to long term.

Sometimes the best trades do not come from the initial wave of volatility, but from the second—when the dust settles, and the market begins to reprice in a more measured manner.

The same applies to releases of quantitative data. You must quickly determine whether the data is bullish or bearish for your market—and assess whether it presents a trade opportunity now or is better utilized to form a longer-term view.

Here's something important to consider: the right fundamental announcement can also cause the market to distort significantly. When volume decreases and reactions become exaggerated, the price can overshoot considerably. These are the moments when counter-trend opportunities often emerge—just as we discussed in the Technical Analysis chapter.

Trading news relies on discipline and patience as much as on speed. Truly market-moving events offer multiple opportunities across various timeframes. Your task is to identify which ones suit your style and which to disregard.

In the Market Preparation section, we examined the broad spectrum of information that influences each market. Pair that foundation with the principles outlined here, and you possess everything needed to be a professional fundamental trader: prepared, selective, and always in tune with the bigger picture.

Because when you can marry the what from the charts with the why from the fundamentals, you're no longer just reacting to the markets—you're in harmony with the markets.

6.3 Seasonality

'Tis the Season(al) to be jolly

I'll admit—I was about ten years into my trading career before I really started paying attention to seasonality.

Certainly, I noticed a few recurring patterns in the financial markets I traded, but not nearly as many as you could identify in commodities and agriculture. The one that remained prominent in my mind early in my career was the old stock market adage:

"Sell in May, go away, and come back on St. Leger's Day."

Even my dad used to say it to me. It always felt like a nursery rhyme—something passed down through generations.

But beneath the sing-song simplicity lay a practical observation: markets tended to quieten over the summer. The idea was that you should sell your shares at the end of May, take the summer off, and then return in September when volumes increased again. Traditionally, the "restart" was marked by the St. Leger Stakes horse race in Doncaster—the final event of the British flat racing season and, for many in the City of London, a social signal that the summer lull was over.

Of course, it's not a perfect rule; no seasonal pattern is. But the fact that sayings like this persist over decades demonstrates just how strong and enduring some seasonal tendencies can be.

Catchy rhymes aside, let's be clear on what we actually mean by seasonality in trading:

Seasonality refers to a market's recurring price patterns at particular times of the year, caused by predictable cycles in supply, demand, weather, economic activity, or human behavior.

It doesn't mean prices will behave the same way each year; markets are never so predictable. What it implies is that certain forces tend to operate at the same time, year after year, creating probabilities that traders can analyze and leverage.

Seasonality exists because real-world markets are connected to natural cycles. Long before markets displayed only numbers on screens, traders in the Chicago pits dealt with crops in the ground, weather forecasts on the horizon, and inventories stored in silos.

Traders Understood:

Weather and Harvest Cycles (Agriculture)
Crops are planted and harvested at fixed times of the year. Planting limits supply, while harvesting floods it. Weather shocks—droughts, freezes, storms—tend to occur in certain months.

Storage and Inventory Dynamics (Commodities)
Grain elevators, oil tanks, and gas storage facilities all follow seasonal cycles of filling and drawing down. Inventories increase in some months, decrease in others, and prices often move together.

Consumption Patterns (Energy & Food)
Natural gas demand rises in the winter heating season, gasoline demand increases in the summer driving season, and food commodities often follow seasonal consumption peaks.

Fiscal and Reporting Calendars (Equities & Fixed Income)
Companies publish earnings quarterly. Governments announce budgets and spending reviews on fixed annual schedules. Investors rebalance portfolios at year- and quarter-end.

Human Behavior (Across Markets)
Traders go on summer holidays. Funds adjust their positions at tax deadlines. Year-end optimism drives rallies. These behavioral patterns recur as predictably as harvests.

In short, seasonality exists because life is seasonal.

Markets mirror the world they price—and the world operates in cycles. Recognizing these cycles and knowing when they are most significant provides traders with an extra advantage.

6.3.1 Classic Seasonal Patterns

Seasonality shows up everywhere once you start looking. Some of the best-known patterns include:

The Santa Claus Rally (Equities)
Stock markets often drift higher into the final week of December, aided by low volumes, festive optimism, and portfolio rebalancing.

The January Effect (Equities)
Historically, small-cap stocks often outperformed in January as new money flowed in and funds rebalanced after the year-end.

Harvest Pressure (Grains)
Corn, wheat, and soybeans often experience downward pressure during harvest time, as supply floods the market—a pattern that Chicago pit traders built their careers on.

Driving Season (Oil)
U.S. gasoline demand generally increases during the summer months as Americans take to the roads, often pushing up petrol and crude oil prices.

Winter Heating Season (Natural Gas)
Demand for natural gas rises sharply in colder months, causing significant seasonal fluctuations linked to weather forecasts and storage levels.

These aren't guaranteed trades—nothing in markets ever is. But they emphasize a vital point: markets don't just react to charts and headlines; they also respond to the calendar.

When you grasp those seasonal rhythms, you can predict when opportunity is most likely to arise—and ready yourself to act when history has the potential to repeat itself.

Mastering the Seasonals

The most successful seasonal traders have always been drawn to the commodity markets—because commodities are directly linked to cycles of planting, harvest, storage, consumption, and weather.

One of the most renowned names in this field is Larry Williams, a Chicago trading pit veteran who became legendary for his skill in spotting and exploiting seasonal movements. Williams amassed his fortune by making large, calculated bets on recurring commodity patterns—such as when cattle prices tended to rise during grilling season, or when grain prices softened due to harvest pressure.

He wasn't just gambling; he developed a systematic approach. Williams examined decades of price history, identified the most consistent patterns, and then executed trades when those seasonal tendencies aligned with broader fundamentals and technical signals. He demonstrated that if you had the discipline to study the calendar and act on probabilities, seasonality could be a powerful edge capable of generating a fortune.

While stocks, bonds, and currencies have seasonal tendencies, commodities wear their seasonality on their sleeve. They're directly tied to real-world cycles like:

Agriculture: planting, growing, and harvesting seasons.

Energy: heating in winter, driving in summer.

Livestock: feed cycles, breeding patterns, and seasonal demand for meat.

Soft commodities (coffee, sugar, cocoa): weather in producing countries, seasonal consumption peaks (think Christmas chocolate or summer ice cream).

These natural and behavioral rhythms create patterns that can be measured, studied, and, more importantly, traded.

6.3.2 How to Find Seasonal Trades in Commodities

So, how do you truly identify and utilize these seasonal tendencies as a trader? Here's the process:

Use Seasonality Tools and Databases to study historical patterns over time.

Professional seasonal traders use databases that aggregate years of price data to highlight recurring monthly or weekly patterns.

Many platforms now chart "seasonal averages" to indicate when a commodity usually rises or falls. I have used a platform called Seasonalgo, which offers a blended average over multiple years.

The chart below shows the current price and year-to-date (YTD) movement of Sugar futures (black line) and three blended averages of the market movement until the contract's expiry.

Red line = 5-year average of the market's movement
Green line = 10-Year average of the market's movement
Blue line = 15-year average of the market's movement

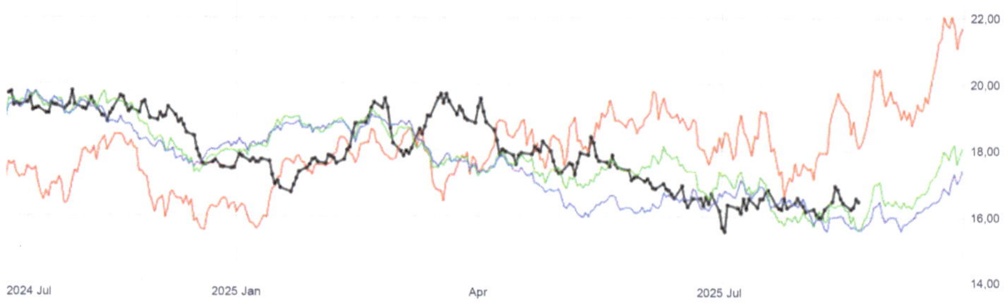

As you can see, all averages approaching the end of the contract expiry tend to be higher.

If you don't know what trade you should be looking to do, by looking at this chart, we will cover more in the practice section.

6.3.3 Connect Seasonality to Fundamentals

Always question the reason behind the pattern. Is it related to planting/harvest, storage withdrawals, or consumption demand?

The most effective seasonal trades are those supported by clear supply and demand fundamentals.

This is where you can link the farming data with the Commitment of Traders (CoT) report we discussed earlier in the book. If the seasonal trend aligns with farmer behavior and positioning in the CoT report, you have a stronger case. The more data you can gather behind an idea, the higher the likelihood of success.

Combine with Technicals

Never trade seasonality in isolation. Use technical confirmation, trendlines, support/resistance levels, and breakouts to refine your timing.

I often overlay seasonal charts with my technical setups when trading commodities. Seeing a seasonal pattern align with a clear technical structure gives me the confidence to act. (I'll show you a full worked example of this in the Practice section later in the book.)

Mind the Macro
A significant macro shock can override any seasonal trend. Central bank policies, wars, recessions, or black swan events can entirely reverse expectations.

The same applies to every trading idea. To paraphrase Mike Tyson: "Everyone has a plan until they get punched in the face." In the markets, that punch often results from a major macro shift.

Personally, I treat seasonality as one part of a trader's toolkit, not the whole toolbox.

Seasonality is one of the market's quiet forces—always present, often unnoticed. It doesn't forecast the future, but it shifts the odds in your favor by emphasizing when supply, demand, and human behavior are most likely to drive prices in a certain direction.

What makes seasonality so influential isn't that it guarantees a move—nothing in trading does. It's that it reliably shifts the odds in your favor.

When you recognize that natural gas demand has increased in 18 of the past 20 winters, or that sugar tends to rally in Q1 as Brazilian weather uncertainty peaks, you're no longer trading blindly. You're trading with probabilities in your favor.

And just as Larry Williams demonstrated, when those probabilities are examined, layered, and applied year after year, they can be turned into a genuine, repeatable advantage.

For us as traders, seasonality isn't a standalone system. It's an additional advantage—one that becomes most effective when it aligns with strong fundamentals and clear technicals. Used correctly, it provides a level of confidence and foresight that many traders never attain.

But even with fundamentals, technicals, and seasonality working together, there's one final piece of the puzzle when it comes to identifying a trade: price action. Because ultimately, every trade depends on how the market moves in real time—the candles, the structure, and the behavior of price itself.

6.4 Trading Price Action

The Price is King
This fourth method of trade identification is quite distinct from the others. It's short-term in character, does not always follow a predictable pattern, and demands that you "read the heartbeat" of the market in real-time.

At its core, price action trading involves recognizing when there is a two-way struggle for direction within a confined price range. It occurs when the market compresses, and all the noise from buyers and sellers is squeezed into a narrow band.

The result?

An opportunity to trade the order flow with low risk and quick results.

These price action trades can show up in many ways:

Quiet periods—summer months, national holidays, or thin overnight sessions.

Ahead of major events—hours before non-farm payrolls, central bank announcements, or crop reports.

Just before a major open, like the build-up into the NYSE cash session.

After violent spikes—when a sharp move higher or lower causes traders to scramble to exit losing positions, while others step in to fade what they see as overbought or oversold levels.

Using technical analysis, you often observe this kind of action forming around key support or resistance levels. The market pushes up against a ceiling or down towards a floor, and instead of a straightforward breakout, you see repeated failed attempts, wicks in both directions, and a growingly noisy cluster of candles.

When one side finally yields, the move can be explosive—either a breakout that proceeds smoothly, or a sharp snapback as trapped traders rush to cover. This is where the discipline of trading the price action becomes crucial; once the market breaks, the trade is over.

The challenge for new traders is that price action doesn't provide a straightforward indicator signal. It's about learning to recognize when the order flow is changing, when momentum is shifting, and when the market is signaling "something is about to happen."

6.4.1 A Trader's First School: Scalping

When I first began as a junior trader, we learned the basics of this kind of trading. On the trading floor, it was called something that stuck: scalping.

The term "scalping" derives from the practice of making small profits from the market—one tick here, one tick there—repeatedly. It involved loading your order book across multiple markets, attempting to get filled on both sides, and securing a tiny profit on each trade before anyone else could.

It was intense, stressful, and sometimes catastrophic. If you misheard a market-moving comment or failed to pull your orders in time, you could be left holding the wrong side of the market as it ran away from you.

Back then, in the early days of electronic screen trading, scalping was a rite of passage. Today, highly sophisticated market-making algorithms dominate this space, executing strategies much faster and more efficiently than a human ever could.

But that doesn't mean the style has vanished. There are still committed traders who seek to capitalize on moments when buyers and sellers need to do their business and are prepared to offer a price or two to get it done. For them, price action remains king—it's just about spotting those small windows of imbalance and being quick enough to seize the opportunity.

6.4.2 Introducing the Price Ladder

When it comes to trading price action—and for the majority of my trade execution—I use what's known as a price ladder to view the market.

Price ladders are common in professional trading and are now included in most retail brokerage platforms. They allow you to see the market in its purest form: who's bidding, who's offering, and where transactions are actually happening.

You can customize a ladder with all kinds of extra information and tools for execution, which we'll explore in the execution section of this book. For now, I want to keep it simple and show you the basic structure.

Here's what you'll see on a basic ladder:

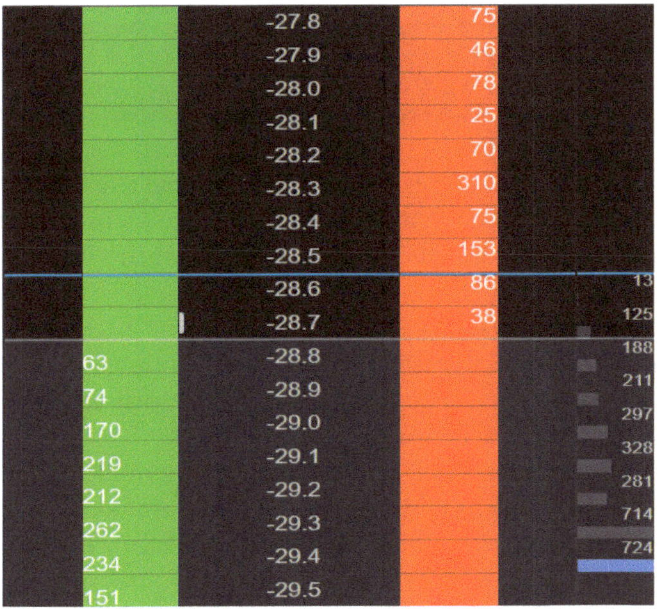

Bid column (left)—This is where the buyers are. If you want to buy the market, this is where you do your business.

Price column (middle)—This shows the actual traded prices, updating in real-time as the market fluctuates.

Ask column (right)—This is where the sellers are. If you want to sell to the market, this is your side.

Traded quantity (far right)—For our price action example, this is the critical piece. It shows how many contracts have traded at each price since the market opened.

Think of it as a footprint of where the real battles between buyers and sellers have taken place.

With just these four elements, you have everything you need to start reading the tug-of-war of price action: where liquidity sits, where volume is clustering, and which side might be running out of steam.

Reading price action on a ladder is relatively straightforward once you know what to look for.

Consider the example we're working with. The key feature is the volume traded between – 29.4 and – 29.3. At both of these prices, more than 700 contracts have changed hands, more than double the volume at the next most traded price of 29.1.

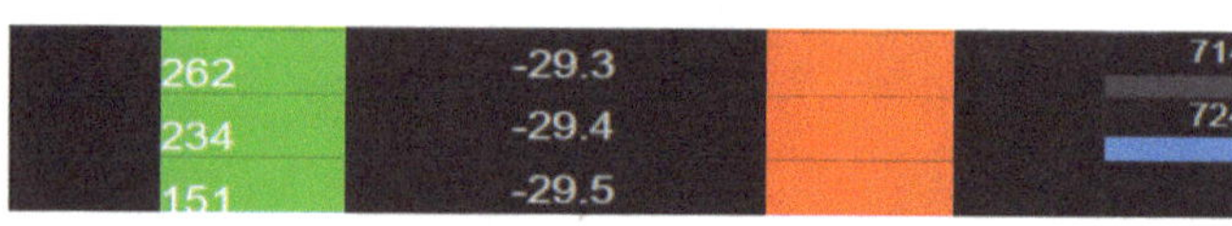

Now, hindsight in trading is always perfect. I can't tell you whether you could have sat on both the bid and the offer and made a profit a few times, or if the market simply traded 700 lots at one price, then 700 lots at the next, and moved higher.

That detail doesn't matter.

What matters is this: when you observe concentrated volume at a tight cluster of prices, you've identified a classic price action zone. That's the footprint of buyers and sellers engaged in serious business.

This is exactly what a price action trading opportunity looks like. Your role as the trader is to identify these zones as they form—not with hindsight, but in real time—and decide how you want to engage with them.

Moving from Identification to Execution

We've now finished the final step in identifying a trade. Through technical analysis, fundamentals, seasonality, and price action, you've developed the tools to spot opportunities in any market environment.

But identification is only the first step. The true skill of trading lies in what follows—how you choose to execute and then manage that trade.

This is where everything you developed during the preparation phase—mindset, resilience, patience, and discipline—comes to the surface. Many people can predict what might happen in the market. Analysts, commentators, and casual observers can all spot opportunities. However, what distinguishes a trader from a mere observer is the ability to act on those opportunities consistently and with control.

Execution is where preparation meets process. It's the moment where analysis becomes decision, where conviction turns into commitment, and where your mindset and discipline are tested in real time.

With that in mind, let's move to the next stage of the professional process—the art and discipline of executing a trade.

7

Executing a Trade

Trade execution is where ideas turn into results. You can analyses charts, monitor fundamentals, and spot seasonality all day—but none of it counts until you place a trade. Execution is the act of turning your conviction into action in the market. It's where traders distinguish themselves from analysts, commentators, or spectators.

There are many ways to execute a trade, but as with most aspects of trading, execution is a skill developed through practice, discipline, and repetition. In this chapter, we'll break down execution into its core elements and provide you with the tools to build confidence and consistency in this vital part of the process.

We'll begin by examining the theory behind execution: why order placement is more than simply clicking "buy" or "sell," and how execution choices can influence your risk, your returns, and even your mindset. From there, we'll look into the different order types available to traders—including market and limit orders, stop orders, and advanced combinations—and how each can be utilized to help you execute with accuracy and purpose.

Risk, which lies at the very core of execution, will be a primary focus. We'll examine stop loss techniques, position sizing, and risk controls that turn execution from a gamble into a reliable, repeatable process.

Finally, we'll look at some of the classic execution profiles you'll meet in your own trading and among professionals: the hesitant trader who struggles to take action, the overconfident trader who trades too aggressively, and the disciplined trader who develops an edge by executing consistently.

S. Warner-Baker, *Learn to Trade Like a Professional*,
https://doi.org/10.1007/978-3-032-20125-6_7

By recognizing these profiles, you'll learn not just how to execute a trade, but how to do it in a way that matches the professional standards you are aiming for.

Execution is the ultimate test in trading. In the pages ahead, you'll discover how to overcome hesitation, manage your risk effectively, and approach each trade with confidence and clarity.

7.1 The Three Golden Rules of Trade Execution

At its core, trade execution isn't complicated. Remove the jargon and distractions, and it boils down to three essential rules that every professional trader follows:

Entry—When and how you get into the trade.
Execution begins with clarity. A strong entry doesn't mean you're simply "buying because it looks good"—it signifies entering at a specific point, guided by your analysis, with a clear rationale. Good entries improve your chances, providing the best possible start to manage the trade.

Exit—When and how you take profits.
Every trade requires a plan for where you'll exit if things go your way. This isn't about perfection—no one ever sells at the absolute top or buys at the absolute bottom. You need to visualize where you would like to close your trade and ensure you have the order in place.

Stop—Where do you get out if your trade doesn't go your way?
The stop is your insurance policy. It's the line in the sand that prevents one poor trade from turning into a career-threatening mistake. Professionals don't argue with stops; they respect them. A stop-loss is not a sign of failure—it's a sign of discipline, ensuring you can trade another day.

Together, these three rules form the foundation of execution theory. Get them right, and you shift from being reactive to being structured and professional. Get them wrong—or worse, ignore them—and trading quickly turns into guesswork, driven by emotion and hindsight.

Let's examine some order types. This will help me explain the theory behind the golden rules of execution a bit more.

7.1.1 May I Take Your Order (Type)

Market Orders vs Limit Orders

The very first dilemma every trader confronts in trade execution is straightforward:

Should I get in (or out) immediately, or wait for a better price?

That decision comes down to two main types of orders: the market order and the limit order. Both are vital tools, each with its own advantages and disadvantages.

Market Order

A market order is the instruction to buy or sell immediately at the best available price.

Pros:

Instant execution—you're in or out without delay.

Useful when speed matters, for example, in fast-moving markets or when cutting a loss.

Cons:

You have no control over the exact price you'll get.

In thin or volatile markets, slippage can result in paying more (or receiving less) than anticipated.

Think of a market order as saying: "Just get me in (or out), whatever the price is right now."

Limit Order

A limit order is the instruction to buy or sell at a specific price or better.

Pros:

Full control over the entry or exit level.

It can help you avoid overpaying on entries or leaving profits on the table at exits.

Cons:

No guarantee of execution—if the market never reaches your price, you simply won't trade.

In fast-moving conditions, you may miss the trade entirely.

A limit order is essentially saying: "I'll trade, but only if I can do it on my terms."

Market and limit orders form the foundation of execution. All advanced order types you will encounter later—such as stop orders, stop-limits, iceberg orders, and others—are built upon these two. Understanding the difference between them is the first step to trading with confidence and control.

Let's examine a straightforward example of a buy market order in action, using the price ladder—a tool many professional traders rely on to view market depth and execute trades in real time.

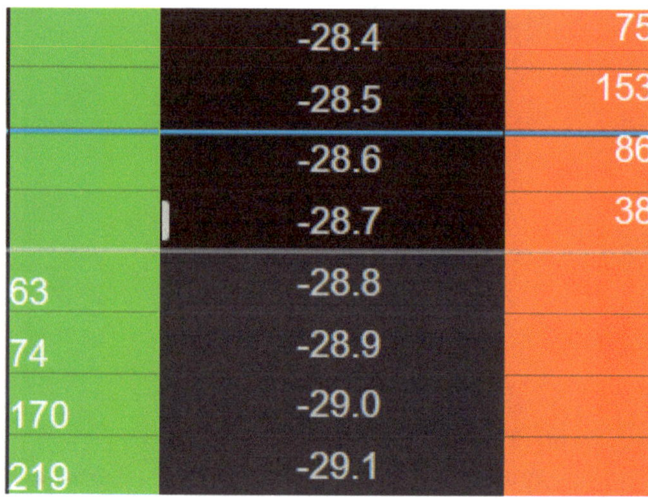

Buy side

Market buy

The current best offer (the lowest price at which someone is willing to sell) is −28.7, and 38 contracts are available at that level.

If you place a market buy order for 10 contracts, you'll be filled immediately at −28.7—the full quantity at the best available price.

If you place a market buy order for 50 contracts, the first 38 contracts will be filled at −28.7, and the remaining 12 contracts will 'lift market' and be filled at the next best offers— −28.6.

Limit buy

If the current best offer is −28.7, you can place a buy limit order at any price below that—for example, −28.8, −28.9, or lower. Your order will appear on the left-hand column of the ladder, queued behind any other buyers already waiting at that price.

Your order is now resting in the book, visible to the market, but not yet filled.

Execution depends on someone else hitting your bid—i.e., selling into the market at your chosen price.

There's no guarantee this will occur, especially in rapidly changing markets or when you're too distant from the current price.

But you retain complete control over your entry level. You have specified your risk and price in advance. This is helpful when establishing your terms and planning your trades.

Sell side

Market sell

By now, you might already be putting the pieces together: if you purchase at the best offer, then to sell at market, you hit the best bid.

Suppose the current best bid is −28.8, with 63 contracts resting there from other traders wanting to buy.

If you place a sell market order for 10 contracts, your order will hit the bid, and all 10 contracts will be filled immediately at −28.8.

If, however, you sell 100 contracts, here's what happens:

The first 63 contracts will be filled at −28.8 (the volume currently available at the best bid).

The remaining 37 contracts will 'hit market', being filled at −28.9 in this case, or at other prices where buyers are waiting.

The larger your order compared to the available liquidity, the more price levels it will traverse—potentially causing slippage.

This is why market orders are regarded as aggressive. You accept whatever price the market is currently offering to ensure execution.

Limit sell

A limit sell order is the opposite of the buy limit you've just seen. Instead of passively waiting to buy below the market, you're now passively waiting to sell above it.

The current best offer is −28.7; you want to sell but don't want to take the current bid—you want a better price.

So, you place a limit sell order at −28.6, one tick above the market.

Your order will appear on the right-hand column of the ladder—the offer side—at −28.6.

You've now told the market: "I'm willing to sell, but only at this price or better."

Your order is now visible to other participants who are sitting in the queue at that price.

To be filled, a buyer must lift your offer—in other words, a market buy order must hit your price.

If that happens, your order (or the portion of it that matches) will be filled at your chosen level.

But if the market never trades up to −28.6, or it moves lower, your order will remain unfilled.

7.1.2 Market Liquidity and Why it Matters

Having covered market orders and limit orders, it's essential to mention liquidity. It's a concept you need to understand early in your trading journey because it directly influences how—and how effectively—your trades are executed.

Liquidity refers to how easily you can buy or sell in a market without causing a significant price change.

A liquid market has:

Plenty of buyers and sellers.
Tight bid/offer spreads (the small gap between buy and sell prices).
Large volumes are available at each price level on the ladder.
The ability to trade larger sizes without moving the market much.

Examples of highly liquid markets: S&P 500 futures, EUR/USD, U.S. Treasuries. The book has focused primarily on liquid markets.

An illiquid market has:

Fewer participants.
Wider bid/offer spreads.
Small volumes sit at each price level.
A much higher risk of slippage when executing market orders.

Examples of illiquid markets include thin commodity spreads, niche single stocks, and low-volume cryptocurrencies. Futures contracts that are coming close to expiry

Why does this matter?

In liquid markets, market orders are generally safer—you're more likely to get the price you see, with minimal slippage.

In illiquid markets, limit orders are often essential—they protect you from paying too much or selling too cheaply.

Professionals always match their trade size to the depth of the market. Get this wrong, and you risk turning a good idea into a costly mistake.

The bottom line is that low liquidity makes clean execution more difficult. That's why professionals rely on different order types and execution strategies—to work with, not against, the liquidity in front of them.

7.1.3 Beyond the Basics: Advanced Order Types

So far, we've covered the basics—market and limit orders—the simplest way to say "get me in" or "get me out". But thanks to the digitization of the trading world, we now have access to far more advanced order types. These tools let you refine your execution, manage risk automatically, and operate with greater precision than ever before.

Here are some of the most widely available order types—and the ones I've used most throughout my trading career:

GTD (Good Till Day)
Your order remains active until the end of the trading session. If it hasn't been filled by the close, it is automatically cancelled.

GTC (Good Till Cancelled)
Unlike GTD, these orders stay active until you cancel them manually. Useful if you want to keep an order running for several days or weeks.

Iceberg Order
Only part of your order is visible on the book at any given time. For example, you might want to sell 1,000 contracts but only display 50 at a time, hiding your full size from the market. These are very useful in illiquid markets, so your size doesn't scare away other market participants.

OCO (Order Cancels Order)
A paired order where executing one automatically cancels the other. Professional traders use these frequently; there's nothing worse than forgetting to cancel an order in your plan and losing money because of it.

Pay-Up
An order that instructs the system to improve your bid or offer by a set number of ticks to increase the likelihood of a fill. If you are working a bid or

an offer at market and your trade isn't filled, the order can 'pay-up' to the next price to secure a fill.

Stop-Loss Orders (Market or Limit)
Stop-Market: When your stop price is triggered, a market order is sent, guaranteeing execution but not the price.

Stop-Limit: When triggered, a limit order is sent, giving you price control but no guarantee of being filled.

Trailing Stop
A dynamic stop order that moves with the market. If the market moves in your favor, the stop adjusts to lock in more profit; if it moves against you, the stop holds and protects your downside.

Ghost Order
An order type sometimes offered by advanced platforms that allows you to place an order visible only to you, not to the market. Execution occurs once conditions are met, but other traders cannot see it resting on the book.

Conditional Orders
These trigger only when specific conditions are met (price, time, volume, or a combination). They allow you to program your execution in advance rather than reacting in the moment. It is a very basic form of algorithmic trading that we can utilize if the system you are using supports it. If this occurs in the market, then execute accordingly.

The key point here is not to use every order type just because it exists.

Professionals select the most suitable tool for the trade idea, market conditions, and liquidity. When used effectively, these orders can enhance your execution skills; if used poorly, they can complicate matters and cause you to chase your tail.

7.1.4 Trading is a Risky Business—Execution Risks

Identifying trades is entirely risk-free. At that stage, you're only risking your time and a bit of mental energy. However, as soon as you move from idea to execution, everything shifts. That's when you trade your effort for market risk.

I've always told traders that the simplest and most accurate definition of trading risk is this:

> "How much are you prepared to lose on a trade?"

From that point onward, everything else falls into place. Once you define your maximum loss, you can determine whether you have allocated your risk wisely through your execution choices.

We've already looked at some of the risks tied to execution:

Liquidity risk—the danger of moving the market when liquidity is thin.

Order-type risk—the risk of slippage when using market orders, versus the potential of missing fills when using limit orders.

Stop-order risk—the importance of having a predefined exit if the market goes against you.

The stop order is non-negotiable among these. It's, by far, the most crucial part of your risk framework. Without it, you're trading blindly, and one poor decision can erase weeks, months, or even years of progress.

The second essential element is position sizing. A stop becomes pointless if your trade size is too large because even a "controlled" loss can turn into a disaster. Position size and stop placement are interconnected: one influences the other.

Classic risk theory suggests you should never risk more than 2% of your account on a single trade.

For example, if your trading account is £50,000, your maximum risk per trade would be £1,000. If your stop-loss is 10 ticks away and each tick is worth £50, that means you could take two contracts for the trade (10 ticks × £50 × 2 contracts = £1,000 risk). This kind of framework allows traders to manage risk mathematically and prevent catastrophic losses.

Over the years, I've approached risk a little differently and coached traders with a different mindset. My guiding principle has always been:

Never let a bad trade ruin your day, never let a bad day ruin your week, and never let a bad week ruin your month.

I base my approach on the concept of recoverable losses. This has helped me keep my downside risk under control across thousands of trades. I use it both for individual markets and as a broad view of my trading risk.

For example:

If I've never earned more than £1000 in a specific market, I don't trade very often; then it makes no sense for me to lose more than that.

In fact, my loss shouldn't even exceed my average daily gain in that market over the past few months.

This gives me a dynamic, relative view of risk. Losses are always compared against realistic gains—keeping them recoverable. It ensures I never dig a hole so deep in any one market, day, or week that it undermines my long-term consistency and my overall trading goals.

I believe theory offers a framework, but practice requires flexibility. The best traders utilize both—a structured foundation and a personal philosophy that keeps risk aligned with their performance.

While you are on your own trading journey and getting to grips with risk, you will inevitably develop your own philosophy along the way. Risk management isn't a one-size-fits-all solution—it's partly science, partly art. The science provides structure (like the 2% rule or technical stop placement), while the art comes from experience—learning what keeps you consistent, disciplined, and able to return day after day.

What matters most is that you create a framework that keeps your losses recoverable, your emotions under control, and your capital safe. Because as long as you can remain in the game, you always have the chance to win.

7.1.5 Classic Execution Profiles

A highly recommended read on this topic is The Art of Execution by Lee Freeman-Shor. In it, he explains how investors behave when implementing their ideas, categorizing them into profiles that emphasize both strengths and weaknesses. I've always found his framework compelling—and it translates well into the trading world too.

Here are some of the execution profiles you'll encounter—not only in others but also in yourself. Recognizing these tendencies is essential for progressing from amateur to professional.

The Hesitant Trader
This trader finds it difficult to take action. They recognize the setup, overthink, and often miss the chance altogether. Like the "Rabbit" in Freeman-Shor's work, they freeze when it's time to act. Hesitation usually stems from fear of loss, and the solution lies in the process. Clear rules for entry, exit, and stop-losses lessen emotional strain and make execution straightforward rather than personal.

The Overconfident Trader
This trader enjoys increasing their position size and swinging big, often excessively so. They resemble the "Hunter" or even the "Raider"—charging into the market

with conviction but lacking discipline. Overconfidence can lead to occasional spectacular wins, but without consistent risk management, it's a quick path to blow-ups. The lesson: size your positions based on your stops, not your ego.

The Impatient Trader
Similar to the "Rabbit," but instead of freezing, they jump in too early. They can't wait for confirmation and often chase the market. This is the trader who always wants to be in a trade, even when the edge isn't there. Impatience kills edge—the discipline is to wait for your pitch, like an Assassin patiently lining up the shot.

The Disciplined Trader
This is the professional standard: a clear plan, predefined stop, appropriate size, and consistent execution. The disciplined trader doesn't need excitement; they need repeatability. They operate more like the "Assassin" in The Art of Execution—deliberate, precise, and willing to wait as long as it takes for the right opportunity.

The Adaptive Trader
A rarer but valuable profile. This trader learns from mistakes, evolves, and adapts their style as market conditions change. They share DNA with what Freeman-Shor calls the "Connoisseur"—selective, thoughtful, and capable of combining patience with boldness when the odds are favorable. The adaptive trader is not inflexible, but they never forsake discipline.

Knowing which execution profile you favor helps you identify your weaknesses in real time. Are you hesitating? Are you rushing? Are you pressing for too much size? Or are you executing steadily, regardless of the outcome?

By cultivating awareness of your execution style, you'll learn not just how to place trades, but how to do so in a manner that aligns with the professional standard you aim for.

Execution is the moment when analysis turns into action—when ideas meet the market. By mastering order types, understanding liquidity, setting clear stops, sizing positions properly, and recognizing your own execution profile, you give yourself the best chance of starting each trade on solid ground. But placing a trade is only half the battle. The real test begins once you're in the market. From that point onwards, it's no longer about spotting or entering a trade—it's about how you manage it.

8

Managing a Trade

A good friend of mine and trading veteran, Dan Gramza, has always described managing trades as "trying to stay within the eye of a storm when you're sailing a ship." It's the perfect image. Around you, the waves are crashing, the wind is howling, and everything is unpredictable. But in the center—the eye—there is calm. Your job as a trader is to keep your ship steady in that calm, no matter how violent the storm around you.

I'll never forget my first storm. I was about six months into my professional trading career, finally starting to feel like I understood what I was doing. I had my positions in the market, my orders placed, and a sense of control. Then, out of nowhere, a central banker made an offhand comment about moving interest rates—and the market went berserk.

Within seconds, my positions reversed against me, and the resting orders I had placed were executed rapidly. I found myself making too many trades, completely out of control, like a rabbit caught in the headlights of an approaching car. In less than 10 minutes, my first six months of hard-earned gains were wiped out. I sat there, numb and devastated, wondering how it had all fallen apart so quickly.

But that moment was my rite of passage—the harsh yet essential lesson every trader encounters sooner or later. The lesson was simple but unforgettable: be prepared for anything and learn how to manage your trades for any scenario, because the markets can and will surprise you.

That's what this chapter is about—how to find your calm amidst the storm, how to protect yourself when the unexpected occurs, and how to manage trades in a way that keeps you in the game.

S. Warner-Baker, *Learn to Trade Like a Professional*,
https://doi.org/10.1007/978-3-032-20125-6_8

For me, the most important aspects of trade management rest on two main pillars: process and psychology. Process encompasses the mechanics—mindset, understanding the market environment, stop-losses, risk management, and adherence to your plan. Psychology involves the internal struggles—obsession, fear, panic, complacency, ego, denial, and greed.

In the pages ahead, we'll examine both pillars. We'll begin with the practical aspect: how to use stops effectively, how to size and modify positions, and how to manage trades in accordance with the market environment. Then we'll shift to psychology, where we'll confront the traps that cause most traders to fail—from holding onto losing positions to closing winners too early. Finally, we'll integrate all of this with a set of fundamental rules to help you stay balanced when markets are anything but.

8.1 Stop Losses: The Foundation of Trade Management

If there's one rule that differentiates professional traders from amateurs, it's this: always know where you're getting out before you get in.

As we've mentioned before—and I often remind myself nearly every day—the great Bruce Kovner, one of the most successful hedge fund managers of the last century, expressed it perfectly:

"Whenever I enter a position, I have a predetermined stop. I know where I'm getting out before I get in. It's the only way I can sleep."

The stop loss acts as your safety net. It sets the maximum amount you are prepared to lose on a trade and, more importantly, enforces that decision automatically. Without it, every losing trade risks spiraling out of control. With it, your downside is clearly defined, monitored, and manageable.

There are three key principles to using stops effectively:

Set Them Beyond the Noise
Placing your stop too close is like putting it in the middle of traffic—it's likely to be hit by normal market fluctuations. Stops should be set beyond key technical levels (support, resistance, ranges) at points that are more difficult for the market to reach casually. Remember: the market is clever. It hunts for obvious stop levels. We'll cover this more in the Practice section, but for now, know that your stop placement must defend you against both randomness and predators.

Respect Them Without Hesitation

The biggest mistake traders make isn't setting stops—it's moving them when the market gets close. The moment you override your stop, you've abandoned discipline. The stop is there to protect you from yourself. Over the years, when I've had to discipline traders for excessive losses, the number one excuse I've heard is: "I missed my stop." It's true this can happen in fast-moving markets—but there's no excuse for staying in afterwards. The next step must be to exit immediately. No hesitation. No questions asked.

Use Them to Size Your Position

Your stop distance should directly dictate your position size. If your stop is 10 ticks away and you only want to risk £500, you can calculate exactly how many contracts to trade. This keeps your risk consistent, no matter the market. This is the art of growing as a trader: as you build confidence and profits, your acceptable loss size can increase—but it must always remain controlled.

Stops are not about admitting defeat—they're about staying in the game. If you get stopped out, you can always re-enter if conditions improve. But if you hold on without one, you may not get that second chance.

Here's the key point I emphasize to junior traders: you must always think in terms of recoverable losses. This is where many beginners go wrong. They let a single trade run so far against them that it wipes out days, weeks, or even months of progress. Once a loss becomes unrecoverable within a realistic timeframe, you've broken the golden rule of risk.

A professional doesn't judge a stop by ego or just the market—they assess it based on what can be recovered. This rule helps you avoid digging a hole too deep to get out of, and it ensures you stay in the game long enough to seize the next opportunity.

The truth is, not all trades will be winners. Accepting this fact—and managing stops effectively—is not just part of the trading process; it's the key to long-term survival.

8.2 Scaling Risk: Adding and Reducing Positions

If stops are about protecting your downside, then scaling is about managing your exposure once you're in a trade. It's a key skill in trade management—and for me, it remains an ongoing challenge: when do I add to my position, and when do I start reducing it? Like most aspects of trading, it can either sharpen your edge or erode your account, depending on your approach.

At its simplest, scaling is the act of adding to a winning trade or reducing size when conditions change.

Adding to Winners

The idea of adding to a winning position often divides opinion. Some traders avoid doing so, fearing they will give back profits. Others view it as the key to maximizing their edge when the market moves in their favor. Many traders I've coached—and some of the most legendary fund managers—often add when the trade is going their way. It's as if the move in their favor confirms their conviction, and they want to maximize the opportunity.

There's a common saying in trading that you should never add to a losing position. In most trading teachings, this is called negative averaging, although it has been normalized under the softer label of fading in. Fading in means executing more of the same trade at better prices to improve your average entry. Done mindlessly, it's one of the fastest ways to blow up a trading account. But if it's part of a plan—as it often is for me—it can be a structured way to build into a position over a range of prices. Remember: you will never buy the exact low or sell the exact high. Fading in gives me the room I need for execution most of the time.

Adding more when the market has proven you right requires courage and conviction. However, it must be accompanied by discipline: adjusting your stop as you increase your size and planning your exit accordingly.

When done correctly, scaling into winners enables you to pyramid positions and build on gains. When done recklessly, it becomes ego-driven risk. This is exactly the type of trader behavior that, when executed with skill, can move you from the lower leagues to the main event.

Scaling Out of a Trade

Just as important as knowing when to add is knowing when to reduce. Markets change. Liquidity dries up, volatility spikes, or new information emerges. Professionals don't wait for disaster—they cut size proactively to bring risk back in line with the new reality.

Scaling out is also a valuable tactic when your profit target hasn't been achieved, but the market continues to trade within a narrow range. During these times, I often focus on the price action rather than my initial plan, scaling out into strength and re-entering if the circumstances warrant it.

Reducing doesn't mean abandoning the trade. It means you're actively managing your plan. You'll never know with certainty if it was the "right" decision at the end of the day or week, but you'll know you made controlled adjustments in response to changing conditions. And that's what professional risk management looks like.

The Balance
Scaling is all about maintaining balance. Being too cautious can lead to premature exits from profitable trades. Going too aggressively risks damaging strong positions with overly large allocations. The skill lies in adjusting size carefully, always guided by stops and risk limits. There is no definitive right or wrong—much depends on your beliefs, experience, and methods. That's why effective trade management is such a key indicator of long-term success.

One of the guiding principles I share with traders is this:

"Never let a bad trade get worse and never let a good trade turn into a loser."

I approach my trades with a defensive mindset first. It might not always seem glamorous, but that's why I've been in the game all these years.

Scaling in and out isn't about chasing excitement or snatching profits. It's about fine-tuning risk in real time—pressing when conditions align and pulling back when they don't.

8.3 Stay on Course in the Eye of the Storm

Once you're in the market, mindset becomes your greatest ally—or your greatest weakness. Execution gets you into the trade, but mindset shapes how you manage everything that follows: the waiting, the swings, the surprises, and the pressure.

A strong mindset hinges on balance. You need conviction in your ideas, but also the flexibility to admit when you are wrong. You require the courage to hold onto winners, but the humility to cut losers. Too much of one and not enough of the other, and you risk falling into the traps that undo most traders.

There are three mindset shifts I consider essential for managing trades:

Detach from the Outcome
Once the trade is underway, your job isn't to predict or hope—it's to manage. The market will do what it wants. Your role is to follow your process: monitor risk, respect stops, and make adjustments calmly.

Stay Calm in Uncertainty
Every trade feels different once you're in it. P&L fluctuates up and down. News impacts the market. A sudden spike can seem like the end of the world. Your role is to stay in the "eye of the storm"—calm while the market swirls around you. That means managing your emotions, staying focused, and trusting your plan.

Trade What You See, Not What You Feel
Feelings tempt you to interfere—to close too early, to increase size out of greed, or to hold back out of stubbornness. The process keeps you grounded in reality. Anchor decisions in evidence: the chart, the order flow, and the rules you set before you entered.

The Storm Clouds That Threaten Mindset
These are the forces that pull traders out of the eye of the storm:

Obsession:
Becoming married to a trade. I've experienced this and done it more times than I can count. Once you've laid the groundwork, it's easy to fixate on that one position. But your mental capacity is limited—don't let one of the thousands of trades you'll make overwhelm your mind.

Fear:
The paralysis is caused by focusing only on what can go wrong. To survive, you need to be anti-fragile—to take knocks and keep moving forward. It's okay if trades go wrong; that's why you have a stop. No trader has 100% winners, but those with longevity know exactly where to get out.

Panic:
The loss of control when volatility spikes and emotions take over. This is where your plan keeps you grounded. Human panic is evident in every major market move—it creates opportunity, but if you panic as a trader, it almost always results in poor decisions.

Complacency:
The risky "I know what I'm doing" attitude. Markets swiftly penalize overconfidence. Even now, I hesitate to call myself an "expert"—the markets are always evolving, and I am just a small part of a vast system. Gratitude and humility prevent me from becoming complacent.

Ego:
The desire to be right at all costs. The market consumes egos for breakfast. The most successful traders I've met are also the most humble—a stark contrast to what you often see on social media.

Denial:
Refusing to stop out, ignoring your plan, and hoping the trade "comes back." Hope is essential at a macro level—optimism drives your career. But on a micro level, "hope trading" is dangerous. If you're hoping your stops get hit at a better level, you're in trouble.

Greed:
Snatching profits as soon as they appear, cutting winners short. It's human nature: we dislike admitting we're wrong, so we move stops. And when we're right, we seek the dopamine rush of locking in gains. Both are natural impulses you must learn to manage.

Every one of these traps has the same cure: stick to the plan.

I have those very words framed above my screens. I practice what I preach. When you built your trade idea, you decided the entry, the stop, the risk, and the conditions under which you'd exit. That plan acts as your anchor. In the heat of the market, when the storm clouds gather, the plan keeps you steady.

Mindset in trade management isn't about being emotionless. It's about recognizing these traps when they arise—obsession, fear, panic, complacency, ego, denial, greed—and choosing to follow your plan rather than your emotions.

8.4 Golden Rules for Managing Trades

To finish this chapter, here are the golden rules I live by and teach every trader I've coached. Keep them close—print them, frame them, or pin them above your screens:

Respect the Stop
Never move it further away. If it's hit, you're out. No exceptions.
Size to Survive
Position size must always reflect your stop distance and account for risk. Risk only what is recoverable.
Never Let a Bad Trade Get Worse
Don't add to losing trades out of denial or hope. Average only if it's part of a pre-defined plan.

Press Only When the Market Proves You Right
Increase trading size when your idea and market structure align perfectly.
Scale Out Proactively
Take risk off when conditions change, volatility spikes, or targets are near.
Detach From the Outcome
Your job is to follow the process, not to predict the future.
Don't Chase or Snatch
Don't chase markets out of FOMO. Don't snatch profits too early out of greed. Let your plan decide.
Hope Has No Place in a Trade
Be optimistic about your career, but never "hope" an individual trade comes back.
Stay Humble
No one is greater than the market. Gratitude and humility help to keep complacency and ego at bay.
Stick to the Plan
Entry, stop, target, and risk were established before you entered. That plan is your anchor—trust it.
You are the Manager
Managing trades isn't about achieving perfection. It's about maintaining control—keeping losses manageable, allowing winners to develop, and ensuring emotions don't sway your decisions. Follow these principles, and you'll increase your chances of staying in the game long enough to succeed.

This part of the process is where discipline, psychology, and process meet. It's the space where the market tests you in real time—and where your ability to respect stops, manage size, scale with discipline, and keep your mindset steady ultimately determines your outcome.

But once the trade is over—win, lose, or scratch (break even)—your job isn't finished. The final step of the process is just as important as the first: evaluating the trade.

Evaluation is where lessons are learned, edges are sharpened, and progress is made. It's how you turn individual trades into long-term growth. In the next chapter, we'll break down exactly how to review your trades, record them effectively, and refine your process so that each trade—no matter the outcome—brings you closer to becoming a professional.

9

Evaluating a Trade

Win or Learn

The mantra I have instilled at my trading education company, Teach the World to Trade, is simple: “Win or Learn.”

We find out which one it is during the evaluation stage of the process. If you’ve reached this point, you’ve already done the hard work: identified the trade, executed it, and managed it in real time. Now comes the final step—to look back. Not to beat yourself up or celebrate unquestioningly, but to extract lessons that will sharpen your edge as we move forward.

Here’s the truth: if you’ve made it to evaluation, you’ve already improved your trading experience and increased your chances of success moving forward. That alone is a win.

In this chapter, we’ll cover how to:

Journal your trades effectively without drowning in detail.

Review your performance objectively, separating process from outcome.

Spot recurring patterns in your behavior—good and bad.

Build feedback loops that make you a better trader every single day by applying a growth mindset.

Because evaluation isn’t about judgment, it’s about learning. It’s how each trade—whether it made money or lost it—becomes part of your purposeful practice and fuels your growth as a professional.

S. Warner-Baker, *Learn to Trade Like a Professional*,
https://doi.org/10.1007/978-3-032-20125-6_9

9.1 The Power of the Journal

As I write this, I see three separate journals on my desk—places where I actively record and review my trades, my days, my weeks, my months, and even my years. I even carry a journal with me on holiday, and I had one with me in the hospital when my daughter was born. To say I believe in the power of journaling is an understatement.

We have so many thoughts, emotions, and distractions swirling around us in the markets—and just as many when we step out of them—that it's impossible to remember all the necessary details of our process and emotions without writing them down.

My first attempt at journaling wasn't even about trading. After university, when I was travelling around South America, I thought of myself as a bit of an Ernest Hemingway—jotting down my thoughts as I went. I was definitely not a writer (and certainly never imagined I'd end up writing a book), but even then I knew this: those words were for me, and no one else. That remains my main piece of advice about journaling: it's for you, and it's there to help you improve. Don't overthink it. Whatever resonates with you and helps you grow as a trader, use it.

For about a year, I even wrote the same phrase at the top of every page:

"Don't trade like an idiot!"

The first step in analyzing a trade is keeping a journal. A trading journal isn't just a diary of wins and losses—it's the foundation of ongoing improvement. Done properly, it helps you repeat what works, fix what doesn't, and build resilience through every trade.

Think of it as your personal growth engine. As I've said many times, trading is "Win or Learn." The journal is where the learning is captured.

What to Record

Your journal doesn't need to be complicated, but it does need to be consistent. At a minimum, record:

Trade Rationale—Why did you take the trade? What was your setup, your logic, your plan?

Market Conditions—What was happening at the time? Volatility, liquidity, news, and broader context.

Emotional State—How did you feel before, during, and after the trade? Nervous, confident, fearful, calm?

Strategy Used—Was this technical, fundamental, seasonal, or price action-based?

Outcome—Entry, stop, target, result—profit, loss, or scratch.

Lessons Learned—What would you do differently next time? What worked well?

Effective Journaling

From coaching hundreds of traders, I've found that the best journals share these qualities:

Consistent Entries—Write something after every trade.
Detail-Oriented—Enough information to learn from, without overloading.
Objective—Record facts, not excuses.
Reflective—Don't just log the trade, review it.
Action-Oriented—Note what you'll change or repeat going forward.

The Growth Mindset in Action

The journal is where you adopt a growth mindset. A losing trade isn't failure—it's feedback. A winning trade isn't just a celebration—it's a chance to recognize what you did well and repeat it. Every entry is an opportunity to practice, review, and improve.

Over time, your journal becomes more than just a record—it transforms into a roadmap of your development as a trader. It documents not only your trades but also your thought process, discipline, and growth. It serves as proof that you are either winning or learning—and in both cases, progressing.

9.1.1 Reviewing Performance: Process Vs Outcome

One of the biggest mistakes traders make when reviewing their trades is judging everything solely by the outcome. If it made money, it must have been a good trade. If it lost money, it must have been a poor trade. This way of thinking is dangerous—and it's not how we as professionals assess performance.

A good trade isn't judged by whether it made money. Instead, a good trade is one where you followed your process: you identified the setup, sized the position correctly, placed the stop in the right spot, and executed according to plan. If you did all of that and still lost money, that's not failure—that's trading. Losses are part of the game, as I've mentioned a few times already.

Similarly, a poor trade isn't justified just because it turned a profit. Perhaps you ignored your stop loss, took an overly large position, or entered poorly in pursuit of a quick gain. You got lucky—and luck is not a reliable strategy.

When you review your performance, ask yourself two key questions:

What mistake did I make that taught me something?

Did I follow my process? Was my analysis sound, my execution disciplined, and my risk defined?

Is my current learning strategy working?

What can I learn? Was there something in the market I didn't account for? Did emotions creep into my decisions? Did I break my rules? If so, why?

This is where your journal becomes especially valuable. By recording both the facts (entry, stop, outcome) and the context (thoughts, emotions, conditions), you provide yourself with the material to distinguish luck from skill.

The aim of reviewing your performance is not to pat yourself on the back for successes or punish yourself for failures. The aim is to sharpen your edge by recognizing patterns—the habits you want to repeat and the errors you need to eliminate.

It's all part of your journey to profitability. And like anything of real value, that path doesn't come for free—it must be documented, studied, and refined through consistent practice.

9.1.2 Spotting Recurring Patterns

Once you've journaled your trades and reviewed them against your process, the next step is to step back and look for patterns. Not patterns in the charts—but patterns in your own behavior.

Over the years, I've noticed many in myself and the traders I've mentored. Many of these habits repeat themselves. While writing this book, I even discussed some of these patterns with my coach. He played devil's advocate, suggesting that what I might see as a "bad habit" could actually be part of what has helped me stay in the game for so long. That gave me food for thought.

For me, the biggest recurring pattern has always been impulse trading—executing trades on a whim without following my process. It's one of the reasons I wrote "don't be an idiot" at the top of my journal for over a year. Those impulsive trades consistently led to poor quality outcomes, and journaling was the only way I could clearly see the damage they caused.

Every trader has tendencies. Some are strengths you want to reinforce; others are blind spots you need to address. The evaluation stage is where these tendencies become visible. Every trade will teach you something—the goal is to discover that best version of yourself, the one who trades effectively, and then repeat that behavior as often as you can.

Positive Patterns
Look for the behaviors that consistently contribute to strong results:

Do you trade best at certain times of day or in certain markets?
Do you stick to your stops without hesitation?
Do you perform better when you prepare thoroughly the night before?
Are your biggest wins the trades where you scaled in with discipline?

These are clues to what you should do more of. They form the foundations of your edge.

Negative Patterns
Equally important is spotting the habits that cost you money:

Do you tend to chase trades after missing the first move?
Do you snatch at profits too quickly?
Do you hold losers too long out of denial or hope?
Do you oversize when you feel "certain" about an idea?

These behaviors repeat until you address them. Awareness is the first step to breaking the cycle.

Markets may change, but human behavior remains persistently consistent. The traders who succeed are those who recognize their own patterns and act accordingly. That's where evaluation becomes so valuable: it's not about reviewing a single trade in isolation, but about connecting the dots across numerous trades.

Even as a coach, I've found that the traders who succeed most aren't the ones who depend only on my advice—they're those who learn to evaluate themselves more effectively than I ever could and grow beyond what seemed possible.

Your journaling offers the raw data. Identifying recurring patterns is the analysis. Together, they provide the insight needed to strengthen what works, eliminate what doesn't, and continually sharpen your edge.

9.1.3 Building Feedback Loops

Journaling and reviewing your trades are only worthwhile if they lead to progress. Writing things down and identifying patterns is the analysis, but improvement comes from creating feedback loops that turn those insights into action.

Think of a feedback loop as a cycle:

Trade → you execute according to your process.
Record → you capture what happened, including facts and emotions.
Review → you analyze what worked and what didn't.
Adjust → you feed that lesson into your next trade.

Then you repeat. Again, and again.

This exemplifies the growth mindset in action, as psychologist Carol Dweck emphasized in her research and her book Mindset. Her studies demonstrated that people who see mistakes as chances to learn rather than proof of failure consistently perform better than those who seek only validation. They endure longer, adapt more swiftly, and ultimately succeed more. In trading, adopting that mindset means every trade—whether wins or losses—becomes a stepping stone towards mastery.

Over time, these loops build up. Small adjustments add up to significant improvements. The trader who embraces feedback loops doesn't just trade—they develop. When I held monthly reviews with traders in my office, we reviewed their evaluations and looked for tiny gains. It often came down to identifying positive or negative feedback loops in their trading and making small changes to enhance performance. When these are combined, they lead to exponential growth.

Process, Not Perfection

The goal isn't to eliminate mistakes entirely—that's impossible. The aim is to reduce their frequency and severity while reinforcing the behaviors that make you profitable. If you notice you keep chasing trades, your process should include a rule to pause before entering. If you see that preparation the night before improves your results, your routine should include a nightly review habit.

Positive vs Negative Feedback Loops

Not all feedback loops work in your favor.

Positive feedback loops strengthen good habits. For instance, documenting how adhering to your stop loss preserved capital makes you more likely to respect stops next time. Over time, these small reinforcements build lasting discipline.

Negative feedback loops entrap you in destructive patterns. For instance, if you seize quick gains and then emotionally reward yourself for being "right," you reinforce a habit that harms you in the long term. If left unchecked, these loops embed harmful behaviors until they become normal.

The key is awareness: build and strengthen your positive loops and identify and break the negative ones.

Resilience Through Reflection
Feedback loops also build resilience. When you see losses in the context of learning, they lose their sting. A bad trade isn't just pain—it's information. As long as you're feeding that information back into your process, you're getting better.

Growth Mindset in Action
This is where the growth mindset truly comes into play. You're not merely reacting to trades; you're utilizing each one as fuel for deliberate, conscious practice. Over time, your journal shifts from being a record of the past to a blueprint for the future.

Evaluation is where trading genuinely evolves. It's the stage where you close the loop on each trade, draw the lesson, and carry it forward. Consistently doing this means you don't just trade more—you trade better.

It might seem like a lot of effort at first, especially if you're pressed for time or trading multiple times a day. But like everything in trading, once you've established the habit, it becomes second nature. Over time, you'll learn to identify lessons swiftly and apply them effectively—and those small, steady improvements will compound into something far greater.

Moving from Process to Practice

With the final part of this section covered, we complete the professional trading process: identify, execute, manage, and evaluate. Each stage builds on the last, forming a cycle of preparation, discipline, and growth. This is the framework professionals rely on, and it's the structure that transforms trading from a gamble into a craft.

But process alone isn't enough. Knowing the steps in theory is one thing—living them in the heat of the market is another. To truly build consistency, you need to move from theory into practice. That means drills, exercises, and deliberate repetition until the process becomes second nature.

In the next section, we'll put everything into practice. You'll learn how to intentionally rehearse the process, develop routines and checklists that keep you focused, and refine your skills through structured drills and exercises. This is where the route to profitability truly begins—not just understanding how professionals trade, but training yourself to do it repeatedly with confidence and control.

Part III

Practice

10

Practicing the Process

"You can't learn to play golf without hitting any golf balls."

That line comes from my good friend Steve Ward—an expert in trader coaching and, to this day, someone I still consider a mentor. Of course, Steve wasn't really talking about the art of knocking a small white ball around a field with a long stick. He was talking about trading. His point was simple: if you don't execute a trade, you don't get to manage a trade, and you'll never uncover the lesson that will make you better next time.

I've carried that idea with me throughout my career, and it sits neatly alongside my own motto—the one we live by at Teach the World to Trade: Win or Learn. But to win or learn, you first have to trade.

Many years into my career, I discovered the work of psychologist Carol Dweck and her research on the growth mindset. What stood out most to me was her idea of purposeful practice: the idea that genuine improvement doesn't arise from mindless repetition, but from structured, deliberate effort. It's not just about making more trades; it's about doing them with intent—testing your process, reviewing your performance, and targeting specific skills for enhancement.

Reflecting on my trading journey, it was heavily based on practice, with the theory often catching up much later. It was very much a game of trial and error in those early days—picking up bits of information that only became essential after the market had taught me an expensive lesson. Many times, those lessons cost me a few ticks before I finally understood.

When I've spoken with traders while working on this book, we often laugh about those early years. We recall the intensity of that first twelve months:

S. Warner-Baker, *Learn to Trade Like a Professional*,
https://doi.org/10.1007/978-3-032-20125-6_10

pushing each other to reach higher and higher trading volumes, month after month. Unknowingly, we were forcing ourselves to practise as much as possible, even in what we would later recognize as a relatively low-risk environment. The small trading sizes we began with were nothing compared to what was in store for us in the years ahead—but the repetitions laid the foundation.

That experience taught me something important: practice is vital, but it works best when paired with the right theory. That's why I've built my training differently. I focus on providing traders with the right amount of theory as a foundation, and only then guide them into methodical practice. That balance offers them the best chance to develop their skills without unnecessary trial-and-error, and to shape themselves into consistent, professional traders.

This chapter is where theory meets practice. Where you take what you know and begin to train it—repeatedly, intentionally, and with structure.

10.1 A Word on Risk Before You Begin

Before we dive into drills, reps, and structured practice, we need to pause on one crucial reality: trading carries real financial risk.

It is possible to lose part or even all of your capital. In fact, if you dive straight into live trading without a clear process or without first practicing in a safe environment, the odds are stacked against you.

That's why everything in this section is designed to be practised in a risk-free environment first. Whether it's a demo account, a trading simulator, or paper trading with clear rules and timestamps, the aim is to train your process without paying unnecessary tuition fees to the market.

Nearly every trading platform nowadays offers simulation features across all major markets. Use them. Treat them seriously. The discipline you apply during simulated practice will be the same discipline you carry into the live market.

Think of it as a flight simulator for pilots: no one allows a trainee pilot to fly a passenger jet without hundreds of hours of simulated flights. Traders should treat their craft no differently.

When I ran training programs, I required junior traders to spend at least a month in eight-hour simulator sessions before they placed a single live order. The goal wasn't to protect the firm's capital—it was to safeguard the trader's confidence and to instill the correct behaviors before pressure was introduced.

Graduate programs at the world's largest investment banks follow the same principle. New hires often spend two full years learning to identify, execute, manage, and evaluate trades in controlled environments before they're ever permitted to trade real money.

It's not only a disclaimer—it's a fact. Simulation and deliberate practice form the foundation of professional performance. They develop muscle memory, emotional control, and process discipline long before real capital is at risk.

10.2 Preparing the Mental Athlete for Practice in the Markets

In my recent development, I've moved beyond market drills and adopted a mental athlete approach to trading. This recognizes that performance at the screen doesn't only stem from charts, orders, or risk parameters—it also depends on the body and mind you bring into the market each day.

I've focused on refining four pillars of my trading and developed a framework that I subsequently introduced to an international network of professional traders in a previous role.

Nutrition—Eating in a way that sustains energy, prevents spikes and crashes, and enhances focus. Personally, I fast overnight for about 14 hours, drinking only water and black coffee until lunchtime, and I avoid processed foods whenever possible. Simple, consistent changes like this have made a significant difference to my energy levels and mental clarity.

Movement—It's easy to spend hours glued to the screen watching the markets, but I've learnt that focus and decision-making begin to decline after about 90 minutes. Now, I set a timer to remind myself to step away, move, or stretch. I set daily fitness targets, and I consider them as important as my trading goals.

Mindfulness—Meditation and breathing exercises help me stay calm and centered, especially before and during trading sessions. I first adopted this idea from Ray Dalio, the hedge fund legend who meditates twice daily whenever possible. Incorporating that habit genuinely transformed my life and enhanced the quality of each day.

Recovery—Prioritizing sleep has been a real game-changer. Avoiding technology for at least 30 minutes before bed helps me switch off and sleep deeply. Investing in a quality mattress and pillow has probably been one of the best investments I've ever made in my personal assets.

Just like an elite athlete prepares before a competition, performs during it, and recovers afterwards, I try to approach trading in the same way. When I align these elements with market practices, I trade more effectively, think more clearly, and adapt more quickly.

Holistic practice isn't separate from market practice—it's the foundation that enables the market work to be carried out at a consistently high standard. If I had a time machine, this would be the advice I'd give to my younger self without hesitation. It's the missing link that would have elevated my performance much earlier.

10.3 Understanding Trader Profiles

Before you can practice effectively, you need to understand what kind of trader you are—or at least what type you're aiming to become.

Each trading style requires a slightly different rhythm, skill set, and approach to practice. Over the years, I have worked across four broad profiles that encompass most professional and retail trading styles.

My own trading journey has experimented with all types of trading. I started as a scalper—trading high volume for low returns, focused on accuracy and speed—before gradually developing my approach to incorporate longer-term, hedge-fund-style macro strategies. None of these styles is superior to the others; they demand different ways of thinking, preparing, and practicing.

The Scalper

The scalper thrives on movement. They operate in seconds and minutes, aiming to capture small price shifts with high frequency and tight control.

Scalping demands supreme focus, rapid pattern recognition, and emotional steadiness under pressure.

Strengths
Exceptional reaction speed and focus.
Deep understanding of order-book behavior and market microstructure.
Discipline to cut losing trades instantly.

Challenges
Mental fatigue and burnout from constant decision-making.
Over-trading in quiet conditions.
Maintaining composure after rapid wins or losses.

The Day/Macro Trader

The day trader—or short-term macro trader—holds positions for hours rather than minutes.

They mostly end each day flat, combining technical analysis with awareness of economic releases, policy shifts, and intraday sentiment.

Strengths
Strong preparation and structure.
Ability to link intraday moves to broader macro themes.
Consistent routine for pre-market planning and post-market review.

Challenges
Over-anticipating news outcomes.
Emotional swings between morning and afternoon sessions.
Pressure to trade daily, regardless of the opportunity.

The Swing Trader

The swing trader operates over days or weeks, capturing moves within broader trends or seasonal cycles.

They rely on patience and conviction, letting probability and timing do the work rather than constant activity.

Strengths
Ability to see the bigger picture and trade narratives, not noise.
Emotional stability during periods of consolidation.
Effective risk sizing and position management.

Challenges
Boredom and the temptation to over-manage trades.
Allowing unrealized profits to turn into losses through hesitation.
Managing overnight and weekend risk.

The Investor/Fund Manager

The investor or fund manager approach takes the longest-term view, holding positions for months or years.

They focus on capital allocation, diversification, and consistent performance rather than daily price action.

Strengths
Patience, foresight, and an understanding of economic cycles.
Skill in constructing balanced portfolios across asset classes.
Focus on compounded, risk-adjusted returns.

Challenges
Maintaining conviction through drawdowns and market regime changes.
Avoiding over-diversification and benchmark chasing.
Balancing research depth with timely decision-making.

Who's it going to be?
Every trader exists somewhere along this spectrum, and many progress through various stages as their capital, confidence, and time horizons develop. A scalper might one day become a swing trader; a swing trader could grow into an investor.

Once you have practised each trading style, you'll notice how your skills begin to overlap across different types. The discipline and accuracy of a scalper enhance a swing trader's timing. The patience of an investor refines the insight of a day trader. Mastery in trading often arises from understanding—and combining—the strengths of each approach.

The aim isn't to choose one box and remain there; it's to understand which profile best suits your personality, resources, and lifestyle at this moment.

A scalper needs rapid feedback and constant focus.
A day trader thrives on structure and preparation.
A swing trader relies on patience and conviction.
An investor leans on foresight and strategic balance.

Knowing where you stand on that scale helps you apply the right process—one that aligns with your time horizon, temperament, and ultimate goals.

Similarly, matching your trading ideas to your profile will make your plans clearer and more effective. A swing trader should focus on multi-day opportunities rather than scalp entries; an investor should think in terms of quarters rather than sessions. Aligning your ideas with your style fosters consistency, confidence, and ultimately, better results.

10.4 Setting Targets and Bringing Lag Indicators to Life

Once you understand your trader profile and the trading style that suits you best, the next step is to define what success looks like—and how you will measure it.

In earlier chapters, we discussed the concept of lag indicators—the visible results of consistent practice, such as profits, account growth, or performance metrics.

They're called lag indicators because they follow your process. They appear after the work is completed.

You can't control the outcome of a single trade, but you can manage the quality of your preparation, execution, and review. Concentrate on those, and the lag indicators will eventually catch up.

That said, it's essential to set clear, realistic targets that guide your practice.

Targets create structure. They give your process something to aim for and your performance something to measure against.

My personal lag indicator is straightforward: to earn twice my annual expenses each year.

At the beginning of each year, I sit down and work out my total expenses—everything from mortgage and bills to food, insurance, and savings. Once I have that total, I double it.

My reasoning is straightforward: if I earn twice what I need, I will always have enough for a good life.

It provides me with breathing room—not just to live comfortably, but to cover any large or unforeseen expenses without having to revise my targets mid-year. If a significant expense arises—a holiday, home improvement, or investment—it's already planned for in my budget.

That figure becomes my annual target, which I then break down into monthly and weekly milestones to track and review.

It's not about pursuing money for its own sake—it's about making sure the process aligns with a clear, tangible outcome that reflects financial independence and sustainability.

From that point onwards, I allow my process to take control. The market will behave as it does, and all I can do is manage my risk, execute my edge, and honestly review my performance.

Now, with twenty years of trading experience, I have a wealth of my own data to rely on when setting realistic yet challenging goals.

If you're reading this before entering the market for real, you need to think the same way: what is realistically achievable, and what is my vision?

Millionaires aren't made overnight; they're forged through hard work and commitment, not just in trading but in any profession.

Focus on small, steady progress over time; that's essential. But always remain true to your vision.

Rewinding twenty years, my aim was straightforward: to establish a lasting career in trading.

That became my guiding principle, and the winning trades followed.

10.5 The Checklist: Your Daily Compass

So, we have established a vision of where we aim to be as traders.

We've considered the different profiles we might fit into, aligned our mindset, and established our process.

Now it's time to hit the markets ...

Not yet.

Slow it down.

Before placing any order, organize your checklist.

This is one of my non-negotiable daily routines before I trade—without exception. It centers me, calms my mind, and guarantees I trade deliberately, not impulsively.

The checklist acts as the link between preparation and performance. It transforms knowledge into organization, and organization into reliable action.

The Origin of the Checklist

The story of the checklist doesn't start in trading—it starts in aviation, and it is a favorite of mine.

In 1935, Boeing was testing its new Model 299 bomber—the most advanced aircraft of its era. During a demonstration flight, the plane crashed shortly after take-off, killing two crew members.

The investigation found no mechanical failure. The cause was pilot error—the test pilot, one of the most experienced aviators in the Air Corps, had forgotten a crucial step.

The aircraft was too complex for even the best pilots to rely solely on memory.

So, Boeing engineers devised something revolutionary for its time: a straightforward, written checklist.

It wasn't glamorous, but it was effective. Pilots now had a structured routine to follow—a list of essentials to complete before take-off, during flight, and before landing.

That one idea revolutionized aviation safety. The same pilots who once believed checklists were unnecessary went on to fly the Model 299 (later known as the *B*-17) for over 1.8 million miles without a single incident.

The principle remains universal: when the stakes are high and the environment is intricate, structure is essential.

Trading is no different. Markets move quickly—pressure mounts. Distractions grow.

The checklist is your flight plan—your pre-trade routine that prevents costly errors and maintains consistency under pressure.

Your Trading Checklist

Your checklist should reflect the key stages of the trading process—Identify, Execute, Manage, Evaluate—while encouraging clear thinking before you trade.

From my own routine, it looks something like this:

Market Review

What markets am I observing today?
What's the current direction—bullish, bearish, ranging, or close to turning?
What's the price now, and where is my target price?
What information is already priced in, and what could still surprise the market?
Which types of trades are on my trade watchlist?

Fundamentals to Watch

What are the key data points, reports, or events that could drive markets today?

What are the main themes across UK, EU, and US macroeconomics, or key commodities and assets such as oil, bonds, and stock indices?

What might shift sentiment or volatility?

Trade Preparation

What is my trading size for each trade?
Are there any hero trades I've executed recently that I can emulate—disciplined examples worth repeating?
What is my aim for each trade—centered on process, not profit?
What is my daily risk limit, and what is my maximum drawdown tolerance?

The checklist isn't about creating rigidity; it's about creating consistency.

It's what keeps your emotions from hijacking your decisions and prevents you from trading on impulse rather than intent.

10.6 Follow the money, not the impulse

Impulse trading is costly. The checklist acts as your safeguard against it—a straightforward framework that encourages you to slow down, remain patient, and base your decisions on logic rather than emotion.

Patience, discipline, and consistency might seem straightforward, but they are the foundation of professional trading.

Every elite trader I've ever worked with—regardless of market or style—follows some form of checklist; use yours as your daily compass, and over time it will become more than a list—it will become a staple guide for your trading day.

Personally, I keep all of this recorded in different spreadsheets and notebooks that I prefer to fill in by hand. There's something about putting pen to paper that helps me link theory with practice.

Many traders I've worked with prefer to keep detailed digital spreadsheets—recording their checklists, indicators, trade logs, and evaluation notes. Others, like me, find that writing by hand slows the mind just enough to foster focus and awareness.

It doesn't matter whether it's digital or handwritten—what matters is that you record, review, and reflect.

Writing connects intention to action. It's how process becomes habit.

An example of my own checklist:

Market	Direction	Price now	Target	Fundamentals to watch	Trade watchlist	Trading size	Goal
Gold	Bullish	4125	4500	Trade war	Sell level at 4185	2 Lots	$1000
Oil	Bearish	60.82	60	Economic slowdown	Sell into strength	5 Lots	$5000
10 Year T-Note	Bullish	113	114	Rate cuts	Look for a bullish reversal	10 Lots	$5000

This is a simple structure, but it's one I use every day.

It keeps me accountable to my process, helps me see opportunities clearly, and reminds me to approach the market with discipline rather than impulse.

A completed checklist like this isn't just a record—it's a snapshot of your thoughts before the trade. Over time, these pages tell the story of your growth as a trader.

In the next section, I'll share what my trading blueprint looks like—the structure I use to check in on my own performance—and the daily checklist I still complete by hand before every trading session.

10.7 Trading Blueprint

Working down from our lag measure, as we've already discussed, we need to fill our lead measure bucket to reach the goal. This creates the blueprint for our trading week—the structured framework that links our long-term outcomes to our daily actions.

My own lag measure is to earn twice my annual expenses each year. The next step is simple: identify as many trades in the markets as possible that have a higher than 50% chance of success.

That is the very essence of a trader's job: constant identification.

Using all the skills and techniques developed over a career—the ones we've explored throughout this book—the trader's primary role is to identify opportunity.

I try not to set a strict number for how many trades I should find in a day. Some days there will be too many to keep up with; on others, just a few. What matters is the quality, not the quantity.

It's important to emphasize that I only seek setups with over 50% probability—because, in theory, that's all I require.

If I'm 51% correct during my trading career, and I handle the rest of the process properly, I'll succeed.

To stay aligned, I dedicate time daily to technical and fundamental analysis, observing price action, and reviewing seasonality. This structured routine naturally leads to execution.

I'll note down my trading ideas and levels whenever one passes the "identifying" column of my process. From there, I'll evaluate whether it's a trade that needs to be acted on immediately or if it's better to wait for a more favorable price.

At this stage, I also assess how much risk I am willing to accept—the trade size and the distance to my stop, which determines the point at which I am proved wrong.

The probability factor I assign to each trade directly influences how I execute it, as does the profile it fits—whether it's a scalp, day trade, swing, or position play.

Once execution is complete, we naturally transition to the management phase, where we establish contingency plans to adjust risk and highlight upcoming scenarios that could impact the market in the near future.

When the trade concludes, we move into the final stage—evaluation, or as we say at Teach the World to Trade: Win or Learn.

This is where the lessons live.

We ask: How could I have made more? How could I have lost less? What did the market teach me this time?

Those answers become the raw material for growth—the inputs that shape your personal Golden Rules and deepen your professionalism as a trader.

So at the end of each trading day, you can assess your primary and most crucial lead measure:

Did you identify as many high-probability trades as you could in the trading session?

The trading blueprint summary

Level	Measure type	Focus	Example	Frequency
Vision	Long-Term Goal	Your "why"—the reason you trade and what success means to you.	Build a sustainable trading career, achieve financial independence, and teach others.	Ongoing
Lag measure	Outcome	The result follows from a consistent process and discipline.	Earn double my annual outgoings.	Annual
Lead measures	Process inputs	The daily and weekly actions that drive the outcome.	Identify as many trades as possible with > 50% probability of success; journal and review performance.	Daily/Weekly
Daily practice	Habit building	The structured work that develops skill and consistency.	Technical, fundamental, price action, and seasonal analysis; execution drills; review checklist.	Daily
Trading process	Execution framework	The flow that turns knowledge into action.	Identify → Execute → Manage → Evaluate.	Every Trade
Reflection	Continuous improvement	Turning lessons into learning—the "Win or Learn" mindset.	Review trades, extract key insights, update Golden Rules.	Daily/Weekly/Monthly

How to Use the Blueprint

Your blueprint is another anchor—a clear visual reminder of what drives results.

The further down you go, the more control you have.

You can't force a lag measure (profit), but you can influence every lead measure beneath it through consistent, structured practice.

Each layer supports the next.

Your daily habits feed your lead measures, which in turn produce your lag measures, ultimately moving you closer to your vision.

Trading success isn't random—it's the result of alignment.

When your daily work aligns with your long-term vision, you're on the professional path to profitability. From there, it's about putting in the effort to develop the trading skills that cover the bills—and that naturally leads us into the next chapter.

11

Trader Drills to Build Trading Skills

In his work on elite performance, Brian Cain—one of the world's leading mental performance coaches—often says:

"You don't rise to the occasion; you fall to the level of your training."

He's right.

You can't think your way to consistency—you have to train your way there.

As Cain puts it, "You do drills to build skills."

The same principle applies to professional athletes, pilots, or soldiers as to traders.

The markets are your arena. Your drills are the repetitions that embed discipline, focus, and emotional control—the real edge behind long-term profitability.

Everything we've constructed so far—your process, checklist, lead measures, and blueprint—forms the framework.

Now it's time to put it to work.

In this chapter, we'll take the professional trading process—Identify, Execute, Manage, Evaluate—and transform it into a series of structured practice drills aimed at accelerating your skill development.

Each drill has a purpose: to enhance precision, recognize patterns, adapt skills, and maintain composure under pressure, which sets professionals apart from amateurs.

When you commit to drills, you move from knowing to doing.

And when you practice deliberately, you move from doing to mastering.

Let's build the skills that pay the bills.

S. Warner-Baker, *Learn to Trade Like a Professional*,
https://doi.org/10.1007/978-3-032-20125-6_11

11.1 Identify: Drills to Strengthen Your Market Awareness

We need to begin by identifying opportunities in the markets—sifting through the noise and selecting ideas that align with our blueprint and trading style.

This phase is about training your eyes and ears so that scanning the markets becomes second nature. Over time, you develop pattern recognition built through hours and hours of repetition, until your analysis becomes instinctive.

The goal here isn't to predict; it's to understand. To see the market clearly, filter out distractions, and focus on what matters.

Drill 1: Technical Analysis

Objective:

To train your technical eye to spot direction, structure, and opportunity across multiple timeframes.

Method:

During your designated trading session, choose at least three markets you favor—ideally a mix from the money, food, and energy markets we discussed earlier.

Use your technical analysis skills to identify the market's direction across three timeframes: daily, 60-minute, and 10-minute.

Identify any pivot points or key areas of support and resistance where the market might reverse or accelerate.

Watch for any candlestick patterns we discussed earlier (such as hammers, shooting stars, or over-extensions).

Write your observations clearly on your checklist—direction, key levels, patterns, and overall bias.

Purpose:

Repetition fosters recognition. Over time, you'll observe recurring patterns in market behavior, volatility, and how the price responds to key levels.

The goal isn't prediction—it's familiarity. The more familiar you are with how markets move, the faster and more accurately you'll recognize opportunity when it appears.

Drill 2: Fundamental Awareness

Objective:

Enhance your ability to link macro events, news flow, supply and demand, and key themes to potential trading opportunities.

Method:

Choose one market from each sector: money, food, and energy.

For example: UK Bonds, Coffee, and Natural Gas.

Identify the main macroeconomic themes influencing those markets this week. (Consider interest rate expectations, inflation data, geopolitical tensions, or energy supply issues.)

Note the scheduled economic releases on the calendar that could influence your chosen markets—central bank statements, employment figures, inventory reports, or crop data.

Examine the expected data and consider whether it is bullish or bearish, above or below the forecast.

Find out whether there's a current market theme. For example:

Rising inflation expectations have become an issue, resulting in interest rates expected to remain higher for longer—and bond prices falling.

Major coffee-producing regions anticipate a poor harvest this year, driving prices higher than normal.

The weather is milder than usual, so demand for heating (and consequently gas) is lower, and natural gas prices keep falling.

Make short notes on your checklist:

What's the theme?

Which markets are affected—just the one you've highlighted, or others as well?

What's already priced in, and what could still surprise?

If possible, follow the news flow in real time (using Bloomberg, Reuters, X.com, or a live economic calendar) and watch how the markets respond.

Purpose:

This drill trains you to understand the reason behind the market's movement.

It's not about prediction—it's about recognizing cause and effect: how economic data, sentiment, supply and demand, and policy expectations ripple through asset classes.

With practice, you'll begin instinctively connecting price movements to the macro environment, enabling you to spot higher-probability trade opportunities that align with both technical and fundamental factors.

Personally, I find this the most fascinating part of the job—piecing together the information puzzle and relating it to the prices moving on the screen.

Drill 3: Price is King

Objective:

Develop your skill to interpret live market behavior—the movement, rhythm, and balance between buyers and sellers—so you can identify shifts in momentum before they become obvious on the chart.

Method:

Choose a market from your daily checklist and open a candlestick chart, trading ladder, or DOM (Depth of Market).

Observe how the price reacts around key levels you identified earlier—support, resistance, or pivot points.

Do large bids or offers appear and hold?

Is volume increasing or drying up as price tests a level?

How fast are trades printing on the tape?

Watch for price-action clues that reveal who's in control:

Sharp rejections or long wicks → potential reversal.

Tight consolidations after an impulsive move → potential continuation.

Heavy trading at one price with little movement → balance or absorption.

Record what you see every 15 minutes for one full session.

Note time, level, volume behavior, and outcome (did price break or hold?).

At the end of the session, review your notes and mark where your observations aligned with the next move and where they did not.

Purpose:

This drill develops market intuition—the kind of natural understanding that can't be learned from a textbook.

Over time, you'll start to notice the difference between real momentum and noise, between a healthy trend and fatigue.

Price action reading is where structure meets instinct.

You're not predicting; you're listening—learning to hear the market breathe.

When that becomes second nature, your timing, confidence, and trade selection all improve dramatically.

Drill 4: Seasonal Set-Ups

Objective:

To develop an understanding of how seasonal patterns influence markets and learn how to use this knowledge to identify higher-probability trading opportunities.

Method:

Select one or two markets from your checklist—preferably from the energy or food sectors, where seasonality often has a considerable impact.

(Think: natural gas, corn, cocoa, oil, wheat, or sugar.)

There are seasonal patterns in the money markets, too, but they are usually less noticeable.

Use a seasonality analysis tool such as Seasonalgo.com—a paid-for but comprehensive service used by many professional traders.

If you don't have access, there are free alternatives like TradingView's Seasonal Indicator, or you can conduct your own back testing using historical price data.

Look for recurring trends over multiple years:

When does the market typically rally or sell off?

Are there consistent patterns tied to supply and demand cycles, weather, harvests, or production schedules?

Cross-check the seasonal tendency against current fundamentals and technicals:

If seasonality suggests a bullish phase, does current price action confirm or contradict it?

If the market is behaving differently this year, what might be driving the deviation?

Record your findings in your trading journal or checklist:

Typical seasonal direction (bullish or bearish).
Average duration of the move.
Key months or weeks when the pattern repeats.
Whether it aligns with or contradicts your current trade ideas.

Purpose:

This drill enhances your contextual awareness—helping you recognize when probabilities tend to shift in your favor.

Seasonality doesn't forecast the future, but it offers a historical advantage—a method to compare typical patterns with current developments.

Combined with technical, fundamental, and price-action analysis, it provides a four-dimensional view of the market.

Like a professional, you start thinking in terms of patterns, probabilities, and cycles.

As always, repetition is the key. The more seasonal patterns you examine, the more instinctive your grasp of market rhythm will become.

Drilling Down to find those opportunities

The ability to identify opportunities consistently is the foundation of trading success.

When you hone your analytical eye through repetition—across technicals, fundamentals, price action, and seasonality—you build the instinct and confidence to act with precision when the market offers an opportunity.

Once you grasp the why and how of identifying trades, you'll find yourself continually tuned in to what's happening globally—and how it might relate to a market and an opportunity.

11.2 Execute: Drills to Build Precision and Control

Execution is when your analysis meets the market—the moment when theory becomes action.

This stage isn't just about luck, speed, or instinct—it's about control. Precision in entry, discipline in exit, and consistency in risk.

The following drills aim to reinforce those mechanics through repeated practice.

Master these, and you'll execute with the confidence and calm of a professional.

Drill 1: Entry—Heading into the Eye of the Storm

Objective:

To develop consistency in timing and confidence when taking trades.

Method:

Select one market and one setup—technical, fundamental, or seasonal.

Identify your entry level in advance and mark it clearly on your chart.

Set alerts at your selected price and wait for confirmation from your rules—for example, a candlestick close, a volume shift, a breakout, or a pullback.

Set a limit order at the price you plan to enter the trade at, letting the market come to you instead of chasing it.

Simultaneously, place a market order in the simulation aligned with your intended trade direction.

If you're waiting to buy at a certain level, get long at market in the sim.

If you're waiting to sell, go short at market in the sim.

Record every trade in your journal—note what confirmed your entry and how it felt: calm, rushed, hesitant, or uncertain.

Purpose:

This drill develops patience under pressure, but it also checks if you're being too cautious with your entries.

By running a simulated market position alongside your planned limit entry, you'll quickly see how often your setups succeed without you, helping you balance patience with assertiveness.

You're training yourself to step calmly into the market when conditions are right—not before. Over time, you'll learn to trust your process, not your impulse, and find confidence in the eye of the storm.

Drill 2: Exit—Knowing When to Drop Anchor

Objective:

To build consistency and composure in taking profits—exiting trades with control, not emotion.

Method:

Before you enter any trade, clearly define your exit level.

Be realistic—is the timeframe you can hold the trade in line with your intended target?

Have you previously managed a move of that size, or are you optimistic about it?

Are there technical levels that could prevent your exit from being executed as planned, or challenge your target price along the way?

Place your target order immediately after entry, whether it's a Good Till Cancelled (GTC) limit order or a Good Till Day (GTD) order that cancels at the end of the session.

Ensure your order is correctly set and remains active for the required time. This is a rookie mistake I've had to correct for junior traders many times. If you exit the trade before the order is fulfilled, remember to remove it!

Set an alert a few ticks before your target price. When it triggers, do nothing—just observe the market and stay alert for any sudden price movements.

Let the market come to you—don't shift your target unless genuinely new, significant information warrants it.

Once the price hits your target, exit without hesitation. This goes without saying—it's the embodiment of the stick to the plan mantra.

In your SIM account, keep a shadow position open to see how far it could have extended. This helps you develop awareness of the difference between opportunity and discipline.

Even when I'm trading live, I still use my sim account to practise process work—and this is one of the drills I repeat.

Purpose:

This drill teaches you the art of leaving the market with grace.

You're guiding yourself to follow a plan, not a feeling. Every trader is tempted to overstay the move, but consistency emerges from knowing when enough is enough.

By practicing fixed exits and monitoring both the emotional and financial outcomes, you'll learn two invaluable lessons:

Profit is a by-product of discipline and patience, not desire.

There's always another trade—but there's only one process.

Over time, you'll stop chasing the last tick and begin mastering the moment when it's time to drop anchor and prepare to sail again.

Drill 3: Stop Loss—When to Abandon Ship

Objective:

To develop the discipline to define, respect, and execute your stop loss—recognizing when to cut a trade that's no longer valid, without hesitation or emotion.

Method:

Define your stop before entry.

Identify the precise price level that disproves your idea—this should be determined by market structure, not money.

Or, determine it where your risk tolerance allows the loss without harming your trading account or your mental well-being.

Ask yourself:

What price level would invalidate my reasoning for this trade?
Is the cost of the trade—my stop—greater than the gains from my target?

This is what we refer to as the profit/loss ratio. Personally, I operate on a minimum of 1:1, meaning my potential loss and gain should always be equal. That ratio is usually reserved for short-term scalping.

For longer-term profiles, you should aim for a much higher profit-to-loss ratio—ideally 2 or 3 to 1 or more, as long as it's realistic.

Those who frequently fail tend to trade with a ratio below 1:1. If you find yourself in this situation, regard it as a warning sign.

Place your stop immediately after entry.

Whether you use a Good Till Cancelled (GTC) stop order or a Good Till Day (GTD) stop for intraday trades, make sure it's there from the start.

You'll face the trader's dilemma:

A market stop guarantees the exit, but not the price.

A limit stop guarantees the price, but not the certainty of execution.

Choose your method deliberately—both have a role depending on volatility and your time horizon.

Do not wait to "see how it goes."

That's how traders sink their ships.

Use your SIM account to test various stop placements—such as structural, duration-based, and fixed-percentage—and to experiment with market versus limit stops.

Analyze which method best fits your trading strategy and personality.

When the stop is hit, exit without debate.

No justification.

No, "it might bounce."

No, "I can't get out here, this is a great level."

And most importantly, do not rely on the market returning to your stop and then reaching your target.

The market has spoken. The idea was wrong—and that's okay. Not every trade will be a winner. It's something I still need to emphasize to traders with years of experience—including myself.

Purpose:

This drill is about risk discipline and emotional control.

You're not training to avoid losses—you're training to handle them professionally.

Every trader faces setbacks. The professionals endure them more quickly, subtly, and efficiently.

Knowing when to abandon ship safeguards your capital, confidence, and career.

By practicing disciplined stops, you learn two fundamental truths about trading:

Capital preservation is essential for longevity—you must stay in the game.

You can't catch the next wave if you're still bailing out the last one.

Over time, this drill develops emotional resilience—the composed acceptance that being wrong isn't failure, it's feedback.

The sooner you cut a losing trade, the sooner you're ready to seize the next opportunity.

Drill 4: Trade Size—The Weight of Conviction

Objective:

To align your position size with conviction, risk tolerance, and market conditions—developing the discipline to size your trades systematically rather than emotionally.

Method:

Predefine three position sizes:

Small: exploratory or scalping ideas—test trades with minimal risk.
Medium: standard trades that fit your process and meet your criteria.
Large: high-conviction trades supported by multiple factors—technical, fundamental, and seasonal alignment, along with a proven track record of success.

Assign rules to each size.

Small: risk 0.25–0.5% of your account, or around 5% of what you would allow yourself to lose in a day.
Medium: risk around 1%, or roughly 20% of your daily loss limit.
Large: up to 2% when conviction is strong and the setup is clear, or up to 50% of your daily loss limit.

Base your decision on process, not feeling.
Ask yourself: What makes this trade more deserving of risk?
If you can't provide at least two independent confirmations—such as a technical setup aligning with a macro theme—it's not a "large" trade.
Adjust for volatility and liquidity.
Use tools like the Average True Range (ATR) or recent trading ranges to normalize your position size.
Higher volatility or thin liquidity results in smaller positions; lower volatility permits slightly larger ones.
This keeps your risk consistent regardless of market conditions.
Use your SIM account to practise scaling size correctly—gradually increasing exposure only when your process remains consistent.

Purpose:

This drill develops risk awareness, self-control, and professional consistency.
When trade size reflects process, not impulse, you eliminate one of the main causes of inconsistent trading results.
Size is confidence quantified.
It reflects your preparation, conviction, and respect for risk.
When you learn to size trades correctly—not too large due to overconfidence and not too small out of fear—your trading psychology stabilizes.

You'll discover that profitability doesn't only stem from winning trades, but also from knowing precisely how much of yourself to invest in each one.

This is not a black-and-white decision, but with practice, you'll discover a suitable range of sizes for each market and trade type you carry out.

And most importantly, each trade you make provides valuable data to improve your approach.

The Art of Execution

Execution is the key divider—it's where traders start to shape their identity.

Every trader can identify a chart pattern, read a headline, or form an opinion, but only a professional can convert those insights into disciplined, repeatable action.

The drills in this section—entry, exit, stop loss, and trade size—are where your theory meets practical application.

They're the moments when your process is tested under pressure and where habits are either made or broken.

The truth is, good execution is seldom exciting. It's not about heroic calls or lucky streaks.

It's about maintaining consistency under pressure—remaining calm enough to let the market come to you, confident enough to take your profits, disciplined enough to accept your losses, and self-aware enough to know exactly how much risk you can manage.

Every drill here aims to develop rhythm—helping you think, act, and respond to the markets like a professional.

Over time, you'll observe your reactions slow, your decisions become more precise, and your results turn less volatile—not because you've discovered a secret, but because you've ceased resisting the process.

Remember:

Entries are about patience—waiting for your moment.

Exits are about discipline—knowing when enough is enough.

Stops are about humility—accepting when you're wrong and moving on.

Trade size is about balance—matching your conviction to your control.

Execution isn't something you "get right" once—it's a skill you rehearse every single day.

The best traders I've worked with still practice these fundamentals because they understand that consistency arises from repetition, and results follow disciplined execution.

11.3 Management: Drills to Get You That Promotion!

Trade management is where traders are forged, sharpening their ability to withstand the pressure of a position moving against them and to make the correct decision under stress, with a clear mind and a plan. It's where traders either develop or give back their profits, adapting in moments of market chaos when needed.

Once you have taken a position, your role shifts. You are no longer the analyst or the executor; you become the ultimate risk manager.

Your task now is to supervise your position, make adjustments when needed, and remain calm while the market does what it does best: move unpredictably.

This stage of trading is about control through awareness.

You don't control the market; you manage your risk exposure, your choices, and your response to shifting market conditions.

The drills that follow are designed to help you manage risk dynamically and professionally, fading in and out, adjusting exposure, and handling your emotions while trading.

They'll train you to remain present, objective, and adaptable under pressure—the true marks of a professional.

Drill 1: Fading in—Building Exposure with Purpose

Objective:

To build the ability to expand into a role systematically, without emotion or impulse, using predefined rules.

Method:

Identify a solid trade idea that suits your profile using the techniques we've discussed, or try one of your own.

Start with a small initial position (e.g. 25–50% of your intended size).

As the market moves in your favor and confirms your idea, add to your position at pre-planned price levels; alternatively, if the market moves against you, have a pre-determined entry zone where you'll add more to improve your average entry price.

Example: Add at + 25% and + 50% of your intended move, or on the flip side, at—10% and—20%.

Adjust stops on earlier entries to protect capital as exposure builds.

Use limit orders for scaling, never market orders. You want to participate in structure, not chase price.

Purpose:

This drill builds confidence in adding to winners while maintaining structure and control and finessing your entry.

It's almost impossible to buy low and sell high every time you trade; that's why I often scale into my positions over a range of prices.

You're learning to manage success the same way you manage risk, with intent, not emotion.

Scaling should feel calm, deliberate, and earned, never reactive or greedy.

Drill 2: Fading Out—Reducing Exposure the Professional Way

Objective:

To practise taking partial profits and reducing size strategically as a trade develops, locking in gains while keeping opportunity alive.

Method:

Predefine fade-out levels when planning your trade—for example, at 1:1 and 2:1 reward-to-risk ratios, or at technical levels that may challenge your trade as it progresses further onside.

As the price nears these levels, take partial profits (e.g. 25–50%) using limit orders.

Move stops on the remaining position to break even or better.

Continue trailing stops based on structure (e.g., previous swing lows/highs) as the trend develops.

Purpose:

Fading out teaches strategic detachment—you're securing profits while keeping calm.

It turns emotional wins into managed outcomes and helps you build consistency in both P&L and mindset.

Drill 3: Adjusting Risk Mid-Trade—Managing the Heat

Objective:

To develop your skill in managing exposure dynamically without panicking or interfering unnecessarily.

Method:

As the trade unfolds, monitor whether volatility or market structure has changed meaningfully.

If the market moves in your favor:

Consider tightening your stop to lock in gains.
Avoid moving stops too aggressively—don't strangle a healthy trade.

If the market moves against you, but your analysis still stands:

Avoid doubling down impulsively.
Reduce the trade size or hedge instead.

Practice this in simulation: execute ten trades where you adjust mid-trade based solely on structure, not on emotion.

A useful exercise is to envisage market-moving scenarios that could cause prices to fluctuate and plan your response—a surprise central bank comment, a geopolitical headline, or an unexpected policy change.

Purpose:

This drill helps you stay adaptive without losing control.

It teaches you to respond to what is actually happening—not to what you wish would happen. The price is the absolute king, and no matter how good your plan is, you must trade the market wherever it moves.

Drill 4: Emotional Management—the Calm Within the Chaos

Objective:

To develop the mental awareness to remain composed while managing live trades—especially when emotions begin to surface.

Method:

Before each session, jot down one emotional goal (e.g. "Stay patient through pullbacks").

During live trades, observe your physical signals—tense shoulders, shallow breathing, quick clicking of the nearest pen—and deliberately reset.

When you sense tension building, pause and take three deep breaths before making any decision.

I use this daily in my own trading: four seconds in, four seconds hold, four seconds out, four seconds pause.

It's a powerful way to keep a level head throughout the day.

After the trade, journal not only the result but also how well you managed your state.

Purpose:

Managing trades means managing yourself.

The market doesn't evaluate your analysis; it assesses your capacity to remain calm under pressure.

When you master emotional regulation, you no longer need to force control over the market because you have gained control over yourself.

That's what separates the amateur from the professional.

The CEO of You

Trade management is where professionalism genuinely reveals itself. You must simultaneously balance the numerous roles of a trader and then make the correct decision at the right moment, under pressure.

You're an economist, a technical analyst, a market maker, an execution broker, a risk manager, a fund manager, a coach—and more—all combined. And the final decision always lies with you.

It's what I love about trading—the buck starts and ends with you.

You've already done the hard work—you've analyzed, executed, and committed.

Now it's about protecting capital, nurturing winners, and staying calm in the storm.

The best managers don't react—they respond.

They don't panic—they adjust.

And above all, they understand that the goal isn't to control the market—it's to manage the risk and let the market handle the rest.

It's the ultimate test of temperance and discipline.

Countless times, I've made the wrong decision when managing a trade—but each one taught me something valuable.

Those lessons formed the basis of my own trading guidebook—insights gained in real time, not just theory. And that's what brings us to the final stage of the process: Evaluation.

Because no matter how well you prepare, execute, or manage, the real growth occurs when you review.

Evaluation is where experience becomes wisdom.

It's where lessons from every win and loss are turned into progress—refining your edge, sharpening your process, and boosting your belief.

In the next section, we'll explore how to complete the cycle—how to journal, measure, and learn from your trades in a way that speeds up mastery.

This is where professionals distinguish themselves from participants.

It's time to turn results into reflection—and reflection into growth.

11.4 Evaluation: Drills to Help You Win or Learn

Every trader desires to succeed, but the most skilled traders understand that genuine progress comes from learning.

Winning demonstrates what's achievable; losing reveals what steps to take afterwards.

As the founder of Teach the World to Trade, I articulated our mantra plainly: Win or Learn.

I've mentioned it repeatedly throughout this book—and I follow it every day.

Looking back, my own start in the markets was exactly that: win or learn, a game of trial and error.

Now, after years in the profession, I can identify the process by name and add a bit more color.

There is no failure when you treat trading as an ongoing learning process.

Each trade becomes a test—not of your ability to predict, but of your ability to prepare, execute, manage, and review with discipline.

Evaluation is where that learning happens.

It's where you learn the lesson from the market—the feedback that shapes your next decision, your next improvement, your next win.

When you evaluate properly, you stop being reactive and start becoming reflective.

You turn every mistake into a message and every result into data.

Every professional I've worked with—from junior recruits to fund managers—treats evaluation as non-negotiable.

It's no coincidence that traders who fail are often the ones who never take their journaling and evaluation seriously.

Evaluation is the quiet moment after the chaos—where experience becomes wisdom and process turns into precision.

Just as a CEO reviews their company's performance, a trader must review their own, not only the P&L but also the decisions, emotions, and behaviors that caused it.

Remember, you are the analyst, the execution broker, the risk manager, the coach, and the CEO—and your evaluation functions as the board meeting that decides what happens next.

The Role of Evaluation in the Process

Hopefully, with the help of the previous pages, you've built a process you can practice.

You can identify opportunities, execute with intent, and manage with composure.

Evaluation is what ties it all together.

It's the link between one trade and the next—the point where you take everything that happened and turn it into insight.

Without evaluation, you're simply repeating trades.

With it, you're refining yourself.

Evaluation allows you to:

- Review what worked and what didn't—without ego or emotion.
- Identify patterns in your performance.
- Strengthen your process one decision at a time.
- Reconnect with your purpose after both wins and losses.

The best traders don't just analyze markets—they analyze themselves, and above all, they do it consistently.

Evaluation Drills

The drills that follow are intended to help you practice the final stage of the process—structured self-mastery.

They'll assist you in learning from each trade, so your market tuition fees are never wasted.

Drill 1: Rapid Review—The Two Questions That Matter

Objective:

Transform every trade—whether you win or lose—into a learning opportunity by emphasizing improvement over outcome.

Method:

After closing each trade, resist the urge to judge it as good or bad.
Open your trading journal and answer two simple questions:

1. How could I have made more?
2. How could I have lost less?

Be specific. Did you:
Enter too early or too late?
Set the wrong stop distance?
Trade too much size—or not enough?
Miss a key piece of fundamental or technical information?
Hold too long or cut too soon?
Write the answer in plain language—one or two sentences only.
This isn't a novel; it's a diagnostic tool.
Add one short action point for the next trade. For example:
"Wait for confirmation on the one-hour chart before entering."
"Trail stops behind technical structure rather than fixed ticks."
"Trade 50% more or less on the first entry of this trade type."
At the end of the week, read your notes back-to-back.
If you see the same issue appear three times, that becomes your next focus area.

Purpose:

This drill builds self-awareness and accountability.
The two questions strip away noise and ego, leaving only the lessons that matter.

It's a daily practice of purposeful reflection—not a post-mortem, but a tune-up.

Over time, you'll notice your answers get shorter and your improvements sharper.

You stop repeating mistakes and start refining instinct.

Professional traders don't seek perfection; they seek progress.

This exercise guarantees that every trade—whether a win or a loss—moves you one step closer along that path.

Drill 2: Process Breakdown—Identify Which Step Failed

Objective:

To precisely identify where in your trading process things went right or wrong, transforming vague feedback ("I traded badly") into targeted improvement ("my management broke down").

Method:

After finishing your Rapid Review, take one more step back.

Look at each trade through the four pillars of your process:

Identify—Did I find a high-quality opportunity using my framework?

Execute—Did I follow my entry rules with precision and patience?

Manage—Did I handle the position as planned, or did emotion take control, and did I overthink the situation?

Evaluate—Did I record and review the trade properly afterwards?

For every losing or suboptimal trade, mark which phase broke down.

"Execution error—entered before confirmation."

"Management lapse—moved stop emotionally."

"Identification gap—ignored conflicting fundamentals."

Highlight the root cause of the failure—not just the symptom.

Was it a lack of preparation? Emotional decision-making? Poor time management? Fatigue or distraction?

At the end of the week, count how many trades failed at each stage.

The phase with the highest number of breakdowns becomes your focus for next week's practice.

In your journal, write one line under each heading: for example,

"Next week's focus: improve execution timing by waiting for confirmation."

"Next week's focus: tighten risk control—never add more size mid-trade."

Purpose:

This drill transforms evaluation from vague reflection into structured feedback.

It helps you analyze your own process like a professional coach would—identifying weak links and turning them into training priorities.

The aim isn't to eradicate errors; it's to identify them more quickly and correct them intentionally.

By approaching each phase of trading as a separate skill, you'll become more consistent, more accountable, and far less reactive.

Over time, you'll start to recognize patterns instantly—even while a trade is live—because you've trained your mind to observe your own process in motion.

That's when you shift from being a trader who follows a process to a trader who embodies the process.

Drill 3: SWOT Your Trading Week

Objective:

To step back from individual trades and analyze your overall weekly performance through a professional lens—identifying strengths, weaknesses, opportunities, and threats that shape your growth as a trader.

Method:

Set aside time each week—ideally on Friday after the close or during the weekend—for your personal trading debrief.

This is your board meeting with yourself. Treat it seriously.

Open your trading journal and review the week's entries as a whole, rather than as isolated trades.

Identify patterns: recurring mistakes, consistent successes, emotional tendencies, or missed opportunities.

Complete a simple SWOT analysis for the week:

S—Strengths

What did I do well this week?

Which parts of my process were consistent?

Did I stay disciplined under pressure?

Where did I feel most confident and composed?

Which market did I excel in?

W—Weaknesses

Where did I deviate from my process?

Did I take any trades out of boredom, revenge, or FOMO?

Was my preparation thorough enough each morning?

Did fatigue, emotion, or environment impact performance?

O—Opportunities

What did I learn that could strengthen my edge next week?

Are there markets, strategies, or setups I've noticed potential in but haven't explored yet?

Is there a specific drill or skill I can revisit to sharpen my execution?

T—Threats

What could derail my progress if left unchecked?

Am I overtrading, under-resting, or losing confidence?

Are there external factors—stress, time pressure, distractions—I need to manage better?

Write your SWOT in your journal each week—brief, honest notes are all that's required.

Then conclude each category with a single line labelled "Action."—for example.

Strength: "Keep using the pre-market checklist."

Weakness: "Reduce screen time after two losses."

Opportunity: "Revisit seasonal setups in energy markets."

Threat: "Improve sleep routine before trading sessions."

Purpose:

This drill helps you step back from daily noise and see the bigger picture of your performance.

It's not about self-criticism—it's about the all-important self-awareness.

A weekly SWOT keeps your development strategic. It emphasizes what to continue doing, what to address, and what to be alert for.

You start to run your trading like a business—reviewing data, analyzing risk, and making course corrections before problems escalate.

Over time, these weekly reflections compound.

You'll begin identifying recurring strengths to focus on, weaknesses to remove, and opportunities you might otherwise overlook in the hurry of daily trading.

This analysis also forms the foundation of many traders' weekly or monthly coaching sessions—a tool that has benefited hundreds of professionals over the years.

Drill 4: The Growth Mindset Audit—Turning Mistakes into Methods

Objective:

To enhance resilience and foster growth by reframing mistakes, struggles, and setbacks as intentional opportunities for improvement.

Method:

At the end of your trading week, review your journal and identify three trades that challenged you most—emotionally, financially, or mentally.

These aren't necessarily your biggest losers; they're the ones that taught you the most.

For each trade, answer these five Growth Mindset questions:

What was my intention going into this trade
What actually happened?
What did I learn from this?
How will I apply that lesson next time?
How will I measure if the change worked?

If a trade goes wrong, don't see it as failure—see it as feedback. The first trading psychologist I ever worked with used this phrase, and it has stayed with me ever since.

Example: "I moved my stop too soon." becomes → "I need to trust my initial analysis and reduce mid-trade interference."

For each lesson, create one new behavior or micro-goal for the week ahead.

"Write down my stop level before placing the trade."

"When anxious, use the 4 × 4 breathing drill before acting."

End the exercise by reading your notes aloud—yes, out loud.

Speaking them aloud makes the lesson genuine. It shifts the mistake from feeling to action.

Purpose:

This drill changes how you perceive setbacks. Instead of dodging them, you start to embrace them as disguised lessons.

A trader with a fixed mindset avoids pain; a trader with a growth mindset learns from it.

By intentionally transforming your mistakes into strategies, you craft a personalized manual for growth—a dynamic record that develops alongside you.

Over time, this practice builds unshakable self-trust.

You stop fearing mistakes because you understand they are merely raw material for your next stage of growth.

As one of my mentors once told me:

The difference between a professional and an amateur isn't that the pro makes fewer mistakes—it's that they learn more quickly from each one.

When you start auditing yourself this way, you no longer fear losing.

You start fearing not learning.

Drill 5: The Golden Rules—Write, Refine, Repeat

Objective:

Maintain your trading process by regularly updating your personal Golden Rules—the distilled lessons and principles that guide your decisions in every market condition.

Method:

Set a recurring time each week—ideally after your SWOT or Growth Mindset Audit—to review your notes and extract valuable lessons.

Ask yourself: "What rule would have prevented this mistake?" or "What principle made this week work well?"

For every meaningful insight, write one Golden Rule—short, clear, and actionable.

Some of my own as I write this

"Don't over-scalp positions, keep the majority of your trade on for the medium term.'

"Make sure to check the 15-day moving average before entering an Oil trade."

"Believe in yourself based on your success rate and increase your trading size."

"Complete your checklist before you trade each day."

Keep your Golden Rules somewhere visible—in your trading journal, pinned above your desk, or at the bottom of your pre-trade checklist. This is where mine sit!

Repetition builds reinforcement.

Once a month, revisit your list and ask:

Does this rule still serve me?
Have I outgrown it?
Does it need refining or replacing?
When you break a rule, don't beat yourself up—use it as a signal to do a deeper review.
Write: "Which part of me ignored this, and why?"

Purpose:

Your Golden Rules are your compass—the principles that keep you grounded when the market tests your patience, focus, and discipline.
Over time, this list becomes your personal trading doctrine—another trading blueprint forged from your own successes and scars.
It's not something copied from another trader; it's something shaped through experience, reflection, and iteration.
The best traders I've worked with can summarize their entire philosophy in a few simple rules—each one written in the ink of lessons learned the hard way.
Updating and reviewing your Golden Rules is how you stay sharp.
It's how you turn short-term experience into long-term wisdom.
Because when your rules evolve with you, your process becomes stronger, more consistent, and uniquely your own.
Write your own How to Trade Like a Professional book, one trade at a time!

The Man (or Person) in the Mirror

Like Michael Jackson once sang, "I'm looking at the man in the mirror, I'm asking him to change his ways."
Now, I promise I'm not one to sing this to myself during evaluation sessions—honest—, but he has a point.
It perfectly sums up what we aim to accomplish with the evaluation drills you've just finished.
All aspects of our practice can be evaluated critically.
Every trade, decision, and emotion provides a lesson—a guide we can use to perform better next time.
That's what this stage is all about: marginal gains.
The small, gradual improvements that, when combined, lead to significant results over time.

It reminds me of the story of the Great Britain cycling team, who, under Sir Dave Brailsford's philosophy of "the aggregation of marginal gains", looked for every possible advantage—from nutrition and bike design to something as simple as bringing their own pillows to competitions so they'd sleep better.

That same mindset applies to trading.

When you examine closely enough, you'll discover dozens of tiny details that can enhance your performance: better preparation, sharper risk management, cleaner entries, and more mindful breaks.

Individually, each one appears small. Collectively, they can revolutionize your results.

And now and then, in those reflections, you'll hit the jackpot—a golden rule that changes everything.

A single insight that helps you save or earn a great deal of cash.

That's what the man (or woman) in the mirror is for.

Not judgment.

Not ego.

Just honest reflection and a commitment to being slightly better tomorrow than you were today.

A Rage for Mastery

Before we move on to the next chapter, I want to leave you with a final thought from one of my favorite performance coaches, Brian Cain, who has dedicated his career to understanding what drives high performance.

He states, "The most important thing anyone can do is have a rage for mastery—a passion for getting better, for learning and applying what you learn."

That single line encapsulates the essence of everything in this chapter.

Becoming a professional trader isn't about natural talent or luck. It's about that constant drive to improve—the daily commitment to refine your craft, to learn from every trade, and to keep applying those lessons until excellence becomes instinct.

Every drill, reflection, and evaluation you've undertaken here is meant to fuel that hunger for mastery.

The more you practise intentionally, the more fluent you become in your own process—until trading no longer feels like effort, but expression.

That passion for improvement is what distinguishes those who dabble from those who endure.

It's what keeps you grounded on the bad days and humble on the good ones.

And it's precisely the mindset you'll need for what's ahead—because we're about to confront the biggest presence in every trader's journey.

Risk Management

It's the elephant in the trading room—the silent partner in every decision you make, the force that shapes every outcome.

You cannot ignore it. You cannot outwit it.

But you can learn to understand, respect, and handle it professionally.

So, let's examine the subject that dominates the capital markets—and influences every decision we make, both in trading and in life.

12

Risk vs Reward

12.1 Reframing Risk

If there's one principle that sets professionals apart from the masses, it's how they think about risk. Most new traders are fixated on reward—the life-changing profit target, the big win, the dream of catching that perfect move and cruising into the sunset in a brand-new Lambo! It's natural. Every chart looks like a story of opportunity. Every uptick feels like confirmation. But professional traders learn early that the only thing you can truly control in markets is your risk. Everything else—reward, outcome, and timing—is firmly beyond your control. You can tilt the odds in your favor through preparation and process, but you can't dictate how or when the market will move.

That's why risk isn't something we fear or avoid; it's something we manage with precision and respect. When I'm deciding whether to take a trade—whether it's in the energy, food, or money markets—I always begin with one question: How much am I willing to lose to find out if I'm right? That single question defines everything that follows—position size, stop distance, time horizon, and emotional stance. It sets the boundaries for the trade before the trade even exists.

Many retail traders believe professionals are fearless. The reality is that we are far more cautious. We don't avoid risk—we assess it, control it, and act deliberately. Every trade we make is a calculated risk, an experiment with a known cost. Think of risk as the cost of opportunity.

S. Warner-Baker, *Learn to Trade Like a Professional*,
https://doi.org/10.1007/978-3-032-20125-6_12

Just as a business pays for raw materials to produce a product, a trader "pays" risk to participate in the market. If you pay too much, your business becomes unprofitable. If you refuse to pay at all, you'll never make anything. The trick is finding that sustainable middle ground—a relationship with risk that's affordable, repeatable, and scalable. When I was very young, my father would take me to the wholesalers in East London's East End to buy imported clothes from India and South-East Asia. I'd watch him sift through hundreds of items, trying to decide which ones would sell. This was my very first exposure to risk: if he got the trade wrong, he'd be left with a product he couldn't sell and would have to take a loss.

There are thousands of examples like this in both business and personal life. Once you understand market risk and the trading process, it's no different from the risk decisions made every day by people worldwide. For me, risk lies at the heart of every conversation I have with students and professionals alike. It's not the dark side of trading; it's the heartbeat of it. The better you understand risk, the freer you become as a trader—because you stop trying to control what you can't and start mastering what you can. And here's the paradox: The more control you try to have over outcomes, the more emotionally entangled you become. But the more you focus on managing risk, the calmer, more consistent, and ultimately more profitable you become.

Trading, at its core, is the art of managing uncertainty. Risk is simply the measure of that uncertainty—and the cost we pay to stay in the game long enough for our edge to unfold.

How Much Are You Willing to Lose?

Before I ever look at a chart, I have a clear idea of how much I'm willing to lose in a market during the day. I call this a hard stop. That might sound counterintuitive to someone chasing opportunity, but for professionals, it's the only place to start. Knowing your loss limit keeps you rational when emotions threaten to take over. It defines your process, protects your capital, and—more importantly—safeguards your confidence.

Every trade has a cost of discovery—the price you pay to find out if your idea works. If you can keep that cost small and consistent, you give yourself countless chances to learn and grow. But if you take excessive risks, you narrow your learning window and reduce your chances of survival.

Defining Your Line in the Sand

A common belief is that traders risk between 1 and 2% of their total account on any individual trade. That number isn't set in stone—it's simply a sensible guideline. It helps keep your drawdowns manageable and your emotions under control. With a 1% risk, you can be wrong ten times in a row and still have the ability to trade the following day. That's the only statistic that genuinely matters: how long can you stay in the game?

On the trading floor, things were quite different. We followed a system based on hard stops—the maximum loss a trader could tolerate in a single trading day. It was adjusted according to experience and performance over time. All junior traders started with the same limit on their first day. As traders became profitable, the hard stop would be increased; if results turned negative, the limit would be decreased.

It wasn't an ideal risk metric, but it enabled the core principles of trading discipline to function: perform well, and your trading size—and your drawdown tolerance—expand; perform poorly, and both diminish. It's a model I continue to follow today, based on one simple principle:

No single trade should ruin your day. No day should spoil your week. No week should destroy your month. And no month should spoil your year.

I've seen traders destroy perfectly good accounts not because their ideas were flawed but because their sizing was reckless. They fell into the trap of thinking that conviction justified exposure. It doesn't. The market doesn't care how confident you feel; it only cares about how much you're willing to lose before it proves you wrong.

When I was teaching recruits on the trading floor, I used to tell them: "Find the number that hurts a little, but doesn't scar."

Manage your losses carefully—if you've never earned that amount in a day, week, or month, then you shouldn't be risking losing it.

That's your real risk tolerance.

If a loss hardly bothers you, you're probably not pushing yourself out of your comfort zone. If it haunts you all weekend, you're trying to hit harder than you can swing. The sweet spot is where a loss is just enough to make you review your process—but not enough to shake your confidence. Unfortunately, as you improve as a trader, those numbers grow—as does the opportunity for greater gains.

Financial vs Psychological Risk Capacity

This is where most traders misunderstand themselves. They believe risk is purely a mathematical issue—a matter of percentages and stops. But it's also profoundly psychological. Your financial risk capacity is what your account can manage. Your psychological risk capacity is the extent to which your mind and emotions can handle stress. The smaller of the two should always determine your position size.

Some traders with six-figure accounts can only handle losing a few hundred pounds before they spiral. Others can withstand a series of thousand-pound losses with complete composure. The difference isn't wealth—it's self-awareness. That's why I encourage every trader I work with to journal their emotional state after every losing trade. Write down how you felt. Did you want to recover the money immediately? Did you rationalize breaking your rules? Did you feel numb, angry, or detached?

Over time, you will recognize your emotional breakeven point—the level of loss that begins to impair your decision-making. Once you identify that point, you gain genuine control and a foundation to build upon.

Consistency Over Conviction

I've traded through every type of market—high volatility in oil, sluggish interest-rate spreads, explosive moves in natural gas—and one thing stays the same: professionals never let conviction override discipline. They understand that a solid process is far more valuable than a strong opinion.

By defining risk in advance, you free yourself from the chaos of uncertainty. You have already accepted the worst-case scenario before the trade even begins. That's what allows professionals to trade with calm objectivity.

So, before you ever ask, "How much can I make?," train yourself to ask, "How much am I willing to lose to find out I am right?"

This one question, answered honestly, will determine everything about the trader you become.

Duration and Time-Based Risk

We often think of risk as a fixed number—the amount we're willing to lose on a trade. However, risk isn't fixed; it changes with every passing hour you stay in the market. The longer your trade remains open, the more variables can shift. What seems like a solid trade at 9 a.m. can be entirely different by 3 p.m., once new data, sentiment, or positioning enters the market. I call this time-dependent risk. It's the quiet multiplier that gradually influences every position you hold.

Time as a Multiplier of Uncertainty

From the moment you execute a trade, each passing minute raises risk. You're exposed to news, sentiment, data releases, and even random shocks unrelated to your initial thesis. A short-term scalp in crude oil might encounter headline risk from a surprise OPEC statement. A three-day position in gold could suddenly be affected by a shift in Treasury yields or a dollar surge. Holding natural gas over the weekend exposes you to weather updates that can dramatically alter the supply–demand picture by Monday morning. The key point is simple: time increases uncertainty.

Professional traders understand this instinctively. That's why intraday traders often operate with much tighter stops—not just in price, but in time. They often say, "If it hasn't gone by now, it's not going to." They recognize that momentum diminishes, liquidity shifts, and conditions change. A trade that doesn't move as expected often signals that either the market disagrees or your timing is off. Either way, time itself becomes a form of feedback.

Exposure Time and Opportunity Cost

One of the most important questions you can ask yourself as a trader is: "How long am I willing to be wrong?" This question defines your exposure time—the duration you're willing to keep risk active before cutting it. Exposure time isn't just about safeguarding capital; it's also about freeing up focus and opportunity. Every trade you hold consumes mental bandwidth. If you're stuck in a slow, uncertain position for days, you might miss a clearer, higher-probability setup elsewhere. The traders I work with constantly weigh the trade-off between patience and opportunity cost. I've observed this happen many times across markets.

Traders, for example, often hold on to Brent positions long after the structure has shifted, waiting for a move that never materializes. Meanwhile, a fresh opportunity in gold or stock indices appears right under their noses. We often call this "being married to a trade." It's common—and should be recognized and addressed as quickly as possible. If you're going to commit capital, also commit focus. And if the market isn't rewarding that focus within a reasonable timeframe, withdraw it and redeploy elsewhere.

Aligning Trade Duration with Strategy

Different strategies demand different time horizons—and your risk structure must match the one you are using.

Scalpers and intraday traders operate on a minute-to-minute and hour-to-hour basis. They rely on tight stops, high precision, and quick feedback loops. Their risk per trade is minimal, but their trading frequency is high.

Swing traders operate over days and weeks. They accept greater overnight exposure and news volatility, so they trade smaller positions and set wider stops.

Position traders concentrate on weeks or months. They are less concerned with intraday fluctuations and more focused on macro trends—interest-rate cycles, seasonal spreads, and shifts in supply and demand.

The risk occurs when traders unintentionally mix these timeframes. They begin a trade with an intraday outlook but end up holding it for days because they do not want to accept a loss. That's no longer a trade—it's a hostage situation. Developing professional discipline involves aligning your expected duration with your planned risk. If you want to hold positions for longer, you must accept that your stop and position size will need to be adjusted accordingly.

Knowing When to Let Time Work for You

Of course, time isn't always the enemy. Sometimes, time is your greatest ally—when the structure of a trade aligns with your conviction, and you have enough patience to let it develop.

In the STIR markets, for instance, many of the most successful trades I've ever made in EURIBOR didn't pay off immediately. They matured as positioning shifted, yield curves adjusted, and macro catalysts materialized. In those cases, time was an advantage.

But here's the difference: those trades were planned that way from the beginning. They had the scope, the reasoning, and the risk limits to justify holding them.

That's the professional distinction—whether you're using time intentionally as part of your advantage, or because you're emotionally stuck in a losing trade.

The Time–Risk Equation

In simple terms, risk rises as time passes—not always in a straight line, but often exponentially during volatile conditions. A trade open for five hours isn't five times riskier than a one-hour trade; it can be much more. That's why professionals monitor not just price exposure but also time exposure—how long their capital remains active and vulnerable to change. So next time you find yourself justifying a position as "just taking longer than expected," ask yourself: "Is time still working for me, or against me?" As a trader, every hour you wait is an hour during which your capital and confidence are exposed to forces beyond your control.

12.2 Probability and Expectancy

Most people think trading is about prediction. They believe success comes from accurately forecasting where the market will go next. It's a comforting illusion—the idea that certainty exists if you analyze thoroughly. Professionals understand better. We don't predict; we prepare. Trading isn't about being right or wrong—it's about managing probabilities. Every trade you make is an experiment with a probable outcome, not a guaranteed one. The sooner you accept that fact, the sooner you can start thinking like a professional.

Thinking in Probabilities

A professional trader does not judge success by whether a trade wins or loses. Instead, they judge it by whether they followed their process correctly and if the trade had a positive expectation.

Expectancy is a straightforward yet powerful concept. It indicates what you can expect to earn, on average, for each pound you risk across a series of trades.

The formula is straightforward:

Expectancy = (Win Rate × Average Win) – (Loss Rate × Average Loss)

If you win 40% of the time and your average winning trade is twice the size of your average losing trade, you remain profitable over the long term.

This is the mathematics of consistency—the reason why disciplined traders who manage their losses outperform those who chase high win rates. Think of it as your track record as a trader; it's a valuable lag measure to keep yourself accountable to.

Amateurs want to be right. Professionals want to make money.

Building Positive Expectancy

Let's examine two examples:

Trader A wins 70% of the time but risks £1,000 to make £500.
Trader B wins only 40% of the time but risks £500 to make £1,500.

Over 100 trades, Trader A will likely end up break-even or in loss after costs, while Trader B will gradually grow their account with each successful run.

That's expectancy in action—it's not about how often you win, but about the quality of your wins.

Fewer high-quality, high-risk: Reward (R:R) trades will always outperform a steady stream of low-quality wins that fail to cover their losses.

This is where discipline and self-awareness come into play. The traders who endure the longest are those who understand their edge and consistently focus on it, without deviation or emotion. I have observed this many times in successful traders, and it is proof of this principle.

The Law of Large Numbers

Professional traders base their entire mindset on the law of large numbers—the statistical principle that over a sufficiently large sample, your results will tend to follow your edge.

If your system has a positive expectancy, the key is not to win every trade—it's to place enough trades for the edge to reveal itself.

That's why emotional resilience is crucial in trading. You must be able to cope with losing streaks without abandoning your process.

When I trade calendar spreads on the short-term interest rate curve, I can go days or even weeks without spotting a clear opportunity. Patience was part of the advantage. But once the opportunity arose—when curve steepening and macro headwinds aligned—it paid off multiple times over the small losses sustained along the way.

Expectancy rewards consistency, not excitement.

Understanding Probability in Context

Probability isn't a fixed number—it depends on the situation.

A trade setup that succeeds 70% of the time during stable volatility may only succeed 50% of the time in turbulent markets. That's why professionals don't treat probabilities as fixed; they continually update them based on market behavior.

If volatility spikes, liquidity vanishes, or a central bank meeting is imminent, the probability distribution shifts—and so should your sizing and expectations.

This is where professional traders and traditional bookmakers resemble each other: both constantly recalibrate odds. But traders face an extra challenge—the game itself keeps changing.

The skill lies in recognizing when your probabilities are most dependable and when they are affected by noise.

The Edge Multiplier

I often describe expectancy as your edge multiplier. The stronger your process and the cleaner your risk management, the higher the multiplier. Here's how it manifests in practice:

- Poor process, weak discipline = expectancy near zero or negative.
- Structured process, controlled risk = positive expectancy that compounds over time.
- Exceptional process, self-awareness, and patience = professional-level performance where compounding takes over.

Expectancy isn't glamorous, but it is the quiet engine behind every consistent trader. It turns trading from a game of guesses into a process based on probabilities.

The journey from Prediction to Process

Once you start thinking in probabilities, you no longer need to be right—and that's when trading becomes simpler. You stop tying your identity to individual outcomes and begin trusting your edge to play out over time. When a trade results in a loss, you don't spiral—you record it, learn from it, and move forward. When a trade succeeds, you don't celebrate—you acknowledge that your process functioned as intended. Over time, this mindset gathers more benefits than any single trade ever could. Because trading isn't about perfect prediction—it's about disciplined repetition. Your goal isn't to win today; it's to trade well enough to be here still tomorrow.

12.3 Value at Risk (VaR)

When you start thinking in probabilities, it's natural to want a framework that helps quantify them—a way to translate "how risky is this trade?" into something you can actually measure. That's where Value at Risk, or VaR, comes in. For many retail traders, VaR sounds like a complex institutional tool—something used by banks, hedge funds, or risk departments buried deep in compliance reports. But stripped down to its core, VaR is simply a way of asking a very practical question:

"With X per cent confidence, what's the most I could lose over a Y period of time?"

It's not a perfect model—no risk model is—, but it's one of the best starting points for understanding exposure. It helps translate volatility into potential loss, providing a frame of reference for how much risk you're actually bearing. Understanding VaR in Plain English: Let's simplify.

Imagine you hold a £100,000 trading account. You run a daily VaR calculation at a 95% confidence level and find a result of £1,500. That means that, under normal market conditions, there's a 95% probability you won't lose more than £1,500 in a day—and a 5% chance you could lose more. That small tail, the 5%, is where surprises, shocks, and slippage live.

That's what the world's professionals plan for; the 95% figure is what helps risk managers sleep well at night, as it provides a downside parameter they can rely on to keep trading floors and hedge funds operating. VaR doesn't eliminate uncertainty, but it does help you understand it. It enables you to compare different trades and strategies using the same language—risk expressed as potential loss. Whether you're trading oil, gold, or short-term rates, you can use VaR to gauge how volatile your portfolio truly is, and how much capital you should allocate.

Why Institutions Use It

At the institutional level, VaR is the cornerstone of risk management. Every trading desk—from equities to energy to fixed income—operates within a VaR limit. It ensures that no individual trader, strategy, or book can take on more risk than the firm can withstand. If a trader's VaR exceeds that limit, positions are automatically reduced, often without discussion. This protects the firm from one person's overconfidence—or conviction—turning into a disaster.

When I led trading teams, we analyzed VaR metrics daily. They provided a clear picture of our risk exposure, the relationships between our positions, and our capacity to take on additional trades. This fostered discipline, transparency, and accountability at the desk. Retail traders often dismiss this kind of structure as "too corporate", but that discipline is what allows professionals to operate effectively. You don't need a PhD or a team of quants to understand the principles of VaR—you need to adopt the mindset: measure, monitor, and manage.

Adapting VaR for Individual Traders

You don't need sophisticated software or databases to implement VaR thinking. You can estimate it conceptually using volatility, position size, and timeframe. Here's a simple method:

Estimate volatility by examining the average true range (ATR) or standard deviation of recent price movements. Multiply by a confidence factor—such as 1.65 for 95% confidence, or 2.33 for 99%—and adjust for position size and holding period.

Example: You're trading gold futures. The recent daily standard deviation is $20 per ounce. A one-lot position equals 100 ounces.

Your daily volatility exposure is approximately $2,000. With 95% confidence, your VaR could be around $3,300 ($2,000 × 1.65).

This indicates, statistically, how much you could lose in one day under normal conditions.

Now, if you plan to hold that trade for five days, the expected risk increases proportionally with time—roughly by the square root of time ($\sqrt{5} \approx 2.24$), bringing the total potential exposure closer to $7,400.

You don't need to calculate that precisely every time. I know I don't, but simply understanding that risk increases over time and with volatility helps you make smarter choices.

Where the Model Ends—and You Begin

No model can predict the future. VaR assumes that tomorrow will resemble yesterday—and we all know markets seldom behave that politely. That's why professionals don't rely solely on VaR; they also conduct stress tests—scenarios that ask, "What if the unthinkable happens?" What if gold gaps $50 overnight? What if OPEC makes an unexpected decision? What if a flash crash wipes out liquidity in the spreads? These aren't hypothetical; they're survival drills. They remind us that models are only as valuable as the humility behind them.

Acknowledging the Experts

I am fortunate to bring my experience, knowledge, and friendship to this topic. If you wish to explore further, I recommend looking into the work of Professor Carol Alexander, one of the world's foremost experts on financial risk and modelling.

Carol has written extensively on volatility, VaR, and the mathematics underpinning market behavior, and her research has influenced how institutions and regulators consider systemic risk. She is also a friend, and her academic rigor has helped bridge the gap between theory and practical trading.

For traders seeking to go beyond intuition and gain a deeper understanding of how risk operates—mathematically, statistically, and emotionally—her work is an excellent starting point.

Incorporating VaR into Your Process

Most traders aim not just to become a risk quant, but to think like one. You don't need to run daily models or publish reports, but you should understand what you might lose and how this loss varies across different market conditions. Start simply: comprehend how volatility impacts exposure. Adjust your sizing and stops as volatility changes. Don't see risk as a fixed figure; view it as a dynamic element that demands ongoing attention. Over time, this approach makes you your own risk manager—someone who isn't daunted by uncertainty but is guided by it.

12.4 The Risk–Reward Equation

If risk is the cost of doing business, then reward is your return on investment. The professional game is built on balancing the two—ensuring that every pound you risk has a logical, consistent, and realistic expectation of reward. This is the most basic, yet most powerful concept in trading: the risk–reward ratio. For me, this single number—the relationship between what you're willing to lose and what you aim to gain—dictates whether a trade is even worth your attention. It's the filter that turns random ideas into structured opportunities.

The Professional Ratio

Every trader has a minimum risk–reward threshold.

Mine is usually 1:2 or better—meaning for every £1000 I risk, I want the potential to make £2,000 or more.

That's not greed; it's probability management.

A 1:2 ratio means I can be wrong more than half the time and still make money.

A 1:3 ratio means I can be wrong even more often—yet still come out ahead.

That's how professionals endure long losing streaks and keep growing their equity curves. It's not because they're right all the time—it's because when they're right, it genuinely makes a difference.

If your trades consistently have poor risk–reward ratios—for example, risking £1,000 to make £500—you've already lost before you start. You would need an extraordinary win rate to break even, and markets rarely allow you to sustain that.

Asymmetry Is Everything

The appeal of trading lies in its asymmetry—the fact that your downside can be managed, while your upside can be unlimited. When you establish a trade correctly, your potential reward should, by design, surpass your risk. That's the asymmetry professionals aim for—and it's where compounding genuinely begins. I like to think of each trade as a small asymmetric bet on probability. If I lose, I lose a known amount. If I win, I win a multiple. Repeat that process a hundred times, and the law of large numbers works in your favor.

This is also why many traders find it psychologically difficult, because asymmetry feels uncomfortable. You often face small losses and wait for larger wins to make up for them. It seems illogical. It requires patience. But that's the nature of professional trading—a gradual process of small losses and occasional big wins. In other words, learn to accept the challenge; this is where resilience is necessary.

Evaluating Reward in Context

Not all "reward" is created equal.

The quality of potential reward matters just as much as its size.

A trade with a 1:3 ratio due to high volatility isn't necessarily better than a calm, structured setup with a 1:2 ratio.

Professionals consider probability alongside potential—because the more volatile the environment, the harder it is actually to capture that reward.

When I'm assessing trades, I don't just ask, "What could I make?"

I ask:

- How likely am I to realize that profit?
- How much time will it take?
- What could disrupt the move?

A 1:3 textbook setup that demands perfect timing and sentiment is less useful than a clear, consistent 1:2 trade you can repeat daily or weekly.

Consistency compounds. Rarity doesn't.

Trade Selection Through Ratios

One of the most practical approaches to applying this thinking is to use risk–reward as your trade filter. Before you buy or sell, visualize the setup. Mark your stop—the point where your trade thesis is invalidated—and your target—the level offering fair reward for the risk involved. If the distance to your target is not at least twice the distance to your stop, pass on the trade. This simple habit will contribute more to your profitability than any technical indicator.

This rule has saved me numerous times on the trading screens and has kept many of my traders in the game for over a decade. There were days when markets were dull—when I was tempted to force a trade out of boredom. But having that rule stopped me. If the reward wasn't there, I moved on. The missed trade was never a loss. The forced trade usually was.

The Emotional Edge

Risk–reward isn't just mathematical—it's psychological. Understanding that you've built asymmetry into your trade provides emotional clarity. You can accept losses calmly because you know your winners will compensate. This shifts you from a "win or lose" mindset to the long-term perspective of expectancy. Here, psychology and process come together. When you are selective with your trades, your focus improves. You begin making fewer, higher-quality trades—and your confidence increases. It's not about increasing the number of trades; it's about improving their quality.

12.5 The Power of Process to Help the Psychology of Risk

Here's my approach:

1. Define the risk—the price point where your trade thesis becomes invalid.
2. Set the target—a realistic level that is at least twice the distance from the risk.
3. Calculate the ratio—if it's below 1:2, skip the trade.
4. Size accordingly—risk only what fits within your daily or weekly limit.
5. Review outcomes—not just the result, but whether the ratio worked out as expected.

Over time, this discipline develops structure, confidence, and consistency—the three key elements every trader needs to succeed in the long term.

When you understand expectancy, probability, and VaR, the risk–reward ratio becomes your guide in decision-making. You stop chasing trades and start selecting them. This distinguishes amateurs from professionals. Amateurs think in terms of hope; professionals think in terms of ratios. They know every trade must justify its place at the table—and only those with positive asymmetry earn a seat.

Building a Healthy Relationship with Risk
At some stage in every trader's journey, risk stops being just a number on a trading platform or spreadsheet and becomes a relationship—one that must be understood, respected, and managed daily. You can't trade effectively if you fear risk, and you can't survive if you ignore it. The goal isn't to eliminate risk; it's to foster a healthy respect for it—to see it as the price of staying in the game long enough for your idea to unfold.

From Fear to Respect
Early in my career, I wasn't quite sure how to manage risk. There was an unspoken fear on the first trading floor I worked on that if you lost too much

money or didn't manage risk properly, you'd lose your job. For a first role straight out of university, that pressure was intense. Every losing trade felt like a personal failure—a dent in my confidence and, at times, my sense of self. I believed that if I could find the perfect setup or system, I could avoid losing altogether—I just needed to practice and learn from my mistakes. But there is no perfect system.

There are only probabilities, and the goal is to keep nudging those probabilities further in your favor with each trade. The professionals I learned from never spoke about avoiding losses; they spoke about managing them. They expected them. They even planned for them. Unlike during winning streaks, you always knew when a trader was "up against it"; that's when mental-athlete training and a solid plan matter most. That shift—from fear to respect—is one of the defining moments in a trader's evolution.

When you stop treating losses as threats and start treating them as tuition, the game changes; you stop flinching at uncertainty and start working with it. You begin to spiral upward instead of feeling trapped in a loop you can't escape. Every profession has its cost of learning. In trading, that cost is expressed in money—a metric we all relate to. Friends often tell me, "I don't know how you can do it; losing all that money would terrify me." My reply is always the same: "If it were easy, everyone would be doing it."

Losing Well

If risk is unavoidable, then loss is unavoidable too—and your attitude towards loss will shape your long-term success. One of the first questions I asked as a novice trainee was to a senior trader: *"Is there anyone out there who's never lost?"* "Not a chance," he replied. Two decades later, I still haven't met a trader with a perfect record. The best traders I've worked with aren't those who avoid losing streaks; they're the ones who handle them with grace, resilience, and quiet optimism.

- They don't spiral after a losing day.
- They don't double down to try and win it back.
- They close the laptop, take a breath, and come back the next morning ready to execute the process again.
- They understand that one loss—or even a series of losses—doesn't define who they are. It simply reflects the inherent randomness of the business.
- They know the markets can remain irrational longer than anyone can stay solvent—a mantra that has shaped my trading approach for years.

If you learn to accept losses gracefully—with acceptance, curiosity, and discipline—you become almost emotionally invincible. When losses no longer shake your confidence, your focus improves significantly. That's the emotional edge that sets professionals apart: the ability to trade calmly amid the storm.

Risk as a Teacher

The market has an incredible way of teaching you the same lessons until you finally listen. When you overtrade, it humbles you. When you get greedy, it corrects you. When you lose discipline, it reminds you who's really in charge. I've learned more from my losing trades than from my winning ones. Every drawdown, every hard-stop hit, every painful stretch where nothing worked—all of it shaped the risk framework I live by today.

I vividly remember, about six months into my career, being wiped out by a market move following a sudden central bank shift. In a single day, I lost the profits I had amassed over the previous six months. I was gutted, but it taught me invaluable lessons—chief among them: never become complacent; the market can do whatever it wants, whenever it wants.

That's the paradox of progress in this business: you develop through facing discomfort. If you shy away from risk, you miss out on growth. That's where progress resides—just beyond your comfort zone. If you approach risk wisely, you gain the confidence that only experience can provide.

Detachment from Outcomes

A key part of building a healthy relationship with risk is detachment—not in a cold, mechanical manner, but in an emotionally intelligent way. You can't control the outcome of any individual trade. What you can control is the quality of your preparation, your process, and your response. Detach your self-worth from your P&L. I still don't check my P&L during the day and only review it weekly or monthly.

I've always advised my traders to do the same. Keep your emotions separate from each tick on the screen; take regular breaks to avoid living through every market move. Don't let your identity be defined by the outcome of a single day. You're managing a process that can always be enhanced. Sometimes it succeeds, sometimes it doesn't—win or learn. That's what professional composure looks like. It's not indifference—it's perspective.

You'll make thousands of trades in your life; one day's outcome won't define your career. When you trade with detachment, your decisions become clearer, quicker, and more aligned with your edge. You're no longer reacting to fear or greed; you're responding to structure and logic—a state I call zen-like trading.

The Resilient Mindset

At the heart of trading lies a simple truth: you can't avoid uncertainty—but you can build resilience within it. It's one of the defining traits of successful traders. The markets will test you mentally and financially; the key is being able to recover and face the challenge when conditions turn against you. Resilience allows you to keep showing up after a loss, a poor week, or a period where nothing seems to work. It's the quiet confidence that says, I've seen this before, and I'll find my rhythm again. You have a process you trust—one that improves the more you practice. It all depends on you.

My resilience grew from reminding myself: someone less committed and less prepared than me is making money in these markets—so why not me? I'm optimistic you'll feel the same after reading this book.

12.6 The Importance of Risk

The reason I emphasize risk so much here—and at the end of the book—is simple: without a strong relationship with risk, nothing else works. Many traders I've taught over the years rush in without preparation, a process, or any real respect for risk. Put everything together in the order I've outlined to improve your chances of success. The best setups, the most advanced strategies, the sharpest analysis—all of it falls apart if you can't manage exposure or handle loss.

Risk management isn't the dull side of trading; it is trading. It's the ongoing internal dialogue I continue to have with myself and with every trader I mentor. It's the foundation upon which every profitable career is built. It's what keeps you alive long enough to benefit from the compounding that transforms skill into mastery.

By now, you've seen how each element of professional trading connects:

- Defining what you're willing to lose gives you clarity.
- Understanding time and exposure keeps you objective.
- Thinking in probabilities and expectancy removes the need to be right.
- Quantifying risk through VaR grounds your intuition in logic.
- Applying risk–reward discipline aligns your process with long-term success.
- Building a healthy relationship with risk ensures you can sustain it all.

When you assemble these pieces, trading ceases to feel chaotic and becomes controlled. You're no longer pursuing outcomes—you're managing exposure and letting consistency do its work. That's what true professionalism in trading means: clarity amidst uncertainty. Essentially, risk acts as a mirror. It reflects who you are when the market pushes back. Your relationship with risk reveals your discipline, patience, humility, and confidence in your process. If you learn to manage that relationship with honesty and composure, there's nothing in this game you can't handle.

There is no way to eliminate risk in trading, but with careful thought and practice, we can learn to control ourselves within it. If there's one thread that connects everything in this book, it's this: professional trading is not about predicting markets—it's about mastering yourself. Risk becomes your greatest teacher, your discipline's daily companion, and the guide of your journey to freedom. When you learn to respect risk, you stop trying to conquer the market and begin working in harmony with it.

That's the beginning of mastery—and the mindset that will carry you into the final chapter.

13

The End Is Just the Beginning

The Journey So Far

When you first opened this book, you took the initial step towards thinking, operating, and improving like a professional trader. You've built the foundations of Preparation, learning to master your mindset, understand the markets, and develop habits that promote consistency. You've learned the Process—how professionals identify, execute, manage, and evaluate trades with structure and discipline. And you've explored Practice—the stage where knowledge transforms into skill through repetition, reflection, and refinement.

This three-part journey reflects how professional traders are trained in real trading environments. It's a process meant not to make you rich overnight but to make you capable—capable of performing under pressure, adapting to uncertainty, and improving with each trade you undertake.

The purpose of this book is to demonstrate that professional trading isn't reliant on luck, prediction, or even flawless analysis. It's about understanding the rules of the game and mastering oneself.

13.1 Transitioning From Knowing to Doing

We have, on our journey, realized that markets don't reward knowledge—they reward execution.

The difference between understanding something and taking action is where most traders fail.

S. Warner-Baker, *Learn to Trade Like a Professional*,
https://doi.org/10.1007/978-3-032-20125-6_13

Bridging that gap is where professionalism begins.

The truth is straightforward: trading isn't about beating the market; it's about aligning yourself with it.

You can't control what the market does—only how you prepare, respond, and learn.

The successful traders you've read about in this book didn't succeed because they knew more—they succeeded because they did more of the right things, more consistently, for longer.

They persisted with their process through each stage of doubt, and that steadiness became their advantage.

Consistency is not a coincidence.

It's the result of structure, awareness, and review.

13.2 The Reality of Professional Trading

If it were easy, everyone would be doing it!

Every trader, regardless of experience, encounters fear, uncertainty, and loss. Professionals handle these differently. They don't avoid losses—they expect them. They don't chase outcomes—they manage processes. They don't blame the market—they study their response to it. Over time, you'll realize that trading tests your character far more than it tests your strategy.

Markets are mirrors. They reflect your habits, beliefs, and emotions about yourself. Your task is to keep improving the person looking into that mirror through good habits, discipline, and energy.

13.3 Next Steps: Building a Professional Pathway

You now have the framework—Preparation, Process, and Practice—but mastery only emerges when you make it your own.

Here's how to move forward:

1. *Keep a Trading Journal*

- Record not just your trades, but your thoughts before and after them.
- Track your state of mind, decision quality, and adherence to process.
- Review weekly to spot what's improving and what's drifting.

2. *Review with Structure*

- Use your evaluation template from Chap. 9.
- Score yourself not on profit, but on process execution.
- Reward discipline, not outcome.

3. *Schedule Practice Time*

- Allocate time for deliberate drills—execution, order entry, seasonality analysis, price action review.
- Practice when markets are closed; prepare when others are distracted.

4. *Develop Your Network*

- Surround yourself with traders who take their craft seriously.
- Share insights, review trades together, and learn collectively.
- Remember: environment shapes behavior.

5. *Revisit Your Purpose*

- The markets will test your why.
- When it feels hard—and it will—return to the reason you started.
- You're not just learning to trade; you're learning to grow.

If you follow this structure, your growth becomes inevitable; skip it, and results will become unpredictable.

The choice, as ever, is yours; you are the one steering your destiny.

13.4 Paying It Forward

As you grow, think about how you can help others do the same. Trading is often a solitary activity, but the most successful traders I have known never worked alone. They mentored, shared, and encouraged—and in doing so, they furthered their own mastery.

When you teach, you learn twice. When you serve, you become stronger.

I attribute much of my own longevity in the markets to the ongoing teaching and reinforcement of trading's fundamental principles. The next generation of traders will require more role models to demonstrate that trading can be ethical, structured, and sustainable—that it can be a craft, not a gamble.

Be one of them.

13.5 The End Is Just the Beginning—Final Word

The knowledge, wisdom, theory, and experience in this book are the culmination of a blessed career in trading the financial markets—all stemming from early curiosity as a boy and developing into a fascination as a young man entering the workforce.

I have experienced both luck and misfortune. I've faced challenge after challenge, but resilience, hard work, optimism, honesty, and a good sense of humor have shaped a successful trading career—one in which I've earned more than I imagined as a child from a council estate, brought up in a working-class family, attending underprivileged schools with, frankly, terrible teachers.

Over time, I've come to understand my craft well enough to share it. As soon as I realized I could help others succeed, I sought to do so—mentoring traders who are now great friends, opening doors for hundreds of young people who once had no idea how markets work, and watching them shape their own lives. The joy of seeing their careers flourish in capital markets is priceless. It's worth more than any successful trade.

If this book has provided you with anything—clarity, courage, or simply a better question to ask when you next sit down to trade—then it has fulfilled its purpose.

The end is just the beginning.

Close the book. Open your journal. Define your risk. Make the next right trade.

As an old-school trader used to say to me when he left the office each day: "Stay lucky!"

References

Blas, J., & Farchy, J. (2021). *The world for sale: Money, power and the traders who barter the earth's resources*. Penguin Random House.

Cain, B. (2020). *One percent better: A story about how to close the gap from where you are to where you want to be*. Rodale Books.

Covey, S. R., McChesney, C., & Huling, J. (2012). *The 4 disciplines of execution: Achieving your wildly important goals*. Free Press.

Douglas, M. (2000). *Trading in the zone: Master the market with confidence, discipline and a winning attitude*. Prentice Hall Press.

Duckworth, A. (2016). *Grit: The power of passion and perseverance*. Scribner.

Dweck, C. S. (2006). *Mindset: The new psychology of success*. Random House.

Freeman-Shor, L. (2015). *The art of execution: How the world's best investors get it wrong and still make millions*. Harriman House.

Hill, N. (1937). *Think and grow rich*. The Ralston Society.

Lambert, C. (2011). *Candlestick charts: An introduction to using candlestick charts*. Harriman House.

Lewis, M. (1989). *Liar's Poker*. W. W. Norton & Company.

Maloney, M. (2008). *Guide to investing in gold and silver: Protect your financial future*. Business Plus.

Rogers, J. (2004). *Hot commodities: How anyone can invest profitably in the world's best market*. Random House.

Schwager, J. D. (1989). *Market wizards: Interviews with top traders*. Harper Business.

Steenbarger, B. N. (2002). *The psychology of trading: Tools and techniques for minding the markets*. John Wiley & Sons.

Taleb, N. N. (2001). *Fooled by randomness: The hidden role of chance in life and in the markets*. Texere.

S. Warner-Baker, *Learn to Trade Like a Professional*,
https://doi.org/10.1007/978-3-032-20125-6

Taleb, N. N. (2007). *The black swan: The impact of the highly improbable*. Random House.

Thomas, E. (2022). *You owe you: Ignite your power, your purpose, and your why*. HarperCollins Leadership.

Ward, S. (2014). *The bulletproof trader: Evidence-based strategies for overcoming setbacks and sustaining high performance in the markets*. Harriman House.

Index

A
Agricultural commodities, 201, 234, 245–246
Altcoins, 161

B
Bitcoin, 131–133, 135, 137–138, 142–143
Bonds, 31, 36, 38–39, 44
Breakout, 270, 300
Brent Crude, 174–176, 182–183
Bretton Woods, 52

C
Calendar Spreads, 68
Checklist, 342
Cocoa, 205–209
Coffee, 212–213, 215–216
Commodities, xiii, 33, 49, 87, 101, 167, 197, 201, 220, 297
Continuous improvement, 13
Corn, 221, 223–224
Counter-trend, 186, 262, 277, 284
COVID-19, 32, 45, 119, 169, 207
Cryptocurrencies, 54, 131–132, 150, 155, 163, 166

D
DeFi, 7, 145, 149–152, 161
Deliberate practice, 335

E
Energy markets, 167, 177, 249
Equities, 33, 119
Ethereum, 132, 145–146, 148, 154

F
Feeder cattle, 242
Financial freedom, xi
Fixed Income, 38, 70
FTSE, ix, 104, 109

G
GameStop, 125
Gold, 51–52, 63, 71, 73, 75–76, 78–79, 81
Golden Rules, 306, 323, 370

S. Warner-Baker, *Learn to Trade Like a Professional*,
https://doi.org/10.1007/978-3-032-20125-6

H

Hunt Brothers, 84

I

Indices, 105, 108, 121–124, 126, 129–130
Inefficiencies, 27–28, 165
Interest rates, 30–32, 36, 39, 43, 53, 55, 60–61, 63–64, 66–67

J

Journaling, 17, 326–327, 329

L

Lean hog, 237, 239
Light Sweet Crude, 174
Live cattle, 242

M

Managing risk, xi
Market Structure, 4, 180, 261, 324

N

Natural gas, 167, 193–196, 296, 378
Nixon Shock, 74

O

2020 Oil Crash, 180
Oil markets, 169, 172, 177, 187

P

Pathway to profitability, xii
Paying It Forward, 395
Personal growth, xi
Practice, xii
Precious metals, 71, 77, 101
Preparation, xii
Process, xii
Professional mindset, xii

S

Self-mastery, x
Skill development, 347
Soybeans, 231–234
Structured practice, 347
Sugar, 198, 201–203

T

Trading process, xi
Trendlines, 265, 268
Trends, 41, 45, 61, 103, 203, 261, 276, 339, 351

W

Wheat, 226, 229
WTI crude, 179, 181–183, 186
WTI-Brent spread, 175

Y

Yasuo Hamanaka, 100

FSC
www.fsc.org
MIX
Papier | Fördert
gute Waldnutzung
FSC® C083411

Kolibri 360 GmbH
Ferdinand-Jühlke-Straße 7
99095 Erfurt, Deutschland
produktsicherheit@kolibri360.de